# *Betty Crocker's*
# EASY COOKING
# for Family and Friends

## MORE THAN 350 DELICIOUS
## EVERYDAY RECIPES

RODALE

This edition published by arrangement with Wiley, Inc.

Printed in the United States of America

**GENERAL MILLS, INC.**
**Betty Crocker Kitchens**
Manager, Books: Lois Tlusty
Recipe Development: Betty Crocker Kitchens Home Economists
Food Stylists: Betty Crocker Kitchens Food Stylists
Photography and Illustrations: Photographic Services Department
Cover photograph by Photographic Services Department

Edited by Kathy Everleth
Book design by Carol Angstadt

**Library of Congress Cataloging-in-Publication Data**

    Betty Crocker's easy cooking for family and friends : more than 350 delicious everyday recipes.
        p.     cm.
    Includes index.
    ISBN 1–57954–691–9 hardcover
    1. Cookery.   I. Crocker, Betty.
   TX714.B475   2004
   641.5—dc21                      2003001490

2  4  6  8  10  9  7  5  3  1  hardcover

Cover photos: Crunchy Herb-Baked Chicken (page 249), Baked Brie with Sun-Dried Tomatoes (page 208), Beef Kabobs with Chilied Plum Sauce (page 158), and Luscious Lemon Bars (page 388)

For more great ideas, visit www.bettycrocker.com.

# CONTENTS

# INTRODUCTION

Whether you're cooking a weeknight meal for your family, making a last-minute lunch for a gang of kids, or preparing dinner for a group of friends, you'll be ready for anything with *Betty Crocker's Easy Cooking for Family and Friends*. With recipes for everything from drinks to desserts, this book makes it all easy for you.

Basically, if you make everyone feel welcome and comfortable in your home and serve them yummy food, they'll enjoy themselves. That's what cooking for family and friends is all about. And you *can* do it, whether you're on a casserole or a caviar budget.

Of course, you've gotten off to a good start by picking up this book. Here you'll find all kinds of recipes, plus decorating ideas to add flair to your table and tips for making every meal and occasion fun and enjoyable.

As you get started, remember: The recipe is your friend! Not only is it your step-by-step guide to fixing good food, the recipe also gives you great ideas and helpful information. If you read through the entire recipe before beginning to cook, you'll feel confident, organized and well-prepared when trying a recipe for the first time. This will give you the opportunity to make sure that you have all the ingredients, utensils and pans needed to prepare the recipe. Plus, you'll know if the recipe makes as many servings as you need and how much time the food needs to cook or bake. (For recipes ready in 30 minutes or less, look for the QUICK symbol.) After reviewing the recipe, you'll be ready to cook with confidence. And if you ever need a little extra help or more tips and recipes, don't forget that you can always visit www.bettycrocker.com.

As an added bonus, I've included my special "Good Times—Guaranteed!" chapter (see page 407). Here you'll find my favorite tried-and-true tips for easy entertaining. From buffet table settings to quick napkin folds to simple centerpieces, I share all of my best ideas for making every occasion sparkle.

With this book in hand, bringing your loved ones together for a memorable meal will be easy and enjoyable, and you'll have more time to relax and share in the fun. After all, that's really what it's all about. So here's to you and to many happy meals with family and friends!

*Betty Crocker*

# $\mathcal{C}$ASUAL $\mathcal{M}$EALS

You'll be ready with a delicious meal any day of the week with these terrific recipes at your fingertips. Read on for sandwiches for the big game, pizza for a night of videos, pasta for a quick dinner and more—a wide variety that's great for every day!

◀ Chicken and Sweet Potato Curry (page 60)

# BEVERAGES

## APPLE-KIWI SMOOTHIES

**QUICK**   Prep: 10 min        2 servings

1   small apple, peeled and cut into chunks

1   kiwifruit, peeled and cut into chunks

4   medium strawberries, stems removed

1   container (6 ounces) strawberry low-fat yogurt

⅓   cup apple juice

**1.** Place all ingredients in blender or food processor.

**2.** Cover and blend on high speed about 30 seconds or until smooth.

**1 SERVING:** Calories 155 (Calories from Fat 10); Fat 1g (Saturated 1g); Cholesterol 5mg; Sodium 55mg; Carbohydrate 36g (Dietary Fiber 3g); Protein 4g

# TRIPLE-CHOCOLATE MALTS

**QUICK**  Prep: 5 min        2 servings

¾ **cup fat-free (skim) chocolate milk**

¼ **cup reduced-calorie chocolate-flavored syrup**

1 **tablespoon natural-flavor malted milk powder**

1½ **cups fat-free chocolate frozen yogurt**

**1.** Place milk, chocolate syrup and malted milk powder in blender. Cover and blend on high speed 2 seconds.

**2.** Add frozen yogurt. Cover and blend on low speed about 5 seconds or until smooth.

**1 SERVING:** Calories 245 (Calories from Fat 10); Fat 1g (Saturated 0g); Cholesterol 5mg; Sodium 145mg; Carbohydrate 52g (Dietary Fiber 0g); Protein 7g

# CHOCOLATE MILK SHAKES

**QUICK**  Prep: 10 min        2 servings

¾ **cup milk**

¼ **cup chocolate-flavored syrup**

1½ **cups vanilla ice cream**

**1.** Place milk and syrup in blender. Cover and blend on high speed 2 seconds.

**2.** Add ice cream. Cover and blend on low speed about 5 seconds or until smooth.

**1 SERVING:** Calories 340 (Calories from Fat 115); Fat 13g (Saturated 8g); Cholesterol 50mg; Sodium 160mg; Carbohydrate 50g (Dietary Fiber 1g); Protein 7g

***Lighter Chocolate Milk Shakes:*** For 1 gram of fat and 275 calories per serving, use fat-free (skim) milk and substitute fat-free frozen yogurt for the ice cream.

***Berry Milk Shakes:*** Substitute strawberry or cherry topping or frozen strawberries or raspberries in syrup, thawed and undrained, for the chocolate-flavored syrup.

---

**COOKING TIP**

• Turn these shakes into malts by adding about 1 tablespoon natural-flavor or flavored malted milk powder before blending.

---

# *H*OT CHOCOLATE

**QUICK**   Prep: 5 min; Cook: 15 min          6 servings

> 3   **ounces unsweetened baking chocolate**
>
> 1½   **cups water**
>
> ⅓   **cup sugar**
>
>      **Dash of salt**
>
> 4½   **cups milk**

**1.** Heat chocolate and water in 1½-quart saucepan over medium heat, stirring constantly, until chocolate is melted and mixture is smooth.

**2.** Stir in sugar and salt. Heat to boiling; reduce heat. Simmer uncovered 4 minutes, stirring constantly. Stir in milk. Heat just until hot (do not boil because skin will form on top).

**3.** Beat with hand beater until foamy, or stir until smooth. Serve immediately.

**1 SERVING:** Calories 220 (Calories from Fat 100); Fat 11g (Saturated 7g); Cholesterol 15mg; Sodium 150mg; Carbohydrate 24g (Dietary Fiber 2g); Protein 8g

***Lighter Hot Chocolate:*** For 1 gram of fat and 120 calories per serving, substitute ⅓ cup baking cocoa for the chocolate and use fat-free (skim) milk. Mix cocoa, sugar and salt in saucepan; stir in water. Continue as directed in step 2.

# APPETIZERS

## $\mathscr{H}$OT CRAB DIP

**QUICK**  Prep: 10 min; Bake: 20 min        About 2½ cups dip

- 4  medium green onions, trimmed and sliced
- 1  clove garlic, peeled and finely chopped
- 1  package (8 ounces) cream cheese, at room temperature
- ¼  cup grated Parmesan cheese (1 ounce)
- ¼  cup mayonnaise or salad dressing
- ¼  cup dry white wine or apple juice
- 2  teaspoons sugar
- 1  teaspoon ground mustard
- 1  can (6 ounces) crabmeat, drained
- ⅓  cup sliced almonds
-    Assorted crackers or sliced raw vegetables, if desired

**1.** Heat the oven to 375°.

**2.** Mix onions, garlic, cream cheese, Parmesan cheese, mayonnaise, wine, sugar and mustard in ungreased casserole.

**3.** Flake crabmeat with fork, and remove any tiny pieces of shell. Stir crabmeat into cheese mixture in casserole. Sprinkle with almonds.

**4.** Bake uncovered 15 to 20 minutes or until hot and bubbly. Serve with crackers.

**1 SERVING (1 TABLESPOON):** Calories 45 (Calories from Fat 35); Fat 4g (Saturated 2g); Cholesterol 10mg; Sodium 50mg; Carbohydrate 1g (Dietary Fiber 0g); Protein 2g

***Hot Artichoke-Crab Dip:*** Drain 1 can (14 ounces) artichoke heart quarters in a strainer, then coarsely chop. Stir into cheese mixture with crabmeat.

### COOKING TIP

• You can use 6 ounces imitation crabmeat, coarsely chopped, for the canned crabmeat in this recipe.

**FLAKING CRABMEAT**

Use a fork to flake the crabmeat, and remove any tiny pieces of shell.

# $\mathcal{L}$AYERED VEGETABLE AND AIOLI APPETIZER

Prep: 15 min; Bake: 20 min    12 servings

- **4 ounces fat-free cream cheese, softened**
- **½ cup fat-free mayonnaise**
- **2 cloves garlic, peeled and finely chopped**
- **½ teaspoon grated lemon peel**
- **Dash of ground red pepper (cayenne)**
- **2 medium bell peppers (green, red or yellow), cut into 1½-inch pieces**
- **1 small red onion, peeled and coarsely chopped**
- **1 cup mushrooms**
- **2 tablespoons crumbled chèvre (goat) cheese**
- **2 tablespoons chopped fresh basil leaves**
- **Crackers, if desired**

**1.** Heat oven to 450°. Mix cream cheese, mayonnaise, garlic, lemon peel and red pepper in medium bowl until smooth. Cover and refrigerate while preparing vegetables.

**2.** Mix bell peppers, onion and mushrooms in medium bowl. Spray with olive oil–flavored cooking spray 2 or 3 times; toss to coat. Spread in ungreased jelly roll pan, 15½ × 10½ × 1 inch. Bake uncovered 15 to 20 minutes or until vegetables are tender; cool slightly.

**3.** Spread cream cheese mixture on serving platter. Top with vegetables. Sprinkle with chèvre cheese and basil. Serve with crackers.

**1 SERVING:** Calories 25 (Calories from Fat 0); Fat 0g (Saturated 0g); Cholesterol 0mg; Sodium 135mg; Carbohydrate 4g (Dietary Fiber 1g); Protein 2g

# FOCACCIA WEDGES

**QUICK** Prep: 15 min; Bake: 12 min     6 servings

1 **can (10 ounces) refrigerated pizza crust dough**

3 **cloves garlic, peeled and finely chopped**

½ **teaspoon dried rosemary leaves, crumbled**

1 **large sweet onion (Bermuda, Maui, Spanish or Vidalia), peeled, thinly sliced and separated into rings**

¾ **cup grated fat-free Parmesan cheese (3 ounces)**

¼ **teaspoon salt, if desired**

1. Heat oven to 400°. Spray cookie sheet with olive oil–flavored cooking spray. Roll or pat pizza dough into 13 × 9-inch rectangle. Sprinkle with garlic and rosemary. Arrange onion rings evenly over dough. Sprinkle with cheese.

2. Bake about 12 minutes or until cheese just begins to brown. Lightly spray focaccia with cooking spray; sprinkle with salt. Cut into 6 wedges. Serve immediately.

**1 SERVING:** Calories 165 (Calories from Fat 20); Fat 2g (Saturated 1g); Cholesterol 5mg; Sodium 440mg; Carbohydrate 35g (Dietary Fiber 3g); Protein 5g

## Interesting Dippers

When deciding what to serve with dips, dunks and spreads, you'll find lots of dippers to choose from. Check out the variety of crackers now available. Look for different sizes, shapes, colors and flavors. Scan the snack aisle, too. Big pretzel sticks, flavored chips and snacks in unusual shapes will also work well. Fresh vegetables are always a crisp and colorful option. Try zucchini slices, radishes cut into rose shapes or baby corn on the cob (found in jars near the canned vegetables). Whatever you choose, keep in mind that dippers should be sturdy enough to stand up to the dip without breaking. ■

# CHEESE TRIANGLES

Prep: 20 min; Bake: 20 min        35 appetizers

1  **pound feta cheese**

2  **eggs, slightly beaten**

¼  **cup finely chopped chives**

¼  **teaspoon white pepper**

1  **package (6 ounces) frozen phyllo sheets, thawed**

¼  **cup (½ stick) margarine or butter, melted**

1. Heat oven to 350°. Grease cookie sheet. Crumble cheese in small bowl; mash with fork. Stir in eggs, chives and pepper until well mixed.

2. Cut stack of phyllo sheets lengthwise into thirds. Cover with waxed paper, then with damp towel to prevent them from drying out. Use 2 sheets of phyllo for each strip. Place 1 heaping teaspoon cheese mixture on end of strip; fold phyllo strip end over end, in triangular shape, to opposite end. Place on cookie sheet. Repeat with remaining phyllo and cheese mixture. (Triangles can be covered and refrigerated up to 24 hours at this point.) Brush margarine over triangles.

3. Bake about 20 minutes or until puffed and golden.

**1 SERVING:** Calories 60 (Calories from Fat 40); Fat 4.5g (Saturated 2.5g); Cholesterol 25mg; Sodium 190mg; Carbohydrate 3g (Dietary Fiber 0g); Protein 3g

# MUSHROOM PITA BITES

QUICK   Prep: 5 min; Bake: 10 min        8 servings

2  **pita breads (6 inches in diameter)**

2  **cups sliced mushrooms (about 5 ounces)**

1  **small red onion, thinly sliced**

1  **small green bell pepper, chopped**

2  **tablespoons chopped fresh or 2 teaspoons dried basil leaves**

1  **cup finely shredded mozzarella cheese (4 ounces)**

1  **tablespoon grated Parmesan cheese**

1. Heat oven to 425°. Split each pita bread around edge in half, using knife. Place pita rounds, cut sides up, on ungreased cookie sheet. Top with mushrooms, onion, bell pepper, basil and cheeses.

2. Bake 8 to 10 minutes or until cheese is melted. Cut each pita round into 8 pieces.

**1 SERVING:** Calories 100 (Calories from Fat 35); Fat 4g (Saturated 2g); Cholesterol 10mg; Sodium 150mg; Carbohydrate 11g (Dietary Fiber 2g); Protein 5g

# CHEESY POTATO SKINS

Prep: 15 min; Bake: 1 hr 15 min; Broil: 11 min          8 servings

**4  large potatoes (about 2 pounds)**

**2  tablespoons butter or stick margarine, melted (see tip)**

**1  cup shredded Colby-Monterey Jack cheese (4 ounces)**

**½  cup sour cream**

**8  medium green onions, trimmed and sliced**

1. Heat oven to 375°. Prick potatoes in several places with fork. Bake potatoes 1 hour to 1 hour 15 minutes or until tender. Let stand until cool enough to handle.

2. Cut potatoes lengthwise into fourths; carefully scoop out pulp, leaving ¼-inch shells. Save potato pulp for another use.

3. Set oven control to broil. Place potato shells, skin sides down, on rack in broiler pan. Brush with butter. Broil with tops 4 to 5 inches from heat 8 to 10 minutes or until crisp and brown. Sprinkle cheese over potato shells. Broil about 30 seconds or until cheese is melted. Serve hot with sour cream and green onions.

**1 SERVING:** Calories 180 (Calories from Fat 90); Fat 10g (Saturated 7g); Cholesterol 30mg; Sodium 120mg; Carbohydrate 19g (Dietary Fiber 2g); Protein 6g

***Lighter Cheesy Potato Skins:*** For 5 grams of fat and 135 calories per serving, decrease cheese to ½ cup and use fat-free sour cream.

---

**COOKING TIP**

• Margarine spreads with at least 65% vegetable oil can be used.

## COOKING TIPS

• If you can't find cream cheese with roasted garlic, use ¼ cup regular cream cheese at room temperature, and stir in ¼ teaspoon garlic powder.

• If you buy cooked chicken pieces or cook your own chicken, you will need 2 or 3 chicken breast halves.

# Mediterranean Chicken Quesadillas

**QUICK**    Prep: 10 min; Bake: 5 min        16 servings

**4**  flour tortillas (8 or 10 inches in diameter)

¼  cup reduced-fat cream cheese with roasted garlic, softened

½  pound cooked chicken or turkey (from the deli); about 1 cup, cut into ½-inch pieces

**3**  roma (plum) tomatoes, chopped

**1**  cup shredded mozzarella cheese (4 ounces)

½  cup crumbled feta cheese (2 ounces)

    Chopped fresh cilantro or parsley, if desired

    Sliced ripe olives, if desired

    Sliced jalapeño chili, if desired

    Salsa, if desired

1. Heat oven to 450°.

2. Place 2 tortillas on ungreased cookie sheet. Spread about 2 table-spoons cream cheese over each of the 2 tortillas. Top with chicken, tomatoes, mozzarella cheese and feta cheese. Top with the 2 re-maining tortillas.

3. Bake about 5 minutes or just until cheese is melted. To serve, cut each quesadilla into 8 wedges. Sprinkle with cilantro. Garnish each wedge with an olive or jalapeño chili slice, using toothpick to hold the olive or chili in place. Serve with salsa.

**1 SERVING:** Calories 95 (Calories from Fat 45); Fat 5g (Saturated 2g); Cholesterol 20mg; Sodium 160mg; Carbohydrate 7g (Dietary Fiber 0g); Protein 6g

## SPECIAL TOUCH

### Menu, Buffet or Place Cards

You will need:

**Selected image to copy**

**8½ × 11-inch sheets overhead transparency film** (available at copy center or office supply stores)

**Blank cards or card stock**

**Adhesive tape**

1. Photocopy an image onto transparency film.

2. Cut out desired shape in card.

3. Tape image onto back of card.

*Tip:* Before cutting out the desired shape in the cards, you can print a menu or other names on the cards using a computer.

# $\mathcal{S}$PINACH QUESADILLAS WITH FETA CHEESE

**QUICK**  Prep: 15 min; Cook: 12 min        16 servings

4 fat-free flour tortillas (8 inches in diameter)
¼ cup reduced-fat cream cheese with roasted garlic, softened
2 cups frozen chopped spinach, thawed and squeezed to drain
1 tablespoon finely chopped red onion
¼ cup crumbled feta cheese (1 ounce)
2 tablespoons fat-free sour cream
  Cherry tomato halves, if desired
  Sliced ripe olives, if desired

**1.** Spread 2 tortillas with cream cheese. Layer tortillas with spinach, onion and feta cheese. Top with remaining 2 tortillas; press lightly.

**2.** Spray 12-inch nonstick skillet with cooking spray; heat over medium heat. Cook each quesadilla in skillet 2 to 3 minutes on each side or until light golden brown.

**3.** Cut each quesadilla into 8 wedges. Top with sour cream, tomato halves and olives. Secure with toothpicks. Serve warm.

**1 SERVING:** Calories 45 (Calories from Fat 10); Fat 1g (Saturated 1g); Cholesterol 5mg; Sodium 130mg; Carbohydrate 7g (Dietary Fiber 0g); Protein 2g

# OVEN-FRIED CHICKEN CHUNKS WITH PEANUT SAUCE

Prep: 10 min; Bake: 25 min        8 servings

- 1½ **cups cornflakes cereal, crushed**
- ½ **cup Reduced Fat Bisquick® baking mix**
- ¾ **teaspoon paprika**
- ¼ **teaspoon salt**
- ¼ **teaspoon pepper**
- 1 **pound boneless, skinless chicken breasts, cut into 1-inch pieces**
- **Peanut Sauce (below)**

**1.** Heat oven to 400°. Line jelly roll pan, 15½ × 10½ × 1 inch, with aluminum foil.

**2.** Mix all ingredients except chicken and Peanut Sauce in 2-quart resealable plastic food-storage bag. Shake about 6 chicken pieces at a time in bag until coated. Shake off any extra crumbs. Place chicken pieces in pan. Spray with cooking spray.

**3.** Bake uncovered 20 to 25 minutes or until coating is crisp and chicken is no longer pink in center. Serve with Peanut Sauce.

**1 SERVING:** Calories 120 (Calories from Fat 25); Fat 3g (Saturated 1g); Cholesterol 35mg; Sodium 240mg; Carbohydrate 10g (Dietary Fiber 0g); Protein 13g

## PEANUT SAUCE

- ½ **cup fat-free plain yogurt**
- ¼ **cup reduced-fat peanut butter**
- ½ **cup fat-free (skim) milk**
- 1 **tablespoon soy sauce**
- ⅛ **teaspoon ground red pepper (cayenne), if desired**

Mix all ingredients in 10-inch nonstick skillet. Cook over medium heat 3 to 4 minutes, stirring occasionally, until mixture begins to thicken.

**CUTTING A CHICKEN WING**

Use a sharp knife or kitchen scissors to cut chicken wing at joints to make 3 pieces. Discard tips.

# ℬUFFALO CHICKEN WINGS

Prep: 15 min; Bake: 30 min          24 servings

12  chicken wings (about 2 pounds)
 2  tablespoons margarine or butter
 ½  cup all-purpose flour
 ½  teaspoon salt
 ¼  teaspoon pepper
 1  cup barbecue sauce
 1  tablespoon red pepper sauce
 ½  teaspoon Cajun seasoning
 ¼  teaspoon ground cumin
 1  bottle (8 ounces) blue cheese dressing, if desired
    Celery sticks, if desired

1. Cut each chicken wing at joints to make 3 pieces. Discard tips. Cut and discard excess skin from chicken with kitchen scissors or knife.

2. Heat oven to 425°. Place margarine in rectangular pan and place in oven about 1 minute or until melted.

3. Mix flour, salt and pepper in a large heavy-duty resealable plastic food-storage bag. Place chicken in bag, seal bag and shake until chicken is completely coated with flour mixture. Place chicken in a single layer in pan.

4. Bake uncovered 20 minutes. While the chicken is baking, mix barbecue sauce, pepper sauce, Cajun seasoning and cumin in small bowl.

5. Remove chicken from oven and turn pieces over with tongs. Pour sauce mixture over chicken, spooning sauce over chicken pieces if necessary to coat completely.

6. Continue baking uncovered about 10 minutes longer or until juice of chicken is no longer pink when cut in center of thickest pieces. Serve with blue cheese dressing and celery sticks.

**1 SERVING:** Calories 70 (Calories from Fat 35); Fat 4g (Saturated 1g); Cholesterol 15mg; Sodium 170mg; Carbohydrate 3g (Dietary Fiber 0g); Protein 5g

• To save time, make and bake the meatballs and freeze them up to 3 months, or purchase frozen meatballs from your super-market. Heat sauce ingredients to boiling, then stir in frozen meatballs. Simmer uncovered for about 20 minutes or until meatballs are hot.

• When serving appetizers, con-sider using two trays for each ap-petizer served. When one tray is on the buffet table, the empty tray can be refilled in the kitchen to quickly replace the other when needed.

# $\mathcal{S}$WEET-AND-SOUR MEATBALLS

Prep: 10 min; Bake: 15 min; Cook: 20 min     30 meatballs

- 1   medium onion, peeled and finely chopped
- 1   pound ground beef
- ⅓  cup dry bread crumbs
- ¼  cup milk
- ¼  teaspoon salt
- ⅛  teaspoon pepper
- 1   egg
- 1   jar (9½ ounces) sweet-and-sour sauce

**1.** Heat oven to 400°.

**2.** Mix onion, beef, bread crumbs, milk, salt, pepper and egg in large bowl. Shape mixture into thirty 1-inch meatballs.

**3.** Place meatballs in ungreased rectangular pan. Bake uncovered about 15 minutes or until beef in center of meatball is no longer pink and juice of beef is clear.

**4.** Place meatballs and sweet-and-sour sauce in saucepan. Heat to boiling over medium-high heat, stirring occasionally. Once mixture is boiling, reduce heat just enough so mixture bubbles gently. Cover and cook about 15 minutes or until sauce and meatballs are hot. Serve hot with toothpicks.

**1 MEATBALL:** Calories 40 (Calories from Fat 20); Fat 2g (Saturated 1g); Cholesterol 15mg; Sodium 70mg; Carbohydrate 2g (Dietary Fiber 0g); Protein 3g

***Salsa Meatballs:*** Substitute 1 jar (12 ounces) salsa for the sweet-and-sour sauce. Garnish with sliced green onions, if desired.

# BREADS

## Mountain Bran Muffins

Prep: 10 min; Bake: 20 min; Stand: 3 min          12 muffins

- 1 cup buttermilk
- 1 egg
- 2½ cups Mountain Bran Mix (below)
- ½ cup chopped walnuts
- ½ cup raisins

**1.** Heat oven to 400°. Grease bottoms only of 12 medium muffin cups, 2½ × 1¼ inches, or line with paper baking cups.

**2.** Prepare Mountain Bran Mix. Beat buttermilk and egg in large bowl. Stir in Mountain Bran Mix just until moistened; fold in walnuts and raisins.

**3.** Divide batter evenly among muffin cups (about seven-eighths full). Bake until golden brown or toothpick inserted in center comes out clean, 18 to 20 minutes. Let stand 3 minutes; remove muffins from pan.

**1 MUFFIN:** Calories 190 (Calories from Fat 65); Fat 7g (Saturated 1g); Cholesterol 20mg; Sodium 220mg; Carbohydrate 31g (Dietary Fiber 3g); Protein 4g

### MOUNTAIN BRAN MIX

- 3 cups all-purpose flour
- 3 cups Fiber One® cereal, finely crushed
- 2 cups packed brown sugar
- 1½ teaspoons baking soda
- 1½ teaspoons baking powder
- 1½ teaspoons salt
- ½ cup shortening

Mix flour, cereal, brown sugar, baking soda, baking powder and salt in 4-quart bowl. Cut in shortening until mixture resembles coarse crumbs. Cover and store in cool, dry place no longer than 1 month.

**COOKING TIP**

• The Mountain Bran Mix recipe makes about 7½ cups, which is enough for 3 dozen muffins.

# Sweet Corn Bread Muffins

Prep: 10 min; Bake: 25 min          12 muffins

   1  **cup milk**
  ¼  **cup (½ stick) margarine or butter, melted**
   1  **egg**
1¼  **cups cornmeal**
   1  **cup all-purpose flour**
  ½  **cup sugar**
   1  **tablespoon baking powder**
  ½  **teaspoon salt**

**1.** Heat oven to 400°. Grease bottoms only of 12 medium muffin cups, 2½ × 1¼ inches, or line with paper baking cups.

**2.** Beat milk, margarine and egg in 3-quart bowl. Stir in remaining ingredients all at once just until flour is moistened (batter will be lumpy).

**3.** Fill muffin cups about three-fourths full. Bake until golden brown and a toothpick inserted in center comes out clean, 20 to 25 minutes.

**1 MUFFIN:** Calories 175 (Calories from Fat 45); Fat 5g (Saturated 1g); Cholesterol 20mg; Sodium 290mg; Carbohydrate 29g (Dietary Fiber 1g); Protein 4g

# CHEDDAR AND GREEN ONION BISCUITS

**QUICK**  Prep: 15 min; Bake: 11 min        8 biscuits

1⅓  **cups all-purpose flour**

1½  **teaspoons baking powder**

½  **teaspoon salt**

¼  **teaspoon baking soda**

¼  **teaspoon ground mustard**

4  **medium green onions, trimmed and sliced**

⅓  **cup shredded reduced-fat Cheddar cheese (1½ ounces)**

¾  **cup buttermilk**

3  **tablespoons vegetable oil**

1. Heat oven to 450°. Spray cookie sheet with cooking spray. Mix flour, baking powder, salt, baking soda and mustard in medium bowl. Stir in onions and cheese. Mix buttermilk and oil; stir into flour mixture until soft dough forms.

2. Drop dough by 8 spoonfuls onto cookie sheet. Bake 9 to 11 minutes or until golden brown. Serve warm.

**1 BISCUIT:** Calories 120 (Calories from Fat 45); Fat 5g (Saturated 1g); Cholesterol 0mg; Sodium 300mg; Carbohydrate 16g (Dietary Fiber 1g); Protein 4g

## Some Like It Hot: Reheating Your Bread

It is always a treat when warm bread is served at a meal. You can freshen up room-temperature loaves of bread by heating them in the oven.

For a crisper crust, place the loaf right on the oven rack. Heat it in a 300° oven about 20 minutes or until the crust is crisp and warm. For a softer crust, wrap the loaf in aluminum foil before popping into the oven. You also can heat coffee cakes in aluminum foil the same way and then frost and decorate.

Bread slices and rolls can be warmed in the microwave, but you must be very careful so they don't overheat and become tough or hard. Breads heated in the microwave become dry and tough faster than bread heated in a conventional or toaster oven, so plan to eat them right away. ■

# $\mathcal{S}$OUR CREAM BREADSTICK TWISTS

Prep: 20 min; Bake: 12 min        12 breadsticks

- **2 cups all-purpose flour**
- **3 teaspoons baking powder**
- **½ teaspoon salt**
- **⅓ cup shortening**
- **1¼ cups sour cream**
- **2 tablespoons chopped fresh or freeze-dried chives**
- **2 tablespoons margarine or butter, melted**
- **¼ cup poppy seeds**

**1.** Heat oven to 450°.

**2.** Mix flour, baking powder and salt in large bowl. Cut in the shortening, using pastry blender or crisscrossing 2 knives, until mixture looks like fine crumbs.

**3.** Stir in sour cream and chives until dough leaves side of bowl and forms a ball.

**4.** Turn dough onto lightly floured surface. Gently roll dough in flour to coat all sides. Shape dough into a ball. Knead dough by curving your fingers around and folding dough toward you, then pushing it away with heels of your hands, using a quick rocking motion. Repeat 10 times, turning dough each time.

**5.** Roll dough into a 12 × 8-inch rectangle. Cut rectangle crosswise into 12 breadsticks, each about 1 inch wide. Carefully pick up both ends of each breadstick, and twist dough. Place breadsticks about 1 inch apart on ungreased cookie sheet. Brush breadsticks lightly with margarine. Sprinkle with poppy seeds.

**6.** Bake 10 to 12 minutes or until golden brown. Immediately remove breadsticks from cookie sheet to wire cooling rack. Serve warm.

**1 BREADSTICK:** Calories 195 (Calories from Fat 115); Fat 13g (Saturated 6g); Cholesterol 20mg; Sodium 240mg; Carbohydrate 17g (Dietary Fiber 1g); Protein 3g

---

**COOKING TIP**

- For a flavor twist, get creative with other toppers on these breadsticks. Instead of sprinkling with poppy seeds, try sesame seeds, grated Parmesan cheese or coarse salt.

---

**ROLLING DOUGH**

Use a rolling pin to roll the dough into a 12 × 8-inch rectangle.

**CUTTING AND SHAPING BREADSTICKS**

Use a sharp knife to cut rectangle of dough crosswise into 12 breadsticks, each about 1 inch wide. Carefully pick up both ends of each breadstick, and twist dough.

**COOKING TIP**

• For fun variety, after rolling the balls in margarine, roll them in a cinnamon and sugar mixture or in a savory blend of fragrant herbs.

# PULL-APART BREAD

Prep: 20 min; Rise: 30 min; Bake: 30 min; Cool: 2 min        12 servings

**3½ to 3¾ cups all-purpose flour**
**2 tablespoons sugar**
**½ teaspoon salt**
**1 package active dry yeast**
**1 cup milk**
**¼ cup (½ stick) margarine or butter**
**1 egg**
**¼ cup (½ stick) margarine or butter, melted**

**1.** Grease 12-cup Bundt cake pan or tube pan, 10 × 4 inches.

**2.** Mix 1½ cups of the flour, the sugar, salt and yeast in 3-quart bowl. Heat milk and ¼ cup margarine in 1-quart saucepan over medium-low heat, stirring frequently, until very warm (120° to 130°). Add milk mixture and egg to flour mixture. Beat on low speed until moistened; beat 3 minutes on medium speed. Stir in enough remaining flour to make dough easy to handle.

**3.** Turn dough onto lightly floured surface. Knead until smooth and elastic, about 5 minutes. Shape dough into 24 balls. Dip each ball of dough into the melted margarine. Layer evenly in pan. Cover and let rise in warm place until double, 20 to 30 minutes.

**4.** Heat oven to 350°. Bake until golden brown, 25 to 30 minutes. Cool 2 minutes; invert onto heatproof serving plate. Serve warm.

**1 SERVING:** Calories 220 (Calories from Fat 80); Fat 9g (Saturated 2g); Cholesterol 20mg; Sodium 220mg; Carbohydrate 31g (Dietary Fiber 1g); Protein 5g

# $\mathcal{F}$IERY FOUR-PEPPER BREAD

Prep: 10 min; Cycle time

| 1½-pound recipe (12 slices) | | 2-pound recipe (16 slices) | |
|---|---|---|---|
| ¾ | cup plus 3 tablespoons water | 1¼ | cups water |
| 1 | tablespoon red pepper sauce | 1½ | tablespoons red pepper sauce |
| 1 | tablespoon chopped jalapeño chili | 1½ | tablespoons jalapeño chili |
| 2 | tablespoons margarine or butter, softened | 2 | tablespoons margarine or butter, softened |
| 3 | cups bread flour | 4 | cups bread flour |
| ¼ | teaspoon medium grind black pepper | ½ | teaspoon medium grind black pepper |
| ½ | teaspoon crushed red pepper | ¾ | teaspoon crushed red pepper |
| 1 | tablespoon sugar | 2 | tablespoons sugar |
| 1 | teaspoon salt | 1¼ | teaspoons salt |
| 1½ | teaspoons bread machine or quick active dry yeast | 2¼ | teaspoons bread machine or quick active dry yeast |

**1.** Make 1½-pound recipe with bread machines that use 3 cups flour, or make 2-pound recipe with bread machines that use 4 cups flour.

**2.** Measure carefully, placing all ingredients in bread machine pan in the order recommended by manufacturer.

**3.** Select Basic/White cycle. Use Medium or Light crust color. Do not use Delay cycles. Remove baked bread from pan, and cool on wire rack.

**1 SLICE:** Calories 140 (Calories from Fat 20); Fat 2g (Saturated Fat 0g); Cholesterol 2mg; Sodium 230mg; Carbohydrate 28g (Dietary Fiber 1g); Protein 4g

# DOUBLE-GARLIC POTATO BREAD

Prep: 10 min; Cycle time

| 1½-pound recipe (12 slices) | 2-pound recipe (16 slices) |
|---|---|
| 1 cup water | 1¼ cups water |
| 2 tablespoons margarine or butter, softened | 3 tablespoons margarine or butter, softened |
| 1 egg | 1 egg |
| 3 cups bread flour | 4 cups bread flour |
| ⅔ cup mashed potato mix seasoned with roasted garlic (dry) | ⅔ cup mashed potato mix seasoned with roasted garlic (dry) |
| 1 tablespoon sugar | 1 tablespoon sugar |
| 1½ teaspoons salt | 1½ teaspoons salt |
| ¼ teaspoon garlic powder | ¼ teaspoon garlic powder |
| 2½ teaspoons bread machine or quick active dry yeast | 2 teaspoons bread machine or quick active dry yeast |

**1.** Make 1½-pound recipe with bread machines that use 3 cups flour, or make 2-pound recipe with bread machines that use 4 cups flour.

**2.** Measure carefully, placing all ingredients in bread machine pan in the order recommended by manufacturer.

**3.** Select Basic/White cycle. Use Medium or Light crust color. Do not use Delay cycles. Remove baked bread from pan, and cool on wire rack.

**1 SLICE:** Calories 150 (Calories from Fat 20); 2g Fat (Saturated Fat 0g); Cholesterol 0mg; Sodium 320mg; Carbohydrate 30g (Dietary Fiber 1g); Protein 4g

## COOKING TIPS

• For good texture and volume, slightly less yeast is needed in the 2-pound loaf than is needed in the 1½-pound loaf.

• If you don't have roasted garlic mashed potato mix, use the same amount of unflavored mashed potato mix and increase the garlic powder to ½ teaspoon.

# OLD-WORLD RYE BREAD

Prep: 15 min; Cycle time; Rest: 10 min; Rise: 45 min; Bake: 28 min
1 loaf, 16 slices

⅔ **cup water**
2 **tablespoons vegetable oil**
⅔ **cup buttermilk**
2¼ **cups bread flour**
1 **cup rye flour**
⅓ **cup mashed potato mix (dry)**
2 **tablespoons packed brown sugar**
1¼ **teaspoons salt**
1 **teaspoon caraway seed**
2 **teaspoons bread machine or quick active dry yeast**
**Cornmeal**
**Additional caraway seed, if desired**

**1.** Measure carefully, placing all ingredients except cornmeal and additional caraway seed in bread machine pan in the order recommended by manufacturer.

**2.** Select Dough/Manual cycle. Do not use delay cycles.

**3.** Remove dough from pan, using lightly floured hands. Cover and let rest 10 minutes on lightly floured surface.

**4.** Grease large cookie sheet; sprinkle with cornmeal. Roll dough into 25-inch rope. Curl rope into coil shape; tuck end under. Place on cookie sheet. Cover and let rise in warm place 30 to 45 minutes or until double. (Dough is ready if indentation remains when touched.)

**5.** Heat oven to 400°. Brush water over loaf; sprinkle with cornmeal and additional caraway seed. Bake 23 to 28 minutes or until loaf is golden brown and sounds hollow when tapped. Remove from cookie sheet to wire rack; cool.

**1 SLICE:** Calories 125 (Calories from Fat 30); Fat 3g (Saturated 1g); Cholesterol 2mg; Sodium 160mg; Carbohydrate 23g (Dietary Fiber 2g); Protein 3g

# SANDWICHES AND PIZZAS

## CHIPOTLE—BLACK BEAN BURRITOS

**QUICK**    Prep: 10 min; Cook: 7 min          4 servings

|   |   |
|---|---|
| 1 | large onion, peeled and chopped |
| 6 | cloves garlic, peeled and finely chopped |
| 1 | can (15 ounces) black beans, rinsed, drained and mashed |
| 1 to 2 | teaspoons finely chopped chipotle chilies in adobo sauce, drained |
| 4 | fat-free flour tortillas (6 or 8 inches in diameter) |
| ½ | cup shredded reduced-fat mozzarella cheese (2 ounces) |
| 1 | large tomato, chopped |

1. Spray 10-inch nonstick skillet with cooking spray; heat over medium-high heat. Cook onion and garlic in skillet about 5 minutes, stirring occasionally, until onion is tender. Stir in beans and chilies; cook until hot.

2. Place one-fourth of the bean mixture on center of each tortilla. Top with cheese and tomato. Fold one end of tortilla up about 1 inch over filling; fold right and left sides over folded end, overlapping. Fold remaining end down. Place seam side down on serving platter or plate.

**1 SERVING:** Calories 255 (Calories from Fat 25); Fat 3g (Saturated 2g); Cholesterol 8mg; Sodium 600mg; Carbohydrate 49g (Dietary Fiber 9g); Protein 16g

# CHICKEN-PESTO SANDWICHES

**QUICK**    Prep: 10 min; Broil: 20 min          6 sandwiches

- 6  boneless, skinless chicken breast halves (about 1¾ pounds)
- ½  teaspoon salt
- 2  tablespoons chopped fresh or 2 teaspoons dried oregano leaves
- 1  round focaccia bread (about 10 inches in diameter)
- 1  container (7 ounces) refrigerated pesto
- 6  slices tomato
- 1½  cups shredded spinach

**1.** Flatten each chicken breast half to ¼-inch thickness between sheets of plastic wrap or waxed paper. Sprinkle with salt and oregano.

**2.** Set oven control to broil. Place chicken on rack in broiler pan. Broil with tops 4 to 6 inches from heat 15 to 20 minutes, turning once, until juice is no longer pink when centers of thickest pieces are cut.

**3.** Cut focaccia horizontally in half; cut into 6 wedges. Spread pesto on cut sides of bread. Layer chicken, tomato and spinach on bottom wedges. Top with top wedges.

**1 SANDWICH:** Calories 530 (Calories from Fat 250); Fat 28g (Saturated 5g); Cholesterol 85mg; Sodium 1090mg; Carbohydrate 34g (Dietary Fiber 3g); Protein 38g

# CHICKEN QUESADILLA SANDWICHES

Prep: 25 min; Cook: 6 min per quesadilla          4 servings

- **2 teaspoons vegetable oil**
- **1 pound boneless, skinless chicken breasts**
- **¼ cup chopped fresh cilantro**
- **¼ teaspoon ground cumin**
- **8 flour tortillas (8 to 10 inches in diameter)**
- **1 cup shredded Monterey Jack cheese (4 ounces)**
- **1 can (4 ounces) chopped green chilies, drained**
- **Salsa, if desired**

1. Heat oil in 10-inch nonstick skillet over medium-high heat. Cook chicken, cilantro and cumin in oil 15 to 20 minutes, turning chicken once and stirring cilantro mixture occasionally, until juice of chicken is no longer pink when centers of thickest pieces are cut. Shred chicken into small pieces; mix chicken and cilantro mixture.

2. Spray 1 side of 1 tortilla with cooking spray; place sprayed side down in same skillet. Layer with one-fourth of the chicken mixture, ¼ cup of the cheese and one-fourth of the chilies to within ½ inch of edge of tortilla. Top with another tortilla; spray top of tortilla with cooking spray.

3. Cook over medium-high heat 4 to 6 minutes, turning after 2 minutes, until light golden brown. Repeat with remaining tortillas, chicken mixture, cheese and chilies. Cut quesadillas into wedges. Serve with salsa.

**1 SERVING:** Calories 495 (Calories from Fat 180); Fat 20g (Saturated 7g); Cholesterol 75mg; Sodium 690mg; Carbohydrate 50g (Dietary Fiber 3g); Protein 32g

# ℬARBECUED ROAST BEEF SANDWICHES

**QUICK**  Prep: 5 min; Cook: 10 min          6 sandwiches

1  **cup barbecue sauce**

1  **pound thinly sliced cooked roast beef, cut into 1-inch strips (3 cups)**

6  **hamburger buns, split**

**1.** Heat barbecue sauce in medium saucepan just to boiling.

**2.** Stir beef into sauce. Cover and simmer about 5 minutes or until beef is hot.

**3.** Fill buns with beef mixture.

**1 SANDWICH:** Calories 270 (Calories from Fat 55); Fat 6g (Saturated 2g); Cholesterol 55mg; Sodium 540mg; Carbohydrate 30g (Dietary Fiber 1g); Protein 25g

# ℋAMBURGERS PARMIGIANA

**QUICK**  Prep: 5 min; Cook: 10 min          4 servings

1  **pound ground beef**

1  **small onion, peeled and chopped**

2  **tablespoons grated Parmesan cheese (½ ounce)**

½  **teaspoon garlic salt**

1  **jar (15½ ounces) chunky-style spaghetti sauce**

½  **cup shredded mozzarella cheese (2 ounces)**

4  **slices French bread, toasted, or 2 hamburger buns, split and toasted**

**1.** Mix ground beef, onion, Parmesan cheese and garlic salt. Shape into 4 patties, each about ½ inch thick.

**2.** Cook in 10-inch skillet over medium heat, turning frequently, until desired doneness; drain.

**3.** Pour spaghetti sauce over patties, heat until hot. Top each patty with 2 tablespoons mozzarella cheese; let stand until cheese begins to melt. Serve on French bread.

**1 SERVING:** Calories 465 (Calories from Fat 215); Fat 24g (Saturated 9g); Cholesterol 75mg; Sodium 980mg; Carbohydrate 35g (Dietary Fiber 2g); Protein 30g

# ITALIAN SAUSAGE CALZONE

Prep: 15 min; Bake: 20 min; Cool: 5 min          4 servings

½ **pound bulk Italian sausage**

1 **small onion, peeled and chopped**

⅓ **cup pizza sauce**

1 **can (2 ounces) mushroom stems and pieces, drained**

2 **cups Original Bisquick® baking mix**

⅓ **cup hot water**

1 **tablespoon vegetable oil**

1 **cup shredded mozzarella cheese (4 ounces)**

¼ **cup grated Parmesan cheese (1 ounce)**

1 **egg white**

1. Heat oven to 450°.

2. Cook and stir sausage in large skillet over medium heat until brown; drain. Stir in onion, pizza sauce and mushrooms; reserve.

3. Mix baking mix, hot water and oil until dough forms. Roll into 12-inch circle on cloth-covered surface dusted with baking mix. Place on ungreased cookie sheet.

4. Top half of the circle with mozzarella cheese, sausage mixture and Parmesan cheese to within 1 inch of edge. Fold dough over filling; press edge with fork to seal. Brush with egg white. Bake until golden brown, 15 to 20 minutes. Cool 5 minutes; cut into wedges.

**1 SERVING:** Calories 515 (Calories from Fat 260); Fat 29g (Saturated 10g); Cholesterol 50mg; Sodium 1620mg; Carbohydrate 41g (Dietary Fiber 2g); Protein 24g

# WHOLE WHEAT VEGETABLE CALZONE

Prep: 15 min; Bake: 25 min; Rest: 5 min        6 servings

**Whole Wheat Calzone Dough (below)**
1    **package (10 ounces) frozen chopped broccoli**
⅓    **cup creamy Italian dressing**
½    **teaspoon salt**
1    **package (3 ounces) cream cheese, softened**
1    **cup sliced mushrooms, or 1 jar (4½ ounces) sliced mushrooms, drained**
2    **carrots, shredded**
1    **medium tomato, chopped**
½    **small green bell pepper, chopped**
1    **egg, beaten**

**1.** Heat oven to 375°.

**2.** Prepare Whole Wheat Calzone Dough. Divide into 6 equal pieces. Pat each into 7-inch circle on lightly floured surface, turning dough over occasionally to coat with flour.

**3.** Rinse frozen broccoli in cold water to separate; drain. Mix dressing, salt and cream cheese until well blended (mixture will appear curdled). Stir in broccoli and remaining vegetables.

**4.** Top half of each circle with ⅔ cup vegetable mixture to within 1 inch of edge. Fold dough over filling; fold edge up and pinch to seal. Place on greased cookie sheet; brush with egg. Bake until golden, 25 minutes.

**1 SERVING:** Calories 350 (Calories from Fat 155); Fat 17g (Saturated 5g); Cholesterol 50mg; Sodium 770mg; Carbohydrate 47g (Dietary Fiber 9g); Protein 11g

## WHOLE WHEAT CALZONE DOUGH

1    **package active dry yeast**
1    **cup warm water (105° to 115°)**
1    **tablespoon sugar**
2    **tablespoons vegetable oil**
1    **teaspoon salt**
2½ to 3    **cups whole wheat flour**

Dissolve yeast in warm water in large bowl. Stir in sugar, oil, salt and 1 cup of the flour. Beat until smooth. Mix in enough remaining flour to make dough easy to handle. Turn dough onto lightly floured surface; knead until smooth and elastic, about 5 minutes. Cover with bowl and let rest 5 minutes.

# $\mathcal{G}$REEK PIZZA

Prep: 15 min; Rest: 5 min; Bake: 30 min    6 servings

**Crust (below)**

1  **cup shredded Kasseri or mozzarella cheese (4 ounces)**

1  **package (10 ounces) frozen chopped spinach, thawed and squeezed dry**

½  **pound ground lamb**

1  **tablespoon snipped fresh oregano leaves or 1 teaspoon dried oregano leaves**

1  **medium tomato, chopped**

½  **cup crumbled feta cheese**

½  **cup Greek or ripe olives, cut up**

1  **tablespoon olive oil, if desired**

**1.** Place oven rack in lowest position of oven. Heat oven to 425°.

**2.** Prepare Crust; sprinkle remaining ingredients except olive oil evenly over top to within ½ inch of edge. Bake until crust is golden brown, 25 to 30 minutes. Drizzle with 1 tablespoon olive oil if desired.

**1 SERVING:** Calories 415 (Calories from Fat 160); Fat 18g (Saturated 7g); Cholesterol 45mg; Sodium 780mg; Carbohydrate 46g (Dietary Fiber 3g); Protein 20g

## CRUST

1  **package active dry yeast**

1  **cup warm water (105° to 115°)**

2½  **cups all-purpose flour**

2  **tablespoons olive or vegetable oil**

1  **teaspoon sugar**

1  **teaspoon salt**

**1.** Dissolve yeast in warm water in 2½-quart bowl. Stir in remaining ingredients; beat vigorously 20 strokes. Let rest 5 minutes.

**2.** With floured fingers, press dough in greased 12-inch pizza pan or into 11-inch circle on greased cookie sheet

**COOKING TIP**

• Kasseri cheese is a Greek cheese made from sheep or goat's milk. It has a sharp, salty flavor and melts beautifully. Plus, the cheese itself is hard, so it is perfect for shredding. Look for this creamy, gold-colored cheese, sold in blocks, in your grocer's refrigerator or at speciality cheese shops.

## SERVING TIP

• You can also serve this Italian classic mozzarella and tomato pizza as an appetizer. For bite-size portions, cut pizza into small squares instead of wedges.

# *P*IZZA MARGHERITA

**QUICK**    Prep: 10 min; Bake: 20 min        8 servings

- 1  can (10 ounces) refrigerated pizza crust dough
- 2  cups shredded mozzarella cheese (8 ounces)
- 2  roma (plum) tomatoes, sliced
- ¼  teaspoon salt
- ⅛  teaspoon pepper
- ¼  cup chopped fresh basil leaves
- 1  tablespoon olive or vegetable oil

**1.** Heat oven to 425°. Lightly grease cookie sheet with shortening.

**2.** Unroll pizza crust dough. Press dough into 12-inch circle on greased cookie sheet, pressing from center to edge so edge is slightly thicker than center.

**3.** Sprinkle 1 cup of the cheese over dough to within ½ inch of edge.

**4.** Arrange tomatoes on cheese. Sprinkle salt, pepper and 2 table-spoons of the basil over tomatoes and cheese. Sprinkle with remaining 1 cup cheese. Drizzle with oil.

**5.** Bake about 20 minutes or until crust is golden brown and cheese is melted. Sprinkle with remaining 2 tablespoons basil. To serve, cut pizza into wedges.

**1 SERVING:** Calories 190 (Calories from Fat 70); Fat 8g (Saturated 4g); Cholesterol 15mg; Sodium 380mg; Carbohydrate 30g (Dietary Fiber 1g); Protein 11g

# ℬBQ CHICKEN PIZZA

**QUICK**  Prep: 8 min; Bake: 12 min          6 servings

- **3  packages (8 ounces each) Italian bread shells or 6 pita breads (6 inches in diameter)**
- **¾  cup barbecue sauce**
- **1½  cups cut-up cooked chicken**
- **¾  cup shredded smoked or regular Cheddar cheese (3 ounces)**
- **6  tablespoons chopped red onion**

Heat oven to 450°. Place bread shells on ungreased large cookie sheet. Spread barbecue sauce on bread shells to within ¼ inch of edges. Top with chicken and cheese. Sprinkle with onion. Bake 7 to 12 minutes or until cheese is melted.

**1 SERVING:** Calories 275 (Calories from Fat 70); Fat 8g (Saturated 4g); Cholesterol 45mg; Sodium 650mg; Carbohydrate 34g (Dietary Fiber 2g); Protein 19g

# MAIN DISHES

## $\mathcal{V}$EGETABLE—CHEDDAR CHEESE SOUP

**QUICK**   Prep: 10 min; Cook: 8 min          8 servings

½ cup margarine or butter

2 medium carrots, finely chopped

1 small onion, peeled and finely chopped

1 stalk celery, finely chopped

2 medium zucchini, cut into 2-inch strips

½ cup all-purpose flour

1 teaspoon dry mustard

2 cups chicken broth

2 cups half-and-half

3 cups shredded Cheddar cheese (12 ounces)

**1.** Heat margarine in Dutch oven until melted. Cook carrot, onion and celery in margarine until softened. Stir in zucchini and cook about 2 minutes or until crisp-tender. Mix flour and mustard; stir into vegetable mixture.

**2.** Gradually stir in chicken broth and half-and-half. Cook over medium heat, stirring constantly until mixture boils; boil 1 minute. Slowly stir in cheese until melted.

**1 SERVING:** Calories 400 (Calories from Fat 295); Fat 33g (Saturated 15g); Cholesterol 65mg; Sodium 710mg; Carbohydrate 13g (Dietary Fiber 2g); Protein 15g

# ITALIAN CHICKEN AND BEAN SOUP

Prep: 15 min; Cook: 25 min        4 servings

- 1 **tablespoon olive or vegetable oil**
- ½ **pound boneless, skinless chicken breast halves, cut into ½-inch pieces**
- ½ **teaspoon Italian seasoning**
- 2 **cans (14½ ounces each) ready-to-serve chicken broth**
- 2 **cups water**
- ½ **cup uncooked small pasta shells**
- ½ **cup uncooked juniorettes (small spiral pasta)**
- 1 **can (15 to 16 ounces) kidney beans, rinsed and drained**
- 1 **small red bell pepper, coarsely chopped**
- 1 **medium zucchini, cut into 1-inch pieces**

**1.** Heat oil in 3-quart saucepan over medium-high heat. Add chicken; sprinkle with ¼ teaspoon of the Italian seasoning. Cook, stirring frequently, 3 to 5 minutes or until browned.

**2.** Add broth and water. Heat to boiling. Add pasta, kidney beans and bell pepper. Heat to boiling; reduce heat. Cook uncovered 10 to 12 minutes, stirring occasionally, until pasta is tender. Stir in remaining ¼ teaspoon Italian seasoning and the zucchini. Cook 3 to 5 minutes or until zucchini is crisp-tender.

**1 SERVING:** Calories 375 (Calories from Fat 70); Fat 8g (Saturated 1g); Cholesterol 35mg; Sodium 1400mg; Carbohydrate 53g (Dietary Fiber 9g); Protein 31g

# CREAMY TOMATO-BEEF NOODLE SOUP

**QUICK**   Prep: 5 min; Cook: 20 min          4 servings

1  **pound ground beef**
1  **small onion, peeled and chopped**
2  **cups tomato juice**
1  **can (10¾ ounces) condensed cream of celery soup**
1¼  **cups water**
¾  **teaspoon chopped fresh or ¼ teaspoon dried marjoram leaves**
½  **cup frozen green peas**
⅛  **teaspoon pepper**
1  **bay leaf**
1  **cup uncooked egg noodles**

**1.** Cook beef and onion in 4-quart Dutch oven over medium heat about 10 minutes, stirring occasionally, until beef is brown; drain.

**2.** Stir in remaining ingredients except noodles. Heat to boiling. Stir in noodles; reduce heat. Simmer uncovered about 10 minutes, stirring occasionally, until noodles are tender. Remove bay leaf.

**1 SERVING:** Calories 370 (Calories from Fat 180); Fat 20g (Saturated 8g); Cholesterol 85mg; Sodium 1080mg; Carbohydrate 24g (Dietary Fiber 2g); Protein 25g

# ITALIAN SAUSAGE SOUP

**QUICK** Prep: 10 min; Cook: 20 min        6 servings

1   **pound turkey Italian sausage links, cut into 1-inch pieces**

2½   **cups water**

1   **can (10½ ounces) condensed beef broth**

1   **can (28 ounces) whole Italian-style tomatoes, undrained**

2   **cups broccoli flowerets or 1 bag (14 ounces) frozen broccoli flowerets, thawed**

1   **cup uncooked penne pasta**

1   **medium onion, chopped**

1   **clove garlic, peeled and finely chopped**

½   **teaspoon dried basil leaves**

¼   **teaspoon fennel seeds, crushed**

¼   **teaspoon pepper**

**1.** Cook sausage in 4-quart Dutch oven over medium-high heat, stirring occasionally, until brown; drain.

**2.** Stir in remaining ingredients, breaking up tomatoes. Heat to boiling; reduce heat to medium-low. Cover and cook about 15 minutes, stirring occasionally, until pasta is tender.

**1 SERVING:** Calories 240 (Calories from Fat 90); Fat 10g (Saturated 3g); Cholesterol 45mg; Sodium 820mg; Carbohydrate 22g (Dietary Fiber 3g); Protein 18g

# $\mathcal{A}$SIAN NOODLE BOWL

Prep: 15 min; Cook: 19 min       4 servings

¼ cup barbecue sauce

2 tablespoons hoisin sauce

1 tablespoon peanut butter

Dash of ground red pepper (cayenne), if desired

1 tablespoon vegetable oil

1 small onion, peeled and cut into thin wedges

½ small red bell pepper, chopped

2 cups broccoli flowerets or 1 bag (14 ounces) frozen broccoli flowerets, thawed

¾ cup water

1 package (10 ounces) Chinese curly noodles

1 can (14 ounces) baby corn nuggets, drained

¼ cup chopped peanuts

1. Mix barbecue sauce, hoisin sauce, peanut butter and red pepper in medium bowl; set aside.

2. Heat oil in skillet over medium heat 1 to 2 minutes. Cook onion and bell pepper in oil 2 minutes, stirring frequently. Stir in broccoli and water. Cover and cook 4 to 6 minutes, stirring occasionally, until broccoli is crisp-tender when pierced with fork.

**3.** Cook and drain noodles as directed on package.

**4.** Meanwhile, stir corn and sauce mixture into vegetable mixture. Cook uncovered 3 to 4 minutes, stirring occasionally, until mixture is hot and bubbly.

**5.** Spoon noodles into 4 individual serving bowls. Spoon vegetable mixture over noodles. Sprinkle with peanuts.

**1 SERVING:** Calories 325 (Calories from Fat 45); Fat 5g (Saturated 1g); Cholesterol 0mg; Sodium 510mg; Carbohydrate 67g (Dietary Fiber 6g); Protein 9g

## SPECIAL TOUCH

### Vellum Place Mats

You will need:

**Spray adhesive**

**8½ × 11-inch sheets lightweight decorative art paper**

**11 × 17-inch sheets vellum paper**

**Skeleton leaves (available at art store) or dried leaves**

1. Spray adhesive onto back side of lightweight paper; place on vellum and press lightly.

2. Spray adhesive onto backs of leaves; press lightly onto vellum in desired design.

# $\mathcal{T}$USCAN PASTA AND BEANS

Prep: 20 min; Cook: 15 min    6 servings

3 cups uncooked gemelli (twist) pasta (12 ounces)

2 medium yellow or red bell peppers, chopped

½ pound green beans, cut into 1-inch pieces

1 medium onion, peeled and chopped

2 cloves garlic, peeled and finely chopped

1 can (14½ ounces) diced tomatoes with Italian herbs, undrained

½ cup fat-free vegetable or chicken broth

1 tablespoon chopped fresh or ½ teaspoon dried rosemary leaves, crumbled

2 cups lightly packed chopped escarole or spinach leaves

1 can (15 to 16 ounces) great Northern beans, rinsed and drained

2 tablespoons red wine vinegar

Shredded Parmesan cheese, if desired

**1.** Cook and drain pasta as directed on package.

**2.** Meanwhile, spray 4-quart Dutch oven with cooking spray; heat over medium-high heat. Cook bell peppers, green beans, onion and garlic in Dutch oven about 7 minutes, stirring occasionally, until vegetables are crisp-tender.

**3.** Stir tomatoes, broth and rosemary into vegetable mixture; reduce heat. Simmer uncovered about 3 minutes or until vegetables are tender. Stir in escarole and great Northern beans. Simmer uncovered about 3 minutes or until escarole is wilted. Toss vegetable mixture and pasta. Sprinkle with vinegar and cheese.

**1 SERVING:** Calories 340 (Calories from Fat 20); Fat 2g (Saturated 0g); Cholesterol 0mg; Sodium 200mg; Carbohydrate 74g (Dietary Fiber 10g); Protein 17g

#  ESTO WITH PASTA

**QUICK** Prep: 15 min; Cook: 12 min    4 servings

- 3 **cups uncooked rigatoni pasta (8 ounces)**
- 1 **cup fresh basil leaves**
- 2 **cloves garlic, peeled**
- ⅓ **cup grated Parmesan cheese (1½ ounces)**
- ⅓ **cup olive or vegetable oil**
- 2 **tablespoons pine nuts or walnut pieces**
  **Grated Parmesan cheese, if desired**

**1.** Cook and drain pasta as directed on package.

**2.** Meanwhile, rinse basil leaves with cool water and pat dry thoroughly with paper towel or clean, dry kitchen towel.

**3.** Place basil leaves, garlic, ⅓ cup cheese, oil and pine nuts in blender. Cover and blend on medium speed about 3 minutes, stopping blender occasionally to scrape sides, until smooth.

**4.** Place pasta in large serving bowl. Immediately pour pesto over hot pasta and toss until pasta is well coated. Serve with additional cheese.

**1 SERVING:** Calories 440 (Calories from Fat 215); Fat 24g (Saturated 4g); Cholesterol 5mg; Sodium 160mg; Carbohydrate 46g (Dietary Fiber 2g); Protein 12g

***Cilantro Pesto:*** Substitute ¾ cup firmly packed fresh cilantro leaves and ¼ cup firmly packed fresh parsley leaves for the 1 cup fresh basil.

***Spinach Winter Pesto:*** Substitute 1 cup firmly packed fresh spinach leaves and ¼ cup firmly packed fresh basil leaves, or 2 tablespoons dried basil leaves, for the 1 cup fresh basil.

**COOKING TIP**

• Store pesto airtight in the refrigerator up to 5 days or in the freezer up to 1 month. Cover and store immediately because its color will darken as it stands.

# $\mathcal{P}$ENNE PASTA WITH MARINARA SAUCE

Prep: 15 min; Cook: 39 min    8 servings

- **2** tablespoons olive or vegetable oil
- **2** medium onions, peeled and chopped
- **2** large cloves garlic, peeled and finely chopped
- **1** small green bell pepper, chopped
- **1** can (28 ounces) whole tomatoes, undrained
- **1** can (15 ounces) tomato sauce
- **2** tablespoons chopped fresh or 2 teaspoons dried basil leaves
- **1** tablespoon chopped fresh or 1 teaspoon dried oregano leaves
- **½** teaspoon salt
- **½** teaspoon fennel seeds
- **¼** teaspoon pepper
- **1** package (16 ounces) uncooked penne pasta (about 5⅓ cups)
  **Grated Parmesan cheese, if desired**

**1.** Heat oil in large saucepan over medium heat 1 to 2 minutes. Cook onions, garlic and bell pepper in oil 2 minutes, stirring occasionally.

2. Stir in tomatoes with their liquid, and break up with a spoon or fork. Stir in tomato sauce, basil, oregano, salt, fennel seeds and pepper. Heat to boiling. Reduce heat just enough so mixture bubbles gently and does not spatter.

3. Cover and cook 35 minutes, stirring about every 10 minutes to make sure mixture is just bubbling gently and to prevent sticking. Lower heat if sauce is bubbling too fast.

4. After tomato sauce has been cooking about 20 minutes, cook and drain pasta as directed on package. Serve pasta with marinara sauce. Sprinkle with cheese.

**1 SERVING:** Calories 290 (Calories from Fat 45); Fat 5g (Saturated 1g); Cholesterol 0mg; Sodium 620mg; Carbohydrate 56g (Dietary Fiber 5g); Protein 10g

## SPECIAL TOUCH

### Pasta Bowl Basket Charger

You will need:

**Shallow basket or large terra-cotta saucers**

**Natural excelsior or straw**

**Dinner plates**

1. Line the baskets or saucers with the excelsior or straw.

2. Place the dinner plates on top.

# PASTA PRIMAVERA

**QUICK**   Prep: 10 min; Cook: 15 min        4 servings

8  ounces uncooked fettuccine or linguine
1  tablespoon olive or vegetable oil
2  medium carrots, peeled and cut crosswise into think slices
1  small onion, peeled and chopped
1  cup broccoli flowerets
1  cup cauliflowerets
1  cup frozen green peas
1  container (10 ounces) refrigerated Alfredo sauce
   Grated Parmesan cheese, if desired

**1.** Cook and drain pasta as directed on package.

**2.** Heat oil in skillet over medium-high heat 1 to 2 minutes. Add carrots, onion, broccoli flowerets, cauliflowerets and peas. Stir-fry with a turner or large spoon 6 to 8 minutes, lifting and stirring constantly, until vegetables are crisp-tender.

**3.** Stir Alfredo sauce into vegetable mixture. Cook over medium heat, stirring constantly, until hot.

**4.** Stir fettuccine into the vegetable mixture. Serve with cheese.

**1 SERVING:** Calories 520 (Calories from Fat 280); Fat 31g (Saturated 12g); Cholesterol 100mg; Sodium 690mg; Carbohydrate 51g (Dietary Fiber 6g); Protein 15g

# Pasta Yields

When preparing pasta, allow ½ to ¾ cup cooked pasta per side-dish or appetizer serving. If you plan to make pasta your main dish, allow 1¼ to 1½ cups per serving. Two ounces (⅔ cup) dried pasta will yield approximately 1 cup of cooked pasta. This yield will vary slightly depending on the shape, type and size of pasta. To measure 4 ounces of spaghetti easily, make a circle with your thumb and index finger, and fill it with pasta.

| Pasta Type | Uncooked Amount | Cooked Amount | Servings |
|---|---|---|---|
| **Short Pastas** Macaroni, Penne, Rotini, Shells, Wagon Wheels | 6 to 7 ounces | 4 cups | 4 to 6 |
| **Long Pastas** Capellini, Linguine, Spaghetti, Vermicelli | 7 to 8 ounces | 4 cups | 4 to 6 |
| **Noodles** | 8 ounces | 4 to 5 cups | 4 to 6 |

# RATATOUILLE POLENTA BAKE

Prep: 25 min; Bake: 45 min; Stand: 5 min      6 servings

1 medium onion, peeled and coarsely chopped
1 medium green bell pepper, coarsely chopped
1 small unpeeled eggplant (1 pound), chopped
1 medium zucchini, chopped
½ teaspoon salt
¼ teaspoon pepper
1 can (14½ ounces) Italian-style stewed tomatoes, undrained
1 tube (16 ounces) refrigerated plain polenta (or any flavor)
2 tablespoons shredded Parmesan cheese
¾ cup finely shredded reduced-fat mozzarella cheese (3 ounces)
¼ cup chopped fresh parsley

**1.** Heat oven to 375°. Spray 12-inch nonstick skillet with cooking spray; heat over medium-high heat. Cook onion and bell pepper in skillet 2 minutes, stirring occasionally. Stir in eggplant, zucchini, salt and pepper. Cook 3 to 4 minutes, stirring occasionally, until vegetables are tender. Stir in tomatoes, breaking up with spoon; reduce heat to low. Cook 3 minutes, stirring occasionally.

**2.** Spray rectangular baking dish, 11 × 7 × 1½ inches, with cooking spray. Cut polenta into ¼-inch slices. Arrange over bottom of dish, overlapping and cutting to fit where necessary. Sprinkle with Parmesan cheese. Spoon vegetable mixture evenly over top.

**3.** Cover and bake 30 minutes. Sprinkle with mozzarella cheese and parsley. Bake uncovered about 15 minutes or until cheese is melted and casserole is bubbly. Let stand 5 minutes before serving.

**1 SERVING:** Calories 205 (Calories from Fat 35); Fat 4g (Saturated 2g); Cholesterol 10mg; Sodium 500mg; Carbohydrate 39g (Dietary Fiber 6g); Protein 9g

# CREAMY CORN AND GARLIC RISOTTO

Prep: 10 min; Cook: 25 min        4 servings

3¾ cups fat-free vegetable or chicken broth

4 cloves garlic, peeled and finely chopped

1 cup uncooked Arborio or regular long-grain rice

2 cups frozen whole kernel corn

⅓ cup grated fat-free Parmesan cheese (3 ounces)

¼ cup shredded reduced-fat mozzarella cheese (1 ounce)

¼ cup chopped fresh parsley

**1.** Heat ⅓ cup of the broth to boiling in 10-inch skillet. Cook garlic in broth 1 minute, stirring occasionally. Stir in rice and corn. Cook 1 minute, stirring occasionally.

**2.** Stir in remaining broth. Heat to boiling; reduce heat to medium. Cook uncovered 15 to 20 minutes, stirring occasionally, until rice is tender and creamy; remove from heat. Stir in cheeses and parsley.

**1 SERVING:** Calories 340 (Calories from Fat 35); Fat 4g (Saturated 2g); Cholesterol 10mg; Sodium 1200mg; Carbohydrate 69g (Dietary Fiber 4g); Protein 11g

# $\mathcal{S}$EA SCALLOP STIR-FRY

**QUICK**  Prep: 20 min; Cook: 8 min        4 servings

1  **package (3 ounces) Oriental-flavor ramen noodle soup mix**

1  **tablespoon olive or vegetable oil**

¾  **pound asparagus, cut into 1-inch pieces**

1  **large red bell pepper, cut into thin strips**

1  **small onion, peeled and chopped**

2  **cloves garlic, peeled and finely chopped**

¾  **pound sea scallops, halved**

1  **tablespoon soy sauce**

2  **tablespoons lemon juice**

1  **teaspoon sesame oil**

¼  **teaspoon red pepper sauce**

**1.** Reserve seasoning packet from noodles. Cook and drain noodles as directed on package.

**2.** Meanwhile, heat olive oil in wok or 12-inch skillet over high heat. Add asparagus, bell pepper, onion and garlic; stir-fry 2 to 3 minutes or until vegetables are crisp-tender. Add scallops; stir-fry until white.

**3.** Mix contents of reserved seasoning packet, the soy sauce, lemon juice, sesame oil and pepper sauce; stir into scallop mixture. Stir in noodles; heat through.

**1 SERVING:** Calories 200 (Calories from Fat 80); Fat 9g (Saturated 1g); Cholesterol 15mg; Sodium 620mg; Carbohydrate 19g (Dietary Fiber 2g); Protein 13g

# RAB CAKES

**QUICK**   Prep: 15 min; Cook: 10 min          4 servings

**Mustard-Dill Sauce or Cilantro Sour Cream (at right)**

¼ **cup mayonnaise or salad dressing**

1 **egg**

2 **slices bread, crusts removed**

2 **medium green onions with tops, thinly sliced**

2 **cans (6 ounces each) crabmeat, drained**

1 **teaspoon ground mustard**

¼ **teaspoon salt**

⅛ **teaspoon pepper**

¼ **cup dry bread crumbs**

2 **tablespoons vegetable oil**

**1.** Prepare Mustard-Dill Sauce or Cilantro Sour Cream.

**2.** Mix mayonnaise and egg in medium bowl. Tear bread into small pieces. You should have about 1¼ cups soft bread crumbs. Add

soft bread crumbs to mayonnaise mixture. Add onions to mayonnaise mixture. Mix thoroughly.

3. Flake crabmeat with a fork and remove any tiny pieces of shell. Add crabmeat to mayonnaise mixture. Stir in ground mustard, salt and pepper. Shape crabmeat mixture into 4 patties.

4. Place dry bread crumbs in shallow dish. Place each patty in this dish of bread crumbs, and turn once to coat both sides. Use your hands to gently press bread crumbs onto patties.

5. Heat oil in skillet over medium heat 1 to 2 minutes. Cook patties in oil about 10 minutes, gently turning patties over once, until golden brown on both sides. You may need to reduce the heat to medium-low if the crab cakes become brown too quickly. Serve crab cakes with sauce.

**1 SERVING:** Calories 430 (Calories from Fat 295); Fat 33g (Saturated 7g); Cholesterol 155mg; Sodium 780mg; Carbohydrate 12g (Dietary Fiber 1g); Protein 22g

**COATING CRAB CAKES**
Place each patty in the dish of dry bread crumbs, and turn once to coat both sides. Use your hands to gently press bread crumbs onto patties.

## MUSTARD-DILL SAUCE

¼ **cup mayonnaise or salad dressing**

¼ **cup sour cream**

1 **tablespoon Dijon mustard**

¾ **teaspoon chopped fresh or ¼ teaspoon dried dill weed**

Mix all ingredients. Cover and refrigerate until serving time.

## CILANTRO SOUR CREAM

½ **cup sour cream**

2 **tablespoons chopped fresh cilantro**

Mix the sour cream and cilantro. Cover and refrigerate until serving time.

#  SOUTHERN-FRIED CATFISH

Prep: 10 min; Cook: 36 min        6 servings

**Vegetable oil**

1¼ **cup cornmeal**

1 **teaspoon salt**

½ **teaspoon ground red pepper (cayenne)**

¼ **teaspoon pepper**

6 **small catfish (about ½ pound each), skinned and pan-dressed**

½ **cup all-purpose flour**

2 **eggs, slightly beaten**

**Lemon wedges, if desired**

**1.** Heat oven to 275°.

**2.** Heat oil (½ inch) in 12-inch skillet over medium-high heat until hot. Mix cornmeal, salt, red pepper and pepper; reserve.

**3.** Coat catfish with flour; dip into eggs. Coat with cornmeal mixture. Fry catfish, 2 at a time, until golden brown, about 6 minutes on each side. Keep warm in oven while frying remaining catfish. Garnish with lemon wedges if desired.

**1 SERVING:** Calories 340 (Calories from Fat 45); Fat 5g (Saturated 1g); Cholesterol 175mg; Sodium 450mg; Carbohydrate 28g (Dietary Fiber 2g); Protein 48g

# VEN-FRIED FISH

**QUICK**   Prep: 15 min; Bake: 10 min        4 servings

**1   pound cod, haddock or other medium-firm fish fillets, about ¾ inch thick**

**¼   cup cornmeal**

**¼   cup dry bread crumbs**

**¾   teaspoon chopped fresh or ¼ teaspoon dried dill weed**

**½   teaspoon paprika**

**¼   teaspoon salt**

**⅛   teaspoon pepper**

**¼   cup milk**

**3   tablespoons butter or stick margarine, melted**

**1.** Move oven rack to position slightly above middle of oven. Heat oven to 500°.

**2.** Cut fish into 2 × 1½-inch pieces. Mix cornmeal, bread crumbs, dill weed, paprika, salt and pepper. Dip fish into milk, then coat with cornmeal mixture.

**3.** Place fish in ungreased rectangular pan, 13 × 9 × 2 inches. Drizzle butter over fish. Bake uncovered about 10 minutes or until fish flakes easily with fork.

**1 SERVING:** Calories 200 (Calories from Fat 90); Fat 10g (Saturated 2g); Cholesterol 55mg; Sodium 390mg; Carbohydrate 9g (Dietary Fiber 1g); Protein 20g

# ℬROILED FISH STEAKS

 Prep: 5 min; Broil: 11 min          4 servings

**4** **small salmon, trout or other medium-firm fish steaks, about ¾ inch thick (1½ pounds)**

**Salt**

**Pepper**

**2** **tablespoons butter or stick margarine, melted**

**1.** Set oven control to broil.

**2.** Sprinkle both sides of fish with salt and pepper. Brush with half of the butter.

**3.** Place fish on rack in broiler pan. Broil with tops about 4 inches from heat 5 minutes. Brush with remaining butter. Carefully turn fish; brush with butter. Broil 4 to 6 minutes longer or until fish flakes easily with fork.

**1 SERVING:** Calories 240 (Calories from Fat 115); Fat 13g (Saturated 3g); Cholesterol 95mg; Sodium 440mg; Carbohydrate 0g (Dietary Fiber 0g); Protein 31g

***Broiled Fish Fillets:*** Substitute 1 pound fish fillets, cut into 4 serving pieces, for the fish steaks. Broil with tops about 4 inches from heat 5 to 6 minutes or until fish flakes easily with fork (do not turn).

# OVEN-BARBECUED CHICKEN

Prep: 10 min; Bake: 1 hr    6 servings

**3 to 3½ pounds cut-up broiler-fryer chicken**

**¾ cup chili sauce or ketchup**

**2 tablespoons honey**

**2 tablespoons soy sauce**

**1 teaspoon ground mustard**

**½ teaspoon prepared horseradish**

**½ teaspoon red pepper sauce**

**1.** Heat oven to 375°.

**2.** Place chicken, skin sides up, in ungreased rectangular pan, 13 × 9 × 2 inches. Mix remaining ingredients; pour over chicken.

**3.** Bake uncovered 30 minutes. Spoon sauce over chicken. Bake uncovered about 30 minutes longer or until juice of chicken is no longer pink when centers of thickest pieces are cut.

**1 SERVING:** Calories 285 (Calories from Fat 115); Fat 13g (Saturated 4g); Cholesterol 85mg; Sodium 800mg; Carbohydrate 16g (Dietary Fiber 1g); Protein 27g

# PESTO CHICKEN AND PASTA

**QUICK**   Prep: 5 min; Cook: 12 min    4 servings

**3 cups uncooked farfalle (bow-tie) pasta (6 ounces)**

**2 cups cubed cooked chicken or turkey breast**

**½ cup pesto**

**½ cup coarsely chopped drained roasted red bell peppers (from 7-ounce jar)**

**Sliced ripe olives, if desired**

**1.** Cook and drain pasta as directed on package, using 3-quart saucepan.

**2.** Mix hot cooked pasta, chicken, pesto and bell peppers in same saucepan. Heat over low heat, stirring constantly, until hot.

**3.** Garnish with olives.

**1 SERVING:** Calories 565 (Calories from Fat 160); Fat 18g (Saturated 4g); Cholesterol 60mg; Sodium 290mg; Carbohydrate 71g (Dietary Fiber 4g); Protein 35g

# CRISPY CHICKEN WITH APRICOT STUFFING

Prep: 20 min; Bake: 1 hr     6 servings

**Apricot Stuffing (below)**

1 **cup crushed cornflakes**

1 **tablespoon chopped fresh or 1 teaspoon dried thyme leaves**

½ **teaspoon salt**

3 to 3½ **pounds cut-up broiler-fryer chicken, skin removed**

2 **eggs, beaten**

**1.** Heat oven to 375°. Grease rectangular pan, 13 × 9 × 2 inches. Prepare Apricot Stuffing. Spoon stuffing into pan.

**2.** Mix cornflakes, thyme and salt in shallow dish. Dip chicken into eggs, then coat with cornflakes mixture. Place chicken on stuffing in pan.

**3.** Cover and bake 30 minutes; turn chicken. Bake uncovered 20 to 30 minutes longer or until juice of chicken is no longer pink when centers of thickest pieces are cut.

**1 SERVING:** Calories 640 (Calories from Fat 305); Fat 34g (Saturated 7g); Cholesterol 160mg; Sodium 1100mg; Carbohydrate 52g (Dietary Fiber 4g); Protein 35g

## APRICOT STUFFING

1 **cup hot water**

¾ **cup chopped pecans, toasted (see page 99)**

¾ **cup chopped dried apricots**

¼ **cup (½ stick) margarine or butter, melted**

1 **medium onion, peeled and chopped**

1 **bag (8 ounces) herb stuffing mix**

Mix all ingredients.

# CHICKEN AND SWEET POTATO CURRY

Prep: 15 min; Cook: 18 min      4 servings

2 tablespoons all-purpose flour

1 tablespoon curry powder

½ teaspoon salt

1 pound boneless, skinless chicken breast halves, cut into 1-inch pieces

1 tablespoon vegetable oil

2 cups peeled and cubed sweet potatoes

1¼ cups apple juice

1 fresh mild chili (about 3 to 4 inches in length), chopped

2 tablespoons apple jelly

**1.** Mix flour, curry powder and salt in heavy-duty resealable plastic food-storage bag. Add chicken; seal bag and shake until chicken is evenly coated.

**2.** Heat oil in 12-inch nonstick skillet over medium-high heat. Add chicken; stir-fry 2 to 3 minutes or until brown. Stir any remaining flour mixture into apple juice. Stir sweet potatoes, apple juice and chili into chicken.

**3.** Cover and cook 10 to 15 minutes, stirring occasionally, until chicken is no longer pink in center and potatoes are tender. Stir in jelly until melted.

**1 SERVING:** Calories 330 (Calories from Fat 70); Fat 8g (Saturated 2g); Cholesterol 70mg; Sodium 370mg; Carbohydrate 41g (Dietary Fiber 4g); Protein 27g

# $\mathcal{S}$WEET-AND-SOUR CHICKEN

**QUICK** Prep: 5 min; Cook: 10 min          4 servings

1 package (10 ounces) frozen breaded fully cooked chicken chunks

¼ cup water

1 bag (16 ounces) frozen broccoli, carrots and water chestnuts

1 can (20 ounces) pineapple chunks, drained

1 jar (9 ounces) sweet-and-sour sauce

**1.** Prepare chicken chunks as directed on package.

**2.** Meanwhile, heat water to boiling in 3-quart saucepan. Add frozen vegetables; reduce heat to medium. Cover and cook 5 to 6 minutes or until hot; drain. Return vegetables to saucepan.

**3.** Stir chicken, pineapple and sweet-and-sour sauce into vegetables in saucepan. Cook over medium heat 3 to 4 minutes, stirring occasionally, until hot.

**1 SERVING:** Calories 415 (Calories from Fat 145); Fat 16g (Saturated 4g); Cholesterol 45mg; Sodium 780mg; Carbohydrate 55g (Dietary Fiber 5g); Protein 18g

# $\mathcal{H}$ONEY-MUSTARD TURKEY WITH SNAP PEAS

Prep: 5 min; Marinate: 20 min; Cook: 12 min          4 servings

1 pound uncooked turkey breast slices, about ¼ inch thick

½ cup Dijon and honey poultry and meat marinade

1 cup baby carrots, cut lengthwise in half

2 cups frozen snap pea pods

**1.** Place turkey in shallow glass or plastic dish. Pour marinade over turkey; turn slices to coat evenly. Cover dish and let stand 20 minutes at room temperature.

**2.** Spray 10-inch skillet with cooking spray; heat over medium heat. Drain most of marinade from turkey. Cook turkey in skillet about 5 minutes, turning once, until brown.

**3.** Add carrots, lifting turkey to place carrots on bottom of skillet. Top turkey and carrots with pea pods. Cover and simmer about 7 minutes or until carrots are tender and turkey is no longer pink in center.

**1 SERVING:** Calories 150 (Calories from Fat 10); Fat 1g (Saturated 0g); Cholesterol 75mg; Sodium 65mg; Carbohydrate 9g (Dietary Fiber 3g); Protein 29g

# ORANGE-TERIYAKI BEEF WITH NOODLES

**QUICK**  Prep: 10 min; Cook: 15 min        4 servings

1   **pound beef boneless sirloin, cut into thin strips**
1   **can (14½ ounces) fat-free beef broth**
¼   **cup teriyaki stir-fry cooking sauce**
2   **tablespoons orange marmalade**
    **Dash of ground red pepper (cayenne)**
1½  **cups frozen snap pea pods**
1½  **cups uncooked fine egg noodles (3 ounces)**

**1.** Spray 12-inch skillet with cooking spray; heat over medium-high heat. Cook beef in skillet 2 to 4 minutes, stirring occasionally, until brown. Remove beef from skillet; keep warm.

**2.** Add broth, teriyaki sauce, marmalade and red pepper to skillet. Heat to boiling. Stir in pea pods and noodles; reduce heat to medium. Cover and cook about 5 minutes or until noodles are tender. Stir in beef. Cook uncovered 2 to 3 minutes or until sauce is slightly thickened.

**1 SERVING:** Calories 265 (Calories from Fat 45); Fat 5g (Saturated 2g); Cholesterol 80mg; Sodium 1210mg; Carbohydrate 28g (Dietary Fiber 2g); Protein 29g

# $\mathcal{I}$TALIAN BEEF KABOBS

Prep: 10 min; Marinate: 1 hr; Broil: 8 min    2 servings

**2    cloves garlic, peeled and finely chopped**

**¼    cup balsamic vinegar**

**¼    cup water**

**2    tablespoons olive or vegetable oil**

**1    tablespoon chopped fresh or 1 teaspoon dried oregano leaves**

**1½    teaspoons chopped fresh or ½ teaspoon dried marjoram leaves**

**1    teaspoon sugar**

**¾    pound beef bone-in sirloin or round steak, 1 inch thick, fat and bone removed and cut into 1-inch pieces**

**1.** Make a marinade by mixing all ingredients except beef in medium glass or plastic bowl. Stir in beef until coated. Cover and refrigerate, stirring occasionally, at least 1 hour but no longer than 12 hours. If you are using bamboo skewers, soak them in water 30 minutes before using to prevent burning.

**2.** Set oven control to broil.

**3.** Remove beef from marinade, reserving marinade. Thread beef on skewers, leaving a ½-inch space between pieces. Brush kabobs with marinade.

**4.** Place kabobs on rack in broiler pan. Broil kabobs with tops about 3 inches from heat 6 to 8 minutes for medium-rare to medium doneness, turning and brushing with marinade after 3 minutes. Discard any remaining marinade.

**1 SERVING:** Calories 195 (Calories from Fat 70); Fat 8g (Saturated 2g); Cholesterol 80mg; Sodium 60mg; Carbohydrate 1g (Dietary Fiber 0g); Protein 30g

**COOKING TIPS**

• To save time, omit the garlic, vinegar, water, oil, oregano, marjoram and sugar, and instead, marinate the beef in ⅔ cup purchased Italian dressing in step 1.

• Although you might be tempted to serve the extra marinade with the cooked kabobs, you should discard any marinade that has been in contact with raw meat. Bacteria from the raw meat could transfer to the marinade.

# PASTA WITH BEEF, BROCCOLI AND TOMATOES

**QUICK**   Prep: 5 min; Cook: 15 min        6 servings

3  **cups uncooked radiatore or rotini pasta (9 ounces)**

¾  **pound beef boneless sirloin, cut into ¼-inch strips**

½  **teaspoon pepper**

1  **package (16 ounces) fresh or frozen broccoli cuts**

1  **can (14½ ounces) diced tomatoes with roasted garlic, undrained**

1  **can (14½ ounces) beef broth**

2  **tablespoons cornstarch**

2  **tablespoons Worcestershire sauce**

**1.** Cook and drain pasta as directed on package.

**2.** Meanwhile, spray 12-inch skillet with cooking spray; heat over medium-high heat. Add beef to skillet; sprinkle with pepper. Cook 2 to 3 minutes, stirring frequently, until brown. Stir in broccoli, tomatoes and broth; reduce heat. Cover and simmer about 10 minutes, stirring occasionally, until broccoli is crisp-tender.

**3.** Mix cornstarch and Worcestershire sauce; stir into beef mixture. Heat to boiling, stirring constantly. Boil and stir 1 minute. Toss beef mixture and pasta.

**1 SERVING:** Calories 270 (Calories from Fat 30); Fat 3g (Saturated 1g); Cholesterol 30mg; Sodium 500mg; Carbohydrate 44g (Dietary Fiber 4g); Protein 21g

# $\mathcal{B}$EEF ENCHILADAS

Prep: 15 min; Cook: 20 min; Bake: 20 min      4 servings

  1  **pound ground beef**
  1  **medium onion, peeled and chopped**
  1  **cup shredded Cheddar cheese (4 ounces)**
 ½  **cup sour cream**
  2  **tablespoons chopped fresh parsley**
 ¼  **teaspoon pepper**
  1  **small green bell pepper, chopped**
  1  **clove garlic, peeled and finely chopped**
  1  **can (15 ounces) tomato sauce**
 ⅔  **cup water**
  1  **tablespoon chili powder**
 1½ **teaspoons chopped fresh or ½ teaspoon dried oregano leaves**
 ¼  **teaspoon ground cumin**
  8  **corn tortillas (5 or 6 inches in diameter)**
     **Sour cream, if desired**
     **Chopped green onions, if desired**

**1.** Heat oven to 350°.

**2.** Cook beef in skillet over medium heat 8 to 10 minutes, stirring occasionally, until beef is brown.

**3.** Place a strainer over a medium bowl, or place a colander in a large bowl. Spoon beef into strainer to drain fat; discard fat. Return beef to skillet. Stir in onion, sour cream, cheese, parsley and pepper. Cover and set aside.

**4.** Place bell pepper, garlic, tomato sauce, water, chili powder, oregano, and cumin in saucepan. Heat to boiling over medium heat, stirring occasionally. Once mixture is boiling, reduce heat just enough so that mixture bubbles gently. Cook uncovered 5 minutes. Pour enough of the mixture into ungreased baking dish to cover bottom.

**5.** Place 2 tortillas between dampened microwavable paper towels or microwavable plastic wrap and microwave on high 15 to 20 seconds to soften them. Dip each tortilla into sauce mixture to coat both sides.

**6.** Spoon about ¼ cup of the beef mixture down one side of each softened tortilla to within 1 inch of edge. Roll tortilla around filling, and place seam side down in ungreased rectangular pan. Repeat with remaining tortillas and beef mixture. Pour any remaining sauce over enchiladas.

**7.** Bake uncovered about 20 minutes or until hot and bubbly. Garnish with sour cream and green onions.

**1 SERVING:** Calories 565 (Calories from Fat 295); Fat 33g (Saturated 16g); Cholesterol 110mg; Sodium 1000mg; Carbohydrate 39g (Dietary Fiber 6g); Protein 34g

**Cheese Enchiladas:** Substitute 2 cups shredded Monterey Jack cheese (8 ounces) for the beef. Add the onion, 1 cup Cheddar cheese, sour cream, parsley and pepper to Monterey Jack cheese. Sprinkle ¼ cup shredded Cheddar cheese over enchiladas before baking.

---

**COOKING TIP**

• To save time, omit the bell pepper, garlic, tomato sauce, chili powder, oregano and cumin. Instead, use a 16-ounce jar of salsa.

---

**FILLING TORTILLAS**

Spoon about ¼ cup of the beef mixture down one side of each softened tortilla to within 1 inch of edge. Roll tortilla around filling, and place seam side down in baking dish.

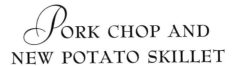

# PORK CHOP AND NEW POTATO SKILLET

Prep: 5 min; Cook: 50 min          6 servings

**6** pork loin or rib chops, ½ inch thick (about 1½ pounds)

**1** can (10¾ ounces) condensed cream of mushroom soup

**1** can (4 ounces) mushroom stems and pieces, undrained

**¼** cup water

**2** tablespoons dry white wine or apple juice

**¾** teaspoon chopped fresh or ¼ teaspoon dried thyme leaves

**½** teaspoon garlic powder

**½** teaspoon Worcestershire sauce

**6** medium new potatoes (about 1½ pounds), quartered

**1** tablespoon chopped pimiento

**1** package (10 ounces) frozen green peas, rinsed and drained

**1.** Spray 10-inch nonstick skillet with nonstick cooking spray; heat skillet over medium-high heat. Cook pork in skillet until brown on both sides.

**2.** Mix soup, mushrooms, water, wine, thyme, garlic powder and Worcestershire sauce; pour over pork. Heat to boiling, stirring oc-casionally; reduce heat. Cover and simmer 15 minutes.

**3.** Add potatoes. Cover and simmer 15 minutes. Stir in pimiento and peas. Cover and simmer about 10 minutes, stirring occasionally, until pork is tender and slightly pink when centers of thickest pieces are cut and peas are tender.

**1 SERVING:** Calories 385 (Calories from Fat 155); Fat 17g (Saturated 6g); Cholesterol 70mg; Sodium 580mg; Carbohydrate 34g (Dietary Fiber 5g); Protein 29g

# ROASTED PORK CHOPS AND VEGETABLES

Prep: 20 min; Bake: 1 hr          4 servings

- **4  pork rib chops, ½ inch thick (1 pound)**
- **2  teaspoons parsley flakes**
- **½  teaspoon dried marjoram leaves**
- **½  teaspoon dried thyme leaves**
- **½  teaspoon garlic salt**
- **¼  teaspoon coarsely ground pepper**
- **6  new potatoes, quartered**
- **4  ounces mushrooms, halved**
- **1  medium green bell pepper, cut into 1-inch pieces**
- **1  medium onion, peeled and cut into thin wedges**
- **1  medium tomato, cut into 8 wedges**

**1.** Heat oven to 425°. Spray jelly roll pan, 15½ × 10½ × 1 inch, with olive oil–flavored cooking spray. Remove fat from pork. Mix parsley, marjoram, thyme, garlic salt and pepper. Spray both sides of pork chops with cooking spray. Sprinkle with 1 to 1½ teaspoons herb mixture. Place in corners of pan.

**2.** Mix potatoes, mushrooms, bell pepper and onion in large bowl. Spray vegetables 2 or 3 times with cooking spray; stir. Sprinkle with remaining herb mixture; toss to coat. Spread evenly in center of pan between pork chops.

**3.** Bake uncovered 45 minutes. Turn pork; stir vegetables. Place tomato wedges over vegetables. Bake uncovered 10 to 15 minutes or until pork is no longer pink when cut near bone and vegetables are tender.

**1 SERVING:** Calories 265 (Calories from Fat 65); Fat 7g (Saturated 2g); Cholesterol 55mg; Sodium 170mg; Carbohydrate 31g (Dietary Fiber 4g); Protein 23g

# Easy Pasta and Sausage

**QUICK**  Prep: 12 min; Cook: 14 min          4 servings

 3  **cups uncooked radiatore (nugget) pasta (9 ounces)**
 4  **turkey Italian sausages, cut into 2-inch pieces**
 1  **large green bell pepper, cut into thin strips**
 1  **cup marinara or spaghetti sauce**
    **Shredded Parmesan cheese, if desired**

**1.** Cook and drain pasta as directed on package.

**2.** Cook sausages in 12-inch skillet over medium heat about 10 minutes, turning occasionally, until no longer pink; drain.

**3.** Stir bell pepper into sausages; cook 2 minutes. Stir in marinara sauce and pasta. Cook about 2 minutes or until hot. Sprinkle with cheese.

**1 SERVING:** Calories 390 (Calories from Fat 90); Fat 10g (Saturated 3g); Cholesterol 35mg; Sodium 690mg; Carbohydrate 60g (Dietary Fiber 4g); Protein 19g

# SALADS AND SIDES

## CARIBBEAN CHICKEN AND BLACK BEAN SALAD

**QUICK** Prep: 20 min        4 servings

Spicy Lime Dressing (below)

2 cups cut-up cooked chicken

¼ cup chopped fresh cilantro

1 large tomato, chopped

1 medium avocado, chopped

1 small yellow summer squash, chopped

1 can (15 ounces) black beans, rinsed and drained

Leaf lettuce

Prepare Spicy Lime Dressing. Toss remaining ingredients except lettuce in large bowl. Pour dressing over lettuce; toss.

**1 SERVING:** Calories 445 (Calories from Fat 205); Fat 23g (Saturated 5g); Cholesterol 60mg; Sodium 630mg; Carbohydrate 40g (Dietary Fiber 10g); Protein 29g

## SPICY LIME DRESSING

¼ cup lime juice

2 tablespoons olive or vegetable oil

1 tablespoon honey

½ teaspoon chili powder

¼ teaspoon ground cumin

¼ teaspoon salt

2 or 3 drops red pepper sauce

Shake all ingredients in tightly covered container.

# CHICKEN AND STRAWBERRY SPINACH SALAD

**QUICK**   Prep: 10 min; Cook: 20 min        4 servings

**Strawberry Dressing (below)**
1 **pound boneless, skinless chicken breast halves**
8 **cups bite-size pieces spinach**
1 **cup strawberries, stems removed and halved**
¼ **cup crumbled Gorgonzola cheese (1 ounce)**
¼ **cup chopped walnuts**

**1.** Prepare Strawberry Dressing. Remove fat from chicken. Spray 8- or 10-inch skillet with cooking spray; heat over medium high heat. Cook chicken in skillet about 15 to 20 minutes, turning once, until juice of chicken is no longer pink when centers of thickest pieces are cut. Remove chicken to cutting board.

**2.** Add dressing to skillet; stir to loosen any pan drippings. Cut chicken into slices. Arrange spinach on individual serving plates. Top with chicken, strawberries and cheese. Drizzle with dressing. Sprinkle with walnuts.

**1 SERVING:** Calories 225 (Calories from Fat 90); Fat 10g (Saturated 3g); Cholesterol 55mg; Sodium 210mg; Carbohydrate 14g (Dietary Fiber 3g); Protein 23g

## STRAWBERRY DRESSING
3 **tablespoons apple juice**
2 **tablespoons strawberry spreadable fruit**
2 **tablespoons balsamic vinegar**

Mix all ingredients until blended.

# THAI CHICKEN SALAD

**QUICK** Prep: 16 min     4 servings

**Honey-Ginger Dressing (below)**

6 cups bite-size pieces assorted salad greens

1½ cups shredded cooked chicken

1 medium carrot, shredded

1 can (14 to 15 ounces) baby corn nuggets, drained

⅓ cup flaked coconut, toasted (page 99)

**1.** Prepare Honey-Ginger Dressing.

**2.** Place salad greens, chicken, carrot and corn in large bowl. Pour dressing over salad; toss until coated.

**3.** Sprinkle with coconut.

**1 SERVING:** Calories 375 (Calories from Fat 190); Fat 21g (Saturated 5g); Cholesterol 45mg; Sodium 750mg; Carbohydrate 32g (Dietary Fiber 4g); Protein 19g

## HONEY-GINGER DRESSING

¼ cup vegetable oil

2 tablespoons balsamic or cider vinegar

2 tablespoons soy sauce

1 tablespoon honey

1 teaspoon grated gingerroot

Shake all ingredients in tightly covered container.

# CHICKEN CURRY COUSCOUS SALAD

Prep: 22 min; Chill: 1 hr        4 servings

**Curry Dressing (below)**
2  **cups cooked couscous**
1  **cup diced cooked chicken**
1  **cup raisins**
1  **medium red or yellow bell pepper, cut into thin strips**
6  **medium green onions, trimmed and chopped**
1  **can (15 to 16 ounces) garbanzo beans, rinsed and drained**
½  **cup chopped roasted almonds**

1. Prepare Curry Dressing.

2. Place remaining ingredients except almonds in large bowl. Pour dressing over salad; toss until coated.

3. Cover and refrigerate about 1 hour or until chilled. Top with almonds.

**1 SERVING:** Calories 710 (Calories from Fat 295); Fat 33g (Saturated 4g); Cholesterol 30mg; Sodium 540mg; Carbohydrate 89g (Dietary Fiber 14g); Protein 28g

## CURRY DRESSING

⅓  **cup olive or vegetable oil**
1  **tablespoon lemon juice**
1  **teaspoon sugar**
½  **teaspoon curry powder**
¼  **teaspoon salt**
⅛  **teaspoon ground allspice**

Shake all ingredients in tightly covered container.

# $\mathcal{C}$HICKEN AND TORTELLINI SALAD

**QUICK** Prep: 12 min        6 servings

- 1 package (9 ounces) refrigerated cheese-filled tortellini
- 6 cups bite-size pieces assorted salad greens
- 3 cups chopped cooked chicken
- ½ cup Italian dressing
- ⅓ cup shredded Parmesan cheese

Cook and drain tortellini as directed on package. Mix tortellini and remaining ingredients except cheese. Sprinkle with cheese.

**1 SERVING:** Calories 325 (Calories from Fat 190); Fat 21g (Saturated 6g); Cholesterol 100mg; Sodium 330mg; Carbohydrate 11g (Dietary Fiber 1g); Protein 24g

# $\int$PICY BEEF SALAD

Prep: 10 min; Cook: 5 min; Marinate: 30 min; Chill: 1 hr     6 servings

- 1 **pound beef boneless sirloin**
- 2 **tablespoons dry sherry or apple juice**
- 1 **tablespoon soy sauce**
- 2 **teaspoons sugar**
- 8 **medium green onions with tops, peeled and cut into ⅛-inch slices**
- 2 **medium tomatoes, coarsely chopped**
- ¾ **pound mushrooms, sliced**
- 1 **small head lettuce, torn into bite-size pieces**
- **Spicy Dressing (at right)**

**1.** Cut and discard most of the fat from the beef. Cut the beef with the grain into 2-inch strips, then cut the strips across the grain into ⅛-inch slices.

**2.** Toss beef, sherry, soy sauce and sugar in a glass or plastic bowl. Cover and refrigerate 30 minutes.

**3.** Heat a skillet over medium-high heat 1 to 2 minutes. Add half of the beef to skillet. Stir-fry about 3 minutes, lifting and stirring constantly, until beef is brown. Remove beef from skillet; drain. Repeat with remaining beef.

**4.** Toss beef and green onions in a large salad or serving bowl. Layer tomatoes, mushrooms and lettuce on the beef. Cover and refrigerate at least 1 hour but no longer than 10 hours.

**5.** Prepare Spicy Dressing. Pour the dressing over the salad, then toss until well coated.

**1 SERVING:** Calories 120 (Calories from Fat 25); Fat 3g (Saturated 1g); Cholesterol 35mg; Sodium 430mg; Carbohydrate 9g (Dietary Fiber 2g); Protein 16g

### SPICY DRESSING

  1  **clove garlic, peeled and finely chopped**
¼  **cup rice vinegar or white wine vinegar**
  2  **tablespoons soy sauce**
  1  **teaspoon finely chopped gingerroot**
  1  **teaspoon sesame oil**
⅛  **teaspoon ground red pepper (cayenne)**

Shake all ingredients in a tightly covered jar or container.

---

## Tips for Tossed Salads

- Choose a variety of greens to create a medley of complementary textures, flavors and colors. For little dashes of flavor, add fresh herbs.

- Mix dark greens with light, crisp greens with tender, and straight greens with curly. Combine pale iceberg with dark green spinach, romaine with curly endive. For color accents, add red leaf lettuce, red cabbage or radicchio.

- Dressing clings much better to dry leaves, so use a salad spinner or paper towel to blot any leftover moisture that may be in the crevices.

- Greens go limp and the edges darken if you cut them with a knife; instead of cutting, tear them into bite-size pieces with your fingers.

- Serve salads family style from a large bowl or in small bowls or on plates for each person. If you're making individual servings, give your artistic flair the go-ahead and arrange the salad attractively on the plate. Try grouping the ingredients or layering them on a bed of greens.

- Tomatoes are watery, so wait until just before tossing to add slices or wedges to a salad so they won't dilute the dressing or cause the greens to go limp. Seeding the tomatoes first will also help.

- Pour dressing over greens just before serving, using only enough to lightly coat the leaves, then toss. Or serve the dressing on the side so each person can add as much or as little as desired. Salads that have been tossed with dressing don't make good leftovers because the salad will become soggy and limp.

- Put the finishing touch on your salad with onion or green bell pepper rings, a sprig of herbs, sliced green or ripe olives, halved cherry tomatoes or a sprinkling of nuts or cheese. ■

# CONFETTI WILD RICE

Prep: 10 min; Cook: 55 min          6 servings

| 1 | tablespoon margarine or butter |
| ½ | cup uncooked wild rice |
| 1½ | cups sliced mushrooms (4 ounces) |
| 2 | medium green onions, trimmed and thinly sliced |
| 1¼ | cups water |
| ½ | teaspoon salt |
| ¼ | teaspoon pepper |
| 1 | package (10 ounces) frozen chopped broccoli, thawed and drained |
| 1 | tablespoon lemon juice |

**1.** Melt margarine in 10-inch nonstick skillet over medium heat. Cook wild rice, mushrooms and onions in margarine about 3 minutes, stirring occasionally, until onions are tender.

**2.** Stir in water, salt and pepper. Heat to boiling, stirring occasionally; reduce heat. Cover and simmer 40 to 50 minutes or until rice is tender; drain if necessary.

**3.** Stir in broccoli and lemon juice. Heat uncovered, stirring occasionally, until hot.

**1 SERVING:** Calories 75 (Calories from Fat 10); Fat 1g (Saturated 0g); Cholesterol 0mg; Sodium 220mg; Carbohydrate 15g (Dietary Fiber 3g); Protein 4g

# PANISH RICE

Prep: 5 min; Cook: 30 min        4 servings

- **2  tablespoons vegetable oil**
- **1  medium onion, peeled and chopped**
- **1  cup uncooked regular long-grain white rice**
- **1  small green bell pepper, chopped**
- **2½ cups water**
- **1  teaspoon salt**
- **¾ teaspoon chili powder**
- **⅛ teaspoon garlic powder**
- **1  can (8 ounces) tomato sauce**

**1.** Heat oil in skillet over medium heat 1 to 2 minutes. Cook onion and rice in oil about 5 minutes, stirring frequently, until rice is golden brown.

**2.** Remove skillet from heat. Stir in bell pepper, water, salt, chili powder, garlic powder and tomato sauce. Heat to boiling over high heat, stirring occasionally.

**3.** Once mixture is boiling, reduce heat just enough so mixture bubbles gently. Cover and cook about 25 minutes, stirring occasionally, until rice is tender and tomato sauce is absorbed. You may have to lower the heat as the mixture becomes thicker.

**1 SERVING:** Calories 265 (Calories from Fat 65); Fat 7g (Saturated 1g); Cholesterol 0mg; Sodium 930mg; Carbohydrate 48g (Dietary Fiber 2g); Protein 5g

---

**COOKING TIP**

- For extra flavor, sprinkle ¼ cup shredded Cheddar cheese over Spanish Rice just before serving.

# BASIL-BAKED NEW POTATOES

Prep: 5 min; Bake: 1 hr 15 min        6 servings

**14 to 18   new potatoes (2¼ pounds)**
**3   medium green onions, trimmed and finely chopped**
**2   tablespoons chopped fresh or 2 teaspoons dried basil leaves**
**2   tablespoons olive or vegetable oil**

**1.** Heat oven to 350°. Spray rectangular pan, 13 × 9 × 2 inches, with nonstick cooking spray.

**2.** Place potatoes in pan. Sprinkle with onions and basil. Drizzle with oil; stir to coat.

**3.** Bake uncovered about 1 hour 15 minutes, stirring occasionally, until potato skins are crispy and potatoes are tender.

**1 SERVING:** Calories 185 (Calories from Fat 45); Fat 5g (Saturated 1g); Cholesterol 0mg; Sodium 10mg; Carbohydrate 35g (Dietary Fiber 3g); Protein 3g

# OVEN-FRIED POTATO WEDGES

Prep: 10 min; Bake: 30 min        4 servings

**¾   teaspoon salt**
**½   teaspoon sugar**
**½   teaspoon paprika**
**¼   teaspoon ground mustard**
**¼   teaspoon garlic powder**
**3   medium baking potatoes (8 to 10 ounces each)**

**1.** Heat oven to 425°. Mix salt, sugar, paprika, mustard and garlic powder.

**2.** Gently scrub potatoes, but do not peel. Cut each potato lengthwise in half; cut each half lengthwise into 4 wedges. Place potato wedges, skin sides down, in ungreased rectangular pan, 13 × 9 × 2 inches.

**3.** Spray potatoes with cooking spray until lightly coated. Sprinkle with salt mixture.

**4.** Bake uncovered 25 to 30 minutes or until potatoes are tender.

**1 SERVING:** Calories 105 (Calories from Fat 0); Fat 0g (Saturated 0g); Cholesterol 0mg; Sodium 450mg; Carbohydrate 24g (Dietary Fiber 2g); Protein 2g

# ℛOASTED VEGETABLES

Prep: 10 min; Bake: 25 min     4 servings

- 1 **medium red or green bell pepper**
- 1 **medium onion, peeled**
- 1 **medium zucchini**
- ¼ **pound mushrooms**
- ¼ **teaspoon salt**
- ⅛ **teaspoon pepper**
- 2 **tablespoons chopped fresh or 2 teaspoons dried basil leaves, if desired**

**1.** Cut bell pepper lengthwise in half, and cut out seeds and membrane. Cut each half lengthwise into 4 strips.

**2.** Cut onion in half. Wrap one half of onion, and refrigerate for another use. Cut remaining half into 4 wedges, then separate into pieces.

**3.** Cut zucchini crosswise into 1-inch pieces. Cut off and discard the end of each mushroom stem, and leave mushrooms whole.

**4.** Heat the oven to 425°. Spray bottom of baking pan with cooking spray. Arrange vegetables in a single layer in sprayed pan. Spray vegetables with cooking spray until lightly coated. Sprinkle with salt, pepper and basil.

**5.** Bake uncovered 15 minutes. Remove pan from oven. Turn vegetables over. Bake uncovered about 10 minutes longer or until vegetables are crisp-tender.

**1 SERVING.** Calories 30 (Calories from Fat 0); Fat 0g (Saturated 0g); Cholesterol 0mg; Sodium 150mg; Carbohydrate 6g (Dietary Fiber 1g); Protein 2g

# CURRIED VEGETABLES

**QUICK**   Prep: 10 min; Cook: 20 min        6 servings

1 tablespoon olive or vegetable oil

1 medium onion, peeled and thinly sliced

1 clove garlic, peeled and finely chopped

2 teaspoons curry powder

1 teaspoon grated gingerroot

¾ cup water

¾ cup apple juice

1 tablespoon soy sauce

1 medium carrot, peeled and cut into ½-inch slices

1 tablespoon cornstarch

1 small bell pepper, cut into thin strips

1 medium zucchini, cut into ½-inch slices

2 cups cauliflowerets

½ cup raisins

**1.** Heat oil in Dutch oven over medium-high heat 1 to 2 minutes. Cook onion, garlic, curry powder and gingerroot in oil, stirring frequently, until onion is tender.

**2.** Stir in water, ½ cup of the apple juice, the soy sauce and carrot. Heat to boiling over high heat. Reduce heat just enough so mixture bubbles gently. Cover and cook 10 minutes.

**3.** Mix cornstarch and remaining ¼ cup apple juice until cornstarch is dissolved. Stir bell pepper, zucchini, cauliflowerets and raisins into carrot mixture. Stir in cornstarch mixture.

**4.** Cover and cook 3 to 5 minutes longer, stirring occasionally, until zucchini is tender.

**1 SERVING:** Calories 115 (Calories from Fat 25); Fat 3g (Saturated 0g); Cholesterol 0mg; Sodium 170mg; Carbohydrate 23g (Dietary Fiber 3g); Protein 2g

• To prepare the squash in a conventional oven, heat oven to 400°. Prick squash with fork; place in ungreased square baking dish, 8 × 8 × 2 inches. Bake uncovered about 1½ hours or until tender. Continue with recipe as directed.

# $\mathcal{S}$PAGHETTI WITH SQUASH

Prep: 15 min; Cook: 20 min; Stand: 10 min     6 servings

1   **medium spaghetti squash (about 3 pounds)**
4   **ounces uncooked spaghetti, broken in half**
¼   **cup chopped fresh parsley**
2   **tablespoons grated Parmesan cheese**
2   **tablespoons margarine or butter, melted**
1   **tablespoon chopped fresh or 1 teaspoon dried oregano leaves**
½   **teaspoon garlic salt**

**1.** Prick squash with fork; place on microwavable paper towel in microwave oven. Microwave on high 8 minutes; turn squash over. Microwave 8 to 11 minutes longer or until tender. Let stand 10 minutes.

**2.** Meanwhile, cook and drain spaghetti as directed on package. Cut squash lengthwise in half; remove seeds and fibers. Reserve one half for another use. Remove spaghetti-like strands with 2 forks.

**3.** Toss squash, spaghetti and remaining ingredients. Return spaghetti mixture to squash shell to serve.

**1 SERVING:** Calories 140 (Calories from Fat 25); Fat 3g (Saturated 1g); Cholesterol 0mg; Sodium 170mg; Carbohydrate 28g (Dietary Fiber 4g); Protein 5g

# $\mathcal{D}$ILLED CARROTS AND PEA PODS

**QUICK**  Prep: 5 min; Cook: 7 min          4 servings

1½  **cups snow (Chinese) pea pods (about 5 ounces)**

1½  **cups baby carrots**

1  **tablespoon margarine or butter**

2  **teaspoons chopped fresh or ½ teaspoon dried dill weed**

⅛  **teaspoon salt**

**1.** Snap off stem end of each pea pod and pull string across pea pod to remove it.

**2.** Add 1 inch water to saucepan. Cover and heat water to boiling over high heat. Add carrots. Cover and heat to boiling again. Once water is boiling, reduce heat just enough so water bubbles gently. Cook covered about 4 minutes or until carrots are crisp-tender. Do not drain water.

**3.** Add pea pods to carrots in saucepan. Heat uncovered until water is boiling again; continue boiling uncovered 2 to 3 minutes, stirring occasionally, until pea pods are crisp-tender. (Pea pods cook very quickly, so be careful not to overcook them.) Drain carrots and pea pods in a strainer, then return to saucepan.

**4.** Stir margarine, dill weed and salt into carrots and pea pods until margarine is melted.

**1 SERVING.** Calories 45 (Calories from Fat 25); Fat 3g (Saturated 1g); Cholesterol 0mg; Sodium 130mg; Carbohydrate 6g (Dietary Fiber 2g); Protein 1g

**COOKING TIP**

• One 6-ounce package of frozen snow (Chinese) pea pods can be substituted for the fresh pea pods. Thaw them before cooking in step 3.

# GREEN BEANS OLÉ

Prep: 10 min; Cook: 25 min        4 servings

1  pound green beans, cut into 1-inch pieces

4  slices bacon, chopped

1  medium onion, peeled and chopped

1  medium tomato, chopped

1  clove garlic, peeled and finely chopped

1  teaspoon chopped fresh or ½ teaspoon dried oregano leaves

½  teaspoon salt

Dash of pepper

2  tablespoons lemon or lime juice

**1.** Place beans in 1 inch water in 2-quart saucepan. Heat to boiling; reduce heat. Simmer uncovered 10 to 15 minutes or until crisp-tender; drain. Immediately rinse with cold water; drain.

**2.** Cook bacon in 10-inch skillet over medium-high heat, stirring occasionally, until crisp. Remove bacon from skillet, reserving 1 table-spoon fat in skillet. Drain bacon on paper towels.

**3.** Cook onion in bacon fat over medium heat, stirring occasionally, until tender. Stir in tomato, garlic, oregano, salt and pepper. Simmer uncovered 5 minutes. Stir in beans; heat through. Drizzle with lemon juice. Garnish with bacon.

**1 SERVING:** Calories 70 (Calories from Fat 25); Fat 3g (Saturated 1g); Cholesterol 5mg; Sodium 410mg; Carbohydrate 11g (Dietary Fiber 4g); Protein 4g

# PEAS AND ALMONDS

QUICK  Prep: 5 min; Cook: 7 min        6 servings

2  tablespoons butter or stick margarine

¼  cup slivered almonds

1  bag (16 ounces) frozen green peas, thawed and drained

½  teaspoon salt

**1.** Melt butter in 10-inch skillet over medium heat. Cook almonds in butter 2 to 3 minutes, stirring occasionally, until light brown.

**2.** Stir in peas and salt. Cook 3 to 5 minutes, stirring frequently, until peas are tender.

**1 SERVING:** Calories 85 (Calories from Fat 45); Fat 5g (Saturated 2g); Cholesterol 5mg; Sodium 270mg; Carbohydrate 10g (Dietary Fiber 4g); Protein 4g

# DESSERTS

## ORANGE CAPPUCCINO BROWNIES

Prep: 20 min; Bake: 20 min; Cool: 15 min          16 brownies

- 1 **cup all-purpose flour**
- 1 **cup sugar**
- ½ **cup baking cocoa**
- 2 **teaspoons instant espresso coffee (dry)**
- ¼ **teaspoon baking powder**
- ½ **cup fat-free cholesterol-free egg product or 2 eggs**
- ¼ **cup (½ stick) margarine or butter, melted**
- 2 **tablespoons water**
   **Orange–Cream Cheese Glaze (below)**
   **Grated orange peel, if desired**

**1.** Heat oven to 350°. Spray square pan, 9 × 9 × 2 inches, with cooking spray. Mix flour, sugar, cocoa, espresso and baking powder in medium bowl. Stir in egg product, margarine and water. Spread in pan.

**2.** Bake 18 to 20 minutes or until center is set and brownies begin to pull away from sides of pan. Cool 15 minutes. Drizzle Orange–Cream Cheese Glaze over brownies. Sprinkle with the orange peel. For brownies, cut into 4 rows by 4 rows.

**1 BROWNIE:** Calories 125 (Calories from Fat 25); Fat 3g (Saturated 1g); Cholesterol 0mg; Sodium 65mg; Carbohydrate 23g (Dietary Fiber 1g); Protein 2g

## ORANGE–CREAM CHEESE GLAZE

- ⅓ **cup powdered sugar**
- ½ **teaspoon frozen orange juice concentrate, thawed, or orange juice**
- ½ **teaspoon grated orange peel**
- 1 **ounce fat-free cream cheese, softened**

Mix all ingredients until smooth.

# Milk Chocolate Fondue

**QUICK** Prep: 15 min; Cook: 5 min        8 servings

1 **package (11½ ounces) milk chocolate chips**

⅔ **cup half-and-half**

2 **tablespoons liqueur (almond, cherry, coffee, hazelnut, Irish cream, orange or raspberry), if desired**

**Dippers (angel food cake cubes, apple wedges, banana slices, brownie cubes, grapes, kiwifruit pieces, mandarin orange segments, maraschino cherries, marshmallows, miniature cream puffs, pineapple cubes, pound cake cubes, strawberries)**

1. Heat chocolate chips and half-and-half in saucepan over low heat, stirring constantly, until chocolate is melted and mixture is smooth. Remove saucepan from heat.

2. Stir in liqueur. Pour mixture into fondue pot and keep warm over low heat.

3. Spear dippers with wooden picks or fondue forks and dip into fondue. If fondue becomes too thick, stir in a small amount of half-and-half.

**1 SERVING:** Calories 255 (Calories from Fat 135); Fat 15g (Saturated 9g); Cholesterol 15mg; Sodium 45mg; Carbohydrate 27g (Dietary Fiber 1g); Protein 4g

***Dark Chocolate Fondue:*** Substitute 1 package (12 ounces) semisweet chocolate chips for the milk chocolate chips.

***White Almond Fondue:*** Substitute 12 ounces vanilla-flavored candy coating (almond bark), chopped, for the milk chocolate chips and decrease half-and-half to ⅓ cup.

---

### COOKING TIP

• To keep fruit from darkening, dip apples and bananas into lemon juice after slicing them.

---

## SPECIAL TOUCH

### Screen Luminaria

You will need:

**8 × 5-inch and 15 × 10-inch rectangles fine metal mesh window screening (window screening is sold in rolls at hardware stores. Cut screening to desired size with scissors or wire cutters)**

**Glass votive (about 2½ inches high) and glass cylinder (about 6 inches high) candleholders**

**Votive (about 2 inches high) and pillar (about 4 to 5 inches high) candles**

**Colored string or thin ribbon**

1. Fold over ½ inch on 1 short edge and 1 long edge of each small rectangle of screening. Fold over 1 inch on both short edges and 1 long edge of each large rectangle of screening.

2. Mold each rectangle of screening around candleholder to form cylinder shape; remove candleholder. Staple short edges of screening together, tucking the unfolded short edge into the corner of the long folded edge.

3. Add votive candles to votive candleholders; place small luminaria screen, folded edge up, over candleholders. Add taller candles to cylinder candleholders; place large luminaria screen, folded edge up, over candleholders. Tie string around centers of luminarias.

COOKING TIP

• Add variety to this elegant dessert by using a mix of fresh raspberries, blueberries and strawberries.

# RASPBERRY CUSTARD CREAM

**QUICK**  Prep: 10 min        4 servings

- **2** containers (6 ounces each) raspberry yogurt
- **1** package (4-serving size) vanilla instant pudding and pie filling mix
- **1** cup whipping (heavy) cream
- **1** cup fresh or frozen (thawed) raspberries
   Additional fresh raspberries for garnish, if desired

**1.** Beat yogurt and dry pudding mix in a medium bowl with electric mixer on low speed 30 seconds.

**2.** Add whipping cream to pudding mixture. Beat on medium speed 3 to 5 minutes, scraping bowl occasionally, until soft peaks form. Soft peaks should be rounded or curled when beaters are lifted from bowl.

**3.** Gently stir 1 cup raspberries into custard.

**4.** Spoon custard mixture into 4 stemmed glasses, dessert dishes or small bowls. Garnish with fresh raspberries. Store covered in refrigerator.

**1 SERVING:** Calories 370 (Calories from Fat 180); Fat 20g (Saturated 12g); Cholesterol 70mg; Sodium 430mg; Carbohydrate 45g (Dietary Fiber 2g); Protein 5g

***Orange-Blueberry Custard Cream:*** Substitute orange yogurt for the raspberry yogurt. Omit raspberries. Stir in 1 cup blueberries.

***Lemon-Strawberry Custard Cream:*** Substitute lemon yogurt for the raspberry yogurt. Omit raspberries. Stir in 1 cup sliced strawberries.

---

### SERVING TIP

● Wine or juice glasses, sundae dishes or clear small bowls all will show off the pretty fruit and custard. And even if they don't match, it will still look great.

---

## SPECIAL TOUCH

### Intertwined Pillars

You will need:

**2 pillar candles (about 8 inches high)**

**About 1 yard colored string, ribbon or raffia**

**Heart button or charm**

**1 sheet (8 × 10 inches) clear glass (from picture frame)**

**Adhesive tape (color-coordinate the tape to match your color scheme. You can also color the tape with permanent markers)**

**4 round napkin rings**

1. Wrap candles together with string. Tie ends of string; attach button.

2. Clean glass; tape edges if sharp.

3. Place glass on napkin rings, making sure 1 ring is under each corner of glass. Arrange candles on glass.

# $\mathcal{F}$RESH BERRY COBBLER

Prep: 5 min; Cook: 5 min; Bake: 15 min     6 servings

½ cup sugar

1 tablespoon cornstarch

4 cups raspberries or blueberries

2 tablespoons water

1 teaspoon lemon juice

1 cup Original Bisquick baking mix

¼ cup milk

1 tablespoon sugar

1 tablespoon margarine or butter, melted

**1.** Heat oven to 425°.

**2.** Mix the ½ cup sugar and cornstarch in saucepan. Stir in raspberries, water and lemon juice. Heat to boiling over medium heat, stirring constantly. Continue boiling 1 minute, stirring constantly. Pour berry mixture into ungreased casserole.

**3.** Stir Bisquick, milk, 1 tablespoon sugar and melted margarine just until blended and a dough forms. Drop dough by 6 spoonfuls onto hot berry mixture.

**4.** Bake about 15 minutes or until the berry mixture is bubbly and topping is light brown.

**5.** Place casserole on wire rack. Cool slightly. Serve warm.

**1 SERVING:** Calories 205 (Calories from Fat 45); Fat 5g (Saturated 1g); Cholesterol 0mg; Sodium 310mg; Carbohydrate 39g (Dietary Fiber 1g); Protein 2g

## COOKING TIPS

• Store raspberries and blueberries in their original container or spread them out in a dish or pan lined with paper towels. Raspberries especially are very fragile, so plan to use them within a day or so to avoid moldy berries.

• For a splashing finish, pass a pitcher of whipping (heavy) cream, half-and-half or eggnog, when it is available, to pour over bowls of warm cobbler. Sprinkle a little ground cinnamon or nutmeg on top for just a hint of spiciness.

**DROPPING DOUGH ONTO BERRY MIXTURE**

Drop dough by 6 spoonfuls onto hot berry mixture.

# CINNAMON APPLE CRISP

Prep: 15 min; Bake: 35 min          6 servings

6  **medium tart cooking apples, such as Granny Smith, Rome Beauty or Greening**

1  **tablespoon lemon juice**

1  **teaspoon ground cinnamon**

1  **cup quick-cooking or old-fashioned oats**

1  **cup packed brown sugar**

¾  **cup all-purpose flour**

½  **cup (1 stick) margarine or butter at room temperature**

   **Ice cream or cream, if desired**

1. Heat oven to 375°. Peel apples if desired. Cut each apple into fourths. Cut core and seeds from center of each fourth. Cut each fourth into slices. You will need about 6 cups of apple slices.

2. Spread apples in square baking pan, 8 × 8 × 2 inches. Drizzle lemon juice over apples. Sprinkle with cinnamon.

3. Mix oats, brown sugar, flour and margarine with fork. The mixture will be crumbly. Sprinkle mixture evenly over apples.

4. Bake 30 to 35 minutes or until topping is golden brown and apples are tender when pierced with fork.

5. Place pan on wire rack. Cool slightly. Serve warm with ice cream.

**1 SERVING:** Calories 450 (Calories from Fat 145); Fat 16g (Saturated 10g); Cholesterol 40mg; Sodium 120mg; Carbohydrate 78g (Dietary Fiber 6g); Protein 4g

# MPOSSIBLE COCONUT PIE

Prep: 10 min; Bake: 55 min        6 servings

| | |
|---|---|
| 2 | **cups milk** |
| ¼ | **cup margarine or butter, softened** |
| 4 | **eggs** |
| ¾ | **cup sugar** |
| ½ | **cup Original Bisquick baking mix** |
| 1½ | **teaspoons vanilla** |
| 1 | **cup flaked or shredded coconut** |

**1.** Heat oven to 350°. Grease glass pie plate, 9 × 1¼ or 10 × 1½ inches.

**2.** Stir all ingredients with fork until blended. Pour into pie plate.

**3.** Bake 50 to 55 minutes or until golden brown and knife inserted in center comes out clean. Refrigerate any remaining pie.

**1 SERVING:** Calories 360 (Calories from Fat 160); Fat 18g (Saturated 8g); Cholesterol 150mg; Sodium 350mg; Carbohydrate 41g (Dietary Fiber 0g); Protein 8g

# CRUNCHY NUT ICE CREAM PIE

Prep: 5 min; Bake: 8 min; Freeze: 4 hr; Cook: 5 min        8 servings

- 1½ **cups ground pecans, walnuts or almonds**
- 3 **tablespoons sugar**
- 2 **tablespoons margarine or butter, softened**
- 1 **quart coffee, chocolate or vanilla ice cream**
  **Rich Chocolate Sauce (below)**

**1.** Heat oven to 400°. Mix pecans, sugar and margarine. Press firmly and evenly against bottom and side of ungreased pie plate, 9 × 1¼ inches. Bake 6 to 8 minutes; cool.

**2.** Spoon ice cream into pie shell. Freeze until firm, about 4 hours. Remove from freezer 10 to 15 minutes before serving. Cut into wedges; spoon Rich Chocolate Sauce over each serving.

**1 SERVING:** Calories 580 (Calories from Fat 360); Fat 40g (Saturated 16g); Cholesterol 125mg; Sodium 120mg; Carbohydrate 49g (Dietary Fiber 2g); Protein 8g

## RICH CHOCOLATE SAUCE

- 1 **package (6 ounces) semisweet chocolate chips**
- ¼ **cup sugar**
- ¼ **cup water**
- ¼ **cup half-and-half**

Heat chocolate, sugar and water in saucepan over low heat, stirring constantly, until chocolate and sugar are melted. Remove from heat; blend in half-and-half. Serve warm or cool.

# CARAMEL-CHOCOLATE PIE

Prep: 15 min; Bake: 10 min; Cook: 10 min; Chill: 1 hr        12 servings

- ½ cup vanilla wafer crumbs (about 25 wafers)
- ¼ cup (½ stick) margarine or butter, melted
- 30 vanilla caramels
- 2 tablespoons margarine or butter
- 2 tablespoons water
- ½ cup chopped pecans, toasted (see opposite page)
- 2 packages (3 ounces each) cream cheese, softened
- ⅓ cup powdered sugar
- 1 bar (4 ounces) sweet cooking chocolate
- 3 tablespoons hot water
- 1 teaspoon vanilla
- 2 cups whipping (heavy) cream
- 2 tablespoons powdered sugar

**1.** Heat oven to 350°. Mix crumbs and ¼ cup margarine. Press mixture firmly against side and bottom of pie plate, 9 × 1¼ inches. Bake 10 minutes; cool.

**2.** Heat caramels, 2 tablespoons margarine and 2 tablespoons water over medium heat, stirring frequently, until caramels are melted. Pour into crust. Sprinkle with pecans. Refrigerate about 1 hour until chilled.

**3.** Beat cream cheese and ⅓ cup powdered sugar until smooth. Spread over caramel layer; refrigerate.

**4.** Heat chocolate and 3 tablespoons hot water over low heat, stirring constantly, until chocolate is melted. Cool to room temperature. Stir in vanilla.

**5.** Beat whipping cream and 2 tablespoons powdered sugar in chilled medium bowl until stiff. Reserve 1½ cups. Fold chocolate mixture into remaining whipped cream. Spread over cream cheese mixture. Top with reserved whipped cream. Refrigerate any remaining pie.

**1 SERVING:** Calories 430 (Calories from Fat 280); Fat 31g (Saturated 16g); Cholesterol 70mg; Sodium 170mg; Carbohydrate 38g (Dietary Fiber 1g); Protein 5g

# Toasting Nuts, Coconut and Sesame Seeds

Toasting brings out the true flavor and adds a wonderful dimension to any recipe that calls for nuts, coconut or sesame seed. A good doneness test, along with color, is when you can smell the toasted aroma. Use it as a signal to watch the nuts or seeds carefully so they don't burn. Remove them immediately from the hot pan or skillet so they don't continue to toast and become too dark or scorch.

## Stove-Top Method

**Nuts:** Sprinkle in an ungreased heavy skillet. Cook over medium heat 5 to 7 minutes, stirring frequently until nuts begin to brown, then stirring constantly until nuts are light brown.

**Coconut:** Sprinkle in an ungreased heavy skillet. Cook over medium-low heat 6 to 14 minutes, stirring frequently until browning begins, then stirring constantly until golden brown.

**Sesame seed:** Sprinkle in an ungreased heavy skillet over medium-low heat 5 to 7 minutes, stirring frequently until browning begins, then stirring constantly until golden brown.

## Oven Method

**Nuts:** Spread in a ungreased shallow pan. Bake uncovered in a 350° oven 6 to 10 minutes, stirring frequently, until nuts are light brown.

**Coconut:** Spread in a ungreased shallow pan. Bake uncovered in 350° oven 5 to 7 minutes, stirring occasionally, until golden brown.

**Sesame seed:** Spread in an ungreased shallow pan. Bake uncovered in 350° oven 8 to 10 minutes, stirring occasionally, until golden brown.

## Microwave Method

**Nuts:** Place 1 teaspoon butter or margarine and ½ cup nuts in a microwavable pie plate. Microwave uncovered on High (100%) 2 minutes 30 seconds to 3 minutes, stirring every 30 seconds, until nuts are light brown.

**Coconut:** Spread ½ cup in a microwavable pie plate. Microwave uncovered on High (100%) 1 minute 30 seconds, stirring every 30 seconds until golden brown. ■

# $\mathcal{J}$TRAWBERRY SHORTCAKES

Prep: 15 min; Stand: 1 hr; Bake: 12 min        6 servings

**1  quart strawberries, sliced**
**½  cup sugar**
**2  cups all-purpose flour**
**2  tablespoons sugar**
**3  teaspoons baking powder**
**1  teaspoon salt**
**⅓  cup shortening**
**¾  cup milk**
**Margarine or butter, softened**
**Sweetened whipped cream**

**1.** Mix strawberries and ½ cup sugar. Let stand 1 hour.

**2.** Heat oven to 450°.

**3.** Combine flour, 2 tablespoons sugar, baking powder and salt in medium bowl. Cut in shortening using pastry blender or criss-crossing 2 knives, until mixture looks like fine crumbs. Stir in milk just until blended.

**4.** Turn dough onto lightly floured surface. Gently smooth into a ball. Knead 20 to 25 times. Roll ½ inch thick. Cut into 3-inch squares or use floured 3-inch cutter. Place about 1 inch apart on ungreased cookie sheet. Bake 10 to 12 minutes or until golden brown.

**5.** Split shortcakes horizontally in half while hot. Spread margarine on split sides. Fill with strawberries; replace tops. Top with strawberries and sweetened whipped cream.

**1 SERVING:** Calories 400 (Calories from Fat 135); Fat 15g (Saturated 5g); Cholesterol 10mg; Sodium 630mg; Carbohydrate 63g (Dietary Fiber 8g); Protein 6g

# OUND CAKE

Prep: 20 min; Bake: 1 hr 20 min; Cool: 2 hr 20 min        24 servings

2½ **cups sugar**

1 **cup (2 sticks) butter or stick margarine, softened (see tip)**

5 **large eggs**

1 **teaspoon vanilla or almond extract**

3 **cups all-purpose (not self-rising) flour**

1 **teaspoon baking powder**

¼ **teaspoon salt**

1 **cup milk or evaporated milk**

**Powdered sugar, if desired**

**1.** Heat oven to 350°. Grease bottom and side of angel food cake pan (tube pan), 10 × 3 × 4 inches, 12-cup Bundt cake pan or 2 loaf pans, 9 × 5 × 3 inches, with shortening; lightly flour.

**2.** Beat sugar, butter, eggs and vanilla in large bowl with electric mixer on low speed 30 seconds, scraping bowl constantly. Beat on high speed 5 minutes, scraping bowl occasionally. Mix flour, baking powder and salt. Beat flour mixture into sugar mixture alternately with milk on low speed, beating just until smooth after each addition. Pour into pan(s).

**3.** Bake angel food or Bundt cake pan 1 hour 10 minutes to 1 hour 20 minutes, loaf pans 55 to 60 minutes, or until toothpick inserted in center comes out clean. Cool 20 minutes; remove from pan(s) to wire rack. Cool completely, about 2 hours. Sprinkle with powdered sugar.

**1 SERVING:** Calories 225 (Calories from Fat 80); Fat 9g (Saturated 5g); Cholesterol 65mg; Sodium 115mg; Carbohydrate 33g (Dietary Fiber 0g); Protein 3g

***Lemon-Poppy Seed Pound Cake:*** Substitute 1 teaspoon lemon extract for the vanilla. Fold 1 tablespoon grated lemon peel and ¼ cup poppy seed into batter.

# ONNIE BUTTER CAKE

Prep: 10 min; Bake: 35–50 min; Cool: 10 min        12 servings

- ⅔  **cup margarine or butter, softened**
- 1¾  **cups sugar**
- 2  **eggs**
- 1½  **teaspoons vanilla**
- 2¾  **cups all-purpose flour (see tip)**
- 2½  **teaspoons baking powder**
- 1  **teaspoon salt**
- 1¼  **cups milk**

**Betty Crocker Rich & Creamy® Chocolate Frosting**

**1.** Heat oven to 350°. Grease and flour rectangular pan, 13 × 9 × 2 inches, or 2 round pans, 9 × 1½ inches. Mix margarine, sugar, eggs and vanilla in large mixer bowl until fluffy. Beat on high speed, scraping bowl occasionally, 5 minutes. Beat in flour, baking powder and salt alternately with milk on low speed. Pour into pan(s).

**2.** Bake rectangular pan 45 to 50 minutes, round pans 30 to 35 minutes or until toothpick inserted in center comes out clean. Cool layers 10 minutes; remove from pan. Cool completely. Frost rectangular or fill and frost rounds with frosting.

**1 SERVING:** Calories 338 (Calories from Fat 110); Fat 12g (Saturated 3g); Cholesterol 40mg; Sodium 440mg; Carbohydrate 53g (Dietary Fiber <1g); Protein 5g

---

**COOKING TIP**

• If using self-rising flour, omit baking powder and salt.

# RASPBERRY JAM CAKE

Prep: 10 min; Bake: 1 hr 15 min; Cool: 10 min; Cook: 5 min        16 servings

| | |
|---|---|
| 1 | cup (2 sticks) margarine or butter, softened |
| ½ | cup granulated sugar |
| ½ | cup packed brown sugar |
| 4 | eggs |
| 1 | jar (10 ounces) red raspberry preserves |
| 3¼ | cups all-purpose flour |
| 1 | teaspoon baking powder |
| 1 | teaspoon baking soda |
| 1 | teaspoon ground nutmeg |
| 1 | teaspoon ground cinnamon |
| ½ | teaspoon salt |
| ¼ | teaspoon ground cloves |
| 1 | cup buttermilk |
| 1 | cup chopped pecans |
| | Caramel Frosting (at right) |

**1.** Heat oven to 350°. Grease and flour tube pan, 10 × 4 inches. Beat margarine and sugars in 3-quart bowl on medium speed, scraping bowl constantly, until blended. Beat on high speed 1 minute. Beat in eggs and preserves until well blended. (Mixture will appear curdled.) Beat in flour, baking powder, baking soda, nutmeg, cinnamon, salt and cloves alternately with buttermilk, beginning and ending with flour mixture, until well blended. Stir in pecans. Pour into pan.

**2.** Bake until toothpick inserted in center comes out clean and top springs back when touched lightly, 70 to 75 minutes. Cool 10 minutes; remove from pan. Cool completely on wire rack. Frost with Caramel Frosting.

**1 SERVING:** Calories 530 (Calories from Fat 220); Fat 24g (Saturated 4g); Cholesterol 55mg; Sodium 430mg; Carbohydrate 75g (Dietary Fiber 1g); Protein 6g

## CARAMEL FROSTING

½ cup (1 stick) margarine or butter

1 cup packed brown sugar

¼ cup milk

2 cups powdered sugar

Heat margarine in 2-quart saucepan until melted. Stir in brown sugar. Heat to boiling, stirring constantly. Boil and stir over low heat 2 minutes; stir in milk. Heat to boiling; remove from heat. Cool to lukewarm. Gradually stir in powdered sugar; beat until smooth and of spreading consistency. If frosting becomes too stiff, stir in additional milk, 1 teaspoon at a time.

# CHOCOLATE SNACK CAKE

Prep: 10 min; Bake: 35 min; Cool: 15 min      9 servings

1½ cups all-purpose (not self-rising) flour

1 cup sugar

¼ cup baking cocoa

1 teaspoon baking soda

½ teaspoon salt

⅓ cup vegetable oil

1 teaspoon white vinegar

½ teaspoon vanilla

1 cup cold water

Ice cream or whipped cream, if desired

**1.** Heat oven to 350°. Grease bottom and side of round pan, 9 × 1½ inches, or square pan, 8 × 8 × 2 inches, with shortening; lightly flour.

**2.** Mix flour, sugar, cocoa, baking soda and salt in medium bowl. Mix oil, vinegar and vanilla. Vigorously stir oil mixture and water into flour mixture about 1 minute or until well blended. Immediately pour into pan.

**3.** Bake 30 to 35 minutes or until toothpick inserted in center comes out clean. Cool 15 minutes. Serve warm or cool with ice cream.

**1 SERVING:** Calories 230 (Calories from Fat 70); Fat 8g (Saturated 1g); Cholesterol 0mg; Sodium 270mg; Carbohydrate 38g (Dietary Fiber 1g); Protein 2g

# Hot Fudge Sundae Cake

Prep: 10 min; Bake: 40 min     9 servings

 1  **cup all-purpose flour**
¾  **cup granulated sugar**
 2  **tablespoons baking cocoa**
 2  **teaspoons baking powder**
¼  **teaspoon salt**
½  **cup milk**
 2  **tablespoons vegetable oil**
 1  **teaspoon vanilla**
 1  **cup chopped nuts, if desired**
 1  **cup packed brown sugar**
¼  **cup baking cocoa**
1¾  **cups very hot water**
     **Ice cream, if desired**

**1.** Heat oven to 350°.

**2.** Mix flour, granulated sugar, 2 tablespoons cocoa, baking powder and salt in ungreased square pan, 9 × 9 × 2 inches. Mix in milk, oil and vanilla with fork until smooth. Stir in nuts. Spread in pan.

**3.** Sprinkle brown sugar and ¼ cup cocoa over batter. Pour water over batter.

**4.** Bake 40 minutes or until top is dry.

**5.** Spoon warm cake into dessert dishes. Top with ice cream. Spoon sauce from pan onto each serving.

**1 SERVING:** Calories 400 (Calories from Fat 100); Fat 11g (Saturated 5g); Cholesterol 30mg; Sodium 240mg; Carbohydrate 71g (Dietary Fiber 1g); Protein 5g

# MENUS FOR CASUAL MEALS

## Snacks and Sweets

Mushroom Pita Bites, **page 10**

Oven-Fried Chicken Chunks with Peanut Sauce, **page 15**

Port wine cheese with hard pretzels

Orange Cappuccino Brownies, **page 87**

Milk Chocolate Fondue, **page 88**

Assorted soft drinks

*Hot Chocolate, **page 6**

**SPECIAL TOUCH:** Try adding grated orange peel, cinnamon, or nutmeg to hot chocolate—with or without mini marshmallows or whipped cream!

## Sit-Down Dinner

Prepared fruit cocktail

Oven-Barbecued Chicken, **page 57**

Baked potatoes with butter and sour cream

Peas and Almonds, **page 86**

Sweet Corn Bread Muffins, **page 20**

Cinnamon Apple Crisp, **page 94**

Wine, coffee and tea

**SPECIAL TOUCH:** Use decorative kitchen towels in place of formal napkins for a casual meal.

## Buffet-Style Party

Layered Vegetable and Aioli Appetizer, **page 8**

Double-Garlic Potato Bread (2-pound recipe), **page 27**

Vegetable–Cheddar Cheese Soup, **page 38**

Penne Pasta with Marinara Sauce, **page 46**

Mesclun with assorted bottled dressings on the side

*Green Beans Olé, **page 86**

Raspberry Jam Cake, **page 104**

Assorted cookies

Assorted soft drinks

**SPECIAL TOUCH:** Arrange sprigs of fresh herbs on serving platters or trays.

## Small Gathering

Celery and carrot sticks with prepared Ranch dip

Tuscan Pasta and Beans, **page 44**

Focaccia Wedges, **page 9**

Spicy Beef Salad, **page 76**

Caramel-Chocolate Pie, **page 98**

Fruit juice spritzers

**SPECIAL TOUCH:** A shallow basket or large terra-cotta saucer makes a perfect pasta bowl charger. For a rustic touch, line the basket first with natural excelsior or straw (page 47).

## For a Larger Crowd

Hot Crab Dip, **page 7**

Sweet-and-Sour Meatballs, **page 18**

*Whole Wheat Vegetable Calzone, **page 34**

*Barbecued Roast Beef Sandwiches, **page 32**

Prepared pasta salad and coleslaw

Pound Cake, **page 102**

Bonnie Butter Cake, **page 103**

Beer and soda

**SPECIAL TOUCH:** Drizzle melted chocolate chips in a simple pattern over one of the cakes.

## Last-Minute Meal

Broiled Fish Steaks, **page 56**

Dilled Carrots and Pea Pods, **page 85**

Quick-cooking brown rice

Raspberry Custard Cream, **page 90**

Iced tea with lemon

**SPECIAL TOUCH:** To brighten up your table in a flash, arrange colorful flowers in a tea kettle or small watering can (see page 422).

*Double recipes that are marked with an asterisk.

# $\mathcal{B}$ACKYARD $\mathcal{B}$ARBECUES

When the sun is out and cold temperatures are gone, take advantage of the weather and take your dinner outdoors! Avoid the oven and keep your kitchen cool on hot days with these great grilling recipes and easy, fun-to-make dishes. Here's everything you need to enjoy fabulous food in the fresh air!

◄ Honey-Mustard Chicken Sandwiches (page 128)

## MAIN DISHES

## SALADS AND SIDES

## DESSERTS

## MENUS

# BEVERAGES

## COOKING TIPS

• To get the most juice from the lemons, let them stand at room temperature or microwave on High for a few seconds before squeezing them.

• Rolling the lemons on a counter while pushing down firmly to break the tissues inside will also release more juice.

## SERVING TIP

• Tastes for sweetness of lemonade vary, so feel free to adjust the sugar to your taste. You may want to make this on the tart side and let guests add sugar if they prefer it sweeter.

**SQUEEZING JUICE FROM LEMONS**

Squeeze and measure juice from lemon halves by placing the juicer over a measuring cup. The juicer also strains out most of the seeds and pulp.

## ᴏLD-FASHIONED LEMONADE

**QUICK**    Prep: 10 min        8 servings

8 to 10  **medium lemons**

6  **cups cold water**

1  **cup sugar**

**Ice**

**Lemon slices for garnish, if desired**

**Maraschino cherries with stems, if desired**

1. Cut lemons in half. Squeeze juice from the lemon halves using a juicer set on a measuring cup. Stop when you have 2 cups of juice. Pour juice through strainer into pitcher to remove any seeds and pulp.

2. Add cold water and sugar to lemon juice in pitcher. Stir until sugar is dissolved.

3. Serve lemonade over ice. Garnish each serving with lemon slice and cherry.

**1 SERVING:** Calories 130 (Calories from Fat 0); Fat 0g (Saturated 0g); Cholesterol 0mg; Sodium 10mg; Carbohydrate 33g (Dietary Fiber 0g); Protein 0g

# ANGY CITRUS PUNCH

**QUICK**   Prep: 10 min        24 servings

1   **can (12 ounces) frozen pineapple-orange juice concentrate, thawed**

1   **can (12 ounces) frozen limeade concentrate, thawed**

1   **can (12 ounces) frozen lemonade concentrate, thawed**

3   **cups cold water**

1   **liter (4¼ cups) lemon-lime soda pop, chilled**

   **Lime, lemon and orange slices, if desired**

**1.** Mix juice concentrates and water in punch bowl.

**2.** Just before serving, stir in soda pop. Float fruit slices in punch.

**1 SERVING:** Calories 125 (Calories from Fat 0); Fat 0g (Saturated 0g); Cholesterol 0mg; Sodium 5mg; Carbohydrate 31g (Dietary Fiber 0g); Protein 0g

**COOKING TIP**

• Make this punch ahead of time by combining the juice concentrates and water in a half-gallon pitcher or large mixing bowl and refrigerating. Just before serving, pour into a punch bowl and add the soda pop and fruit slices.

# UICK CRANBERRY PUNCH

**QUICK**   Prep: 10 min        12 servings

1   **can (6 ounces) frozen pink lemonade concentrate, thawed**

4   **cups cranberry juice cocktail, chilled**

   **Ice**

2   **cans (12 ounces each) ginger ale, chilled**

**1.** Make lemonade in large pitcher as directed on can.

**2.** Stir in cranberry juice cocktail and enough ice to chill. Just before serving, stir in ginger ale.

**1 SERVING:** Calories 110 (Calories from Fat 0); Fat 0g (Saturated 0g); Cholesterol 0mg; Sodium 10mg; Carbohydrate 27g (Dietary Fiber 0g); Protein 0g

**COOKING TIP**

• For festive ice cubes, cut lemon, lime or orange peel into star shapes, and freeze with cranberries in cranberry juice or water in ice-cube trays.

## Chilling Bottled and Canned Drinks

If you just purchased bottled or canned drinks and want to serve them right away, here's how to chill them quickly. Completely submerge them in a bucket or large pot filled with half ice and half water for about 20 minutes. This also works well for carbonated beverages that will be added at the last minute to a punch or used to mix with other ingredients. ∎

# $\mathcal{S}$PARKLING RASPBERRY TEA

**QUICK**    Prep: 5 min        6 servings

**2  cups brewed tea, chilled**

**2  cups raspberry or cranberry-raspberry juice, chilled**

**2  cups sparkling water, chilled**

**Raspberries, lime slices or lemon slices, if desired**

**Fresh mint leaves, if desired**

**1.** Mix tea, juice and water. Serve over ice.

**2.** Garnish with raspberries and mint.

**1 SERVING:** Calories 40 (Calories from Fat 0); Fat 0g (Saturated 0g); Cholesterol 0mg; Sodium 20mg; Carbohydrate 10g (Dietary Fiber 0g); Protein 0g

---

## SPECIAL TOUCH

### Carrots and Flower Pitcher

You will need:

**Clear glass pitcher (3- to 4-quart size or 9 to 10 inches high)**

**1 bunch carrots with tops**

**Yellow or white fresh flowers**

1. Fill pitcher about ¾ full with water.

2. Clean carrots; place in pitcher.

3. Add flowers to pitcher.

*Tip: Keep this arrangement in the refrigerator until you're ready to set it on the table. The carrot tops will stay fresher and prettier longer this way.*

# APPETIZERS

# Gingered Caramel and Yogurt Dip

Prep: 10 min; Chill: 30 min     About 1 cup

- **4 ounces fat-free cream cheese, softened**
- **½ cup vanilla low-fat yogurt**
- **¼ cup plus 1 to 2 teaspoons caramel fat-free topping**
- **1 tablespoon chopped crystallized ginger**
- **Apple slices, if desired**
- **Pear slices, if desired**

1. Beat cream cheese in medium bowl with electric mixer on medium speed until creamy. Beat in yogurt and ¼ cup of the topping until smooth. Cover and refrigerate at least 30 minutes until chilled.

2. Spoon dip into small serving bowl. Drizzle with 1 to 2 teaspoons topping; swirl with tip of knife. Sprinkle with ginger. Serve with apple and pear slices.

**1 SERVING (2 TABLESPOONS):** Calories 60 (Calories from Fat 0); Fat 0g (Saturated 0g); Cholesterol 0mg; Sodium 120mg; Carbohydrate 12g (Dietary Fiber 0g); Protein 3g

**COOKING TIP**

• Dress up this dip by serving it in a hollowed-out red, yellow or green bell pepper half. Baby carrots, halved radishes, bell pepper slices and cucumber spears are tasty vegetables for dipping.

# CAESAR VEGETABLE DIP

Prep: 10 min; Chill: 30 min        About 1¼ cups

½  **cup sour cream**

¼  **cup mayonnaise or salad dressing**

¼  **cup creamy Caesar dressing**

2  **tablespoons shredded Parmesan cheese**

2  **tablespoons chopped red bell pepper**

1  **hard-cooked egg, chopped**

   **Assorted raw vegetables, if desired**

**1.** Mix sour cream, mayonnaise and Caesar dressing until smooth. Stir in cheese.

**2.** Spoon into serving bowl. Sprinkle with bell pepper and egg. Cover and refrigerate 30 minutes to blend flavors if desired. Serve with vegetables.

**1 SERVING (1 TABLESPOON):** Calories 55 (Calories from Fat 45); Fat 5g (Saturated 1g); Cholesterol 15mg; Sodium 65mg; Carbohydrate 1g (Dietary Fiber 0g); Protein 1g

# GGPLANT DIP

Prep: 15 min; Grill: 30 min; Cool: 30 min          About 1½ cups

1 **medium eggplant (about 2 pounds)**
4 to 5 **tablespoons lemon juice**
¼ **cup sesame seed paste (tahini)**
1 **teaspoon salt**
2 **cloves garlic, peeled and crushed**
2 **teaspoons olive or vegetable oil**
2 **tablespoons chopped fresh parsley**
**Paprika**
**Greek or ripe olives, if desired**
**Crackers or toasted pita bread wedges, if desired**

**1.** Brush grill rack with vegetable oil. Heat coals or gas grill for direct heat (see page 144).

**2.** Pierce eggplant in several places with long-tined fork. Cover and grill eggplant 4 inches from medium heat 20 to 30 minutes, turning frequently, until eggplant is very soft and skin is charred. Place eggplant in colander over bowl or in sink about 30 minutes to drain and cool.

**3.** Cut eggplant lengthwise in half. Scoop out and finely chop eggplant pulp. Mix eggplant, lemon juice, sesame seed paste, salt and garlic. Spoon eggplant mixture into shallow serving bowl; flatten top of mixture with back of spoon. Drizzle with oil and sprinkle with parsley and paprika.

**4.** Garnish eggplant dip with olives. Serve with crackers.

**1 SERVING:** Calories 25 (Calories from Fat 20); Fat 2g (Saturated 0g); Cholesterol 0mg; Sodium 100mg; Carbohydrate 2g (Dietary Fiber 1g); Protein 1g

# GUACAMOLE

Prep: 20 min; Chill: 1 hr        About 2¾ cups

2  jalapeño chilies, seeded and chopped, or 2 tablespoons canned chopped green chilies

2  ripe large avocados, pitted, peeled, and mashed

2  tablespoons lime or lemon juice

2  tablespoons finely chopped fresh cilantro

½  teaspoon salt

   Dash of pepper

1  clove garlic, peeled and finely chopped

2  medium tomatoes, finely chopped

1  medium onion, peeled and chopped

   Tortilla chips, if desired

**1.** Mix chilies, avocados and remaining ingredients except tortilla chips in glass or plastic bowl.

**2.** Cover and refrigerate 1 hour to blend flavors. Serve with tortilla chips.

**1 SERVING (1 TABLESPOON):** Calories 10 (Calories from Fat 10); Fat 1g (Saturated 0g); Cholesterol 0mg; Sodium 30mg; Carbohydrate 1g (Dietary Fiber 1g); Protein 0g

*Lighter "Guacamole":* For 0 grams of fat and 5 calories per serving, substitute 1 can (15 ounces) asparagus cuts, drained then blended or processed in food processor until smooth, for avocados. Stir in ¼ cup fat-free mayonnaise.

# SWEET-HOT SALSA

Prep: 20 min; Chill: 4 hr        About 1¾ cups

1   **medium papaya, peeled, seeded and chopped**
1   **small cucumber, peeled and chopped**
1   **small carrot, shredded**
1   **small jalapeño chili, seeded and finely chopped**
1   **tablespoon lime juice**
1   **tablespoon white vinegar**
½   **teaspoon sugar**
¼   **teaspoon salt**

**1.** Mix all ingredients in glass or plastic bowl.

**2.** Cover and refrigerate at least 4 hours to blend flavors but no longer than 2 days. Stir salsa before serving.

**1 SERVING (¼ CUP):** Calories 30 (Calories from Fat 0); Fat 0g (Saturated 0g); Cholesterol 0mg; Sodium 90mg; Carbohydrate 7g (Dietary Fiber 1g); Protein 1g

## SPECIAL TOUCH

### Bird Feeder Vase

You will need:

**Suet bird feeder (about 6 inches wide) with chain**
**Sphagnum moss**
**3 floral water tubes**
**Fresh flowers**

1. Fill bird feeder with moss.

2. Fill tubes with water; place in moss. Place one flower stem in each tube.

3. Hang feeder from chain, or remove chain and place feeder on table.

# Spinach Dip in Bread Bowl

Prep: 15 min; Chill: 1 hour       4½ cups

2   packages (10 ounces each) frozen chopped spinach, thawed
1   can (8 ounces) sliced water chestnuts, drained and chopped
9   medium green onions with tops, trimmed and chopped
1   clove garlic, peeled and finely chopped
1   cup sour cream
1   cup plain yogurt
2   teaspoons chopped fresh or ½ teaspoon dried tarragon leaves
½   teaspoon salt
½   teaspoon ground mustard
¼   teaspoon pepper
1   pound unsliced round bread loaf

**1.** Drain the thawed spinach in a strainer, then squeeze out the excess moisture from the spinach, using paper towels or a clean kitchen towel, until the spinach is dry. Place in a large bowl.

**2.** Add water chestnuts, onions and garlic to the bowl.

**3.** Add the sour cream, yogurt, tarragon, salt, mustard and pepper to the bowl. Mix all ingredients thoroughly. Cover and refrigerate at least 1 hour to blend flavors.

**4.** Just before serving, cut a 1- to 2-inch slice from the top of the loaf of bread. Hollow out the loaf by cutting along the edge with a serrated knife, leaving about a 1-inch shell, and pulling out large chunks of bread. Cut or tear the top slice and the hollowed-out bread into bite-size pieces.

**5.** Fill the bread loaf with the spinach dip, and place on the serving plate. Arrange the bread pieces around the loaf to use for dipping.

**1 SERVING (1 TABLESPOON):** Calories 30 (Calories from Fat 10); Fat 1g (Saturated 1g); Cholesterol 5mg; Sodium 60mg; Carbohydrate 4g (Dietary Fiber 0g); Protein 1g

***Lighter Spinach Dip:*** For 0 grams of fat and 25 calories per serving, substitute ½ cup reduced-fat sour cream for the 1 cup sour cream and 1½ cups plain fat-free yogurt for the 1 cup yogurt.

**COOKING TIP**

• Watch the cheese carefully during grilling to avoid over-cooking.

# ORANGE-ALMOND BRIE

**QUICK**    Prep: 10 min; Grill: 3 min          6 servings

      2  **tablespoons sliced almonds**
    ½  **cup orange marmalade**
      1  **tablespoon Dijon mustard**
      1  **teaspoon white wine vinegar**
8 to 10  **ounce cold round Brie cheese (not creamy)**
      1  **tablespoon margarine or butter, melted**
         **Assorted crackers, if desired**
         **Crisp apple and pear wedges, if desired**

**1.** Brush grill rack with vegetable oil. Heat coals or gas grill for direct heat (see page 144).

**2.** While grill is heating, spread almonds in 8-inch square aluminum foil pan. Grill uncovered 3 to 5 minutes, stirring once or twice, until almonds just start to brown.

**3.** Mix marmalade, mustard and vinegar. Spread marmalade mixture in 6-inch circle on serving plate.

**4.** Brush both sides of cheese with margarine. Cover and grill cheese 4 inches from medium-hot heat 1 to 3 minutes, turning once, until cheese just begins to melt.

**5.** Place cheese on marmalade mixture. Brush lightly with about 1 teaspoon of the marmalade mixture. Sprinkle almonds over cheese and marmalade mixture. Serve cheese with crackers and fruit wedges.

**1 SERVING:** Calories 210 (Calories from Fat 110); Fat 12g (Saturated 7g); Cholesterol 25mg; Sodium 380mg; Carbohydrate 18g (Dietary Fiber 0g); Protein 8g

# $\mathcal{G}$OUDA AND SUN-DRIED TOMATO CHEESE BALL

Prep: 20 min; Chill: 2 hr     About 3 cups

1   tub (8 ounces) soft cream cheese
2   cups shredded Gouda or Colby cheese (8 ounces)
¼   cup chopped fresh chives
¼   cup sliced oil-packed sun-dried tomatoes, drained
¼   teaspoon garlic powder
¾   cup chopped pecans
     **Assorted crackers, if desired**

1. Mix cheeses in medium bowl until blended. Stir in chives, tomatoes and garlic powder.

2. Shape mixture into 1 large or 2 small balls or logs; roll in pecans. Wrap in plastic wrap. Refrigerate until firm, at least 2 hours but no longer than 2 weeks. Serve with crackers.

**1 SERVING (1 TABLESPOON):** Calories 50 (Calories from Fat 35); Fat 4g (Saturated 2g); Cholesterol 10mg; Sodium 60mg; Carbohydrate 1g (Dietary Fiber 0g); Protein 2g

# $\mathcal{F}$IRECRACKER CHICKEN WINGS

Prep: 10 min; Marinate: 1 hr; Grill: 25 min         4 servings

- 12  **chicken wings (2½ pounds)**
- 2  **tablespoons chili powder**
- 1½  **teaspoons dried oregano leaves**
- 1¼  **teaspoons ground red pepper (cayenne)**
- 1  **teaspoon garlic salt**
- 1  **teaspoon ground cumin**
- 1  **teaspoon pepper**
  **Sour cream, if desired**

**1.** Fold wing tips under opposite ends to form triangles.

**2.** Place remaining ingredients except sour cream in resealable plastic food-storage bag. Seal bag and shake to blend seasonings. Add chicken. Seal bag and shake until chicken is coated with seasonings. Refrigerate at least 1 hour but no longer than 24 hours.

**3.** Heat coals or gas grill for direct heat (see page 144). Cover and grill chicken 4 to 6 inches from medium heat 20 to 25 minutes, turning after 10 minutes, until juice of chicken is no longer pink when centers of thickest pieces are cut. Serve chicken with sour cream.

**1 SERVING:** Calories 305 (Calories from Fat 190); Fat 21g (Saturated 6g); Cholesterol 85mg; Sodium 360mg; Carbohydrate 3g (Dietary Fiber 2g); Protein 28g

**COOKING TIP**

• Using a grilling screen prevents the bite-size vegetables from slipping through the grill grids. If a screen is not available, use 2 layers of heavy-duty aluminum foil punched with holes; a cookie sheet is useful to transfer the foil to and from the grill.

# ITALIAN ZUCCHINI BITES

Prep: 15 min; Marinate: 15 min; Grill: 4 min          6 servings (about 24 pieces)

- ½ **cup Italian dressing**
- ½ **teaspoon Italian seasoning**
- ¼ **teaspoon cracked black pepper**
- 2 **medium zucchini, cut into ½-inch slices**
- ¾ **cup grated Parmesan cheese (3 ounces)**

**1.** Mix dressing, Italian seasoning and pepper in shallow nonmetal dish or resealable plastic bag. Add zucchini, turning to coat with marinade. Cover dish or seal bag and let stand at least 15 minutes but no longer than 1 hour.

**2.** Heat coals or gas grill for direct heat (see page 144). Brush grilling screen with vegetable oil.

**3.** Drain zucchini; discard marinade. Toss cheese and 4 to 6 slices zucchini at a time in resealable plastic bag, coating zucchini with cheese.

**4.** Place zucchini on grilling screen. Grill zucchini uncovered 4 inches from medium heat 3 to 4 minutes, turning 2 or 3 times, until cheese is light brown and zucchini is crisp-tender.

**1 SERVING:** Calories 150 (Calories from Fat 115); Fat 13g (Saturated 4g); Cholesterol 10mg; Sodium 340mg; Carbohydrate 4g (Dietary Fiber 1g); Protein 5g

# BREADS

## EXAS TOAST

**QUICK**   Prep: 5 min; Grill: 6 min     4 servings

¼ **cup margarine or butter, softened**

4 **slices white bread, about 1 inch thick**

½ **teaspoon seasoned salt or garlic salt**

**1.** Brush grill rack with vegetable oil. Heat coals or gas grill for direct heat (see page 144).

**2.** Spread margarine on both sides of bread slices. Sprinkle with seasoned salt.

**3.** Grill bread uncovered 4 inches from medium heat 4 to 6 minutes, turning once, until golden brown.

**1 SERVING:** Calories 230 (Calories from Fat 115); Fat 13g (Saturated 3g); Cholesterol 0mg; Sodium 570mg; Carbohydrate 25g (Dietary Fiber 1g); Protein 4g

## RUSCHETTA

**QUICK**   Prep: 10 min; Grill: 6 min     4 servings

½ **cup olive or vegetable oil**

2 **tablespoons chopped fresh or 2 teaspoons dried basil leaves**

2 **cloves garlic, peeled and crushed**

1 **loaf unsliced French bread (about 12 inches), cut horizontally in half**

**1.** Brush grill rack with vegetable oil. Heat coals or gas grill for direct heat (see page 144).

**2.** Mix oil, basil and garlic. Brush or drizzle on cut sides of bread.

**3.** Grill bread uncovered, 4 inches from medium heat about 6 minutes, turning once, until golden brown.

**4.** To serve, cut into ½-inch slices.

**1 SERVING:** Calories 440 (Calories from Fat 270); Fat 30g (Saturated 5g); Cholesterol 0mg; Sodium 440mg; Carbohydrate 38g (Dietary Fiber 2g); Protein 7g

### COOKING TIP

• The name of this traditional Italian garlic bread means "to roast over coals." Olive oil is used generously, and for the best flavor, try extra-virgin oil. If you like, sprinkle the bruschetta with salt and pepper before grilling.

## $\mathcal{S}$ESAME-PARMESAN SLICES

**QUICK**  Prep: 10 min; Grill: 12 min        6 servings

¼ **cup (½ stick) margarine or butter, softened**
½ **cup grated Parmesan cheese (2 ounces)**
6 **slices French or Vienna bread, 1 inch thick**
1 **tablespoon sesame seeds**

**1.** Brush grill rack with vegetable oil. Heat coals or gas grill for direct heat (see page 144).

**2.** Mix margarine and cheese. Spread on both sides of bread slices. Sprinkle both sides with sesame seeds.

**3.** Grill bread uncovered 4 inches from medium heat 10 to 12 minutes, turning once, until golden brown.

**1 SERVING:** Calories 200 (Calories from Fat 110); Fat 12g (Saturated 4g); Cholesterol 5mg; Sodium 420mg; Carbohydrate 18g (Dietary Fiber 1g); Protein 6g

## $\mathcal{B}$LUE CHEESE BREAD

**QUICK**  Prep: 10 min; Grill: 15 min        12 slices

**Blue Cheese Spread (below)**
1 **loaf (1 pound) unsliced French bread**

**1.** Brush grill rack with vegetable oil. Heat coals or gas grill for direct heat (see page 144).

**2.** Prepare Blue Cheese Spread. Cut bread crosswise in half; reserve one half for future use. Cut remaining half diagonally into 1-inch slices. Spread 1 side of each slice with Blue Cheese Spread. Reassemble slices into loaf; wrap securely in 14-inch piece of heavy-duty aluminum foil.

**3.** Cover and grill bread 5 to 6 inches from medium heat 8 to 10 minutes, turning once, until hot. Open foil. Grill bread uncovered 5 minutes longer.

**1 SLICE:** Calories 150 (Calories from Fat 65); Fat 7g (Saturated 2g); Cholesterol 2mg; Sodium 320 mg; Carbohydrate 19g (Dietary Fiber 1g); Protein 4g

## BLUE CHEESE SPREAD

⅓ **cup margarine or butter, softened**
¼ **cup finely crumbled blue cheese (1 ounce)**
1 **clove garlic, peeled and finely chopped**

Mix all ingredients.

# Speedy Microwave-to-Grill Cooking

Combine the talents of your grill with those of your microwave to speed cooking—grilling time generally will be cut in half! Use this cooking combination when grilling bone-in chicken pieces, meaty spareribs, dense raw vegetables such as carrots and potatoes or fresh raw sausage like bratwurst, which are known to overbrown on the outside before the center is cooked.

## To Partially Microwave

- Use microwavable casseroles and dishes with covers to partially cook foods most quickly. If you do not have a cover, use plastic wrap and turn back a corner to allow steam to escape. Meat can be brushed with 2 to 4 tablespoons of your favorite barbecue sauce or marinade before microwaving to add flavor. Add ¼ cup of water or broth to vegetables before microwaving.

- Arrange food with thickest parts to outside edge of dish.

- Cover tightly and microwave on High following the Microwave-to-Grill Guide below.

- Turn over, rotate or stir food after half the microwave time.

- Drain well and immediately place food on the grill to complete cooking.

*Note:* If grilling more than 4 pounds of food, microwave in two batches.

## Microwave-to-Grill Guide

| Food | Time on High Power | What to Look For |
|---|---|---|
| Chicken pieces (bone-in) | 4 to 6 minutes per pound | Edges of pieces will be cooked; parts will be pink but hot |
| Ribs | 6 to 8 minutes per pound | No longer pink; may not be cooked through. |
| Sausage links, raw | 4 to 6 minutes per pound | No longer pink; may not be cooked through. |
| Vegetable pieces, such as potatoes, carrots or winter squash (¾ to 1 inch | 4 to 6 minutes per pound | Softened |

## To Finish on the Grill

As a guide, grill food for about half the time recommended in the recipe. It's possible that additional time may be needed because microwave wattages vary as do grills and grilling conditions, so use the doneness test in the recipe as the final guide.

## Microwave-to-Grill Food Safety

While using the microwave makes grilling quicker, it is especially important to plan preparation time so that food can go directly from the microwave to the grill. Do not refrigerate partially cooked meat, and never let it stand at room temperature before grilling. It's the perfect place for bacteria to grow. Be sure to have the coals ready by the time foods are removed from the microwave. After the food has been microwaved, immediately place it on the grill to complete cooking. ■

# SANDWICHES AND PIZZAS

## *H*ONEY-MUSTARD CHICKEN SANDWICHES

**QUICK**   Prep: 10 min; Grill: 20 min          4 sandwiches

¼  cup Dijon mustard

2  tablespoons honey

1  teaspoon dried oregano leaves

⅛ to ¼  teaspoon ground red pepper (cayenne)

4  boneless, skinless chicken breast halves (about 1¼ pounds)

4  whole-grain sandwich buns, split

4  slices tomato

Leaf lettuce

**1.** Heat coals or gas grill for direct heat (see page 144).

**2.** Mix mustard, honey, oregano and red pepper. Brush on chicken. Cover and grill chicken 4 to 6 inches from medium heat 15 to 20 minutes, brushing frequently with mustard mixture and turning occasionally, until juice of chicken is no longer pink when centers of thickest pieces are cut. Discard any remaining mustard mixture.

**3.** Serve chicken on buns with tomato and lettuce.

**1 SANDWICH:** Calories 275 (Calories from Fat 55); Fat 6g (Saturated 1g); Cholesterol 75mg; Sodium 450mg; Carbohydrate 27g (Dietary Fiber 3g); Protein 31g

# SPICY TURKEY BURGERS

**QUICK**   Prep: 10 min; Grill: 20 min            4 burgers

**Chili-Cheese Spread (below)**

1   **pound ground turkey breast**

1   **small onion, peeled and chopped**

1   **clove garlic, peeled and finely chopped**

2 to 3   **tablespoons canned chopped green chilies**

⅛   **teaspoon salt**

⅛   **teaspoon pepper**

4   **hamburger buns, split**

**1.** Brush grill rack with vegetable oil. Heat coals or gas grill for direct heat (see page 144).

**2.** Make Chili-Cheese Spread. Mix remaining ingredients except buns. Shape turkey mixture into 4 patties, each about ½ inch thick.

**3.** Cover and grill patties 4 to 5 inches from medium heat 15 to 20 minutes, turning once, until turkey is no longer pink in center. Serve on buns with Chili-Cheese spread.

**1 BURGER:** Calories 280 (Calories from Fat 80); Fat 9g (Saturated 2g); Cholesterol 75mg; Sodium 400mg; Carbohydrate 23g (Dietary Fiber 1g); Protein 28g

## CHILI-CHEESE SPREAD

½   **cup shredded reduced-fat Cheddar cheese (2 ounces)**

2   **tablespoons fat-free sour cream**

2   **tablespoons canned chopped green chilies**

Mix all ingredients.

## Burgers at Their Best

Here's how to serve up perfect burgers every time you fire up the grill. Don't press down on a hamburger patty with your spatula while it's cooking. If you do, you'll squeeze out too much of the great-tasting juices that also make the burgers nice and moist! ■

# ℬLUE CHEESE BURGERS

**QUICK**  Prep: 10 min; Grill: 20 min        4 burgers

     1  **pound ground turkey breast**

    ¼  **cup mayonnaise or salad dressing**

     1  **cup crumbled blue cheese (4 ounces)**

     4  **onion or plain hamburger buns, split**

     1  **medium red onion, peeled and sliced, if desired**

**1.** Brush grill rack with vegetable oil. Heat coals or gas grill for direct heat (see page 144). Mix turkey, mayonnaise and blue cheese. Shape mixture into 4 patties, about ¾ inch thick.

**2.** Cover and grill patties 4 to 5 inches from medium heat 15 to 20 minutes, turning once, until turkey is no longer pink in center. Serve on buns with onion slices.

**1 BURGER:** Calories 485 (Calories from Fat 250); Fat 28g (Saturated 9g); Cholesterol 105mg; Sodium 790mg; Carbohydrate 25g (Dietary Fiber 2g); Protein 35g

# ARBECUED BURRITOS

Prep: 25 min; Marinate: 8 hr; Grill: 35 min     6 burritos

- 1 **pound beef boneless top round steak, about 1 inch thick**
-    **Mexican Marinade (below)**
-    **Jicama Salsa (see page 143), if desired**
- 6 **flour tortillas (10 inches in diameter)**
- 1 **cup shredded Cheddar cheese (4 ounces)**
- 1 **medium onion, peeled and chopped**
- 1 **medium tomato, chopped**
- 1 **medium avocado, chopped**
- ¾ **cup barbecue sauce**

**1.** Pierce beef with fork several times on both sides. Prepare Mexican Marinade. Add beef, turning to coat with marinade. Cover dish or seal bag and refrigerate, turning beef occasionally, at least 8 hours but no longer than 24 hours.

**2.** Prepare Jicama Salsa.

**3.** Brush grill rack with vegetable oil. Heat coals or gas grill for direct heat (see page 144). Wrap tortillas in heavy-duty aluminum foil.

**4.** Remove beef from marinade; discard marinade. Cover and grill beef 4 to 5 inches from medium heat 25 to 30 minutes for medium doneness, turning once. Add packet of tortillas for last 5 minutes of grilling, turning occasionally, until warm.

**5.** Cut beef across grain into thin slices. Place beef, cheese, onion, tomato and avocado on center of each tortilla. Fold one end of tortilla up about 1 inch over filling; fold right and left sides over folded end, overlapping. Fold remaining end down. Brush burritos with barbecue sauce.

**6.** Grill burritos uncovered 4 to 5 inches from medium heat 5 minutes, turning once, until hot. Serve burritos with Jicama Salsa.

**1 BURRITO:** Calories 395 (Calories from Fat 160); Fat 18g (Saturated 7g); Cholesterol 60mg; Sodium 690mg; Carbohydrate 37g (Dietary Fiber 4g); Protein 25g

## MEXICAN MARINADE

- 1 **can (5½ ounces) spicy eight-vegetable juice**
- 2 **tablespoons lime juice**
- 1 **tablespoon vegetable oil**
- ¼ **teaspoon salt**

Mix all ingredients in shallow nonmetal dish or resealable plastic bag.

#  BEEF AND VEGGIE PITAS

**QUICK**    Prep: 15 min; Cook: 5 min          4 pitas

**Cheese Sauce or Creamy Italian Sauce (below)**
**Lettuce leaves**
¾  **pound thinly sliced roast beef**
1  **medium cucumber, thinly sliced**
1  **medium tomato, thinly sliced**
1  **medium bell pepper, cut into rings**
1  **medium zucchini, thinly sliced**
4  **thin slices red onion**
4  **pita breads (6 inches in diameter), cut crosswise in half**

Prepare desired sauce. Layer lettuce, beef, cucumber, tomato, bell pepper, zucchini and onion in pita bread halves. Serve with sauce.

**1 PITA:** Calories 515 (Calories from Fat 160); Fat 18g (Saturated 10g); Cholesterol 105mg; Sodium 1300mg; Carbohydrate 46g (Dietary Fiber 3g); Protein 45g

## CHEESE SAUCE

1  **jar (8 ounces) process cheese spread**
2  **tablespoons milk**
¼  **cup chopped tomato**
3  **medium green onions, trimmed and sliced**

Heat cheese spread and milk in 1-quart saucepan over medium heat, stirring constantly, until smooth. Stir in tomato and onions. Serve warm.

## CREAMY ITALIAN SAUCE

½  **cup creamy Italian dressing**
¼  **cup sour cream**
¼  **cup mayonnaise or salad dressing**
¼  **cup milk**

Mix all ingredients.

# $\mathcal{F}$OOT-LONG CONEY DOGS

**QUICK**   Prep: 10 min; Grill: 20 min      6 servings

6  **long hot dogs (each about 12 inches)**
1  **tablespoon margarine or butter, melted**
1  **can (15 ounces) chili with beans**
6  **long hot dog buns, split**
¾  **cup shredded Cheddar cheese (3 ounces)**
1  **large onion, peeled and chopped**

**1.** Brush grill rack with vegetable oil. Heat coals or gas grill for direct heat (see page 144).

**2.** Cut crosswise diagonal slashes ½ inch apart and ¼ inch deep in each hot dog.

**3.** Grill hot dogs uncovered 4 to 5 inches from medium heat 15 to 20 minutes, turning frequently and brushing occasionally with margarine, until hot and slashes begin to open. Remove label and top from can of chili. Place opened can of chili on grill for last 10 minutes of grilling, stirring occasionally, until hot.

**4.** Serve hot dogs on buns with chili, cheese and onion.

**1 SERVING:** Calories 630 (Calories from Fat 335); Fat 37g (Saturated 14g); Cholesterol 60mg; Sodium 1830mg; Carbohydrate 55g (Dietary Fiber 4g); Protein 23g

# *H*EARTY HAM
# AND VEGETABLE SANDWICHES

**QUICK** Prep: 15 min; Grill: 15 min          4 sandwiches

⅓ **cup mayonnaise or salad dressing**

¼ **cup chopped drained pepperoncini peppers**

2 **tablespoons chopped ripe olives**

1 **pound fully cooked ham slice, ½ inch thick**

1 **large red bell pepper, cut into 8 strips**

4 **slices small onion, ¼ inch thick, separated into rings**

4 **whole wheat sandwich buns, split**

**1.** Brush grill rack with vegetable oil. Heat coals or gas grill for direct heat (see page 144).

**2.** Mix mayonnaise, pepperoncini peppers and olives; cover and refrigerate. Cut ham slice into 4 pieces.

**3.** Cover and grill ham, bell pepper strips and onion slices 4 to 6 inches from medium heat about 15 minutes, turning after 5 minutes, until vegetables are crisp-tender. Add buns, cut sides down, for last 2 minutes of grilling, until toasted.

**4.** To serve, spread cut sides of buns with mayonnaise mixture. Fill buns with ham, bell pepper and onion.

**1 SANDWICH:** Calories 445 (Calories from Fat 245); Fat 27g (Saturated 7g); Cholesterol 80mg; Sodium 2060mg; Carbohydrate 24g (Dietary Fiber 4g); Protein 30g

# *N*O-BAKE PESTO CHICKEN PIZZA

**QUICK**   Prep: 10 min; Cook: 5 min          4 servings

1   **tablespoon olive or vegetable oil**
1   **medium stalk celery, chopped**
1   **cup cut-up cooked chicken**
⅓   **cup pesto**
1   **package (8 ounces) Italian bread shells (6 inches in diameter)**
2   **tablespoons freshly shredded Parmesan cheese**
½   **cup shredded lettuce**

**1.** Heat oil in 10-inch skillet over medium-high heat. Cook celery in oil 4 to 5 minutes, stirring occasionally, until crisp-tender; reduce heat. Stir in chicken and pesto. Cook, stirring occasionally, until hot.

**2.** Spoon chicken mixture onto bread shells. Mix cheese and lettuce; sprinkle over chicken mixture. Cut each bread shell in half.

**1 SERVING:** Calories 535 (Calories from Fat 225); Fat 25g (Saturated 6g); Cholesterol 45mg; Sodium 760mg; Carbohydrate 52g (Dietary Fiber 1g); Protein 27g

# ITALIAN SAUSAGE—SPINACH PIZZA

Prep: 30 min; Grill: 5 min        6 servings

¾  **pound bulk Italian sausage**

1  **medium red bell pepper, chopped**

1  **medium onion, peeled and chopped**

½  **package (10-ounce size) fresh spinach leaves, chopped**

1  **pound loaf frozen bread dough, thawed**

1  **tablespoon olive or vegetable oil**

1  **can (6 ounces) Italian-style tomato paste**

1  **cup shredded mozzarella cheese (4 ounces)**

**1.** Brush grill rack with vegetable oil. Heat coals or gas grill for direct heat (see page 144).

**2.** Cook sausage in 10-inch skillet over medium heat about 10 minutes, stirring occasionally, until no longer pink; drain. Stir in bell pepper and onion. Cook about 5 minutes, stirring occasionally, until vegetables are crisp-tender. Stir in spinach; remove from heat. Cover and set aside.

**3.** Divide bread dough into 6 parts. Roll or pat each part into 6-inch round on lightly floured surface. Brush top of each round with oil.

**4.** Grill dough rounds, oil sides down, uncovered 4 to 6 inches from high heat about 2 minutes or until bottoms of crusts are light brown. Remove crusts from grill, and place brown sides up on cookie sheet.

**5.** Spread 2 tablespoons tomato paste on each crust. Top crusts with sausage mixture. Sprinkle with cheese.

**6.** Slide pizzas from cookie sheet onto grill. Cover and grill 3 to 5 minutes or until bottoms of crusts are brown and cheese is melted.

**1 SERVING:** Calories 485 (Calories from Fat 205); Fat 23g (Saturated 9g); Cholesterol 55mg; Sodium 1280mg; Carbohydrate 48g (Dietary Fiber 4g); Protein 25g

# $\mathcal{G}$OAT CHEESE—ARTICHOKE PIZZAS

**QUICK**   Prep: 10 min; Grill: 10 min          4 servings

1   package (3½ ounces) fresh chèvre (goat) cheese (with herbs or plain)

2   packages (8 ounces each) Italian bread shells or 4 pita breads (6 inches in diameter)

1   can (14 ounces) artichoke hearts, drained and cut in half

3   tablespoons chopped drained oil-packed sun-dried tomatoes

2   tablespoons chopped pitted Kalamata olives

1   tablespoon chopped fresh parsley

**1.** Brush grill rack with vegetable oil. Heat coals or gas grill for direct heat (see page 144).

**2.** Spread cheese evenly over each bread shell. Top with remaining ingredients.

**3.** Cover and grill pizzas 4 to 6 inches from medium heat 5 to 10 minutes or until crusts are crisp and vegetables are hot. (If crusts brown too quickly, place a piece of aluminum foil between crusts and grill.)

**1 SERVING:** Calories 290 (Calories from Fat 80); Fat 9g (Saturated 5g); Cholesterol 25mg; Sodium 740mg; Carbohydrate 44g (Dietary Fiber 6g); Protein 14g

---

## Aluminum Foil—A Grill's Best Friend!

Heavy-duty aluminum foil has many uses for grilling. Here are some that you may want to try.

**Saucepan or Bowl:** Mold 3 sheets of heavy-duty aluminum foil around a straight-sided bowl, canister or can of desired size that's upside down. Remove bowl. Press edge of foil tightly or crimp edge down to form a tight rim. Turn foil saucepan over, and place on grill rack to use.

**Cooking Packet:** Center food on half of an 18 × 12-inch sheet of heavy-duty aluminum foil. Fold other half over food so edges meet. Seal edges, making a tight ½-inch fold. Fold again. Allow space on sides for heat circulation and expansion. Repeat to seal each side. After grilling, place foil packet on plate, using tongs or mitts. To serve, cut a large X across top of packet; fold back foil.

**Food Scraper:** Use crumpled aluminum foil (used foil works well) to scrape cooked-on food bits from the grill rack.

**Coals Discarder:** Scoop warm coals onto foil; cool completely. Wrap or tightly fold foil around coals before discarding.

**Food Warmer:** Cover foods after grilling to keep them warm.

**Pan Saver:** Cover the outside of a saucepan or baking pan you plan to use on the grill to keep it from becoming difficult to clean.

**Grill Cover:** If your grill does not have a cover and a recipe recommends one, shape two sheets of heavy-duty aluminum foil in a dome shape the same size as the grill rack. (Form foil over bent coat hangers to easily retain the shape.) ■

# izza Turnovers

Prep: 20 min; Grill: 20 min     4 servings

- 1 **can (10 ounces) refrigerated pizza crust dough**
- ¼ **cup spaghetti sauce**
- 6 **ounces sliced smoked turkey**
- 1 **cup shredded provolone or mozzarella cheese (4 ounces)**
- 4 **medium green onions, trimmed and sliced**
- 2 **tablespoons chopped fresh or 2 teaspoons dried basil leaves**
- 2 **teaspoons olive or vegetable oil**
- ¾ **cup spaghetti sauce**

**1.** Heat coals or gas grill for direct heat (see page 144).

**2.** Roll pizza crust dough on lightly floured surface into 12-inch square. Cut dough into four 6-inch squares. Brush half of each square with 1 tablespoon of the ¼ cup spaghetti sauce to within ½ inch of edges. Top with turkey, cheese, onions and basil. Fold each square in half over filling; press edges to seal. Brush both sides with oil. Place turnovers on double thickness piece of heavy-duty aluminum foil. Do not wrap foil around turnovers.

**3.** Cover and grill turnovers 4 to 6 inches from medium heat about 20 minutes, turning after 10 minutes, until golden brown on both sides. Place ¾ cup spaghetti sauce in small pan or in the can with label removed and heat during last 10 minutes of grilling.

**4.** Serve turnovers with spaghetti sauce.

**1 SERVING:** Calories 435 (Calories from Fat 170); Fat 19g (Saturated 7g); Cholesterol 60mg; Sodium 1040mg; Carbohydrate 42g (Dietary Fiber 2g); Protein 26g

# MAIN DISHES

## CRAB LEGS WITH LEMON-MUSTARD SAUCE

Prep: 20 min; Chill: 1 hr; Grill: 15 min          4 servings

**Lemon-Mustard Sauce (below)**
**3 pounds frozen king crab legs, thawed**
**½ cup (½ stick) margarine or butter, melted**
**Lemon wedges**

1. Prepare Lemon-Mustard Sauce.

2. Brush grill rack with vegetable oil. Heat coals or gas grill for direct heat (see page 144).

3. Carefully cut crab legs lengthwise in half through shell with sharp knife or poultry shears, leaving narrow parts of legs whole.

4. Place crab legs, shell sides down, on grill; brush with margarine. Cover and grill 10 to 15 minutes or until shells turn red and crabmeat turns white and firm.

5. Serve crab legs with Lemon-Mustard Sauce and lemon wedges.

1 SERVING: Calories 565 (Calories from Fat 425); Fat 47g (Saturated 8g); Cholesterol 190mg; Sodium 880mg; Carbohydrate 2g (Dietary Fiber 0g); Protein 34g

### LEMON-MUSTARD SAUCE

¾ **cup mayonnaise or salad dressing**
2 **tablespoons lemon juice**
1 **tablespoon Dijon mustard**
⅛ **teaspoon ground red pepper (cayenne)**

Mix all ingredients. Cover and refrigerate at least 1 hour to blend flavors.

# $\mathcal{G}$RILLED SHRIMP KABOBS

Prep: 10 min; Marinate: 30 min; Grill: 10 min    4 servings

- **1 pound uncooked peeled deveined large shrimp, thawed if frozen**
- **1 cup fat-free Italian dressing**
- **1 medium red onion, peeled and cut into 8 pieces**
- **1 medium green bell pepper, cut into 8 pieces**
- **16 medium cherry tomatoes**
- **16 small whole mushrooms**
- **4 cups hot cooked rosamarina (orzo) pasta**

**1.** Place shrimp and dressing in shallow glass or plastic dish or heavy-duty resealable plastic food-storage bag. Cover dish or seal bag and refrigerate 30 minutes.

**2.** Heat coals or gas grill for direct heat (see page 144). Remove shrimp from marinade; reserve marinade. Thread shrimp, onion, bell pepper, tomatoes and mushrooms alternately on each of four 15-inch metal skewers, leaving space between pieces.

**3.** Grill kabobs uncovered 4 to 6 inches from medium heat 8 to 10 minutes, turning frequently and brushing several times with marinade, until shrimp are pink and firm. Discard any remaining marinade. Serve kabobs with pasta.

**1 SERVING:** Calories 340 (Calories from Fat 25); Fat 3g (Saturated 0g); Cholesterol 160mg; Sodium 740mg; Carbohydrate 56g (Dietary Fiber 5g); Protein 27g

# RED SNAPPER WITH MANGO RELISH

Prep: 10 min; Stand: 30 min; Grill: 10 min    4 servings

**Mango Relish (below)**
**1  pound red snapper, orange roughy or walleye fillets**
**½  teaspoon salt**

**1.** Prepare Mango Relish.

**2.** Brush grill rack with vegetable oil. Heat coals or gas grill for direct heat (see page 144). Spray fish with cooking spray; sprinkle with salt.

**3.** Grill fish 8 to 10 minutes or until fish is light brown and flakes easily with fork. Serve with relish.

**1 SERVING:** Calories 125 (Calories from Fat 10); Fat 1g (Saturated 0g); Cholesterol 50mg; Sodium 380mg; Carbohydrate 11g (Dietary Fiber 1g); Protein 19g

## MANGO RELISH

**1  large mango, cut lengthwise in half, pitted and chopped**
**1  small tomato, chopped**
**2  tablespoons finely chopped red onion**
**½  cup chopped fresh cilantro**
**¼  cup lime juice**

Mix all ingredients in glass or plastic bowl. Cover and let stand 30 minutes.

# GRILLED FISH WITH JICAMA SALSA

Prep: 15 min; Chill: 2 hr; Marinate: 30 min; Grill: 10 min      6 servings

Jicama Salsa (below)

1½ **pounds swordfish, tuna or marlin steaks, ¾ to 1 inch thick**

3 **tablespoons olive or vegetable oil**

1 **tablespoon lime juice**

¼ **teaspoon salt**

⅛ **teaspoon crushed red pepper**

**1.** Prepare Jicama Salsa.

**2.** If fish steaks are large, cut into 6 serving pieces. Mix oil, lime juice, salt and red pepper in shallow glass or plastic dish or heavy-duty resealable plastic food-storage bag. Add fish; turn to coat with marinade. Cover dish or seal bag and refrigerate 30 minutes.

**3.** Heat coals or gas grill for direct heat (see page 144). Remove fish from marinade; reserve marinade. Cover and grill fish 5 to 6 inches from medium heat about 10 minutes, brushing 2 or 3 times with marinade and turning once, until fish flakes easily with fork. Discard any remaining marinade. Serve fish with salsa.

**1 SERVING:** Calories 165 (Calories from Fat 70); Fat 8g (Saturated 2g); Cholesterol 55mg; Sodium 250mg; Carbohydrate 8g (Dietary Fiber 3g); Protein 18g

## JICAMA SALSA

2 **cups chopped peeled jicama (¾ pound)**

1 **tablespoon chopped fresh cilantro or parsley**

1 **tablespoon lime juice**

½ **teaspoon chili powder**

¼ **teaspoon salt**

1 **medium cucumber, peeled and chopped**

1 **medium orange, peeled and chopped**

Mix all ingredients in glass or plastic bowl. Cover and refrigerate at least 2 hours to blend flavors.

## Great Safety Tip

Always serve grilled meat on a clean platter. Never serve cooked meats on the same unwashed platter on which raw meat was carried to the grill. For example, do not carry raw hamburgers to the grill on a platter and then serve the cooked hamburgers on the same unwashed platter. Dangerous bacteria can be transferred to the cooked meat from the raw meat juices. ■

- To seed tomatoes, cut in half crosswise and squeeze gently—the seeds will slide right out.

# GRILLED TUNA WITH SALSA

Prep: 5 min; Chill: 4 hr; Grill: 8 min        6 servings

- **2  medium tomatoes, seeded and chopped**
- **1  small onion, peeled and finely chopped**
- **1  can (4¼ ounces) chopped black olives, drained**
- **¾  cup finely chopped fresh parsley**
- **⅓  cup lemon juice**
- **2  tablespoons vegetable oil**
- **1  clove garlic, peeled and crushed**
- **¼  teaspoon salt**
- **6  tuna or shark steaks (about 5 ounces each)**

**1.** Combine all ingredients except tuna in glass bowl. Cover tightly and refrigerate salsa 2 to 4 hours to blend flavors.

**2.** Brush grill rack with vegetable oil. Heat coals or gas grill for direct heat (see below). Grill fish 4 inches from medium-high heat 3 minutes. Turn steaks and cook 4 to 5 minutes or until tuna turns opaque in center. Remove from grill; keep warm. Serve with salsa.

**1 SERVING:** Calories 280 (Calories from Fat 125); Fat 14g (Saturated 3g); Cholesterol 55mg; Sodium 320mg; Carbohydrate 5g (Dietary Fiber 1g); Protein 34g

## Direct- and Indirect-Heat Grilling

Different recipes for the grill require different kinds of heat, either direct or indirect. Here's the difference:

**In direct-heat grilling,** the food is cooked on the grill rack directly over the heat source—either the evenly distributed hot coals, or directly over the heated burner of a gas grill.

**With indirect-heat grilling,** the food is cooked away from the heat. This is the preferred method for longer-cooking foods, such as whole poultry, whole turkey breasts and roasts. For charcoal grills, place a drip pan directly under the grilling area and arrange the coals around the edge of the firebox. With a dual-burner gas grill, heat only one side and place the food over the burner that is not lit. For a single-burner gas grill, place the food in an aluminum-foil tray or on several layers of aluminum foil and use low heat. ■

# SWORDFISH WITH TOMATO-BASIL BUTTER

Prep: 20 min; Marinate: 15 min; Grill: 15 min     6 servings

**Tomato-Basil Butter (below)**

⅓ **cup balsamic vinegar**

1½ **pounds swordfish, salmon or marlin steaks, 1 to 1½ inches thick**

**Fresh basil leaves, if desired**

**1.** Prepare Tomato-Basil Butter.

**2.** Place vinegar in shallow nonmetal dish or resealable plastic food-storage bag. If fish steaks are large, cut into 6 serving pieces. Add fish, turning to coat with vinegar. Cover dish or seal bag and refrigerate, turning once, at least 15 minutes but no longer than 1 hour.

**3.** Brush grill rack with vegetable oil. Heat coals or gas grill for direct heat (see opposite page).

**4.** Drain fish; discard vinegar. Cover and grill fish 4 inches from medium heat 10 to 15 minutes, turning once, until fish flakes easily with fork.

**5.** Immediately top each steak with Tomato-Basil Butter. Garnish with basil leaves.

**1 SERVING:** Calories 195 (Calories from Fat 115); Fat 13g (Saturated 3g); Cholesterol 60mg; Sodium 150mg; Carbohydrate 1g (Dietary Fiber 0g); Protein 19g

## TOMATO-BASIL BUTTER

¼ **cup (½ stick) margarine or butter, softened**

1 **tablespoon finely chopped shallots**

1 **tablespoon chopped fresh or 1 teaspoon dried basil leaves**

1 **tablespoon finely chopped drained sun-dried tomatoes in oil**

Mix all ingredients. Cover and refrigerate at least 1 hour to blend flavors.

---

**COOKING TIP**

• To save time, you can make Tomato-Basil Butter up to one day ahead. Shape it into 1-inch balls, roll in finely chopped parsley, cover and refrigerate.

---

**COOKING TIP**

- A pan-dressed fish is all ready to cook—it's been gutted and scaled, and usually the head, tail and fins have been removed.

# TROUT WITH ROSEMARY

Prep: 15 min; Grill: 25 min      4 servings

**4 pan-dressed rainbow trout (each about ½ pound)**

**½ teaspoon salt**

**¼ teaspoon pepper**

**4 sprigs rosemary (each about 3 inches long)**

**4 thin slices lemon**

**¼ cup olive or vegetable oil**

**Lemon wedges, if desired**

1. Heat coals or gas grill for direct heat (see page 144). Brush hinged wire grill basket with vegetable oil.

2. Sprinkle cavities of fish with salt and pepper. Place 1 sprig rosemary and 1 slice lemon in each fish. Rub fish with oil. Place fish in basket.

3. Cover and grill fish about 4 inches from medium heat 20 to 25 minutes, brushing 2 or 3 times with oil and turning once, until fish flakes easily with fork.

4. Serve fish with lemon wedges.

**1 SERVING:** Calories 405 (Calories from Fat 205); Fat 23g (Saturated 5g); Cholesterol 150mg; Sodium 430mg; Carbohydrate 1g (Dietary Fiber 0g); Protein 48g

# $\mathcal{S}$OLE FILLETS WITH SPINACH

**QUICK**    Prep: 15 min; Grill: 10 min        4 servings

1 **pound spinach**

1 **teaspoon poultry seasoning**

½ **teaspoon chili powder**

½ **teaspoon salt**

1 to 1½ **pounds sole, flounder or red snapper fillets, ¼ to ½ inch thick**

2 **tablespoons margarine or butter, melted**

**Lemon wedges**

**1.** Heat coals or gas grill for direct heat (see page 144). Spray 13 × 9-inch aluminum foil pan with cooking spray.

**2.** Rinse spinach; shake off excess water, but do not dry. Place about three-fourths of the spinach leaves in pan, covering bottom completely.

**3.** Mix poultry seasoning, chili powder and salt. Lightly rub into both sides of fish. Place fish on spinach, folding thin tail ends under and, if necessary, overlapping thin edges slightly. Drizzle with margarine. Cover fish completely with remaining spinach.

**4.** Cover and grill fish and spinach 4 inches from medium heat 8 to 10 minutes or until fish flakes easily with fork. Check after about 3 minutes; if top layer of spinach is charring, sprinkle with about ¼ cup water.

**5.** Serve fish and spinach from pan with a slotted spoon if desired. Serve with lemon wedges.

**1 SERVING:** Calories 150 (Calories from Fat 65); Fat 7g (Saturated 2g); Cholesterol 55mg; Sodium 510mg; Carbohydrate 3g (Dietary Fiber 2g); Protein 21g

# Honey-Pecan Chicken

Prep: 15 min; Cook: 5 min; Grill: 1 hr 20 min     4 servings

**Honey-Pecan Sauce (below)**

¼ cup (½ stick) **margarine or butter, melted**

2 tablespoons **lemon juice**

2 tablespoons **water**

½ teaspoon **Worcestershire sauce**

¼ teaspoon **salt**

⅛ teaspoon **pepper**

3 to 3½ **pounds whole broiler-fryer chicken, cut into fourths**

**1.** Heat coals or gas grill for direct heat (see page 144).

**2.** Prepare Honey-Pecan Sauce. Mix remaining ingredients except chicken in small 1-quart saucepan. Cook over low heat 5 minutes, stirring occasionally. Mop or brush margarine mixture over chicken.

**3.** Cover and grill chicken, skin sides up, 5 to 6 inches from medium heat 25 to 35 minutes; turn. Mop with margarine mixture. Cover and grill 35 to 45 minutes longer, turning and mopping 2 or 3 times with margarine mixture, until juice of chicken is no longer pink when centers of thickest pieces are cut. Discard any remaining margarine mixture. Serve chicken with Honey-Pecan Sauce.

**1 SERVING:** Calories 560 (Calories from Fat 340); Fat 38g (Saturated 9g); Cholesterol 130mg; Sodium 530mg; Carbohydrate 15g (Dietary Fiber 0g); Protein 40g

## HONEY-PECAN SAUCE

3 tablespoons **honey**

2 tablespoons **margarine or butter, melted**

2 tablespoons **chopped pecans, toasted (see page 99)**

2 teaspoons **lemon juice**

1 teaspoon **mustard**

Mix all ingredients.

## For Extra-Juicy Chicken

Make sure your chicken cooks up extra-moist at your backyard barbecue by using tongs instead of a fork to turn the pieces. A fork will pierce the meat and let too many of the juices run out, thereby drying out the chicken. ∎

# GREEK CHICKEN WITH RED WINE AND GARLIC

Prep: 6 min; Marinate: 1 hr; Grill: 55 min          4 servings

1½ to 2   **pounds broiler-fryer chicken pieces**
   ½   **cup dry red wine or chicken broth**
   3   **tablespoons olive or vegetable oil**
   2   **tablespoons chopped fresh or 1 tablespoon dried basil leaves**
   1   **tablespoon chopped fresh or 1 teaspoon dried mint leaves**
   2   **cloves garlic, peeled and finely chopped**
   1   **jar (4¾ ounces) pitted Kalamata or ripe olives, drained**

**1.** Place chicken in shallow glass or plastic dish. Mix remaining ingredients except olives; pour over chicken. Cover and refrigerate 1 hour.

**2.** Brush grill rack with vegetable oil. Heat coals or gas grill for direct heat (see page 144).

**3.** Remove chicken from marinade; reserve marinade. Cover and grill chicken, skin sides down, 5 to 6 inches from medium heat 15 minutes. Turn chicken; brush with marinade. Cover and grill 20 to 40 minutes longer, brushing occasionally with marinade, until juice of chicken is no longer pink when centers of thickest pieces are cut. Discard any remaining marinade. Serve chicken with olives.

**1 SERVING:** Calories 270 (Calories from Fat 180); Fat 20g (Saturated 4g); Cholesterol 65mg; Sodium 360mg; Carbohydrate 3g (Dietary Fiber 1g); Protein 20g

# $\mathcal{S}$PICY CAJUN GRILLED CHICKEN

Prep: 15 min; Grill: 20 min      8 servings

- ¼ **cup chili powder**
- 2 **tablespoons chopped fresh or 1 tablespoon dried oregano leaves**
- 2 **tablespoons chopped fresh or 1 tablespoon dried thyme leaves**
- 1 **tablespoon packed brown sugar**
- 1 **teaspoon pepper**
- 1 **teaspoon salt**
- 8 **boneless, skinless chicken breast halves (about 2½ pounds)**
- 3 **medium tomatoes, chopped**
- ½ **cup whipping (heavy) cream**
- 1 **clove garlic, peeled and finely chopped**

**1.** Brush grill rack with vegetable oil. Heat coals or gas grill for direct heat (see page 144).

**2.** Mix chili powder, oregano, thyme, brown sugar, pepper and salt; coat both sides of chicken with mixture.

**3.** Cover and grill chicken 4 to 5 inches from medium heat 15 to 20 minutes, turning once, until juice is no longer pink when centers of thickest pieces are cut.

**4.** Heat tomatoes, whipping cream and garlic in 1-quart saucepan over medium-high heat 2 minutes, stirring frequently. Top chicken with tomato mixture.

**1 SERVING:** Calories 215 (Calories from Fat 80); Fat 9g (Saturated 4g); Cholesterol 90mg; Sodium 410mg; Carbohydrate 7g (Dietary Fiber 2g); Protein 28g

# CARIBBEAN CHICKEN WITH SWEET POTATOES

Prep: 25 min; Chill and Marinate: 1 hr; Grill: 25 min        8 servings

**Tropical Fruit Salsa (at right)**
8 **boneless, skinless chicken breast halves (about 2½ pounds)**
1 **cup light rum or apple juice**
¼ **cup honey**
2 **cloves garlic, peeled and crushed**
1 **teaspoon ground allspice**
1 **teaspoon ground cinnamon**
1 **teaspoon ground ginger**
½ **teaspoon salt**
4 **large sweet potatoes or yams, cut into ½-inch slices**

1. Prepare Tropical Fruit Salsa. Place chicken in shallow glass or plastic dish. Mix remaining ingredients except sweet potatoes; pour over chicken. Cover and refrigerate 1 hour.

2. Brush grill rack with vegetable oil. Heat coals or gas grill for direct heat (see page 144). Remove chicken from marinade; reserve marinade. Cover and grill chicken 4 to 5 inches from medium heat 10 minutes. Turn chicken; brush with marinade. Add sweet potato slices to grill. Cover and grill chicken and potato slices 10 to 15 minutes, brushing frequently with marinade, until chicken is no longer pink when centers of thickest pieces are cut. Discard any remaining marinade. Serve chicken and potato slices with salsa.

**1 SERVING:** Calories 245 (Calories from Fat 35); Fat 4g (Saturated 1g); Cholesterol 75mg; Sodium 150mg; Carbohydrate 27g (Dietary Fiber 3g); Protein 28g

## TROPICAL FRUIT SALSA

- 1 **mango, peeled, pitted and chopped**
- 1 **papaya, peeled, pitted and chopped**
- 2 **kiwifruit, peeled and chopped**
- 1 **jalapeño chili, seeded and finely chopped**
- 1 **cup pineapple chunks**
- 1 **tablespoon finely chopped red onion**
- 1 **tablespoon chopped fresh cilantro**
- 2 **tablespoons lime juice**

Mix all ingredients in glass or plastic bowl. Cover and refrigerate 1 to 2 hours to blend flavors.

## CHILI-RUBBED CHICKEN

Prep: 10 min; Marinate: 1 hr; Grill: 20 min        6 servings

- 6 **boneless, skinless chicken breast halves (about 1¾ pounds)**
- 3 **tablespoons tomato paste**
- 2 **tablespoons chili powder**
- 1 **tablespoon white vinegar**
- 1 **teaspoon garlic salt**
   **Two-Tomato Relish (below)**

**1.** Place chicken in shallow glass or plastic dish. Mix tomato paste, chili powder, vinegar and garlic salt. Coat both sides of chicken with tomato paste mixture. Cover and refrigerate 1 hour. Prepare Two-Tomato Relish.

**2.** Brush grill rack with vegetable oil. Heat coals or gas grill for direct heat (see page 144). Cover and grill chicken 4 to 5 inches from medium heat 15 to 20 minutes, turning once, until juice is no longer pink when centers of thickest pieces are cut. Serve with Two-Tomato Relish.

**1 SERVING:** Calories 150 (Calories from Fat 35); Fat 4g (Saturated 1g); Cholesterol 75mg; Sodium 205mg; Carbohydrate 2g (Dietary Fiber 1g); Protein 27g

## TWO-TOMATO RELISH

- 2 **medium tomatoes, chopped**
- 2 **medium yellow tomatoes, chopped**
- 1 **tablespoon red wine vinegar**
- 1 **teaspoon chopped fresh or ¼ teaspoon dried oregano leaves**

Mix all ingredients. Cover and refrigerate until serving.

# CHICKEN AND SUMMER FRUIT KABOBS

Prep: 12 min; Grill: 20 min        6 servings

1   **pound boneless, skinless chicken breasts, cut into 1½-inch pieces**

2   **medium peaches or nectarines, cut into 1-inch wedges**

2   **medium red plums, cut into 1-inch wedges**

1   **medium purple plum, cut into 1-inch wedges**

½   **cup peach or apricot jam**

½   **teaspoon salt**

**1.** Brush grill rack with vegetable oil. Heat coals or gas grill for direct heat (see page 144). Thread chicken, peaches and plums alternately on each of six 10- to 12-inch metal skewers, leaving space between pieces. Mix jam and salt.

**2.** Cover and grill kabobs 4 to 5 inches from medium heat 15 to 20 minutes, turning occasionally and brushing with jam, until chicken is no longer pink in center.

**1 SERVING:** Calories 190 (Calories from Fat 25); Fat 3g (Saturated 1g); Cholesterol 45mg; Sodium 250mg; Carbohydrate 25g (Dietary Fiber 1g); Protein 17g

# $\mathcal{G}$INGERY PEPPER STEAK

Prep: 15 min; Marinate: 1 hr; Grill: 16 min      4 servings

1 **pound beef boneless top sirloin steak, ¾ inch thick**

¼ **cup red wine vinegar**

2 **tablespoons olive or vegetable oil**

2 **tablespoons water**

1½ **tablespoons chopped fresh or 1½ teaspoons dried oregano leaves**

1 **tablespoon grated gingerroot**

2 **teaspoons cracked black pepper**

4 **large cloves garlic, peeled and crushed**

**1.** Cut beef into 4 pieces. Mix remaining ingredients in shallow non-metal dish or resealable plastic food-storage bag. Add beef, turning to coat with marinade. Cover dish or seal bag and refrigerate, turning once, at least 1 hour but no longer than 24 hours.

**2.** Brush grill rack with vegetable oil. Heat coals or gas grill for direct heat (see page 144).

**3.** Remove beef from marinade; discard marinade. Cover and grill beef 4 to 5 inches from medium heat 14 to 16 minutes for medium doneness, turning once.

**1 SERVING:** Calories 220 (Calories from Fat 125); Fat 14g (Saturated 5g); Cholesterol 65mg; Sodium 55mg; Carbohydrate 1g (Dietary Fiber 0g); Protein 22g

**COOKING TIP**

• Look for the freshest gingerroot you can find; it should not be shriveled or cracked, and cut surfaces shouldn't be dried out. Sniff it—gingerroot should smell freshly piquant, not musty.

# BARBECUED LONDON BROIL

Prep: 15 min; Marinate: 8 hr; Grill: 12 min        4 servings

⅓  **cup white vinegar**

⅓  **cup olive or vegetable oil**

3  **tablespoons packed brown sugar**

3  **tablespoons soy sauce**

½  **teaspoon coarsely ground pepper**

2  **medium onions, peeled and sliced**

1  **clove garlic, peeled and finely chopped**

1½  **pounds beef flank steak**

**1.** Mix all ingredients except beef in shallow nonmetal dish or resealable plastic bag. Add beef, turning to coat with marinade. Cover dish or seal bag and refrigerate, turning beef occasionally, at least 8 hours but no longer than 24 hours.

**2.** Brush grill rack with vegetable oil. Heat coals or gas grill for direct heat (see page 144).

**3.** Remove beef and onions from marinade; discard marinade. Place onions in 9-inch round aluminum foil pan. Grill beef uncovered 2 inches from medium heat about 12 minutes for medium-rare doneness, turning once. At same time, add pan of onions to grill, stirring occasionally, until tender.

**4.** Cut beef diagonally across grain into very thin slices. To serve, top with onions.

**1 SERVING:** Calories 300 (Calories from Fat 145); Fat 16g (Saturated 5g); Cholesterol 90mg; Sodium 105mg; Carbohydrate 5g (Dietary Fiber 1g); Protein 35g

# *F*LANK STEAK WITH CHIMICHURRI SAUCE

Prep: 15 min; Marinate: 4 hr; Grill: 16 min        4 or 5 servings

1½ **pounds beef flank steak**

**Chimichurri Sauce (below)**

**1.** Make cuts about ½ inch apart and ⅛ inch deep in diamond pattern in both sides of beef. Place beef in shallow nonmetal dish or resealable plastic food-storage bag.

**2.** Prepare Chimichurri Sauce. Pour 1 cup of the sauce over beef; turn beef to coat with sauce. Cover remaining sauce and set aside to serve with beef. Cover dish or seal bag and refrigerate beef, turning occasionally, at least 4 hours but no longer than 24 hours.

**3.** Brush grill rack with vegetable oil. Heat coals or gas grill for direct heat (see page 144).

**4.** Remove beef from marinade; reserve marinade. Grill beef uncovered 4 to 5 inches from medium heat 12 to 16 minutes for medium doneness, brushing with marinade and turning once. Discard any remaining marinade.

**5.** Cut beef diagonally across grain into thin slices. Serve with remaining sauce.

**1 SERVING:** Calories 500 (Calories from Fat 351); Fat 39g (Saturated 9g); Cholesterol 90mg; Sodium 85mg; Carbohydrate 3g (Dietary Fiber 0g); Protein 34g

## CHIMICHURRI SAUCE

¼ **cup chopped fresh parsley**

1 **cup vegetable oil**

½ **cup white wine vinegar**

½ **cup lemon juice**

1 **teaspoon crushed red pepper**

4 **cloves garlic, peeled and finely chopped**

Shake all ingredients in tightly covered container.

### COOKING TIP

• If you don't have a grill, you can broil the kabobs. Place kabobs on the rack in a broiler pan. Broil with tops about 3 inches from heat 8 to 10 minutes for medium beef doneness, turning and brushing 2 or 3 times with the Italian dressing.

# $\mathscr{B}$EEF KABOBS WITH CHILIED PLUM SAUCE

Cook: 30 min; Grill: 15 min     8 servings

**Chilied Plum Sauce (at right)**

1½ **pounds beef boneless sirloin or round steak, 1 inch thick, cut into 1-inch pieces**

3 **medium zucchini or yellow summer squash, cut into 1-inch slices**

2 **medium bell peppers, cut into 1½-inch pieces**

1 **large onion, peeled and cut into 1-inch pieces**

24 **whole medium mushrooms**

**About ½ cup Italian dressing**

1. Prepare Chilied Plum Sauce. Prepare the coals or a gas grill for direct heat (see page 144).

2. Thread 4 or 5 pieces of the beef on the skewers, alternating with the zucchini, bell peppers, onion and mushrooms, leaving a ½-inch space between pieces.

**3.** Cover and grill the kabobs 4 to 5 inches from medium heat 10 to 15 minutes for medium beef doneness, turning and brushing 2 or 3 times with the Italian dressing. Serve kabobs with sauce for dipping.

**1 SERVING:** Calories 355 (Calories from Fat 135); Fat 14g (Saturated 3g); Cholesterol 55mg; Sodium 440mg; Carbohydrate 34g (Dietary Fiber 3g); Protein 22g

## CHILIED PLUM SAUCE

  1  **can (16½ ounces) purple plums, drained, pitted and finely chopped**

  1  **can (6 ounces) frozen lemonade concentrate, thawed**

  ¼  **cup (½ stick) margarine or butter**

  1  **small onion, peeled and finely chopped**

  ¼  **cup chili sauce**

  1  **tablespoon Dijon mustard**

**1.** Place the plums and lemonade concentrate in the blender. Cover and blend on medium speed until smooth, and set aside.

**2.** Melt the margarine in the saucepan over medium heat 1 to 2 minutes. Cook the onion in margarine about 2 minutes, stirring occasionally, until tender.

**3.** Stir in the plum mixture, chili sauce and mustard. Heat to boiling over medium-high heat. Reduce heat just enough so mixture bubbles gently. Cook uncovered 15 minutes, stirring occasionally. Serve warm, or cover and refrigerate up to 48 hours.

**SERVING TIP**

• For an impressive presentation, line a large serving platter or tray with hot cooked rice or couscous and serve the kabobs on top.

**THREADING THE KABOBS**

Thread 4 or 5 beef pieces on the skewers, alternating with zucchini, bell peppers, onion and mushrooms, leaving a ½-inch space between pieces.

# $\mathcal{T}$ERIYAKI PORK TENDERLOINS

Prep: 10 min; Marinate: 8 hr; Grill: 30 min        6 servings

**2  pork tenderloins (each about ¾ pound)**
**Teriyaki marinade**

**1.** Fold thin end of each pork tenderloin under so that pork is an even thickness; secure with toothpicks. Place pork in resealable plastic food-storage bag or shallow glass or plastic dish. Pour marinade over pork; turn pork to coat with marinade. Seal bag or cover dish and refrigerate at least 8 hours but no longer than 24 hours, turning pork occasionally.

**2.** Brush grill rack with vegetable oil. Heat coals or gas grill for indirect heat (see page 144).

**3.** Remove pork from marinade; reserve marinade. Cover and grill pork over drip pan 4 to 5 inches from medium heat 25 to 30 minutes, brushing occasionally with marinade and turning once, until pork is no longer pink in center. Discard any remaining marinade.

**4.** Remove toothpicks. To serve, cut pork across grain into thin slices.

**1 SERVING:** Calories 160 (Calories from Fat 55); Fat 6g (Saturated 2g); Cholesterol 70mg; Sodium 5mg; Carbohydrate 1g (Dietary Fiber 0g); Protein 25g

# $\mathcal{S}$OUTHWESTERN PORK CHOPS

Prep: 10 min; Marinate: 1 hr; Grill: 12 min        8 servings

**8  pork loin or rib chops, about ½ inch thick (2 pounds)**
**1  tablespoon chili powder**
**1  teaspoon ground cumin**
**¼  teaspoon ground red pepper (cayenne)**
**¼  teaspoon salt**
**1  large clove garlic, peeled and finely chopped**

**1.** Remove fat from pork. Mix remaining ingredients. Rub chili powder mixture evenly on both sides of pork. Cover and refrigerate 1 hour to blend flavors.

**2.** Heat coals or gas grill for direct heat (see page 144). Cover and grill pork 4 to 6 inches from medium heat 10 to 12 minutes, turning frequently, until no longer pink when cut near bone.

**1 SERVING:** Calories 130 (Calories from Fat 55); Fat 6g (Saturated 2g); Cholesterol 50mg; Sodium 115mg; Carbohydrate 1g (Dietary Fiber 0g); Protein 18g

# GRILLED HONEY-MUSTARD PORK CHOPS

**QUICK** Prep: 5 min; Grill: 12 min     4 servings

¼ cup honey

2 tablespoons Dijon mustard

1 tablespoon orange juice

1 teaspoon chopped fresh or ¼ teaspoon dried tarragon leaves

1 teaspoon cider vinegar

½ teaspoon white wine or Worcestershire sauce

Dash of onion powder

4 boneless pork loin chops, ½ inch thick (about 1 pound)

**1.** Mix all ingredients except pork.

**2.** Heat coals or gas grill for direct heat (see page 144). Cover and grill pork 4 to 5 inches from medium coals 10 to 12 minutes, brushing occasionally with honey mixture and turning once, until pork is tender and no longer pink when centers of thickest pieces are cut. Discard any remaining honey mixture.

**1 SERVING:** Calories 285 (Calories from Fat 115); Fat 13g (Saturated 5g); Cholesterol 70mg; Sodium 140mg; Carbohydrate 19g (Dietary Fiber 0g); Protein 23g

## COOKING TIP

• Microwave precooking means faster grilling! Because ribs are precooked, the sweet sauce can be added right at the beginning of grilling.

# GLAZED COUNTRY RIBS

Prep: 15 min; Microwave: 18 min; Grill: 12 min          4 servings

**3  pounds pork country-style ribs, cut into serving pieces**
**½  cup orange juice**
**¾  cup cocktail sauce**
**½  cup orange marmalade**

1. Brush grill rack with vegetable oil. Heat coals or gas grill for direct heat (see page 144).

2. Arrange pork, meatiest pieces to outside edge, in 3-quart microwavable casserole. Add orange juice. Cover and microwave on high 5 minutes. Rearrange and turn over pork, so less-cooked pieces are to outside edge of casserole. Re-cover and microwave 3 minutes; rearrange pork. Re-cover and microwave on medium (50%) 8 to 10 minutes or until very little pink remains.

3. While pork is microwaving, mix cocktail sauce and marmalade; reserve ½ cup to serve with pork.

4. Drain pork; discard cooking liquid. Cover and grill pork 5 to 6 inches from medium heat 10 to 12 minutes, turning and brushing generously with sauce mixture 2 or 3 times, until pork is glazed, browned and no longer pink when cut near bone. Serve pork with reserved sauce mixture.

**1 SERVING:** Calories 740 (Calories from Fat 405); Fat 45g (Saturated 17g); Cholesterol 170mg; Sodium 600mg; Carbohydrate 41g (Dietary Fiber 1g); Protein 44g

# SALADS AND SIDES

## Summer Citrus Fruit Salad

**QUICK** Prep: 15 min     8 servings

1 **cup vanilla yogurt**

1 **tablespoon mayonnaise or salad dressing**

¼ **teaspoon grated orange peel**

2 **tablespoons orange juice**

1 **pint (2 cups) strawberries, hulled and cut lengthwise into slices**

1 **kiwifruit, peeled and cut into pieces**

1 **small bunch seedless green grapes, cut in half**

1 **can (11 ounces) mandarin orange segments, drained**

**1.** Mix the yogurt, mayonnaise, orange peel and orange juice in a bowl.

**2.** Add the fruits to the yogurt mixture. Gently stir until fruits are coated. Cover and refrigerate until serving time.

**1 SERVING:** Calories 90 (Calories from Fat 20); Fat 2g (Saturated 1g); Cholesterol 5mg; Sodium 35mg; Carbohydrate 18g (Dietary Fiber 2g); Protein 2g

# $\mathcal{F}$RESH FRUIT WITH HONEY—POPPY SEED DRESSING

**QUICK**  Prep: 20 min      6 servings

**Honey—Poppy Seed Dressing (below)**

1 **large unpeeled apple or 2 medium apricots or nectarines**

1 **medium orange**

1 **medium pineapple**

1 **small bunch seedless green grapes**

**1.** Prepare Honey—Poppy Seed Dressing.

**2.** Cut the unpeeled apple into slices, or peel and slice the apricots or nectarines. Peel the orange, then cut along the membrane of both sides of one orange section. Remove that section, and continue with the rest of the orange. Cut the pineapple lengthwise into fourths. Cut off the rind and the core. Cut the pineapple into chunks, removing any "eyes" or spots left from the rind. Wash the grapes, and cut in half.

**3.** Mix the fruits and the dressing in a large bowl. Cover and refrigerate until ready to serve. Cover and refrigerate any remaining salad.

**1 SERVING:** Calories 215 (Calories from Fat 90); Fat 10g (Saturated 2g); Cholesterol 0mg; Sodium 5mg; Carbohydrate 32g (Dietary Fiber 2g); Protein 1g

## HONEY—POPPY SEED DRESSING

¼ **cup vegetable oil**

3 **tablespoons honey**

2 **tablespoons lemon juice**

1½ **teaspoons poppy seeds**

Shake all ingredients in a tightly covered jar or container. Shake again before pouring over fruit.

**CUTTING AN ORANGE INTO SECTIONS**

Cut along the membrane of both sides of one orange section. Remove that section, and continue with the rest of the orange.

**PEELING AND CUTTING UP PINEAPPLE**

Cut pineapple lengthwise into fourths. Cut off the rind and the core. Cut pineapple into chunks, removing any "eyes" or spots left from the rind.

**COOKING TIPS**

• Add a twist to this picnic favorite by stirring in 1 cup canned mandarin orange segments, drained. Sprinkle with 2 tablespoons toasted sliced almonds.

• If you don't have a bag of coleslaw mix, you can use 7 cups shredded cabbage and 2 shredded carrots instead.

# $\mathscr{T}$ANGY COLESLAW

Prep: 5 min; Chill: 30 min        8 servings

| | |
|---|---|
| 1 | bag (16 ounces) coleslaw mix |
| 4 | medium green onions with tops, trimmed and thinly sliced |
| ⅓ | cup orange marmalade |
| ¼ | cup rice vinegar or white wine vinegar |
| 1 | tablespoon sugar |
| 1 | tablespoon dark sesame oil |
| 1½ | teaspoons grated gingerroot |
| 1 | teaspoon salt |

**1.** Place the coleslaw mix in a bowl.

**2.** Add onion, marmalade, vinegar, sugar, oil, gingerroot and salt to coleslaw mix. Mix with a large spoon until coleslaw is evenly coated with the dressing.

**3.** Cover and refrigerate at least 30 minutes to blend flavors.

**1 SERVING:** Calories 70 (Calories from Fat 20); Fat 2g (Saturated 0g); Cholesterol 0mg; Sodium 310mg; Carbohydrate 14g (Dietary Fiber 2g); Protein 1g

## SPECIAL TOUCH

### Water or Punch Fishbowl

You will need:

**Small decorative molds, small paper cups or muffin pan with regular-size muffin cups**

**Large fresh flowers (such as carnations, daisies or zinnias)**

**Large clear tray, platter or liner with rim**

**New 1-gallon fishbowl (available at pet store)**

**Lemonade or ice water**

1. Fill molds with water. Place flowers in molds. Freeze until solid. (Distilled water will keep the ice molds clear when they are frozen. You can use tap water if you like, but the molds will be more opaque.)

2. Fill tray ½ full with water. Fill fishbowl with lemonade or ice water, and place in tray.

3. Dip bottoms of molds in warm water to loosen frozen flowers. Remove frozen flowers from molds; float in tray.

# CLASSIC CRUNCHY COLESLAW

**QUICK** Prep: 10 min          8 servings

½ cup sour cream or plain yogurt

¼ cup mayonnaise or salad dressing

1 teaspoon sugar

½ teaspoon dry mustard

½ teaspoon seasoned salt

⅛ teaspoon pepper

1 pound green cabbage, finely shredded or chopped

1 small onion, peeled and chopped

Paprika, if desired

Dill weed, if desired

Mix sour cream, mayonnaise, sugar, mustard, seasoned salt and pepper; toss with cabbage and onion. Sprinkle with paprika or dried dill weed.

**1 SERVING:** Calories 125 (Calories from Fat 100); Fat 11g (Saturated 3g); Cholesterol 20mg; Sodium 180mg; Carbohydrate 6g (Dietary Fiber 2g); Protein 2g

# TRIPLE-CABBAGE SLAW

**QUICK** Prep: 15 min          4 servings

2 cups thinly sliced Chinese (napa) cabbage

1½ cups shredded green cabbage

½ cup shredded red cabbage

1 tablespoon chopped fresh chives

3 tablespoons orange marmalade

2 tablespoons rice vinegar

1 teaspoon grated gingerroot

Mix cabbages and chives in large glass or plastic bowl. Stir marmalade, vinegar and gingerroot until blended. Add to cabbage; toss lightly.

**1 SERVING:** Calories 50 (Calories from Fat 0); Fat 0g (Saturated 0g); Cholesterol 0mg; Sodium 35mg; Carbohydrate 13g (Dietary Fiber 1g); Protein 1g

#  GREEK SALAD

**QUICK**   Prep: 15 min          8 servings

Lemon Dressing (below)

1   **bunch spinach**

1   **head Boston or Bibb lettuce**

3   **medium green onions with tops, trimmed and sliced**

1   **medium cucumber, sliced**

3   **medium tomatoes, cut into wedges**

24   **pitted whole ripe olives (from a 6-ounce can)**

¾   **cup crumbled feta cheese (3 ounces)**

**1.** Prepare Lemon Dressing.

**2.** Remove and discard stems from spinach. Rinse the leaves in cool water. Shake off excess water, and blot to dry, or roll up leaves in a clean, dry kitchen towel or paper towel to dry. Tear leaves into bite-size pieces, and place in bowl. You will need about 5 cups of spinach pieces.

**3.** Separate the leaves from the head of lettuce. Rinse the leaves with cool water. Shake off excess water, and blot to dry. Tear the leaves into bite-size pieces, and add to the bowl.

**4.** Add onion, cucumber, tomatoes and olives to bowl. Break up any large pieces of the cheese with a fork, and add to bowl.

**5.** Pour the dressing over the salad ingredients, and toss with 2 large spoons or salad tongs. To keep salad crisp, serve immediately.

**1 SERVING:** Calories 135 (Calories from Fat 100); Fat 11g (Saturated 3g); Cholesterol 10mg; Sodium 350mg; Carbohydrate 7g (Dietary Fiber 2g); Protein 4g

## LEMON DRESSING

¼   **cup vegetable oil**

2   **tablespoons lemon juice**

½   **teaspoon sugar**

1½   **teaspoons Dijon mustard**

¼   **teaspoon salt**

⅛   **teaspoon pepper**

Shake all ingredients in a tightly covered jar or container. Shake again before pouring over salad.

---

**COOKING TIPS**

• Although the spinach you purchase may be labeled "washed," you should wash it again because it may still contain some sand and dirt. Ready-to-eat spinach, available in bags, does not need to be washed.

• If you do not want to eat the entire salad, save a portion of it in a resealable plastic food-storage bag before adding the dressing. Seal tightly and refrigerate up to two days. Add just enough dressing to the salad to be served to coat the leaves lightly, and refrigerate any remaining dressing.

# $\mathcal{W}$ALDORF SALAD

**QUICK**   Prep: 10 min          4 servings

½ **cup mayonnaise or salad dressing**
1 **tablespoon lemon juice**
1 **tablespoon milk**
2 **medium unpeeled red eating apples, coarsely chopped**
2 **medium stalks celery, chopped**
⅓ **cup coarsely chopped nuts**
  **Salad greens, if desired**

**1.** Mix mayonnaise, lemon juice and milk in medium bowl.

**2.** Stir in apples, celery and nuts. Serve on salad greens. Store remaining salad covered in refrigerator.

**1 SERVING:** Calories 305 (Calories from Fat 250); Fat 28g (Saturated 4g); Cholesterol 15mg; Sodium 180mg; Carbohydrate 14g (Dietary Fiber 3g); Protein 2g

*Lighter Waldorf Salad:* For 13 grams of fat and 170 calories per serving, use reduced-fat mayonnaise and decrease nuts to 2 tablespoons.

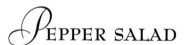

# $\mathcal{P}$EPPER SALAD

Prep: 15 min; Stand: 1 hr 15 min; Grill: 20 min          6 servings

¼ **cup olive or vegetable oil**
6 **medium bell peppers**
½ **teaspoon salt**
¼ **teaspoon pepper**

**1.** Brush grill rack with vegetable oil. Heat coals or gas grill for direct heat (see page 144).

**2.** Cover and grill bell peppers 4 inches from medium heat 15 to 20 minutes, turning frequently, until skin is blistered on all sides. Wrap peppers in clean towel or brown paper bag; cool 15 minutes.

**3.** Remove skin from peppers with knife. Cut peppers lengthwise in half; remove stems and seeds. Cut peppers into ¼- to ½-inch-wide strips; place in nonmetal bowl. Drizzle with oil. Sprinkle with salt and pepper. Cover and refrigerate at least 1 hour but no longer than 3 days.

**1 SERVING:** Calories 100 (Calories from Fat 80); Fat 9g (Saturated 1g); Cholesterol 0mg; Sodium 200mg; Carbohydrate 5g (Dietary Fiber 1g); Protein 1g

# PICY POTATO PLANKS

Prep: 15 min; Cook: 20 min; Grill: 15 min        4 servings

- **3 medium potatoes (about 1½ pounds)**
- **Salt, if desired**
- **⅓ cup margarine or butter**
- **½ teaspoon salt**
- **⅛ teaspoon ground red pepper (cayenne)**
- **⅛ teaspoon garam masala, if desired (see tip)**
- **1 large clove garlic, peeled and crushed**

**1.** Place potatoes in enough water to cover (salted, if desired) in 3-quart saucepan. Cover and heat to boiling. Boil about 15 minutes or until almost tender; drain. Cool slightly.

**2.** Brush grill rack with vegetable oil. Heat coals or gas grill for direct heat (see page 144).

**3.** Heat remaining ingredients to boiling; remove from heat. Cut each potato lengthwise into 4 or 5 slices. Brush potatoes generously with margarine mixture.

**4.** Cover and grill potatoes 4 inches from medium heat about 15 minutes, turning and brushing 2 or 3 times with margarine mixture, until golden brown and tender.

**1 SERVING:** Calories 230 (Calories from Fat 135); Fat 15g (Saturated 3g); Cholesterol 0mg; Sodium 470mg; Carbohydrate 24g (Dietary Fiber 2g); Protein 2g

---

**COOKING TIP**

• Garam masala is an Indian spice mixture. While its recipe is variable, garam masala usually consists of cardamom, cinnamon and cloves and may also include coriander, cumin, nutmeg, mace or pepper.

**COOKING TIPS**

• For 4 servings, use 2 pounds sweet potatoes. For 2 servings, use 2 sweet potatoes, 2 tablespoons margarine or butter and ¼ teaspoon salt.

• For a spicy flavor, stir ¼ teaspoon ground cinnamon or ground red pepper into the margarine mixture.

# Sweet Potato Slices

Prep: 10 min; Cook: 20 min; Grill: 20 min        6 servings

**3   pounds sweet potatoes or yams, peeled and cut into ½-inch diagonal slices**
**⅓   cup margarine or butter, melted**
**½   teaspoon salt**
    **Toasted coconut, if desired**

**1.** Brush grill rack with vegetable oil. Heat coals or gas grill for direct heat (see page 144).

**2.** Heat 1 inch water to boiling in 3-quart saucepan. Add sweet potato slices. Cover and heat to boiling; reduce heat to low. Simmer about 15 minutes or almost tender; drain. Mix margarine and salt in a small bowl.

**3.** Grill sweet potato slices uncovered 4 inches from medium heat about 15 minutes, brushing frequently with margarine mixture and turning once. To serve, sprinkle sweet potatoes with coconut.

**1 SERVING:** Calories 255 (Calories from Fat 90); Fat 10g (Saturated 2g); Cholesterol 0mg; Sodium 330mg; Carbohydrate 43g (Dietary Fiber 5g); Protein 3g

# Herbed Mozzarella Eggplant

**QUICK**    Prep: 15 min; Grill: 12 min        8 servings

**⅓   cup vegetable oil**
**2   tablespoons chopped fresh or 2 teaspoons dried oregano leaves**
**2   tablespoons lemon juice**
**2   cloves garlic, peeled and crushed**
**1   teaspoon salt**
**2   medium eggplants, cut into 1½-inch slices**
**1   cup shredded mozzarella cheese (4 ounces)**

**1.** Brush grill rack with vegetable oil. Heat coals or gas grill for direct heat (see page 144).

**2.** Mix all ingredients except eggplant slices and cheese. Dip eggplant slices into oil mixture, coating both sides.

**3.** Cover and grill eggplant slices 5 to 6 inches from medium heat 8 to 12 minutes, turning and brushing 2 or 3 times with oil mixture, until tender. Top slices with cheese for last 2 minutes of grilling.

**1 SERVING:** Calories 155 (Calories from Fat 110); Fat 12g (Saturated 3g); Cholesterol 10mg; Sodium 370mg; Carbohydrate 10g (Dietary Fiber 3g); Protein 5g

# Timetable for Grilling Vegetables

When grilling veggies, use a grilling pan or screen or heavy-duty foil to keep them from slipping through the grates of the grill. If you're following a recipe that gives specific cooking times, follow those directions for the best results. Otherwise, use the timetable below to help you cook up perfect vegetables every time.

| Vegetable | Grilling Time |
| --- | --- |
| Asparagus spears, whole | 20 minutes |
| Bell peppers, cut into 1-inch strips | 15 minutes |
| Broccoli spears, cut lengthwise in half | 20 minutes |
| Carrots, small whole, partially cooked* | 10 minutes |
| Cauliflowerets, cut lengthwise in half | 20 minutes |
| Cherry tomatoes, whole | 10 minutes |
| Corn on the cob, husked and wrapped in aluminum foil | 20 minutes |
| Eggplant, cut into 1/4-inch slices | 10 minutes |
| Green beans, whole | 15 minutes |
| Mushrooms, whole | 15 minutes |
| Onions, cut into 1/2-inch slices | 10 minutes |
| Pattypan squash, whole | 15 minutes |
| Potatoes, cut into 1-inch wedges, partially cooked* | 15 minutes |
| Zucchini, cut into 3/4-inch pieces | 15 minutes |

*Before grilling, cook in boiling water 10 to 15 minutes or just until crisp-tender.

## COOKING TIPS

• Sprinkling eggplant with salt and letting it stand 30 minutes eliminates the bitter taste often found in eggplant.

• Avoid using the oven for this recipe by heating the spaghetti sauce right in the can. Be sure to remove the label from the can, then open the can and place on the grill rack. Keep an eye on it and stir occasionally. Once it's heated, remove from the heat using oven mitts and spoon out the amount you need.

# $\mathcal{S}$KEWERED RATATOUILLE

Prep: 40 min; Grill: 20 min        6 servings

1   small eggplant, cut into 1-inch chunks
¾   teaspoon salt
2   small zucchini, cut into 1-inch chunks
1   medium green bell pepper, cut into 1-inch chunks
1   small onion, peeled and cut into 1-inch chunks
⅓   cup Italian dressing
1   cup spaghetti sauce or Italian tomato sauce

1. Place eggplant chunks in colander over bowl or sink. Sprinkle with salt. Let drain 30 minutes. Rinse and pat dry.

2. Brush grill rack with vegetable oil. Heat coals or gas grill for direct heat (see page 144).

3. Thread eggplant, zucchini, bell pepper and onion alternately on each of six 10-inch metal skewers, leaving space between each. Brush with dressing.

4. Cover and grill kabobs 4 to 6 inches from medium heat 15 to 20 minutes, turning and brushing twice with dressing, until vegetables are crisp-tender.

5. Heat spaghetti sauce on grill in can with label removed during last 10 minutes of grilling, stirring occasionally. Serve kabobs with spaghetti sauce.

**1 SERVING:** Calories 120 (Calories from Fat 70); Fat 8g (Saturated 1g); Cholesterol 0mg; Sodium 670mg; Carbohydrate 13g (Dietary Fiber 3g); Protein 2g

# Mushrooms with Herbs

Prep: 10 min; Marinate: 1 hr; Grill: 20 min          4 servings

½  **cup olive or vegetable oil**

3  **tablespoons lemon juice**

1  **teaspoon chopped fresh or ¼ teaspoon dried oregano leaves**

1  **teaspoon chopped fresh or ¼ teaspoon dried thyme leaves**

1  **clove garlic, peeled and crushed**

1  **pound large white mushrooms (about 2½ inches in diameter)**

¼  **teaspoon salt**

⅛  **teaspoon pepper**

**1.** Mix oil, lemon juice, oregano, thyme and garlic in large nonmetal bowl or resealable plastic bag. Add mushrooms, stirring to coat with marinade. Cover and refrigerate at least 1 hour but no longer than 8 hours.

**2.** Heat coals or gas grill for direct heat (see page 144).

**3.** Remove mushrooms from marinade (mushrooms will absorb most of the marinade). Cover and grill mushrooms about 4 inches from medium heat 15 to 20 minutes, turning 2 or 3 times, until tender and golden brown. Sprinkle with salt and pepper.

**1 SERVING:** Calories 215 (Calories from Fat 190); Fat 21g (Saturated 3g); Cholesterol 0mg; Sodium 150mg; Carbohydrate 6g (Dietary Fiber 1g); Protein 2g

### COOKING TIP

• You can use smaller mushrooms—just be sure to use a grilling screen or aluminum foil pan, and check for doneness after half the grilling time.

## COOKING TIP

• For a richer flavor, cover the tomatoes and marinate in the refrigerator overnight.

# MARINATED TOMATO SLICES

Prep: 5 min; Chill: 30 min      4 servings

¼ **cup chopped fresh or 2 tablespoons dried basil leaves**

6 **tablespoons olive oil**

2 **tablespoons red wine vinegar**

2 **large tomatoes, sliced**

Mix all ingredients except tomatoes. Pour mixture over tomatoes in glass bowl; chill for at least 30 minutes.

**1 SERVING:** Calories 60 (Calories from Fat 45); Fat 5g (Saturated 1g); Cholesterol 0mg; Sodium 10mg; Carbohydrate 4g (Dietary Fiber 1g); Protein 1g

# Tomato-Artichoke Kabobs

**QUICK**   Prep: 10 min; Grill: 8 min          4 servings

**1   jar (6 ounces) marinated artichoke hearts**

**12   cherry tomatoes**

**1.** Brush grill rack with vegetable oil. Heat coals or gas grill for direct heat (see page 144).

**2.** Drain artichoke hearts; reserve liquid. Thread artichoke hearts and tomatoes alternately on each of four 10- to 12-inch metal skewers, leaving space between pieces. Brush with artichoke liquid.

**3.** Cover and grill kabobs about 4 inches from medium heat 6 to 8 minutes, brushing with artichoke liquid and turning 2 or 3 times, until hot.

**1 SERVING:** Calories 30 (Calories from Fat 10); Fat 1g (Saturated 0g); Cholesterol 0mg; Sodium 105mg; Carbohydrate 6g (Dietary Fiber 2g); Protein 1g

# Corn with Chili-Lime Spread

Prep: 15 min; Grill: 30 min          6 servings

**Chili-Lime Spread (below)**

**6   ears corn (with husks)**

**1.** Prepare Chili-Lime Spread.

**2.** Heat coals or gas grill for direct heat (see page 144).

**3.** Remove large outer husks from each ear corn; turn back inner husks and remove silk. Spread each ear corn with about 2 teaspoons Chili-Lime Spread; reserve remaining spread. Pull husks up over ears; tie with fine wire to secure.

**4.** Grill corn uncovered 3 inches from medium heat 20 to 30 minutes, turning frequently, until tender. Serve corn with remaining spread.

**1 SERVING:** Calories 285 (Calories from Fat 155); Fat 17g (Saturated 4g); Cholesterol 0mg; Sodium 210mg; Carbohydrate 32g (Dietary Fiber 3g); Protein 4g

## CHILI-LIME SPREAD

**½   cup (1 stick) margarine or butter, softened**

**½   teaspoon grated lime peel**

**3   tablespoons lime juice**

**1 to 2   teaspoons ground red chilies or chili powder**

Mix all ingredients.

#  DILLED BABY CARROTS

Prep: 10 min; Grill: 1 hr        4 servings

1   **package (1 pound) baby-cut carrots**
2   **teaspoons dried dill weed**
1   **teaspoon sugar**
1   **teaspoon lemon juice**
1   **tablespoon margarine or butter**

**1.** Heat coals or gas grill for direct heat (see page 144).

**2.** Place carrots on 18 × 12-inch piece of heavy-duty aluminum foil. Sprinkle with dill weed, sugar and lemon juice. Dot with margarine. Wrap foil securely around carrots; punch top of foil once or twice with fork to vent steam.

**3.** Cover and grill foil packet, seam side up, 4 to 6 inches from medium heat about 1 hour or until carrots are tender.

**1 SERVING:** Calories 70 (Calories from Fat 25); Fat 3g (Saturated 1g); Cholesterol 0mg; Sodium 75mg; Carbohydrate 13g (Dietary Fiber 3g); Protein 1g

# DESSERTS

## BRANDIED SKEWERED FRUIT

**QUICK** Prep: 20 min; Grill: 10 min    6 kabobs

½ medium pineapple (about 3-pound size), cut into chunks

3 medium plums, cut in half

3 medium apricots or peaches, cut in half

2 tablespoons margarine or butter, melted

2 tablespoons packed brown sugar

3 tablespoons apricot brandy or apricot nectar

**1.** Brush grill rack with vegetable oil. Heat coals or gas grill for direct heat (see page 144).

**2.** Thread pineapple chunks, 1 plum half and 1 apricot half on each of six 10- to 12-inch metal skewers, leaving space between pieces. Brush with margarine. Sprinkle with brown sugar.

**3.** Grill kabobs uncovered 4 to 6 inches from medium heat about 10 minutes, turning once, until hot. To serve, drizzle with brandy.

**1 KABOB:** Calories 125 (Calories from Fat 35); Fat 4g (Saturated 1g); Cholesterol 0mg; Sodium 45mg; Carbohydrate 23g (Dietary Fiber 2g); Protein 1g

# Spiced Fruit Kabobs

**QUICK**    Prep: 5 min; Grill: 8 min        6 kabobs

¼  **cup (½ stick) margarine or butter**
1  **tablespoon sugar**
½  **teaspoon ground cinnamon**
3  **firm plums**
3  **firm nectarines**
2  **firm medium bananas**

1. Brush grill rack with vegetable oil. Heat coals or gas grill for direct heat (see page 144).

2. Heat margarine, sugar and cinnamon in small pan or food can with label removed, on grill until margarine is melted.

3. Cut plums and nectarines into 4 pieces each; remove pits. Cut bananas into 6 pieces each. Thread fruits alternately on each of six 10- to 12-inch metal skewers, leaving space between pieces.

4. Grill kabobs uncovered 5 to 6 inches from medium heat 6 to 8 minutes, brushing occasionally with margarine mixture and turning 2 or 3 times, until hot.

**1 KABOB:** Calories 130 (Calories from Fat 45); Fat 5g (Saturated 2g); Cholesterol 0mg; Sodium 45mg; Carbohydrate 22g (Dietary Fiber 2g); Protein 1g

# $\mathcal{P}$EARS WITH RASPBERRY SAUCE

**QUICK** Prep: 15 min; Grill: 10 min          6 servings

3 large firm pears
1 tablespoon vegetable oil
1 package (10 ounces) frozen raspberries in syrup, thawed
1 teaspoon lemon juice
3 tablespoons hot fudge sauce, heated, if desired

**1.** Heat coals or gas grill for direct heat (see page 144).

**2.** Peel pears; cut lengthwise in half and remove cores. Lightly brush both sides with oil.

**3.** Cover and grill pears, cut sides up, 4 to 6 inches from medium heat 5 minutes; turn. Cover and grill about 5 minutes longer or until tender.

**4.** While pears are grilling, place raspberries and lemon juice in blender or food processor. Cover and blend on medium speed, stopping blender occasionally to scrape sides, or process about 30 seconds, until well blended. Strain raspberry mixture to remove seeds, if desired. Serve hot pears with raspberry sauce. Drizzle with fudge sauce.

**1 SERVING:** Calories 170 (Calories from Fat 35); Fat 4g (Saturated 1g); Cholesterol 2mg; Sodium 15mg; Carbohydrate 37g (Dietary Fiber 5g); Protein 1g

# $\mathcal{P}$EANUT BUTTER BANANA ROLLS

**QUICK**    Prep: 15 min; Grill: 10 min        4 servings

  4  **flour tortillas (8 inches in diameter)**
 ¼  **cup peanut butter**
 ¼  **cup miniature semisweet chocolate chips**
  2  **small bananas**
  2  **teaspoons margarine or butter, softened**
     **Chocolate-flavored syrup, if desired**

**1.** Heat coals or gas grill for direct heat (see page 144). Soak 4 small bamboo skewers or about 6 toothpicks in water 30 minutes.

**2.** Spread 1 side of each tortilla with peanut butter. Sprinkle with chocolate chips. Cut each banana lengthwise in half. Place 1 banana half on each tortilla. Roll tortilla around banana; secure with wooden skewer. Brush rolls with margarine.

**3.** Grill rolls uncovered 4 to 6 inches from medium heat 8 to 10 minutes, turning once, until golden brown.

**4.** To serve, drizzle banana rolls with chocolate syrup.

**1 SERVING:** Calories 345 (Calories from Fat 155); Fat 17g (Saturated 5g); Cholesterol 0mg; Sodium 300mg; Carbohydrate 44g (Dietary Fiber 4g); Protein 8g

# $\mathcal{S}$UMMER COBBLER

Prep: 15 min; Grill: 30 min     8 servings

¼  **cup (½ stick) margarine or butter, melted**

1¼  **cups Original Bisquick baking mix**

½  **cup sugar**

½  **cup milk**

1  **medium nectarine or peach, sliced**

1  **cup blueberries or blackberries**

¼  **cup sugar**

½  **teaspoon ground cinnamon**

**1.** Heat coals or gas grill for direct heat (see page 144).

**2.** Melt margarine in 9-inch round aluminum foil pan on grill. Mix baking mix, ½ cup sugar and milk; beat 30 seconds. Pour over margarine in pan. Top batter with nectarine and blueberries. Sprinkle with ¼ cup sugar and cinnamon.

**3.** Cover and grill cobbler 5 to 6 inches from medium heat about 30 minutes or until toothpick inserted in center comes out clean.

**1 SERVING:** Calories 230 (Calories from Fat 80); Fat 9g (Saturated 2g); Cholesterol 2mg; Sodium 340mg; Carbohydrate 36g (Dietary Fiber 1g); Protein 2g

---

**COOKING TIP**

• After cobbler is baked, move it to the side of the grill to keep warm until ready to serve.

---

# $\mathcal{P}$OUND CAKE S'MORES

QUICK  Prep: 10 min; Grill: 3 min     4 servings

4  **slices pound cake, 1 inch thick**

20  **miniature marshmallows**

20  **semisweet chocolate chips**

**1.** Brush grill rack with vegetable oil. Heat coals or gas grill for direct heat (see page 144).

**2.** Make horizontal cut in side of each slice of cake, forming a pocket. Fill each pocket with 5 marshmallows and 5 chocolate chips.

**3.** Cover and grill cake 5 to 6 inches from medium heat 2 to 3 minutes, turning once, until golden brown.

**1 SERVING:** Calories 465 (Calories from Fat 245); Fat 27g (Saturated 12g); Cholesterol 115mg; Sodium 90mg; Carbohydrate 51g (Dietary Fiber 1g); Protein 6g

---

**COOKING TIP**

• This version of an old favorite is easy to prepare ahead so it's all ready to cook after the main course is grilled. You can vary the flavor by using different flavors of chips.

---

# Toasted Butter-Rum Pound Cake

**QUICK** Prep: 15 min; Grill: 5 min       8 servings

½ cup sour cream

2 tablespoons packed brown sugar

1 package (10¾ ounces) frozen pound cake

¼ cup rum

¼ cup (½ stick) margarine or butter, softened

½ cup sliced almonds

**1.** Brush grill rack with vegetable oil. Heat coals or gas grill for direct heat (see page 144).

**2.** Mix sour cream and brown sugar; set aside.

**3.** Cut frozen pound cake into 8 slices. For each side, sprinkle with rum, spread with margarine, then press almonds onto margarine. Place cake slices on grilling screen.

**4.** Grill cake uncovered 4 to 6 inches from medium heat about 5 minutes, turning once, until golden brown. To serve, top cake with sour cream mixture.

**1 SERVING:** Calories 295 (Calories from Fat 190); Fat 21g (Saturated 12g); Cholesterol 85mg; Sodium 140mg; Carbohydrate 23g (Dietary Fiber 1g); Protein 4g

# ANGEL FOOD POCKETS

**QUICK** Prep: 10 min; Grill: 2 min 4 servings

**4 slices angel food cake, 1½ inches thick**

**3 tablespoons marshmallow creme**

**1 tablespoon raspberry jam**

**1 tablespoon margarine or butter, melted**

**¼ cup semisweet chocolate chips**

**1.** Heat coals or gas grill for direct heat (see page 144).

**2.** Make horizontal cut in side of each slice of cake, forming a pocket. Mix marshmallow creme and jam; spoon 1 tablespoon mixture into each pocket. Brush both sides of cake with margarine. Place on grilling screen.

**3.** Grill cake uncovered 4 to 6 inches from medium heat 1 minute. Turn; top each slice with 1 tablespoon chocolate chips. Grill uncovered about 1 minute longer or until chocolate is softened. To serve, spread chocolate over tops of cake slices.

**1 SERVING:** Calories 240 (Calories from Fat 55); Fat 6g (Saturated 3g); Cholesterol 0mg; Sodium 390mg; Carbohydrate 44g (Dietary Fiber 1g); Protein 4g

## COOKING TIP

• In place of raspberry jam, use your favorite flavor of jam or preserves in these airy pockets.

# CINNAMON BALLOONS WITH CHOCOLATE SAUCE

Prep: 20 min; Grill: 15 min     5 servings

- 1 can (7½ ounces) refrigerated biscuit dough
- 10 large marshmallows
- ⅓ cup sugar
- ½ teaspoon ground cinnamon
- 2 tablespoons margarine or butter, melted
- ⅓ cup chocolate-flavored syrup

**1.** Heat coals or gas grill for direct heat (see page 144). Grease 9-inch round aluminum foil pan.

**2.** Roll or pat biscuit dough into ten 4-inch circles. Top each with 1 marshmallow. Fold dough around marshmallow to cover completely. Pinch seams to seal.

**3.** Mix sugar and cinnamon. Brush biscuits with margarine; roll in cinnamon-sugar. Place biscuits, seam sides down, in pan.

**4.** Cover and grill biscuits 4 to 6 inches from medium heat about 15 minutes or until light brown. To serve, drizzle biscuits with chocolate syrup. Serve immediately.

**1 SERVING:** Calories 335 (Calories from Fat 100); Fat 11g (Saturated 3g); Cholesterol 0mg; Sodium 590mg; Carbohydrate 57g (Dietary Fiber 1g); Protein 3g

# FLUFFY STRAWBERRY PIE

Prep: 30 min; Chill: 4 hr    8 servings

**Refrigerated pastry for 9-inch pie**
¾ **cup boiling water**
1 **package (4-serving size) strawberry-flavored gelatin**
1 **teaspoon grated lime peel**
½ **cup lime juice (2 limes)**
2 **cups whipping (heavy) cream**
1 **cup powdered sugar**
2 **cups strawberries, slightly crushed**

1. Prepare pastry according to package directions. Cool completely.

2. Pour boiling water on gelatin in large bowl; stir until gelatin is dissolved. Stir in lime peel and lime juice. Refrigerate about 1 hour or until very thick but not set.

3. Beat gelatin mixture with electric mixer on high speed about 4 minutes or until thick and fluffy.

4. Beat whipping cream and powdered sugar in chilled large bowl on high speed until stiff. Fold whipped cream and strawberries into gelatin mixture. Spread in pie crust. Refrigerate about 3 hours or until set. Store covered in refrigerator.

**1 SERVING:** Calories 440 (Calories from Fat 260); Fat 29g (Saturated 14g); Cholesterol 65mg; Sodium 200mg; Carbohydrate 42g (Dietary Fiber 2g); Protein 4g

# $\mathcal{K}$EY LIME PIE

Prep: 20 min; Chill: 30 min; Freeze: 6 hr; Stand: 5 min        8 servings

> **Crunchy Pretzel Crust (at right) or 1 package (6 ounces) ready-to-use graham cracker pie crust**
>
> 2 **packages (8 ounces each) cream cheese at room temperature**
>
> 1 **teaspoon grated lime peel**
>
> ½ **cup Key lime juice or regular lime juice**
>
> 1 **can (14 ounces) sweetened condensed milk**
>
> **Few drops of green food color, if desired**
>
> **Sweetened Whipped Cream (at right) or 1 cup frozen whipped topping, thawed**

**1.** Make Crunchy Pretzel Crust. While crust is chilling, continue with the recipe.

**2.** Beat cream cheese, lime peel, lime juice, milk and food color in a large bowl with electric mixer on medium speed about 1 minute or until smooth.

**3.** Pour lime mixture into crust. Cover and freeze about 6 hours or until filling is firm.

**4.** Let pie stand at room temperature about 5 minutes before cutting into slices. Make Sweetened Whipped Cream. Serve with pie. Cover and freeze any remaining pie.

**1 SERVING:** Calories 590 (Calories from Fat 335); Fat 37g (Saturated 18g); Cholesterol 85mg; Sodium 570mg; Carbohydrate 53g (Dietary Fiber 0g); Protein 11g

## CRUNCHY PRETZEL CRUST

**3 cups small pretzel twists (about 40)**
**½ cup (1 stick) margarine or butter, melted**
**¼ cup granulated sugar**

Place a few pretzels at a time in plastic bag. Seal bag, and crush pretzels into fine crumbs with rolling pin. You should have 1¼ cups of crumbs. Mix crumbs, margarine and sugar in medium bowl. Press firmly and evenly against bottom and side of pie pan. Cover and refrigerate about 30 minutes or until firm.

## SWEETENED WHIPPED CREAM

**½ cup whipping (heavy) cream**
**1 tablespoon granulated or powdered sugar**

Beat whipping cream and sugar in chilled medium bowl with electric mixer on high speed until stiff peaks form.

**CRUSHING PRETZELS**

Place a few pretzels at a time in a plastic bag. Seal bag, and crush pretzels into fine crumbs with rolling pin.

# PINK LEMONADE PIE

Prep: 30 min; Freeze: 4 hr        8 servings

1  **quart (4 cups) vanilla ice cream, softened**
1  **can (6 ounces) frozen pink lemonade concentrate, thawed**
1  **container (4 ounces) frozen whipped topping, thawed**
   **Few drops red food color, if desired**
1  **prepared graham cracker crust**

**1.** Mix ice cream, lemonade concentrate, whipped topping and food color in large bowl. Mound ice cream mixture in crust.

**2.** Freeze about 4 hours or until firm. Let stand at room temperature a few minutes before cutting. (If pie has been frozen for several hours or overnight, remove from freezer about 10 minutes before serving to soften slightly.) Store wrapped in freezer.

**1 SERVING:** Calories 345 (Calories from Fat 155); Fat 17g (Saturated 6g); Cholesterol 30mg; Sodium 250mg; Carbohydrate 45g (Dietary Fiber 0g); Protein 3g

*Yellow Lemonade Pie:* Replace pink lemonade concentrate with regular lemonade concentrate and add a few drops of yellow food color.

# $\mathcal{F}$ROSTY MARGARITA PIE

Prep: 20 min; Freeze: 6 hr     8 servings

**1   cup graham cracker crumbs (12 squares)**

**3   tablespoons powdered sugar**

**¼   cup frozen (thawed) margarita mix concentrate**

**1   pint (2 cups) lime sherbet, softened**

**⅓   cup frozen (thawed) margarita mix concentrate**

**3   tablespoons tequila, if desired**

**1   pint (2 cups) vanilla fat-free ice cream, softened**

**1.** Mix cracker crumbs and powdered sugar. Stir in ¼ cup margarita mix until crumbly. Press mixture firmly against bottom and side of pie plate, 9 × 1¼ inches.

**2.** Mix sherbet, ⅓ cup margarita mix and tequila in large bowl. Gently swirl in ice cream. Spoon mixture into crust; spread evenly. Cover and freeze 4 to 6 hours or until firm.

**1 SERVING:** Calories 200 (Calories from Fat 20); Fat 2g (Saturated 1g); Cholesterol 5mg; Sodium 105mg; Carbohydrate 45g (Dietary Fiber 2g); Protein 2g

# $\mathcal{B}$ANANA SPLIT
## ICE CREAM DESSERT

Prep: 15 min; Freeze: 2 hr 20 min; Stand: 15 min        15 servings

1½  **cups crushed reduced-fat graham crackers (24 squares)**

2  **tablespoons margarine or butter, melted**

2  **ripe medium bananas, mashed**

½  **teaspoon lemon juice**

1  **quart (4 cups) vanilla fat-free ice cream, softened**

¼  **cup hot fudge fat-free topping, warmed**

1½  **cups frozen fat-free whipped topping, thawed**

1  **package (10 ounces) frozen strawberries in light syrup, thawed**

**Fresh strawberries, if desired**

**Banana slices, if desired**

**1.** Spray bottom only of rectangular pan, 13 × 9 × 2 inches, with cooking spray. Mix crushed crackers and margarine until crumbly. Press in bottom of pan. Cover and freeze 20 minutes.

**2.** Mix bananas and lemon juice in medium bowl. Stir in ice cream. Beat with electric mixer on low speed about 30 seconds or until well blended. Spoon evenly over frozen crust. Drizzle hot fudge topping over ice cream mixture; swirl with tip of knife. Cover and freeze about 1 hour or until firm.

**3.** Mix whipped topping and strawberries until well blended. Spread over ice cream mixture. Cover and freeze at least 1 hour until firm.

**4.** Let stand at room temperature 15 minutes before serving. For servings, cut into 5 rows by 3 rows. Garnish with fresh strawberries, banana slices and additional hot fudge topping if desired.

**1 SERVING:** Calories 145 (Calories from Fat 25); Fat 3g (Saturated 1g); Cholesterol 0mg; Sodium 105mg; Carbohydrate 30g (Dietary Fiber 2g); Protein 2g

# $\mathcal{M}$UD PIE

Prep: 20 min; Chill: 30 min; Freeze: 3 hr        10 servings

18  chocolate sandwich cookies, finely crushed

3  tablespoons butter or stick margarine, melted (see tip)

1  quart (2 pints) coffee, chocolate or other flavor ice cream, slightly softened

1  cup hot fudge topping

¼  cup chopped almonds, toasted

Sweetened Whipped Cream (see page 189), if desired

**1.** Mix crushed cookies and butter until well blended. Press on bottom and up side of pie plate, 9 × 1¼ inches. Refrigerate 30 minutes.

**2.** Carefully spread ice cream evenly in crust. Freeze about 1 hour or until firm enough to spread with topping.

**3.** Spread hot fudge topping over top of pie. Sprinkle with almonds. Freeze about 2 hours or until firm. (If pie has been frozen for several hours or overnight, remove from freezer about 10 minutes before serving to soften slightly.) Top with Sweetened Whipped Cream. Store wrapped in freezer.

**1 SERVING:** Calories 395 (Calories from Fat 170); Fat 19g (Saturated 9g); Cholesterol 30mg; Sodium 225mg; Carbohydrate 48g (Dietary Fiber 2g); Protein 5g

---

**COOKING TIP**

• Use a margarine spread with at least 65% vegetable oil.

# Chocolate-Mint Mousse

Prep: 20 min; Freeze: 4 hr     8 servings

**2  cups whipping (heavy) cream**

**¼  cup crème de menthe**

**½  cup chocolate-flavored syrup**

**Baking cocoa, if desired**

**Chopped rectangular chocolate mints or crushed chocolate wafer cookies, if desired**

**1.** Beat whipping cream in a chilled large bowl with electric mixer on high speed until stiff peaks form.

**2.** Gently pour crème de menthe and chocolate syrup over whipped cream. To fold ingredients together, use a rubber spatula to cut down vertically through whipped cream, then slide the spatula across the bottom of the bowl and up the side, turning whipped cream over. Rotate bowl one-fourth turn, and repeat down-across-up motion. Continue mixing in this way just until ingredients are blended.

**3.** Spread whipped cream mixture into ungreased square pan. Cover and freeze at least 4 hours or until mousse is firm.

**4.** Sprinkle cocoa over top of mousse. (If you have a small strainer, place the cocoa in the strainer and shake it over mousse.) To serve, cut mousse into 4 rows by 2 rows. Garnish with chopped candies. Cover and freeze any remaining mousse.

**1 SERVING:** Calories 240 (Calories from Fat 170); Fat 19g (Saturated 12g); Cholesterol 65mg; Sodium 40mg; Carbohydrate 15g (Dietary Fiber 0g); Protein 2g

*Mocha Mousse:* Substitute coffee-flavored liqueur for the crème de menthe. Omit the crushed candies. Garnish each serving with a chocolate-covered coffee bean.

*Frozen Mousse Pie:* Spread the whipped cream mixture in a ready-to-use chocolate-flavored pie crust instead of spreading in the pan. Freeze as directed.

**FOLDING INGREDIENTS INTO WHIPPED CREAM**

To fold ingredients together, use a rubber spatula to cut down vertically through whipped cream, then slide spatula across bottom of bowl and up side, turning whipped cream over. Rotate bowl one-fourth turn, and repeat this down-across-up motion.

# MENUS FOR BACKYARD BARBECUES

## Snacks and Sweets

Orange-Almond Brie, **page 120**

Brandied Skewered Fruit, **page 179**

Pink Lemonade Pie, **page 190**

Old-Fashioned Lemonade, **page 110**

**SPECIAL TOUCH:** Fresh fruit and cheese are a great accompaniment to sweet treats. Add them to dessert plates or serve them on a separate platter.

## Sit-Down Dinner

Grilled Fish with Jicama Salsa, **page 143**

Sweet Potato Slices, **page 172**

Mud Pie, **page 193**

Sparkling Raspberry Tea, **page 112**

Coffee and tea

**SPECIAL TOUCH:** For a pretty centerpiece, fill a clear glass pitcher about ¾ full with water and drop in a clean bunch of carrots with tops and white or yellow fresh flowers (see page 112).

## Buffet-Style Party

Italian Zucchini Bites, **page 124**

Chicken and Summer Fruit Kabobs, **page 154**

Shrimp cocktail

Raw vegetable tray with dip

Key Lime Pie, **page 188**

Quick Cranberry Punch, **page 111**

**SPECIAL TOUCH:** When serving raw vegetables with a dip, line a basket with greens and place the vegetables in the greens in a decorative pattern.

## Small Gathering

Caesar Vegetable Dip, **page 114**

Italian Sausage–Spinach Pizza, **page 137**

Fresh Fruit with Honey–Poppy Seed Dressing, **page 165**

Chocolate-Mint Mousse, **page 194**

Wine and soft drinks

**SPECIAL TOUCH:** For evening gatherings, line your deck or patio with white holiday lights or tiki torches to add ambiance.

## For a Larger Crowd

Spinach Dip in Bread Bowl, **page 118**

*Spicy Cajun Grilled Chicken, **page 151**

Pasta salad

*Tangy Coleslaw, **page 166**

*Summer Cobbler, **page 183**

Vanilla ice cream

Tangy Citrus Punch, **page 111**

**SPECIAL TOUCH:** Belgian endive leaves make great dip scoopers. Keep them refrigerated, wrapped in a damp paper towel inside a plastic bag, for no more than a day or two.

## Last-Minute Meal

Grilled Honey-Mustard Pork Chops, **page 161**

Texas Toast, **page 125**

Bagged ready-to-eat green salad with bottled dressing

Rainbow sherbet

Iced tea with lemon slices

**SPECIAL TOUCH:** Instead of lemon slices, float lime or orange slices or maraschino cherries in iced tea.

*Double recipes that are marked with an asterisk.

# WEEKEND MEALS

Weekends are the perfect time for serving a meal that's special. Impress everyone with this assortment of easy, delicious dishes, and turn your meal into an event to remember!

◀ Spinach-Strawberry Salad (page 269)

# BEVERAGES

# CITRUS SPRITZERS

**QUICK** Prep: 5 min  8 servings

2 cups cold water

1 can (6 ounces) frozen orange juice concentrate, thawed

¾ cup frozen (thawed) grapefruit juice concentrate (from 12-ounce can)

1 bottle (1 liter) sparkling water, chilled

Ice

Orange slices, if desired

Fresh mint leaves, if desired

1. Mix cold water, orange juice concentrate, grapefruit juice concentrate and sparkling water in pitcher.

2. Serve over ice. Garnish each serving with an orange slice and mint leaf.

**1 SERVING:** Calories 80 (Calories from Fat 0); Fat 0g (Saturated 0g); Cholesterol 0mg; Sodium 10mg; Carbohydrate 19g (Dietary Fiber 0g); Protein 1g

**COOKING TIP**

• For an alcoholic version of this party drink, use one chilled bottle (750 ml) of champagne or sparkling white wine instead of the sparkling water.

**SERVING TIP**

• Add extra splash to these spritzers with minted ice cubes. Freeze fresh mint leaves in water in ice-cube trays.

## SPECIAL TOUCH

### Wine Glass ID Bracelets

You will need:

Wine glasses
Colored beads, buttons, small ornaments, or charms
Wire, ribbon or raffia

1. String the beads, buttons, or charms onto the wire.

2. Twist around glass stems.

**Note:** You can also use varied colors of rubber band as a quick on-hand solution.

## Knock-'em-Out Punch

For a finishing touch to your punch, try these delightful additions:

**Garnish punch glasses** with a slice of starfruit on the rim.

**Freeze fresh mint leaves** and whole cranberries in water in ice-cube trays and drop into the punch bowl.

**Make ice cubes** with juice instead of water. When the juice cubes melt, they won't dilute the punch. ◼

# $\mathcal{S}$PARKLING CRANBERRY PUNCH

Prep: 15 min; Freeze: 14 hr        24 servings

**Ice Ring (below), if desired, or ice cubes**
1    **can (12 ounces) frozen lemonade concentrate, thawed**
1½  **cups cold water**
1    **bottle (64 ounces) cranberry juice cocktail, chilled**
4    **cans (12 ounces each) ginger ale, chilled**

**1.** Make Ice Ring. Mix lemonade concentrate and cold water in pitcher. Stir in cranberry juice cocktail. Pour into punch bowl.

**2.** Just before serving, stir in ginger ale. Add ice ring or ice cubes.

**1 SERVING:** Calories 110 (Calories from Fat 0); Fat 0g (Saturated 0g); Cholesterol 0mg; Sodium 10mg; Carbohydrate 27g (Dietary Fiber 0g); Protein 0g

## ICE RING

**Sliced fruit, berries, strips of orange, lemon or lime peel and mint leaves**

**Water or fruit juice**

Choose a ring mold or Bundt cake pan that fits inside your punch bowl. For color, arrange sliced fruit, berries, strips of orange, lemon or lime peel and mint leaves in mold. Slowly add just enough water or fruit juice to partially cover fruit (too much water will make the fruit float); freeze. When frozen, add enough water or fruit juice to fill mold three-fourths full; freeze overnight or at least 12 hours to make sure ice ring is solid. Run hot water over bottom of mold to loosen ice ring. Carefully turn over mold and catch the ice ring as it slips from the mold. Place the ice ring in punch bowl fruit side up.

## SERVING TIPS

• If you don't have a punch bowl, mix all ingredients in a large mixing bowl, and serve punch in tall glasses filled with ice.

• When serving drinks at a buffet, it helps to set up a separate table for drinks, ice and glasses so guests can fill and refill their drinks without going back to the food table.

## UNMOLDING AN ICE RING

When ready to serve punch, run hot water over bottom of mold to loosen ice ring. Carefully turn over mold and catch the ice ring as it slips from the mold. Float ice ring in punch.

• Dress up these frosty drinks by rubbing a slice of lime around the rims of the margarita glasses to moisten, then dipping rims in plain or colored sugar.

# $\mathcal{F}$ROZEN STRAWBERRY MARGARITAS

Prep: 5 min; Freeze: 24 hr        10 servings

- ¾ **cup frozen limeade concentrate (from 12-ounce can), thawed**
- 1 **package (10 ounces) frozen strawberries in syrup, thawed**
- 3 **cups water**
- ¾ **cup tequila**
- 1 **bottle (1 liter) lemon-lime soda, chilled**

**1.** Place limeade concentrate and strawberries with syrup in blender. Cover and blend on medium speed about 30 seconds or until smooth.

**2.** Add water and tequila to strawberry mixture. Stir all ingredients until well mixed. Pour strawberry mixture into plastic container. Cover and freeze at least 24 hours, stirring occasionally, until mixture is slushy.

**3.** For each serving, place about ⅔ cup of slush mixture and about ⅓ cup soda pop in each glass. Stir until mixed.

**1 SERVING:** Calories 125 (Calories from Fat 0); Fat 0g (Saturated 0g); Cholesterol 0mg; Sodium 15mg; Carbohydrate 31g (Dietary Fiber 0g); Protein 0g

***Frozen Raspberry Margaritas:*** Substitute 1 package (10 ounces) frozen raspberries in syrup, thawed, for the strawberries.

## Ruffled Paper Baskets

**Heavy or thick decorative art paper**
**Large taco shell baking pan (7 to 8 inches in diameter)**
**Spray bottle filled with water**
**Tortilla chips, purchased snack mix or candies**

1. Cut art paper into 12-inch circles (circles should be about 2 inches wider than diameter of baking pan used).

2. Lightly spray paper with water. Place paper in baking pan, pressing into ridges; let stand until completely dry. (The art paper must be thick to hold its shape when dry. A little spray starch misted on the back of the paper before pressing it in the pan can help to make it stiffer.) Remove paper basket from pan.

3. Fill baskets with chips.

## COOKING TIPS

- A cooked egg custard rather than uncooked eggs is used to make this eggnog to avoid any food-safety problems associated with uncooked eggs.

- Leftover 'nog? Try blending equal parts fresh fruit and eggnog for a creamy brunchtime smoothie. Or, substitute eggnog for the milk in your favorite quick bread or cake recipe. Delicious! Leftover eggnog will keep, covered, for 2 days.

# Eggnog

Prep: 15 min; Cook: 15 min; Chill: 2 hr          10 servings

**Soft Custard (at right)**
1   **cup whipping (heavy) cream**
2   **tablespoons powdered sugar**
½   **teaspoon vanilla**
½   **cup light rum**
1 or 2   **drops yellow food color, if desired**
    **Ground nutmeg**

**1.** Prepare Soft Custard.

**2.** Just before serving, beat whipping cream, powdered sugar and vanilla in chilled medium bowl with electric mixer on high speed until stiff. Gently stir 1 cup of whipped cream mixture, the rum and food color into custard.

**3.** Pour custard mixture into small punch bowl. Drop remaining whipped cream in mounds onto custard mixture. Sprinkle with nutmeg. Serve immediately. Store covered in refrigerator for up to 2 days.

**1 SERVING (ABOUT ½ CUP):** Calories 155 (Calories from Fat 90); Fat 10g (Saturated 6g); Cholesterol 95mg; Sodium 55mg; Carbohydrate 12g (Dietary Fiber 0g); Protein 4g

## Eggnog Advice

Don't have time to make your own eggnog? You can dress up purchased eggnog instead. Here's the best way, plus some fun flavor variations:

**Place eggnog in a punch bowl** and stir in some rum, if desired, to taste.

**Scoop dollops of cinnamon** or French vanilla ice cream over the eggnog and sprinkle with freshly grated nutmeg.

**For coffee lovers,** make hot cappuccino eggnog. Substitute coffee liqueur for the rum and stir in 1 cup hot espresso coffee. Don't worry if you don't have brewed espresso coffee; any strongly brewed cup of coffee (regular or decaf) will do.

**Freeze small dollops of Sweetened Whipped Cream** (see page 189) by scooping them out onto a cookie sheet and freezing until firm. Keep them handy in a resealable plastic freezer bag. Place one dollop on each drink of eggnog just before serving and sprinkle lightly with ground cinnamon or nutmeg.

**Place plain or chocolate-dipped pirouette cookies** on a serving plate next to the punch bowl—guests can use them as edible stirrers. ∎

## SOFT CUSTARD

**3** large eggs, slightly beaten

**⅓** cup sugar

Dash of salt

**2½** cups milk

**1** teaspoon vanilla

Mix eggs, sugar and salt in heavy 2-quart saucepan. Gradually stir in milk. Cook over medium heat 10 to 15 minutes, stirring constantly, until mixture just coats a metal spoon; remove from heat. Stir in vanilla. Place saucepan in cold water until custard is cool. (If custard curdles, beat vigorously with hand beater until smooth.) Cover and refrigerate at least 2 hours but no longer than 24 hours.

**Nonalcoholic Eggnog:** Substitute 2 tablespoons rum extract and ⅓ cup milk for the rum.

**Lighter Eggnog:** For 4 grams of fat and 100 calories per serving, substitute 2 eggs plus 2 egg whites for the 3 eggs and 2¼ cups fat-free (skim) milk for the milk in the Soft Custard. Substitute 2 cups frozen (thawed) reduced-fat whipped topping for the beaten whipping cream, powdered sugar and vanilla.

# SANGRIA

**QUICK**   Prep: 10 min        8 servings

**⅔** cup lemon juice

**⅓** cup orange juice

**¼** cup sugar

**1** bottle (750 milliliters) dry red wine or nonalcoholic red wine

Lemon and orange slices, if desired

**1.** Strain juices into half-gallon glass pitcher. Stir sugar into juices until sugar is dissolved.

**2.** Stir wine into juice mixture. Add ice if desired. Garnish with lemon and orange slices.

**1 SERVING:** Calories 95 (Calories from Fat 0); Fat 0g (Saturated 0g); Cholesterol 0mg; Sodium 10mg; Carbohydrate 10g (Dietary Fiber 0g); Protein 0g

# APPETIZERS

## CHEESE FONDUE

Prep: 10 min; Cook: 30 min    5 servings

- 2 **cups shredded natural Swiss cheese (8 ounces)**
- 2 **cups shredded Gruyère cheese (8 ounces), see tip**
- 2 **tablespoons all-purpose flour**
- 1 **clove garlic, peeled and halved**
- 1 **cup dry white wine or nonalcoholic white wine**
- 1 **tablespoon lemon juice**
- 3 **tablespoons kirsch, dry sherry, brandy or nonalcoholic white wine**
- 1 **loaf (1 pound) French bread, cut into 1-inch pieces**

1. Place cheeses and flour in resealable plastic food-storage bag. Shake until cheese is coated with flour.

2. Rub garlic on bottom and side of fondue pot, heavy saucepan or skillet; discard garlic. Add wine. Heat over simmer setting or low heat just until bubbles rise to surface (do not boil). Stir in lemon juice.

3. Gradually add cheese mixture, about ½ cup at a time, stirring constantly with wooden spoon over low heat, until melted. Stir in kirsch.

4. Keep warm over simmer setting. If prepared in saucepan or skillet, pour into a fondue pot or heatproof serving bowl and keep warm over low heat. Fondue must be served over heat to maintain its smooth, creamy texture.

5. Spear bread with fondue forks; dip and swirl in fondue with stirring motion. If fondue becomes too thick, stir in ¼ to ½ cup heated wine.

**1 SERVING:** Calories 575 (Calories from Fat 245); Fat 27g (Saturated 16g); Cholesterol 80mg; Sodium 760mg; Carbohydrate 53g (Dietary Fiber 3g); Protein 33g

### COOKING TIPS

• You can substitute 2 cups shredded natural Swiss cheese (8 ounces) for the Gruyère cheese to total 4 cups Swiss cheese.

• Be patient when making cheese fondue, and allow each addition of cheese to completely melt into the wine before adding more.

# SIAGO CHEESE AND ARTICHOKE DIP

**QUICK**    Prep: 15 min; Bake: 15 min        16 servings

1 package (8 ounces) fat-free cream cheese

½ cup fat-free sour cream

2 tablespoons fat-free half-and-half or evaporated fat-free milk

¼ teaspoon salt

¾ cup shredded Asiago cheese (3 ounces)

1 can (14 ounces) artichoke hearts, drained and chopped

4 medium green onions, trimmed and chopped

2 tablespoons chopped fresh parsley

Crisp breadsticks or crackers, if desired

1. Heat oven to 350°. Beat cream cheese in medium bowl with electric mixer on medium speed until smooth. Beat in sour cream, half-and-half and salt. Stir in Asiago cheese, artichoke hearts and onions. Spoon into 1-quart casserole or small ovenproof serving dish.

2. Bake uncovered 10 to 15 minutes or until hot and cheese is melted. Remove from oven; stir. Sprinkle with parsley. Serve with breadsticks.

**1 SERVING (2 TABLESPOONS):** Calories 45 (Calories from Fat 10); Fat 1g (Saturated 0g); Cholesterol 0mg; Sodium 220mg; Carbohydrate 5g (Dietary Fiber 1g); Protein 5g

# BAKED BRIE WITH SUN-DRIED TOMATOES

**QUICK**    Bake: 10 min        Makes 8 servings

1   **round or wedge (8 ounces) Brie cheese (with herbs or plain)**

1   **tablespoon pine nuts, toasted (see page 99)**

3   **tablespoons julienne strips sun-dried tomatoes packed in oil and herbs (from 8-ounce jar)**

1   **tablespoon chopped fresh basil leaves, if desired**
    **Crackers, if desired**

**1.** Heat oven to 350°.

**2.** Lightly brush a round pan with vegetable oil. Do not peel the white rind from the cheese. Place the cheese in center of pan. Bake uncovered 8 to 10 minutes, or until cheese is warm and soft but not runny. (Or place cheese on a microwaveable plate and microwave uncovered on high about 40 seconds.)

**3.** Remove cheese from oven. Carefully move cheese to serving plate using wide spatula or pancake turner. Sprinkle toasted nuts, tomatoes and basil over cheese. Serve with crackers.

**1 SERVING:** Calories 100 (Calories from Fat 70); Fat 8g (Saturated 4g); Cholesterol 20mg; Sodium 250mg; Carbohydrate 1g (Dietary Fiber 0g); Protein 6g

***Baked Brie with Cranberries and Pistachios:*** Omit the pine nuts, tomatoes and basil. Spread ¼ cup whole berry cranberry sauce over the warm cheese. Sprinkle with 1 tablespoon chopped pistachio nuts.

## COOKING TIPS

• To make your own Jerk seasoning, mix ¹/₂ teaspoon ground allspice, ¹/₂ teaspoon garlic powder and ¹/₂ teaspoon dried thyme leaves. Add ¹/₈ teaspoon each of ground red pepper (cayenne), salt and sugar.

• To save time, purchase already peeled mango and papaya slices available in jars in the produce section of your supermarket.

# JAMAICAN SHRIMP

Prep: 20 min; Refrigerate: 1 hr          About 60 servings

**1** can (4 ounces) chopped jalapeño chilies, drained
**3** tablespoons lime juice
**2** tablespoons honey
**2** teaspoons Jerk seasoning
**2** pounds cooked, peeled and cleaned large shrimp
**1** medium mango or 2 medium peaches
**1** medium papaya

**1.** Make a marinade by mixing chilies, lime juice, honey and Jerk seasoning. Stir in shrimp until coated. Cover and refrigerate 1 hour, stirring occasionally. While shrimp are marinating, continue with recipe.

2. Cut mango lengthwise in half, sliding a sharp knife along flat side of seed on one side. Repeat on other side, which will give you two large pieces plus seed. Cut away any flesh from seed. Make lengthwise and crosswise cuts, ½ inch apart, in flesh of each mango half in a crisscross pattern. Be careful not to cut through the peel. Turn each mango half inside out, and cut off mango pieces.

3. Cut papaya lengthwise in half and scoop out seeds using a spoon. Remove peel and cut papaya into ½-inch pieces.

4. Add mango and papaya to shrimp. Mix all ingredients. Serve with toothpicks.

**1 SERVING:** Calories 15 (Calories from Fat 0); Fat 0g (Saturated 0g); Cholesterol 15mg; Sodium 20mg; Carbohydrate 2g (Dietary Fiber 0g); Protein 2g

**CUTTING A MANGO**

Cut mango lengthwise in half, sliding a knife along flat side of seed on one side. Repeat on other side. Cut away any flesh from seed. Cut a crisscross pattern in flesh of each mango half, being careful not to cut through peel. Turn each mango half inside out; cut off mango pieces.

# Shopping for Shrimp

Shrimp cocktail always goes fast at any party—so fast that it's easy to run out before all your guests have had a chance to sample it. This chart will help ensure that you'll always have enough. Shrimp may have descriptive market names, such as "jumbo" or "large," but they're usually sold by count, or number per pound. In general, the smaller the shrimp, the higher the count per pound; the larger the shrimp, the lower the count—and higher the price. Because the market names can vary, look over the sizes, ask the fish manager for suggestions and buy shrimp by the count.

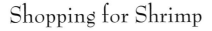

| Shrimp Market Name | Count (Number) Per Pound of Raw Shrimp in Shells |
| --- | --- |
| Super/extra Colossal | Less than 10 |
| Super/extra Jumbo | 16 to 20 |
| Jumbo | 21 to 25 |
| Extra Large | 26 to 30 |
| Large | 31 to 35 |
| Medium Large | 36 to 40 |
| Medium | 41 to 45 |
| Small | 51 to 60 |
| Extra Small to Tiny | 61 to 100 |

**CUTTING A PAPAYA**

Cut papaya lengthwise in half and scoop out seeds using a spoon. Remove peel, using a sharp knife. Cut papaya into ½-inch pieces.

## COOKING TIP

• For a pretty garnish, mix ¼ cup chopped fresh parsley, 2 tablespoons finely chopped red onion, 2 teaspoons capers and 1 teaspoon grated lemon peel. Sprinkle the parsley mixture over top of salmon. Garnish with quartered lemon slices.

# 𝒫OACHED SALMON APPETIZER

Prep: 10 min; Cook: 10 min; Chill: 2 hr        8 servings

1    **small lemon**
1    **small onion**
4    **cups water**
¼    **cup small parsley sprigs**
½    **teaspoon salt**
¼    **teaspoon coarsely ground pepper**
1    **pound salmon fillet**
     **Honey-Mustard Sauce (at right)**
¼    **teaspoon salt**
     **Cocktail bread slices or crackers, if desired**

**1.** Cut lemon crosswise in half. Cut one half into ¼-inch slices. Wrap remaining half in plastic wrap, and refrigerate for another use. Peel onion and cut in half. Cut one half into ¼-inch slices. Wrap remaining half in plastic wrap, and refrigerate for another use.

**2.** Add lemon slices, onion slices, water, parsley sprigs, ½ teaspoon salt and the pepper to 12-inch skillet. Heat to boiling over high heat. Boil 3 minutes, stirring occasionally.

**3.** Reduce the heat to medium-low. Add salmon, with skin side down, to skillet. Cover and cook 5 to 6 minutes or until salmon flakes easily with fork.

**4.** Remove salmon from liquid in skillet, using a slotted spatula. Discard liquid from skillet. Cool salmon completely.

**5.** Cover salmon with plastic wrap and refrigerate at least 2 hours but no longer than 24 hours. While salmon is chilling, prepare Honey-Mustard Sauce.

**6.** Carefully remove skin from salmon. Place salmon on serving plate. Sprinkle with ¼ teaspoon salt. Drizzle sauce over salmon. Serve with bread slices.

**1 SERVING:** Calories 105 (Calories from Fat 45); Fat 5g (Saturated 1g); Cholesterol 30mg; Sodium 220mg; Carbohydrate 4g (Dietary Fiber 0g); Protein 11g

## HONEY-MUSTARD SAUCE

    **2  tablespoons lemon juice**

    **1  tablespoon honey**

    **1  tablespoon Dijon mustard**

    **1  tablespoon olive or vegetable oil**

Stir all ingredients until well mixed.

## SPECIAL TOUCH

### Glitter and Bead Vase

You will need:

    **Clear glass vase (any size)**

    **Spray adhesive or glue**

    **Fine or ultra-fine glitter or small glitter beads**

    **Optional: Round self-adhesive stickers**

1. Clean vase, and dry thoroughly.

2. Cover work surface with newspaper. Spray one side of the vase with adhesive. Sprinkle glitter onto vase while vase is still wet. Shake off excess glitter. Repeat with other side of vase. If using beads, brush all sides of vase with glue. Roll vase in beads.

3. Let stand until vase is completely dry and glitter is set.

*Optional:* To make a polka dot vase, place round stickers onto clean vase. Then spray and apply glitter.

# EASY SALMON PÂTÉ

Prep: 15 min; Chill: 2 hr        16 servings

**1    package (8 ounces) fat-free cream cheese, softened**

**1    can (14¾ ounces) red or pink salmon, drained and flaked**

**3    tablespoons finely chopped red onion**

**2    tablespoons chopped fresh or ¼ teaspoon dried dill weed**

**1    tablespoon Dijon mustard**

**2    tablespoons capers**

**Assorted crackers or pumpernickel cocktail bread, if desired**

**1.** Line 2-cup bowl or mold with plastic wrap. Beat cream cheese in medium bowl with electric mixer on medium speed until smooth. Stir in salmon, 2 tablespoons of the onion, 1 tablespoon of the dill weed and the mustard. Spoon into bowl lined with plastic wrap, pressing firmly. Cover and refrigerate at least 2 hours but no longer than 24 hours.

**2.** Turn upside down onto serving plate; remove bowl and plastic wrap. Garnish pâté with remaining 1 tablespoon onion, 1 tablespoon dill weed and the capers. Serve with crackers.

**1 SERVING (2 TABLESPOONS):** Calories 50 (Calories from Fat 20); Fat 2g (Saturated 0g); Cholesterol 10mg; Sodium 240mg; Carbohydrate 1g (Dietary Fiber 0g); Protein 7g

# ITALIAN STUFFED MUSHROOMS

Prep: 15 min; Cook: 5 min; Bake: 15 min; Broil: 2 min        36 mushrooms

- 36 **medium mushrooms (about 1 pound)**
- 2 **tablespoons margarine or butter**
- 4 **medium green onions with tops, trimmed and thinly sliced**
- ½ **small red bell pepper, chopped**
- 2 **slices bread, torn into small pieces**
- 2 **teaspoons chopped fresh or ½ teaspoon dried oregano leaves**
- ¼ **teaspoon salt**
- ¼ **teaspoon pepper**
   **Grated Parmesan cheese, if desired**

1. Move oven racks so one is in middle of oven and one is near broiler so tops of mushrooms will be 3 to 4 inches from heat. Heat oven to 350°.

2. Twist mushroom stems to remove from caps. Set aside mushroom caps. Finely chop enough of the mushroom stems to measure ⅓ cup.

3. Melt margarine in skillet over medium-high heat. Cook mushroom stems, onions and bell pepper in margarine about 3 minutes, stirring frequently, until onions are softened.

4. Remove skillet from heat. Stir bread into vegetable mixture in skillet. Stir in oregano, salt and pepper.

5. Fill mushroom caps with bread crumb mixture. Place mushrooms, filled sides up, in ungreased baking pan. Sprinkle with cheese. Bake uncovered on middle oven rack 15 minutes. Set oven control to broil. Move pan to top oven rack. Broil about 2 minutes or until tops are light brown. Serve hot.

**1 MUSHROOM:** Calories 20 (Calories from Fat 10); Fat 1g (Saturated 0g); Cholesterol 0mg; Sodium 30mg; Carbohydrate 2g (Dietary Fiber 0g); Protein 1g

**COOKING TIP**

• To make ahead, stuff mushrooms, then cover and refrigerate up to 24 hours before baking. Heat oven to 350°, and continue as directed in step 5.

**FILLING MUSHROOM CAPS**

Fill mushroom caps with bread crumb mixture. Using a small melon baller is an easy way to fill the caps.

**BROILING BELL PEPPERS**

Broil peppers with tops about 5 inches from heat 5 to 7 minutes, turning occasionally, until the skin is blistered and evenly browned but not burned.

# Marinated Peppers, Olives and Cheese

Prep: 15 min; Broil: 7 min; Stand: 20 min; Chill: 4 hr        10 servings

- **6  large red, yellow or green bell peppers**
- **1  cup whole Greek or pitted ripe olives**
- **4  ounce block mozzarella or provolone cheese (1 cup), cut into ½-inch cubes**
- **2  large cloves garlic, peeled and finely chopped**
- **¼  cup olive or vegetable oil**
- **¼  cup lemon juice**
- **2  tablespoons chopped fresh parsley**
- **1  teaspoon chopped fresh or ¼ teaspoon dried oregano leaves**
- **1  teaspoon chopped fresh or ¼ teaspoon dried basil leaves**
- **½  teaspoon salt**
- **⅛  teaspoon pepper**

1. Move oven rack so tops of peppers will be about 5 inches from broiler. Set oven control to broil.

2. Place peppers on rack in broiler pan or directly on oven rack. Broil 5 to 7 minutes, turning occasionally, until skin is blistered and evenly browned but not burned. Place peppers in resealable plastic food-storage bag and close tightly. Let stand 20 minutes.

3. Peel skin from peppers, using a paring knife or your fingers, and remove stems, seeds and membranes. Cut each pepper into ½-inch pieces. Place in bowl.

4. Add olives and cheese to bowl.

5. Place garlic, oil, lemon juice, parsley, oregano, basil, salt and pepper in tightly covered container. Shake well to mix ingredients, and pour over pepper mixture. Gently stir mixture.

6. Cover and refrigerate at least 4 hours, stirring occasionally.

**1 SERVING:** Calories 95 (Calories from Fat 70); Fat 8g (Saturated 3g); Cholesterol 10mg; Sodium 320mg; Carbohydrate 6g (Dietary Fiber 2g); Protein 2g

# $\mathcal{B}$LACK BEAN—CORN WONTON CUPS

**QUICK**   Prep: 20 min; Bake: 10 min        36 wonton cups

- 36 **wonton skins**
- 1 **can (15¼ ounces) whole kernel corn, drained**
- 1 **can (15 ounces) black beans, rinsed and drained**
- ⅔ **cup thick-and-chunky salsa**
- ¼ **cup chopped fresh cilantro**
- ½ **teaspoon ground cumin**
- ½ **teaspoon chili powder**
- ¼ **cup plus 2 tablespoons fat-free sour cream**
- **Fresh cilantro sprigs, if desired**

1. Heat oven to 350°. Gently fit 1 wonton skin into each of 36 small muffin cups, 1¾ × 1 inch. Bake 8 to 10 minutes or until light golden brown. Remove from pan; cool on wire racks.

2. Mix remaining ingredients except sour cream and cilantro sprigs. Just before serving, spoon bean mixture into wonton cups. Top each with ½ teaspoon sour cream and the cilantro sprigs.

**1 WONTON CUP:** Calories 45 (Calories from Fat 0); Fat 0g (Saturated 0g); Cholesterol 5mg; Sodium 90mg; Carbohydrate 10g (Dietary Fiber 1g) Protein 2g

# $\mathcal{S}$UN-DRIED TOMATO BISCOTTI WITH BASIL–CREAM CHEESE TOPPING

Prep: 20 min; Bake: 50 min; Cool: 30 min    32 servings

¼ **cup sun-dried tomato halves (not oil-packed)**

½ **cup fat-free cholesterol-free egg product or 2 eggs**

3 **tablespoons olive or vegetable oil**

2 **cups all-purpose flour**

¼ **cup sugar**

2 **teaspoons baking powder**

¼ **teaspoon salt**

⅛ **teaspoon garlic powder**

**Dash of ground red pepper (cayenne)**

**Basil–Cream Cheese Topping (below)**

¼ **cup crumbled chèvre (goat) cheese (1 ounce)**

**1.** Heat oven to 350°. Pour enough boiling water over dried tomatoes to cover. Let stand 5 minutes; drain, reserving 2 tablespoons liquid. Finely chop tomatoes.

**2.** Mix egg product, oil and reserved tomato liquid until well blended. Stir in flour, sugar, baking powder, salt, garlic powder and red pepper. Stir in tomatoes. Divide dough in half. Shape each half into rectangle, 10 × 3 inches, on ungreased cookie sheet.

**3.** Bake 25 to 30 minutes or until golden brown. Cool on cookie sheet 10 minutes. Cut crosswise into ½-inch slices. Turn slices cut-side down on cookie sheet.

**4.** Bake 10 minutes. Turn biscotti. Bake about 10 minutes longer or until crisp and golden brown. Remove from cookie sheet to wire rack. Cool completely, about 30 minutes.

**5.** Spread each biscotti with about ½ teaspoon Basil–Cream Cheese Topping. Sprinkle with about ½ teaspoon chèvre cheese.

**1 SERVING:** Calories 60 (Calories from Fat 20); Fat 2g (Saturated 1g); Cholesterol 5mg; Sodium 90mg; Carbohydrate 8g (Dietary Fiber 0g); Protein 2g

## BASIL–CREAM CHEESE TOPPING

4 **ounces reduced-fat cream cheese (Neufchâtel), softened**

2 **tablespoons chopped fresh or ½ teaspoon dried basil leaves**

**Dash of garlic powder**

Mix all ingredients until smooth.

# BREADS

## COOKING TIP

• Embellish these scones by sprinkling with coarse decorating sugar crystals or granulated sugar before you bake them.

## SERVING TIP

• Serve these scones on a cake platter with clusters of sugared champagne grapes. To sugar the grapes, brush them with a little corn syrup and lightly sprinkle with granulated sugar.

# $\mathcal{L}$EMON–POPPY SEED SCONES

Prep: 15 min; Bake: 18 min      8 scones

1¾  cups all-purpose flour
¼  cup sugar
2  teaspoons baking powder
¼  teaspoon salt
⅓  cup margarine or butter
   Grated peel of 1 medium lemon (1½ to 3 teaspoons)
1  tablespoon poppy seeds
1  egg
¼  cup half-and-half

1. Heat oven to 400°.

2. Mix flour, sugar, baking powder and salt in medium bowl. Cut margarine into flour mixture, using pastry blender or crisscrossing 2 knives, until mixture looks like fine crumbs.

3. Stir in lemon peel, poppy seed, egg and half-and-half just until mixed and a dough forms. If the dough mixture is not completely moistened, stir in an additional 1 to 2 tablespoons half-and-half.

4. Place dough on lightly floured surface. Gently roll dough in flour to coat all sides. Shape dough into ball. Knead dough by curving your fingers around and folding dough toward you, then pushing it away with heels of your hands, using quick rocking motion. Repeat 10 times, turning dough each time.

5. Place dough on ungreased cookie sheet. Pat dough into 8-inch circle. Cut dough into 8 wedges, but do not separate.

6. Bake 16 to 18 minutes or until golden brown. Carefully separate wedges. Transfer scones to wire rack to cool slightly. Serve warm.

**1 SCONE:** Calories 225 (Calories from Fat 90); Fat 10g (Saturated 6g); Cholesterol 50mg; Sodium 360mg; Carbohydrate 31g (Dietary Fiber 1g); Protein 4g

**Golden Almond Scones:** Omit lemon peel and poppy seeds. Stir in ¼ cup chopped almonds with the egg and half-and-half in step 3. Brush tops of scones with melted margarine, and sprinkle with sliced almonds before baking.

**Cherry-Chip Scones:** Omit lemon peel and poppy seeds. Stir in ⅓ cup chopped dried cherries and ⅓ cup white baking chips with the egg and half-and-half in step 3.

# CURRY RICE DINNER ROLLS

Prep: 15 min; Cycle time; Rest: 10 min; Rise: 40 min; Bake: 20 min    10 rolls

⅔ **cup water**

1 **tablespoon vegetable oil**

2 **cups bread flour**

½ **cup cooked brown rice room temperature or cold**

1 **teaspoon salt**

¾ **teaspoon sugar**

½ **teaspoon curry powder**

1 **teaspoon bread machine or quick active dry yeast**

**Margarine or butter, melted**

1. Measure carefully, placing all ingredients except margarine in bread machine pan in the order recommended by the manufacturer.

2. Select Dough/Manual cycle. Do not use Delay cycles.

3. Remove dough from pan, using lightly floured hands. Knead 5 minutes on lightly floured surface. Cover and let rest 10 minutes.

4. Grease large cookie sheet. Divide dough into 10 equal pieces. Shape each piece into a ball. Place 2 inches apart on cookie sheet. Brush with margarine. Cover and let rise in warm place 30 to 40 minutes or until double. (Dough is ready if indentation remains when touched.)

5. Heat oven to 375°. Bake 15 to 20 minutes or until golden brown. Serve warm, or cool on wire rack.

**1 ROLL:** Calories 160 (Calories from Fat 55); Fat 6g (Saturated 1g); Cholesterol 0mg; Sodium 280mg; Carbohydrate 24g (Dietary Fiber 1g); Protein 3g

## COOKING TIPS

• You'll have better results using cold or room-temperature rice instead of hot cooked rice. Cook the brown rice ahead and cool to room temperature or refrigerate. To cool the rice quickly, spread it out on a cookie sheet or large plate before you refrigerate it. This recipe is also a good way to use any leftover rice you might have on hand.

• To make this recipe ahead, after you have shaped the dough into rolls and placed them on the cookie sheet, cover with plastic wrap. You can refrigerate them from 4 hours up to 48 hours. Before baking, remove the rolls from the refrigerator and remove plastic wrap. Cover with kitchen towel and let rise in a warm place about 2 hours or until double. Bake the rolls as the recipe tells you.

**COOKING TIP**

• For a quicker bread fix-up, spread cheese mixture on French bread slices and place slices, cheese sides up, on the rack in a broiler pan. Broil with tops 2 to 3 inches from heat 1 to 2 minutes or until cheese is melted.

# $\mathcal{H}$OT CHEESE BREAD

**QUICK**    Prep: 5 min; Bake: 20 min        1 loaf (24 slices)

½  **cup (1 stick) margarine or butter at room temperature**

¼  **cup crumbled blue cheese (1 ounce)**

¼  **cup shredded mozzarella cheese (1 ounce)**

1  **loaf (1 pound) French bread**

**1.** Heat oven to 350°.

**2.** Mix margarine, blue cheese and mozzarella cheese.

**3.** Cut bread horizontally in half. Spread cheese mixture over cut sides of bread. Reassemble loaf. Cut bread crosswise into 1-inch slices. Reassemble loaf and wrap securely in heavy-duty aluminum foil.

**4.** Bake about 20 minutes or until cheese is melted. Serve hot.

**1 SLICE:** Calories 180 (Calories from Fat 90); Fat 10g (Saturated 6g); Cholesterol 25mg; Sodium 320mg; Carbohydrate 19g (Dietary Fiber 1g); Protein 5g

**ASSEMBLING LOAF OF BREAD**

Spread cheese mixture over cut sides of bread. Reassemble loaf. Cut bread crosswise into 1-inch slices. Reassemble loaf, and wrap securely in heavy-duty aluminum foil.

**BREAD MACHINE**

# Mediterranean Herbed Bread

Prep: 10 min; Cycle time

### 1½-pound recipe (12 slices)

- 1 cup plus 1 cup water
- 1 tablespoon margarine or butter, softened
- 3 cups bread flour
- 2 tablespoons sugar
- 1 tablespoon dry milk
- 1½ teaspoons salt
- 1 teaspoon chopped fresh basil leaves
- 1 teaspoon chopped fresh oregano leaves
- 1 teaspoon chopped fresh thyme leaves
- 2¼ teaspoons bread machine or quick active dry yeast

### 2-pound recipe (16 slices)

- 1 cup plus 3 tablespoons water
- 1 tablespoon margarine or butter, softened
- 4 cups bread flour
- 2 tablespoons sugar
- 1 tablespoon dry milk
- 1¾ teaspoons salt
- 1½ teaspoons chopped fresh basil leaves
- 1½ teaspoons chopped fresh oregano leaves
- 1 teaspoon chopped fresh thyme leaves
- 2¼ teaspoons bread machine or quick active dry yeast

**1.** Make 1½-pound recipe with bread machines that use 3 cups flour, or make 2-pound recipe with bread machines that use 4 cups flour.

**2.** Measure carefully, placing all ingredients in bread machine pan in the order recommended by the manufacturer.

**3.** Select Basic/White cycle. Use Medium or Light crust color. Remove baked bread from pan, and cool on wire rack.

**1 SLICE:** Calories 135 (Calories from Fat 10); Fat 1g (Saturated 0g); Cholesterol 0mg; Sodium 300mg; Carbohydrate 29g (Dietary Fiber 1g); Protein 4g

### COOKING TIPS

- The same amount of yeast is needed for both the 1½-pound and 2-pound loaves.

- You can substitute dried herbs when fresh herbs aren't available. For the 1½-pound loaf, use ½ teaspoon each of dried basil, oregano and thyme leaves; for the 2-pound loaf, use ¾ teaspoon of each.

## COOKING TIP

• If your bread machine doesn't have a Raisin/Nut signal, add the tomatoes 5 to 10 minutes before the last kneading cycle ends. Check your bread machine's use-and-care book to find out how long the last cycle runs.

**BREAD MACHINE**

# Parmesan Sun-Dried Tomato Bread

Prep: 10 min; Cycle time

### 1½-pound recipe (12 slices)

- 1 cup plus 2 tablespoons water
- 3 cups bread flour
- ½ cup shredded Parmesan cheese
- 1½ cloves crushed garlic
- 2 tablespoons sugar
- 1 teaspoon salt
- 1½ teaspoons dried oregano leaves
- 2 teaspoons bread machine or quick active dry yeast
- ⅓ cup drained and coarsely chopped sun-dried tomatoes (packed in oil)

### 2-pound recipe (16 slices)

- 1¼ cups water
- 4 cups bread flour
- ¾ cup shredded Parmesan cheese
- 2 cloves crushed garlic
- 3 tablespoons sugar
- 1¼ teaspoons salt
- 2¼ teaspoons dried oregano leaves
- 2¼ teaspoons bread machine or quick active dry yeast
- ⅔ cup drained and coarsely chopped sun-dried tomatoes (packed in oil)

**1.** Make 1½-pound recipe with bread machines that use 3 cups flour, or make 2-pound recipe with bread machines that use 4 cups flour.

**2.** Measure carefully, placing all ingredients except tomatoes in bread machine pan in the order recommended by the manufacturer. Add tomatoes at the Raisin/Nut signal.

**3.** Select Basic/White cycle. Use Medium or Light crust color. Do not use delay cycles. Remove baked bread from pan, and cool on wire rack.

**1 SLICE:** Calories 150 (Calories from Fat 20); Fat 2g (Saturated 1g); Cholesterol 5mg; Sodium 270mg; Carbohydrate 29g (Dietary Fiber 1g); Protein 5g

**BREAD MACHINE**

# $\mathcal{D}$ILL WHEAT BREAD

Prep: 10 min; Cycle time

**COOKING TIP**

• The same amount of yeast is needed for both the 1½-pound and 2-pound loaves.

| 1½-pound recipe (12 slices) | 2-pound recipe (16 slices) |
|---|---|
| 1 cup water | 1¼ cups water |
| 2 tablespoons honey | 2 tablespoons honey |
| 2 tablespoons margarine or butter, softened | 2 tablespoons margarine or butter, softened |
| 2 cups bread flour | 2¼ cups bread flour |
| 1½ cups whole wheat flour | 1⅔ cups whole wheat flour |
| 2 tablespoons dry milk | 2 tablespoons dry milk |
| 1 teaspoon salt | 1¼ teaspoons salt |
| 1 teaspoon dried dill weed | 1½ teaspoons dried dill weed |
| 1 teaspoon caraway seeds | 1½ teaspoons caraway seeds |
| 2 teaspoons bread machine or quick active dry yeast | 2 teaspoons bread machine or quick active dry yeast |

1. Make 1½-pound recipe with bread machines that use at least 3 cups flour, or make 2-pound recipe with bread machines that use 4 cups flour.

2. Measure carefully, placing all ingredients in bread machine pan in the order recommended by the manufacturer.

3. Select Whole Wheat or Basic/White cycle. Use Medium or Light crust color. Do not use delay cycles. Remove baked bread from pan, and cool on wire rack.

**1 SLICE:** Calories 165 (Calories from Fat 25); Fat 3g (Saturated 1g); Cholesterol 0mg; Sodium 220mg; Carbohydrate 32g (Dietary Fiber 2g); Protein 5g

**BREAD MACHINE**

# TRIPLE-SEED WHEAT BREAD

Prep: 10 min; Cycle time; Rise: 40 min; Bake: 25 min       1 loaf, 16 slices

- 1 cup plus 1 tablespoon water
- 2 tablespoons margarine or butter, softened
- 1½ cups bread flour
- 1½ cups whole wheat flour
- 2 tablespoons sugar
- 1½ teaspoons salt
- 1½ teaspoons poppy seeds
- 1½ teaspoons sesame seeds
- 1 teaspoon fennel seeds
- 2 teaspoons bread machine or quick active dry yeast
- 1 egg white, beaten
- 1 teaspoon poppy seeds
- 1 teaspoon sesame seeds
- 1 teaspoon fennel seeds

**1.** Measure carefully, placing all ingredients except egg white and 1 teaspoon each poppy seeds, sesame seeds and fennel seeds in bread machine pan in the order recommended by the manufacturer.

**2.** Select Dough/Manual cycle. Do not use Delay cycles.

**3.** Remove dough from pan, using lightly floured hands. Cover and let rest 10 minutes on lightly floured surface.

**4.** Grease large cookie sheet. Roll dough into 20-inch rope. Place on cookie sheet. Curl each end of rope in the opposite direction to form a coiled "S" shape. Cover and let rise in warm place 30 to 40 minutes or until almost double.

**5.** Heat oven to 375°. Brush egg white over loaf; sprinkle with 1 teaspoon each poppy seeds, sesame seeds and fennel seeds. Bake 20 to 25 minutes or until loaf is golden brown and sounds hollow when tapped. Remove from cookie sheet to wire rack; cool.

**1 SLICE:** Calories 100 (Calories from Fat 20); Fat 2g (Saturated 0g); Cholesterol 0mg; Sodium 240mg; Carbohydrate 19g (Dietary Fiber 2g); Protein 3g

# CARAMELIZED ONION BREAD

Prep: 15 min; Cook: 15 min; Cycle time

| 1½-pound recipe (12 slices) | 2-pound recipe (16 slices) |
|---|---|
| ½ cup **Caramelized Onions** (below) | ⅔ cup **Caramelized Onions** (below) |
| 1 **cup water** | 1¼ **cups water** |
| 1 **tablespoon olive or vegetable oil** | 1 **tablespoon olive or vegetable oil** |
| 3 **cups bread flour** | 4 **cups bread flour** |
| 2 **tablespoons sugar** | 2 **tablespoons sugar** |
| 1 **teaspoon salt** | 1 **teaspoon salt** |
| 1¼ **teaspoons bread machine or quick active dry yeast** | 1½ **teaspoons bread machine or quick active dry yeast** |

**1.** Make 1½-pound recipe with bread machines that use 3 cups flour, or make 2-pound recipe with bread machines that use 4 cups flour.

**2.** Prepare Caramelized Onions.

**3.** Measure carefully, placing all ingredients except onions in bread machine pan in the order recommended by the manufacturer. Add onions at the Raisin/Nut signal.

**4.** Select Basic/White cycle. Use Medium or Light crust color. Do not use Delay cycles. Remove baked bread from pan, and cool on wire rack.

**1 SLICE:** Calories 150 (Calories from Fat 10); Fat 1g (Saturated 1g); Cholesterol 0mg; Sodium 320mg; Carbohydrate 31g (Dietary Fiber 1g); Protein 5g

## CARAMELIZED ONIONS

1 **tablespoon margarine or butter**

2 **medium onions, peeled and sliced**

Melt margarine in 10-inch skillet over medium-low heat. Cook onions in margarine 10 to 15 minutes, stirring occasionally, until onions are brown and caramelized; remove from heat.

---

## COOKING TIPS

• If your bread machine doesn't have a Raisin/Nut signal, add the caramelized onions 5 to 10 minutes before the last kneading cycle ends. Check your bread machine's use-and-care book to find out how long the last cycle runs.

• The onions need to cook slowly, so the natural sugar in them can caramelize and develop that delicious delicate sweet flavor. So be patient, and don't increase the heat to make the onions brown more quickly.

# COTTAGE DILL LOAF

Prep: 20 min; Cycle time; Rise: 45 min; Bake: 30 min          1 loaf, 16 slices

1 **cup water**

1 **tablespoon margarine or butter, softened**

½ **cup small curd creamed cottage cheese**

3½ **cups bread flour**

1 **tablespoon sugar**

1 **tablespoon dill seed**

1 **tablespoon instant minced onion**

1 **teaspoon salt**

1½ **teaspoons bread machine or quick active dry yeast**

1 **teaspoon instant minced onion**

1 **teaspoon dill seed**

**1.** Measure carefully, placing all ingredients except 1 teaspoon onion and 1 teaspoon dill seed in bread machine pan in the order recommended by the manufacturer.

**2.** Select Dough/Manual cycle. Do not use Delay cycles.

**3.** Remove dough from pan, using lightly floured hands. Cover and let rest 10 minutes on lightly floured surface.

**4.** Grease large cookie sheet. Shape dough into oval, 12 × 4 inches, tapering both ends slightly. Place on cookie sheet. Cover and let rise in warm place 30 to 45 minutes or until double. (Dough is ready if indentation remains when touched.)

**5.** Heat oven to 375°. Spray water over loaf; sprinkle with 1 teaspoon onion and 1 teaspoon dill seed. Make long slash, ¼ inch deep, down center of loaf, using sharp knife. Bake 10 minutes, spraying 3 times with water. Bake 15 to 20 minutes longer or until loaf is golden brown and sounds hollow when tapped. Remove from cookie sheet to wire rack; cool.

**1 SLICE:** Calories 105 (Calories from Fat 20); Fat 2g (Saturated 0g); Cholesterol 1mg; Sodium 190mg; Carbohydrate 19g (Dietary Fiber 1g); Protein 4g

## COOKING TIPS

• Spraying the loaf with water before and during the first 10 minutes of baking will give you a crustier loaf, and the inside of the bread will be soft and chewy. Use a spray bottle that has a fine mist, so the water is evenly distributed over the loaf.

• The dough may look too dry at the beginning of mixing. Don't add additional liquid, however, until the dough has mixed for a few minutes because as the cottage cheese breaks up, it will add moisture to the dough.

# MAIN DISHES

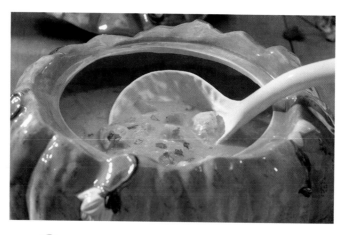

## CHICKEN-CHEESE CHOWDER

Prep: 18 min; Cook: 20 min 6 servings

2 tablespoons margarine or butter
1 small onion, peeled and finely chopped
1½ teaspoons ground cumin
½ pound boneless, skinless chicken breasts, cut into 1-inch pieces
2 large sweet potatoes, peeled and cut into 1-inch pieces
1 can (14½ ounces) ready-to-serve chicken broth
½ cup whipping (heavy) cream
2 teaspoons chili powder
¼ teaspoon salt
1 can (16 ounces) cream-style corn
1 can (4 ounces) chopped green chilies, drained
1 cup shredded Monterey Jack cheese (4 ounces)
Chopped fresh cilantro, if desired

**1.** Melt margarine in 4-quart Dutch oven over medium heat. Cook onion, cumin and chicken in margarine 8 to 10 minutes, stirring occasionally, until chicken is no longer pink in center.

**2.** Stir in sweet potatoes and broth. Heat to boiling; reduce heat to low. Cover and simmer about 8 minutes or until potatoes are tender.

**3.** Stir in remaining ingredients except cheese and cilantro; cook until hot. Gradually stir in cheese just until melted. Sprinkle each serving with cilantro.

**1 SERVING:** Calories 350 (Calories from Fat 160); Fat 18g (Saturated 9g); Cholesterol 65mg; Sodium 825mg; Carbohydrate 32g (Dietary Fiber 4g); Protein 19g

# Spring Arborio Rice and Chicken Soup

Prep: 15 min; Cook: 30 min     6 servings

   2 tablespoons olive or vegetable oil
   1 small onion, finely chopped
   ½ pound boneless, skinless chicken breasts, cut into 1-inch
     pieces
   1 cup uncooked Arborio or other short-grain rice
   6 cups chicken broth
   ¼ cup chopped fresh mint leaves
   3 tablespoons chopped fresh parsley
   1 package (10 ounces) frozen green peas
     Freshly grated Parmesan cheese

**1.** Heat oil in 4-quart Dutch oven over medium heat. Cook onion and chicken in oil, stirring frequently, until chicken is no longer pink in center.

**2.** Stir in rice. Cook 1 minute over medium heat, stirring frequently, until rice begins to brown. Pour ½ cup of the broth over rice mixture. Cook uncovered, stirring frequently, until broth is absorbed. Continue cooking 15 to 20 minutes, adding broth ½ cup at a time and stirring frequently, until rice is creamy and almost tender and 3 cups broth have been used.

**3.** Stir in remaining 3 cups broth, the mint, parsley and frozen peas. Cook over medium heat about 5 minutes or until hot. Serve with cheese.

**1 SERVING:** Calories 280 (Calories from Fat 70); Fat 8g (Saturated 1g); Cholesterol 25mg; Sodium 1110mg; Carbohydrate 36g (Dietary Fiber 3g); Protein 19g

# ITALIAN CHICKEN-LENTIL SOUP

Prep: 15 min; Cook: 40 min      6 servings

  1 tablespoon olive or vegetable oil

  1 pound boneless, skinless chicken breasts, cut into 1-inch pieces

  1 medium onion, peeled and chopped

4½ cups chicken broth

  1 can (28 ounces) Italian-style pear-shaped tomatoes, undrained

  4 medium carrots, thinly sliced

  2 medium yellow summer squash, diced

  1 cup sliced mushrooms (3 ounces)

  1 cup dried lentils (8 ounces), sorted and rinsed

¼ cup chopped fresh or 1 tablespoon dried basil leaves

½ teaspoon salt

¼ teaspoon pepper

   Shredded Parmesan cheese

**1.** Heat oil in 4-quart Dutch oven over medium-high heat. Cook chicken and onion in oil 10 to 12 minutes, stirring occasionally, until chicken is no longer pink in center.

**2.** Stir in remaining ingredients except cheese, breaking up tomatoes. Heat to boiling, stirring occasionally; reduce heat to medium-low. Cover and cook 20 to 25 minutes or until lentils are tender. Serve with cheese.

**1 SERVING:** Calories 260 (Calories from 55); Fat 6g (Saturated 1g); Cholesterol 45mg; Sodium 1230mg; Carbohydrate 32g (Dietary Fiber 11g); Protein 31g

# $\mathcal{R}$IO GRANDE TURKEY SOUP

**QUICK** Prep: 5 min; Cook: 15 min          6 servings

| | |
|---|---|
| 1 | can (28 ounces) whole tomatoes, undrained |
| 1 | jar (16 ounces) thick-and-chunky salsa |
| 1 | can (14½ ounces) fat-free chicken broth |
| 2 to 3 | teaspoons chili powder |
| ½ | bag (16-ounce size) frozen corn, broccoli and red peppers |
| 1 | cup uncooked cavatappi pasta (3 ounces) |
| 2 | cups cut-up cooked turkey or chicken |
| ¼ | cup chopped fresh parsley |

**1.** Heat tomatoes, salsa, broth and chili powder to boiling in 4-quart Dutch oven, breaking up tomatoes. Stir in vegetables and pasta. Heat to boiling; reduce heat.

**2.** Simmer uncovered about 12 minutes, stirring occasionally, until pasta and vegetables are tender. Stir in turkey and parsley; cook until hot.

**1 SERVING:** Calories 220 (Calories from Fat 45); Fat 5g (Saturated 1g); Cholesterol 40mg; Sodium 760mg; Carbohydrate 29g (Dietary Fiber 5g); Protein 20g

# $\mathcal{W}$HOLE WHEAT SPAGHETTI WITH SPICY EGGPLANT SAUCE

**QUICK** Prep: 10 min; Cook: 20 min          4 servings

| | |
|---|---|
| 8 | ounces uncooked whole wheat or regular spaghetti |
| 1 | small eggplant, peeled and cubed |
| 1 | can (14½ ounces) Italian-style stewed tomatoes, undrained |
| 1 | can (8 ounces) tomato sauce |
| ½ | teaspoon crushed red pepper |
| 2 | tablespoons chopped fresh parsley or 2 teaspoons parsley flakes |

**1.** Cook and drain spaghetti as directed on package.

**2.** While spaghetti is cooking, heat eggplant, tomatoes, tomato sauce and red pepper to boiling in 10-inch skillet, stirring occasionally; reduce heat. Simmer uncovered about 15 minutes or until eggplant is tender. Stir in parsley. Serve over spaghetti.

**1 SERVING:** Calories 255 (Calories from Fat 10); Fat 1g (Saturated 0g); Cholesterol 0mg; Sodium 630mg; Carbohydrate 62g (Dietary Fiber 9g); Protein 11g

# $\mathcal{L}$INGUINE WITH RED CLAM SAUCE

Prep: 10 min; Cook: 27 min     6 servings

12 ounces linguine

¼ cup olive or vegetable oil

3 cloves garlic, peeled and finely chopped

1 can (28 ounces) whole Italian-style tomatoes, drained and chopped

1 small red chili, seeded and finely chopped

1 pint shucked fresh small clams, drained and liquid reserved

1 tablespoon chopped fresh parsley

1 teaspoon salt

**1.** Cook and drain linguine as directed on package.

**2.** Meanwhile, heat oil in 3-quart saucepan over medium-high heat. Cook garlic in oil, stirring frequently, until golden. Stir in tomatoes and chili. Cook 3 minutes, stirring frequently.

**3.** Stir in clam liquid. Heat to boiling; reduce heat. Simmer uncovered 10 minutes.

**4.** Chop clams. Stir clams, parsley and salt into tomato mixture. Cover and simmer about 15 minutes, stirring occasionally, until clams are tender. Serve over linguine.

**1 SERVING:** Calories 320 (Calories from Fat 100); Fat 11g (Saturated 1g); Cholesterol 15mg; Sodium 600mg; Carbohydrate 44g (Dietary Fiber 3g); Protein 14g

---

**COOKING TIP**

• You can substitute two cans (6½ ounces each) minced clams, drained and liquid reserved, for the fresh clams in this recipe.

# ANGEL HAIR PASTA WITH SHRIMP

**QUICK** Prep: 5 min; Cook: 10 min    4 servings

1 package (16 ounces) capellini (angel hair) pasta
¼ cup olive or vegetable oil
2 tablespoons chopped fresh parsley
2 cloves garlic, finely chopped
1 small red chili, seeded and finely chopped
⅓ cup dry white wine or vegetable broth
½ teaspoon freshly grated nutmeg
¾ pound uncooked, peeled, deveined small shrimp, thawed if frozen

**1.** Cook and drain pasta as directed on package.

**2.** Meanwhile, heat oil in 4-quart Dutch oven or 12-inch skillet over medium-high heat. Cook parsley, garlic and chili in oil 1 minute, stirring occasionally. Stir in wine, nutmeg and shrimp; reduce heat. Cover and simmer about 5 minutes or until shrimp are pink and firm.

**3.** Mix pasta and shrimp mixture in Dutch oven. Cook over medium heat 2 minutes, stirring occasionally.

**1 SERVING:** Calories 565 (Calories from Fat 170); Fat 19g (Saturated 3g); Cholesterol 215mg; Sodium 160mg; Carbohydrate 75g (Dietary Fiber 3g); Protein 27g

# $\mathcal{G}$ARLIC SHRIMP

**QUICK** Prep: 15 min; Cook: 5 min    4 servings

- 1 **tablespoon vegetable oil**
- 3 **large cloves garlic, peeled and finely chopped**
- 1 **pound uncooked, peeled, deveined medium shrimp, thawed if frozen**
- 1 **large carrot, shredded**
- 2 **tablespoons chopped fresh cilantro**

  **Hot cooked noodles or rice, if desired**

**1.** Heat wok or 12-inch skillet over medium-high heat. Add oil; rotate wok to coat sides. Add garlic; stir-fry 1 minute. Add shrimp; stir-fry 1 minute.

**2.** Add carrot; stir-fry about 3 minutes or until shrimp are pink and firm. Stir in cilantro. Serve with noodles.

**1 SERVING:** Calories 90 (Calories from Fat 35); Fat 4g (Saturated 1g); Cholesterol 105mg; Sodium 130mg; Carbohydrate 3g (Dietary Fiber 1g); Protein 12g

# SAVORY SCALLOPS AND SHRIMP

**QUICK** Prep: 15 min; Cook: 10 min      4 servings

- 2 tablespoons olive or vegetable oil
- 1 clove garlic, peeled and finely chopped
- 1 medium green onion, trimmed and chopped
- 1 medium green bell pepper, chopped
- 1 tablespoon chopped fresh parsley or 1 teaspoon parsley flakes
- 1 pound sea scallops, cut in half
- 1 pound uncooked peeled deveined medium shrimp, thawed if frozen
- ½ cup dry white wine or fat-free chicken broth
- 1 tablespoon lemon juice
- ¼ to ½ teaspoon crushed red pepper

**1.** Heat oil in 10-inch skillet over medium heat. Cook garlic, onion, bell pepper and parsley in oil about 5 minutes, stirring occasionally, until bell pepper is crisp-tender.

**2.** Stir in remaining ingredients. Cook 4 to 5 minutes, stirring frequently, until shrimp are pink and firm and scallops are white.

**1 SERVING:** Calories 220 (Calories from Fat 80); Fat 9g (Saturated 1g); Cholesterol 180mg; Sodium 400mg; Carbohydrate 5g (Dietary Fiber 1g); Protein 31g

# CRABMEAT ROLL-UPS

Prep: 20 min; Bake: 25 min        5 servings

 1  **can (6 ounces) crabmeat, drained and cartilage removed**

½  **cup shredded Swiss or Monterey Jack cheese (2 ounces)**

 1  **small zucchini, shredded**

¼  **cup finely chopped celery**

 1  **small onion, peeled and finely chopped**

 3  **tablespoons chili sauce**

½  **teaspoon salt**

10  **slices white sandwich bread, crusts removed**

 3  **tablespoons butter or stick margarine, melted**

    **Avocado Sauce (below)**

**1.** Heat oven to 350°.

**2.** Mix crabmeat, cheese, zucchini, celery, onion, chili sauce and salt.

**3.** Roll each bread slice to about ¼-inch thickness. Spoon crabmeat mixture across center of each slice. Bring sides of bread up over crabmeat mixture; secure with toothpicks.

**4.** Place roll-ups, seam sides down, in ungreased rectangular baking dish, 13 × 9 × 2 inches. Brush with butter. Bake uncovered about 25 minutes or until golden brown and hot.

**5.** Meanwhile, prepare Avocado Sauce. Serve sauce over roll-ups.

**1 SERVING:** Calories 380 (Calories from Fat 200); Fat 22g (Saturated 10g); Cholesterol 75mg; Sodium 950mg; Carbohydrate 34g (Dietary Fiber 4g); Protein 16g

## AVOCADO SAUCE

½  **cup sour cream**

¼  **teaspoon salt**

 1  **medium tomato, seeded, chopped and drained**

 1  **medium avocado, chopped**

Heat sour cream and salt in 1-quart saucepan over low heat, stirring occasionally, just until warm. Gently stir in tomato. Heat 1 minute; remove from heat. Gently stir in avocado.

# $\mathscr{B}$ROILED SALMON
## WITH HAZELNUT BUTTER

**QUICK** Prep: 10 min; Broil: 12 min; Bake: 6 min          4 servings

**Hazelnut Butter (below)**
**4 salmon fillets (1 to 1½ pounds)**
**½ teaspoon salt**
**⅛ teaspoon pepper**

**1.** Prepare Hazelnut Butter.

**2.** Set oven control to broil. Grease shallow roasting pan or jelly roll pan, 15½ × 10½ × 1 inch.

**3.** Sprinkle both sides of fish with salt and pepper. Place in pan. Broil fish with tops 4 to 6 inches from heat 4 minutes; turn and spread each fillet with about 1 tablespoon Hazelnut Butter. Broil until fish flakes easily with fork, 4 to 8 minutes.

**1 SERVING:** Calories 245 (Calories from Fat 160); Fat 18g (Saturated 3g); Cholesterol 55mg; Sodium 450mg; Carbohydrate 1g (Dietary Fiber 0g); Protein 20g

## HAZELNUT BUTTER

**2 tablespoons finely chopped hazelnuts**
**3 tablespoons margarine or butter, softened**
**1 tablespoon chopped fresh parsley**
**1 teaspoon lemon juice**

Heat oven to 350°. Spread hazelnuts on ungreased cookie sheet. Bake until golden brown, 4 to 6 minutes, stirring occasionally; cool. Mix with remaining ingredients.

*good*

# GLAZED SALMON WITH APPLES

Prep: 10 min; Bake: 25 min     6 servings

- 2 **large apples, sliced**
- 1 **small onion, peeled and sliced**
- 1 **salmon fillet (1½ pounds)**
- 2 **tablespoons Dijon mustard**
- 1 **tablespoon honey**
- ¼ **teaspoon garlic salt**

1. Heat oven to 400°. Mix apples and onion in ungreased rectangular baking dish, 11 × 7 × 1½ inches. Place fish, skin side down, on apple mixture. Mix mustard, honey and garlic salt. Spoon onto fish; spread evenly.

2. Bake uncovered 20 to 25 minutes or until fish flakes easily with fork. Serve apple mixture with fish.

**1 SERVING:** Calories 190 (Calories from Fat 55); Fat 6g (Saturated 2g); Cholesterol 65mg; Sodium 160mg; Carbohydrate 15g (Dietary Fiber 2g); Protein 21g

---

**COOKING TIP**

• Instead of using mango, substitute 4 medium peaches or nectarines if you like.

---

**CUTTING AND SEEDING A JALAPEÑO CHILI**

Cut the stem off the jalapeño chili, then cut off the sides along the ribs, avoiding the seeds. The flesh, ribs and seeds of chilies contain burning, irritating oils. Be sure to wash your hands in soapy water (or wear protective gloves), and be especially careful not to rub your face or eyes until the oils have been washed away.

# BAKED SALMON WITH MANGO SALSA

Prep: 15 min; Bake: 20 min        8 servings

1   **large salmon fillet (about 2 pounds)**
½   **cup lemon juice**
2   **medium mangoes**
1   **medium jalapeño chili**
½   **cup chopped fresh cilantro**

**1.** Heat oven to 400°. Spray baking pan with cooking spray.

**2.** Cut salmon fillet into 8 serving pieces. Place salmon in pan. Drizzle ¼ cup of the lemon juice over salmon.

**3.** Bake uncovered 15 to 20 minutes or until salmon flakes easily with a fork.

**4.** Meanwhile, cut each mango lengthwise in half, sliding a sharp knife along flat side of seed on one side. Repeat on other side, which will give you two large pieces plus seed. Cut away any flesh from seed. Make lengthwise and crosswise cuts, ½ inch apart, in flesh of each mango half in a crisscross pattern. Be careful not to cut through peel. Turn each mango half inside out, and cut off mango pieces (see page 211).

**5.** Cut stem off the jalapeño chili; cut off sides along the ribs, avoiding seeds. Chop enough of chili to measure 2 teaspoons. Wrap any remaining chili in plastic wrap and refrigerate for another use.

**6.** Mix mango, chili, cilantro and remaining ¼ cup lemon juice. Serve over salmon.

**1 SERVING:** Calories 180 (Calories from Fat 55); Fat 6g (Saturated 2g); Cholesterol 65mg; Sodium 60mg; Carbohydrate 11g (Dietary Fiber 1g); Protein 21g

# $\mathcal{S}$OLE WITH ALMONDS

**QUICK**   Prep: 10 min; Bake: 20 min     4 servings

| | |
|---|---|
| 1 | **pound sole or other lean fish fillets, about ¾ inch thick** |
| ⅓ | **cup sliced almonds or chopped walnuts** |
| 3 | **tablespoons margarine or butter at room temperature** |
| 1½ | **tablespoons grated lemon peel** |
| 1½ | **tablespoons lemon juice** |
| ½ | **teaspoon salt** |
| ½ | **teaspoon paprika** |

**1.** Heat oven to 375°. Grease bottom of baking pan with oil.

**2.** Cut fish fillets into 4 serving pieces if needed. Place pieces, skin sides down, in greased pan.

**3.** Mix almonds, margarine, lemon peel, lemon juice, salt and paprika. Spoon over fish.

**4.** Bake uncovered 15 to 20 minutes or until fish flakes easily with fork.

**1 SERVING:** Calories 220 (Calories from Fat 125); Fat 14g (Saturated 2g); Cholesterol 55mg; Sodium 480mg; Carbohydrate 3g (Dietary Fiber 1g); Protein 21g

***Lighter Sole with Almonds:*** For 9 grams of fat and 170 calories per serving, decrease almonds to 2 tablespoons and margarine to 2 tablespoons.

#  BAKED FLOUNDER TERIYAKI

Prep: 10 min; Marinate: 1 hr; Bake: 20 min      6 servings

| | |
|---|---|
| 1½ | **pounds flounder (about 6 small fillets) or other lean fish fillets** |
| 1 | **medium green onion with top, trimmed and thinly sliced** |
| 2 | **cloves garlic, peeled and finely chopped** |
| ⅓ | **cup dry sherry or apple juice** |
| 3 | **tablespoons lemon juice** |
| 2 | **teaspoons finely chopped gingerroot** |
| 1 | **teaspoon vegetable oil** |
| 2 | **teaspoons honey** |
| ¼ | **teaspoon pepper** |

**1.** Spray baking dish, 11 × 7 × 1½ inches, with cooking spray. Cut fish fillets into 6 serving pieces if needed. Place fish in sprayed pan. If pieces have skin, place with skin sides down.

**2.** Mix onion, garlic, sherry, lemon juice, gingerroot, oil, honey and pepper. Spoon over fish. Cover with aluminum foil and refrigerate 1 hour.

**3.** Heat oven to 375°. Bake covered 15 to 20 minutes or until fish flakes easily with fork.

**1 SERVING:** Calories 120 (Calories from Fat 20); Fat 2g (Saturated 0g); Cholesterol 55mg; Sodium 90mg; Carbohydrate 5g (Dietary Fiber 0g); Protein 20g

**COOKING TIP**

• You can substitute other lean fish, such as halibut, red snapper, orange roughy, ocean perch or scrod, for the flounder.

## COOKING TIP

• Baking fish with the skin on helps to hold delicate fish fillets together. Removing the skin after the fish has been cooked is much easier than removing it before cooking. When fish is done, carefully insert a metal spatula between the skin and the flesh, starting at the tail end if the fillet happens to have one. While holding onto a small piece of skin, slide the fish off of the skin.

# *F*LOUNDER WITH MUSHROOMS AND WINE

**QUICK**  Prep: 10 min; Bake: 20 min    4 servings

1 **pound flounder, sole or other delicate fish fillets, about ¾ inch thick**
½ **teaspoon paprika**
½ **teaspoon salt**
⅛ **teaspoon pepper**
1 **tablespoon butter or stick margarine**
½ **cup sliced mushrooms**
⅓ **cup sliced leeks**
⅓ **cup dry white wine or chicken broth**
¼ **cup sliced almonds**
1 **tablespoon grated Parmesan cheese**

**1.** Heat oven to 375°.

**2.** If fish fillets are large, cut into 4 serving pieces. Arrange in ungreased square baking dish, 8 × 8 × 2 inches. Sprinkle with paprika, salt and pepper.

**3.** Melt butter in 10-inch skillet over medium heat. Cook mushrooms and leeks in butter, stirring occasionally, until leeks are tender. Stir in wine. Pour mushroom mixture over fish. Sprinkle with almonds and cheese.

**4.** Bake uncovered 15 to 20 minutes or until fish flakes easily with fork.

**1 SERVING:** Calories 170 (Calories from Fat 70); Fat 8g (Saturated 3g); Cholesterol 60mg; Sodium 420mg; Carbohydrate 3g (Dietary Fiber 1g); Protein 20g

# $\mathcal{S}$EA BASS
## WITH VEGETABLE MÉLANGE

Prep: 30 min; Bake: 25 min     4 servings

1 tablespoon butter or stick margarine

2 medium carrots, cut into 2 × ¼ × ¼-inch strips

1 medium onion, peeled and chopped

1 medium red bell pepper, cut into ¼-inch strips

1 small zucchini, cut into 2 × ¼ × ¼-inch strips

1 teaspoon grated lemon peel

¼ teaspoon salt

⅛ teaspoon dried tarragon leaves, if desired

1 pound sea bass, tilapia, snapper or other medium-firm fish fillets, ¾ to 1 inch thick

2 tablespoons chopped fresh parsley

1 tablespoon butter or stick margarine, melted

1 teaspoon grated lemon peel

1 tablespoon lemon juice

**1.** Heat oven to 425°.

**2.** Melt 1 tablespoon butter in 10-inch nonstick skillet over medium-high heat. Cook carrots and onion in butter 2 minutes, stirring frequently. Stir in bell pepper. Cook 1 minute, stirring frequently. Stir in zucchini, 1 teaspoon lemon peel, the salt and tarragon. Cook 1 minute, stirring frequently; remove from heat.

**3.** Cut fish into 4 serving pieces. If fish has skin, place fish, skin side down, in ungreased rectangular baking dish, 11 × 7 × 1½ inches. Mix remaining ingredients; spread over fish. Spoon vegetable mixture around fish.

**4.** Bake uncovered 20 to 25 minutes or until fish flakes easily with fork. Remove skin from fish before serving if desired.

**1 SERVING:** Calories 200 (Calories from Fat 90); Fat 10g (Saturated 5g); Cholesterol 65mg; Sodium 260mg; Carbohydrate 9g (Dietary Fiber 3g); Protein 21g

# $\mathcal{S}$PINACH-FILLED FISH ROLLS

**QUICK**  Prep: 10 min; Bake: 20 min        4 servings

- **1  pound sole, orange roughy or flounder fillets**
- **1½  cups firmly packed spinach leaves**
- **¼  teaspoon garlic salt**
- **⅓  cup fat-free mayonnaise or salad dressing**
- **½  teaspoon Dijon mustard**
- **¼  cup garlic-flavored croutons, crushed**
-      **Lemon wedges, if desired**

**1.** Heat oven to 400°. Spray square baking dish, 8 × 8 × 2 inches, with cooking spray. If fish fillets are large, cut into 4 serving pieces. Place spinach on fish; sprinkle with garlic salt. Roll up each fillet, beginning at narrow end. Place rolls, with points underneath, in baking dish. Mix mayonnaise and mustard; spoon onto each roll. Sprinkle with crushed croutons.

**2.** Bake uncovered 15 to 20 minutes or until fish flakes easily with fork. Serve with lemon wedges.

**1 SERVING:** Calories 95 (Calories from Fat 10); Fat 1g (Saturated 0g); Cholesterol 45mg; Sodium 300mg; Carbohydrate 5g (Dietary Fiber 0g); Protein 17g

# CRUNCHY HERB-BAKED CHICKEN

*Photo on front cover*

Prep: 20 min; Freeze: 30 min; Bake: 35 min        6 servings

- **6 boneless, skinless chicken breast halves (about ¼ pound each)**
- **1 clove garlic, peeled and finely chopped**
- **¼ cup (½ stick) margarine or butter at room temperature**
- **1 tablespoon chopped fresh chives or parsley**
- **1½ cups cornflakes cereal, crushed (¾ cup)**
- **2 tablespoons chopped fresh parsley**
- **½ teaspoon paprika**
- **¼ cup buttermilk or milk**

**1.** Cut and discard fat from chicken. Rinse chicken under cold water and pat dry with paper towels.

**2.** Mix garlic, margarine and chives. Shape mixture into rectangle, about 3 × 2 inches. Cover and freeze about 30 minutes or until firm.

**3.** Heat oven to 425°. Spray square pan with cooking spray. Flatten each chicken breast half to ¼-inch thickness between sheets of plastic wrap or waxed paper, lightly pounding with flat side of meat mallet.

**4.** Remove margarine mixture from freezer and cut crosswise into 6 pieces. Place 1 piece on center of each chicken breast half. Fold each chicken breast lengthwise over margarine. Fold ends up and secure each end with a toothpick.

**5.** Mix cornflakes, parsley and paprika in shallow bowl. Pour buttermilk into another shallow bowl. Dip chicken, once piece at a time, into milk, coating all sides. Coat all sides with cornflake mixture. Place chicken, seam sides down, in sprayed pan.

**6.** Bake uncovered about 35 minutes or until chicken is no longer pink when cut into center of thickest pieces. Remove toothpicks before serving.

**1 SERVING:** Calories 230 (Calories from Fat 110); Fat 12g (Saturated 6g); Cholesterol 95mg; Sodium 160mg; Carbohydrate 4g (Dietary Fiber 0g); Protein 27g

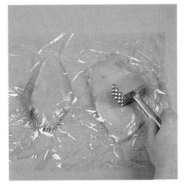

**FLATTENING CHICKEN BREASTS**

Flatten each chicken breast to ¼-inch thickness between sheets of plastic wrap or waxed paper, lightly pounding with flat side of meat mallet.

**FOLDING CHICKEN**

Fold chicken lengthwise over margarine. Fold ends up and secure each end with a toothpick.

# Garlic-Ginger Chicken with Fettuccine

**QUICK** Prep: 10 min; Cook: 18 min     4 servings

1 **package (8 ounces) fettuccine (dry)**

4 **small boneless, skinless chicken breast halves (about 1 pound)**

3 **cloves garlic, peeled and finely chopped**

1 **tablespoon grated gingerroot**

½ **teaspoon salt**

2 **tablespoons dry sherry or apple juice**

1 **tablespoon apple jelly**

2 **tablespoons chopped fresh cilantro**

1. Cook and drain fettuccine as directed on package.

2. Meanwhile, spray 10-inch nonstick skillet with cooking spray; heat over medium-high heat. Cook chicken in skillet about 5 minutes, turning once, until brown. Stir in garlic, gingerroot, salt, sherry and jelly. Turn chicken to glaze with sauce; reduce heat. Cover and simmer about 7 minutes or until juice of chicken is no longer pink when centers of thickest pieces are cut. Remove chicken from skillet.

3. Add fettuccine to sauce in skillet; toss lightly to coat. Serve chicken on fettuccine. Sprinkle with cilantro.

**1 SERVING:** Calories 335 (Calories from Fat 55); Fat 6g (Saturated 1g); Cholesterol 110mg; Sodium 370mg; Carbohydrate 42g (Dietary Fiber 2g); Protein 30g

# CHICKEN IN BRANDY CREAM SAUCE

Prep: 10 min; Cook: 22 min      4 servings

- 1 **tablespoon olive or vegetable oil**
- 4 **boneless, skinless chicken breast halves (about 1¼ pounds)**
- 1 **package (8 ounces) sliced mushrooms**
- 4 **medium green onions, trimmed and chopped**
- ¼ **teaspoon salt**
- ¼ **cup brandy or chicken broth**
- ½ **cup whipping (heavy) cream**
- **Hot cooked spinach fettuccine or regular fettuccine, if desired**

**1.** Heat oil in 10-inch skillet over medium-high heat. Cook chicken in oil 10 to 15 minutes, turning once, until chicken is no longer pink when centers of thickest pieces are cut.

**2.** Stir in mushrooms, onions, salt and brandy. Cook 4 to 5 minutes or until mushrooms are tender and most of the liquid has evaporated. Gradually stir in whipping cream. Cook about 2 minutes or until hot. Serve over fettuccine.

**1 SERVING:** Calories 290 (Calories from Fat 155); Fat 17g (Saturated 7g); Cholesterol 105mg; Sodium 230mg; Carbohydrate 5g (Dietary Fiber 1g); Protein 29g

# CURRY-COCONUT CHICKEN WITH HONEY MUSTARD

**QUICK** Prep: 10 min; Bake: 18 min          6 servings

½ **cup milk**

1 **egg, beaten**

2 **cups shredded coconut**

2 **teaspoons curry powder**

2 **pounds chicken breast tenders**

½ **cup honey**

½ **cup Dijon mustard**

**1.** Heat oven to 375°. Grease jelly roll pan, 15½ × 10½ × 1 inch, or large cookie sheet. Mix milk and egg in bowl. Mix coconut and curry powder in shallow dish. Dip chicken into milk mixture, then coat with coconut mixture. Place in pan.

**2.** Bake uncovered 10 minutes; turn chicken. Bake uncovered 5 to 8 minutes longer or until no longer pink in center. Mix honey and mustard; serve with chicken.

**1 SERVING:** Calories 115 (Calories from Fat 45); Fat 5g (Saturated 3g); Cholesterol 30mg; Sodium 110mg; Carbohydrate 10g (Dietary Fiber 1g); Protein 9g

# ZESTY ITALIAN CHICKEN

Prep: 5 min; Bake: 1 hr     6 servings

**3 to 3½  pound cut-up boiler-fryer chicken**
**¼  cup mayonnaise or salad dressing**
**¼  cup zesty Italian dressing**
**2  tablespoons chopped fresh basil**
**1  tablespoon chopped fresh oregano**
**1  teaspoon chopped fresh rosemary**

**1.** Heat oven to 375°. Place chicken, skin sides down, in ungreased rectangular pan, 13 × 9 × 2 inches.

**2.** Mix remaining ingredients; brush half of mayonnaise mixture on chicken. Cover and bake 30 minutes. Turn chicken; brush with remaining mayonnaise mixture. Bake uncovered about 30 minutes longer or until juice of chicken is no longer pink when centers of thickest pieces are cut. (If chicken browns too quickly, cover with aluminum foil.)

**1 SERVING:** Calories 375 (Calories from Fat 245); Fat 27g (Saturated 6g); Cholesterol 105mg; Sodium 220mg; Carbohydrate 2g (Dietary Fiber 0g); Protein 31

***Zesty Italian Chicken with Sweet Potatoes:*** Peel 4 medium sweet potatoes; cut into 1½-inch pieces. Increase mayonnaise and zesty Italian dressing to ⅓ cup each. Continue as directed in steps 1 and 2; except, after baking chicken 30 minutes, turn chicken and arrange sweet potatoes with remaining mayonnaise mixture. Bake uncovered about 30 minutes longer or until potatoes are tender and juice of chicken is no longer pink when centers of thickest pieces are cut. (If chicken browns too quickly, cover with aluminum foil.)

# Thai Peanut Chicken

Prep: 10 min; Bake: 1 hr     6 servings

**3 to 3½** **pounds cut-up broiler-fryer chicken**

**1½** **cups hot salsa**

**½** **cup peanut butter**

**¼** **cup lime juice**

**2** **tablespoons soy sauce**

**2** **teaspoons grated fresh gingerroot**

**¼** **cup chopped peanuts**

**¼** **cup chopped fresh cilantro**

**1.** Cut and discard fat from chicken. Rinse chicken under cold water, and pat dry with paper towels.

**2.** Heat oven to 375°. Spray rectangular pan with cooking spray. Place chicken, skin side down, in a single layer in sprayed pan.

3. Mix salsa, peanut butter, lime juice, soy sauce and gingerroot. Spoon salsa mixture over chicken.

4. Cover pan with aluminum foil and bake 30 minutes. Remove chicken from oven and turn pieces over with tongs. Spoon sauce from pan over chicken pieces to coat.

5. Continue baking uncovered 20 to 30 minutes longer or until juice of chicken is no longer pink when centers of thickest pieces are cut. Sprinkle with peanuts and cilantro.

**1 SERVING:** Calories 440 (Calories from Fat 270); Fat 20g (Saturated 7g); Cholesterol 85mg; Sodium 700mg; Carbohydrate 11g (Dietary Fiber 4g); Protein 36g

## SPECIAL TOUCH

### Crinkled Paper Chargers

You will need:

**Lightweight decorative art paper, lightweight gift wrap, tissue paper or gold foil**

**Spray adhesive**

**Large flat plates or serving platters**

1. Cut paper into circles 1 inch larger in diameter than the plates to be covered.

2. Spray adhesive onto back of paper; press onto plates and over edges. Smooth paper, pressing from the center out.

3. For serving, place dinner plates on top of papered charger plates.

**LOOSENING CHICKEN SKIN**

Loosen skin from chicken breasts by inserting fingers between the skin and flesh. Gently separate in center, leaving the skin attached at ends.

**STUFFING CHICKEN**

Using your fingers, spread one-fourth of the stuffing evenly between meat and skin of each chicken breast. Smooth skin over breasts, tucking under loose areas.

# Smoked Gouda–Spinach Stuffed Chicken

Prep: 20 min; Bake: 55 min      4 servings

**4 bone-in, skin-on chicken breast halves (2½ to 3 pounds total)**
**Smoked Gouda–Spinach Stuffing (below)**
**½ teaspoon salt**
**¼ teaspoon pepper**
**2 teaspoons margarine or butter, melted**

**1.** Heat oven to 375°. Spray square pan with cooking spray. Make Smoked Gouda–Spinach Stuffing.

**2.** Rinse chicken under cold water and pat dry with paper towels. Loosen skin from chicken breasts by inserting fingers between skin and flesh. Gently separate in center, leaving skin attached at ends.

**3.** Spread one-fourth of the stuffing evenly between meat and skin of each chicken breast, using your fingers. Smooth skin over breasts, tucking under loose areas. Place chicken, skin side up, in sprayed pan. Sprinkle salt and pepper evenly over chicken. Drizzle with margarine.

**4.** Bake uncovered 45 to 55 minutes or until juice of chicken is no longer pink when centers of thickest pieces are cut.

**1 SERVING:** Calories 225 (Calories from Fat 90); Fat 10g (Saturated 5g); Cholesterol 90mg; Sodium 550mg; Carbohydrate 3g (Dietary Fiber 1g); Protein 32g

## SMOKED GOUDA–SPINACH STUFFING

**1 package (10 ounces) frozen chopped spinach, thawed**
**½ cup shredded smoked Gouda or Swiss cheese (2 ounces)**
**¼ teaspoon ground nutmeg**

Drain thawed spinach in a strainer, then squeeze out excess moisture from spinach, using paper towels or a clean kitchen towel, until spinach is dry. Place in medium bowl. Add cheese and nutmeg. Mix all ingredients thoroughly.

***Apple-Hazelnut Stuffed Chicken:*** Omit Smoked Gouda–Spinach Stuffing. Mix ¼ cup chopped hazelnuts (filberts), 1 medium apple, chopped, and 1 package (3 ounces) cream cheese at room temperature. Stuff and bake chicken as directed.

## Easier Chop Jobs

Did you know that frozen nuts are easier to chop than room-temperature nuts? If you need lots of chopped nuts for a recipe, put them in the freezer for at least an hour before chopping them, and you'll make the job go much easier. ▪

# Maple-Glazed Turkey Breast

Prep: 5 min; Bake: 45 min          4 servings

- 1 package (6 ounces) seasoned long-grain and wild rice
- 1½ cups water
- 1 boneless turkey breast (about 1 pound)
- 3 tablespoons maple-flavored syrup
- ½ cup chopped walnuts
- ½ teaspoon ground cinnamon

**1.** Heat oven to 350°.

**2.** Mix uncooked rice, seasoning packet from rice and water in ungreased square baking dish, 8 × 8 × 2 inches. Place turkey breast, skin side up, on rice mixture. Drizzle with maple syrup. Sprinkle with walnuts and cinnamon.

**3.** Cover and bake about 45 minutes or until rice is tender and juice of turkey is no longer pink when center is cut.

**1 SERVING:** Calories 305 (Calories from Fat 90); Fat 10g (Saturated 1g); Cholesterol 75mg; Sodium 170mg; Carbohydrate 25g (Dietary Fiber 1g); Protein 30g

**Slow Cooker Directions:** Decrease water to 1¼ cups. Increase maple-flavored syrup to ¼ cup. Mix uncooked rice, seasoning packet from rice and water in 3½- to 6-quart slow cooker. Place turkey breast, skin side up, on rice mixture. Drizzle with maple syrup. Sprinkle with walnuts and cinnamon. Cover and cook on low heat setting 4 to 5 hours or until juice of turkey is no longer pink when center is cut.

# $\mathcal{B}$EEF MEDALLIONS
## WITH PEAR-CRANBERRY CHUTNEY

Prep: 15 min; Cook: 23 min     4 servings

- **4** beef tenderloin steaks, about 1 inch thick (1 pound)
- **½** large red onion, peeled and thinly sliced
- **2** cloves garlic, peeled and finely chopped
- **2** tablespoons dry red wine or grape juice
- **2** firm ripe pears, peeled and chopped
- **½** cup fresh or frozen cranberries
- **2** tablespoons packed brown sugar
- **½** teaspoon pumpkin pie spice

**1.** Remove fat from beef. Spray 12-inch skillet with cooking spray; heat over medium-high heat. Cook onion, garlic and wine in skillet about 5 minutes, stirring frequently, until onion is tender but not brown.

**2.** Stir in remaining ingredients except beef; reduce heat. Simmer uncovered about 10 minutes, stirring frequently, until cranberries burst. Place chutney in small bowl; set aside.

**3.** Wipe out skillet; spray with cooking spray. Cook beef in skillet over medium heat about 8 minutes for medium doneness, turning once. Serve with chutney.

**1 SERVING:** Calories 250 (Calories from Fat 70); Fat 8g (Saturated 3g); Cholesterol 65mg; Sodium 60mg; Carbohydrate 23g (Dietary Fiber 3g); Protein 25g

www.bettycrocker.com

## COOKING TIP

• When chopping dried cherries and apricots, spray the knife with a little cooking spray so the fruit won't stick. You can also use a kitchen scissors to snip the dried cherries and apricots into small pieces.

# CIDER-GLAZED STUFFED PORK ROAST

Prep: 20 min; Bake: 1 hr 30 min      8 servings

½  **cup dried cherries or cranberries, chopped**

½  **cup dried apricots, chopped**

1  **medium tart cooking apple, such as Granny Smith, Rome Beauty or Greening, peeled and finely chopped**

2  **tablespoons dry bread crumbs**

2  **teaspoons chopped fresh or ½ teaspoon dried rosemary leaves, crumbled**

¼  **teaspoon salt**

3  **pounds pork boneless loin roast**

¼  **cup apple cider**

**Cider Sauce (at right)**

**1.** Heat oven to 350°.

**2.** To make stuffing, mix cherries, apricots, apple, dry bread crumbs, rosemary and salt.

**3.** Starting at narrow side of pork roast and holding blade of knife parallel to work surface, cut lengthwise almost to inside edge of pork (do not cut all the way through). The pork will open like a book. Place 4 pieces of kitchen string on a cutting board at even intervals. Lay pork on top of string. Spoon stuffing mixture evenly into opening of pork. Close opening and tie at even intervals with the string.

**4.** Place pork, fat side up, on rack in roasting pan. Insert meat thermometer so tip is in center of thickest part of pork. Bake uncovered 1 hour to 1 hour 30 minutes, brushing occasionally with apple cider, until thermometer reads 155° and pork is no longer pink when center is cut. Cover pork loosely with a tent of aluminum foil and let stand 10 to 15 minutes or until thermometer reads 160°.

**5.** Meanwhile, prepare Cider Sauce. Serve pork with sauce.

**1 SERVING:** Calories 360 (Calories from Fat 125); Fat 14g (Saturated 5g); Cholesterol 110mg; Sodium 160mg; Carbohydrate 23g (Dietary Fiber 4g); Protein 39g

## CIDER SAUCE

**1¼  cups apple cider**

**2  teaspoons cornstarch**

Mix apple cider and cornstarch in saucepan. Heat to boiling over medium heat, stirring constantly. Boil and stir about 1 minute or until sauce thickens slightly.

**CUTTING THE PORK ROAST**

Starting at narrow side of pork roast and holding blade of knife parallel to work surface, cut lengthwise almost to inside edge of pork (do not cut all the way through). The pork will open like a book.

**STUFFING THE PORK ROAST**

Spoon stuffing evenly into opening of pork. Close opening, and tie at even intervals with pieces of kitchen string.

### COOKING TIP

• For easy cleanup, line the broiler pan with aluminum foil before placing the pork on the rack.

# ℘ECAN-CRUSTED PORK CHOPS

Prep: 15 min; Broil: 25 min        6 servings

6  pork loin or rib chops, about ¾ inch thick (about 2 pounds total)
2  tablespoons Dijon mustard
2  tablespoons mayonnaise or salad dressing
1  tablespoon vegetable oil
1  slice bread, torn into small pieces
½  cup chopped pecans
½  teaspoon salt
4  sprigs fresh parsley or 1 tablespoon parsley flakes

**1.** Cut and discard fat from pork chops.

**2.** Mix mustard, mayonnaise and oil.

**3.** Place bread, pecans, salt and parsley in blender or food processor. Cover and blend on high speed, using quick on-and-off motions, until pecans are finely chopped. Place pecan mixture in shallow bowl.

**4.** Set oven control to broil.

**5.** Spread mustard mixture over all sides of pork, then coat all sides with pecan mixture.

**6.** Place pork on rack in broiler pan. Broil 6 inches from heat about 10 minutes or until brown. Turn pork, and broil 10 to 15 minutes longer or until pork is slightly pink when center is cut.

**1 SERVING:** Calories 280 (Calories from Fat 180); Fat 20g (Saturated 4g); Cholesterol 70mg; Sodium 350mg; Carbohydrate 4g (Dietary Fiber 1g); Protein 24g

## SPECIAL TOUCH

### Simple Fruit Topiary

You will need:

**Small terra-cotta pot (4 to 6 inches in diameter)**

**Spray paint, if desired**

**Floral foam block**

**Fresh pear or apple**

**6- to 7-inch stick or branch**

**About 1 foot ¼-inch-wide ribbon**

**Glue**

**Moss, pebbles, nuts or small candies**

**Additional ribbon, if desired**

1. If desired, spray paint the pot to coordinate with your color scheme.

2. Cut foam into pieces to fit in pot. Press foam firmly in pot. Add water (foam will absorb water which helps to weight down the pot).

3. Pierce small hole in bottom of pear; firmly insert stick. Insert other end of stick into foam in middle of pot. Wrap ribbon around stick. Glue ends of ribbon to stick.

4. Cover foam with moss or pebbles, or line with plastic wrap or tissue and place nuts or candies on top. Tie additional ribbon into bow around top of pot.

# $\mathcal{W}$INE-MARINATED COUNTRY-STYLE RIBS

Prep: 10 min; Cook: 3 min; Marinate: 4 hr; Grill: 1 hr 10 min      6 servings

- **2 tablespoons vegetable oil**
- **1 tablespoon chopped fresh or 1 teaspoon dried rosemary leaves, crushed**
- **1 clove garlic, peeled and finely chopped**
- **½ cup dry red wine or grape juice**
- **1 teaspoon sugar**
- **½ teaspoon salt**
- **¼ teaspoon pepper**
- **3 pounds pork country-style ribs, cut into serving pieces**

**1.** Heat oil in 1½-quart saucepan over medium heat. Cook rosemary and garlic in oil, stirring frequently, until garlic is golden; remove from heat. Stir in wine, sugar, salt and pepper.

**2.** Place pork in glass dish. Pour wine mixture over pork; turn to coat. Cover and refrigerate 4 hours, turning pork occasionally.

**3.** Heat coals or gas grill for direct heat (page 144). Place drip pan under grilling area.

**4.** Remove pork from marinade; reserve marinade. Cover and grill pork over drip pan and 4 to 5 inches from medium heat 1 hour 10 minutes, turning occasionally and brushing with marinade, until pork is tender and no longer pink when center is cut. Discard remaining marinade.

**1 SERVING:** Calories 280 (Calories from Fat 170); Fat 19g (Saturated 6g); Cholesterol 80mg; Sodium 230mg; Carbohydrate 1g (Dietary Fiber 0g); Protein 26g

# $\mathcal{S}$PANISH LAMB AND COUSCOUS

**QUICK**   Prep: 10 min; Cook: 20 min        4 servings

4   lamb sirloin chops, ½ inch thick (about 2 pounds)
1   medium green bell pepper, chopped
1   can (14½ ounces) diced tomatoes, undrained
¼   cup chili sauce
½   teaspoon ground cumin
½   teaspoon dried marjoram leaves
¼   teaspoon garlic powder
¼   teaspoon salt
¼   cup pitted ripe olives, cut in half
2   tablespoons chopped fresh parsley
2   cups hot cooked couscous

1. Spray 12-inch nonstick skillet with cooking spray; heat over medium heat. Cook lamb in skillet, turning once, until brown on both sides.

2. Stir in bell pepper, tomatoes, chili sauce, cumin, marjoram, garlic powder and salt; reduce heat to medium-low. Cover and simmer about 10 minutes or until lamb is light pink in center. Stir in olives; sprinkle with parsley. Serve with couscous.

**1 SERVING:** Calories 310 (Calories from Fat 80); Fat 9g (Saturated 3g); Cholesterol 70mg; Sodium 840mg; Carbohydrate 33g (Dietary Fiber 3g); Protein 27g

# SALADS AND SIDES

## MEDITERRANEAN VEGETABLE SALAD

Prep: 10 min; Chill: 1 hr        6 servings

⅓ cup tarragon or white wine vinegar

3 tablespoons olive or vegetable oil

2 tablespoons chopped fresh or 2 teaspoons dried oregano leaves

½ teaspoon sugar

½ teaspoon ground mustard

½ teaspoon salt

½ teaspoon pepper

2 cloves garlic, peeled and finely chopped

3 large tomatoes, sliced

2 large yellow bell peppers, sliced into thin rings

6 ounces spinach leaves

½ cup crumbled feta cheese (2 ounces)

Kalamata olives, if desired

**1.** Mix vinegar, oil, oregano, sugar, mustard, salt, pepper and garlic. Place tomatoes and bell peppers in glass or plastic container. Pour vinegar mixture over vegetables. Cover and refrigerate at least 1 hour to blend flavors.

**2.** Line serving platter with spinach. Drain vegetables; place on spinach. Sprinkle with cheese. Garnish with olives.

**1 SERVING:** Calories 135 (Calories from Fat 80); Fat 9g (Saturated 2g); Cholesterol 10mg; Sodium 360mg; Carbohydrate 12g (Dietary Fiber 3g); Protein 4g

# $\mathcal{F}$RENCH BREAD SALAD

Prep: 15 min; Chill: 1 hr         6 servings

6  slices day-old French or Italian bread, 1 inch thick, torn into
   1-inch pieces
2  medium tomatoes, chopped
1  medium cucumber, peeled and chopped
1  small onion, peeled and thinly sliced
⅓  cup fat-free red wine vinegar dressing
2  tablespoons chopped fresh or 2 teaspoons dried basil leaves
¼  teaspoon pepper

**1.** Mix all ingredients in glass or plastic bowl.

**2.** Cover and refrigerate, stirring once, at least 1 hour to blend flavors and soften bread. Stir before serving.

**1 SERVING:** Calories 105 (Calories from Fat 10); Fat 1g (Saturated 0g); Cholesterol 0mg;
Sodium 210mg; Carbohydrate 22g (Dietary Fiber 2g); Protein 4g

# PEAR AND BLUE CHEESE SALAD

**QUICK**   Prep: 10 min          4 servings

Cider Vinaigrette (below)
1  medium bunch romaine
2  medium red or green pears
¼  cup crumbled blue cheese (1 ounce)
2  tablespoons chopped walnuts

**1.** Prepare Cider Vinaigrette.

**2.** Remove any limp outer leaves from the romaine and discard. Break remaining leaves off the core, and rinse with cool water. Shake off excess water and blot to dry. Tear leaves into bite-size pieces. You will need about 8 cups of romaine pieces. Place romaine pieces in bowl.

**3.** Cut each pear into fourths. Cut core and seeds from center of each fourth. Cut each fourth into ¼-inch slices and add to romaine. Add cheese and walnuts to romaine.

**4.** Pour vinaigrette over salad and toss. Serve immediately.

**1 SERVING:** Calories 95 (Calories from Fat 55); Fat 6g (Saturated 2g); Cholesterol 4mg; Sodium 180mg; Carbohydrate 10g (Dietary Fiber 2g); Protein 2g

## CIDER VINAIGRETTE

¼  cup olive or vegetable oil
2  tablespoons cider vinegar
½  teaspoon Dijon mustard
¼  teaspoon salt
   Dash of ground pepper

Shake all ingredients in tightly covered jar or container. Shake again before pouring over salad.

# $\mathscr{S}$PINACH-STRAWBERRY SALAD

**QUICK**   Prep: 15 min        4 servings

> Honey-Dijon Dressing (below)
> 1  small jicama
> 2  kiwifruit
> ½  pint (1 cup) strawberries
> 7 to 8  cups ready-to-eat spinach (from 10-ounce bag)
> 1  cup alfalfa sprouts

**1.** Prepare Honey-Dijon Dressing.

**2.** Peel jicama, removing brown skin and a thin layer of flesh just under skin. Cut about half of the jicama into about 1¼-inch sticks to measure about ¾ cup. Wrap remaining jicama, and refrigerate for another use.

**3.** Peel kiwifruit. Cut lengthwise in half, then cut into slices. Rinse strawberries with cool water and pat dry. Remove leaves and cut berries lengthwise into slices. Remove stems from spinach leaves, and tear any large leaves into bite-size pieces. Place spinach, strawberries, alfalfa sprouts, jicama sticks and kiwifruit slices in bowl. Pour dressing over salad and toss. Serve immediately.

**1 SERVING:** Calories 165 (Calories from Fat 90); Fat 8g (Saturated 1g); Cholesterol 0mg; Sodium 45mg; Carbohydrate 28g (Dietary Fiber 8g); Protein 3g

## HONEY-DIJON DRESSING

> 2  tablespoons vegetable oil
> 2  tablespoons honey
> 2  tablespoons orange juice
> 1  tablespoon seasoned rice vinegar or white vinegar
> 1  teaspoon poppy seeds, if desired
> 2  teaspoons Dijon mustard

Shake all ingredients in a tightly covered jar or container. Shake again before pouring over salad.

---

**COOKING TIPS**

• Besides the spinach, packaged mixed salad greens that are already cleaned and ready to use are available in the produce section of the supermarket. A 10-ounce bag is about 8 cups of greens. The Italian variety is especially pretty.

• Cut leftover jicama into sticks and serve with other raw vegetables for a snack or appetizer.

# $\mathcal{M}$ANDARIN SALAD

**QUICK** Prep: 10 min; Cook: 2 min          6 servings

¼ **cup sliced almonds**

1 **tablespoon plus 1 teaspoon sugar**

 **Sweet-Sour Dressing (below)**

½ **small head lettuce, torn into bite-size pieces**

½ **bunch romaine, torn into bite-size pieces**

2 **medium stalks celery, chopped**

2 **tablespoons thinly sliced green onions**

1 **can (11 ounces) mandarin orange segments, drained**

**1.** Cook almonds and sugar in 1-quart saucepan over low heat, stirring constantly, until sugar is melted and almonds are coated; cool and break apart.

**2.** Prepare Sweet-Sour Dressing.

**3.** Toss almonds, dressing and remaining ingredients.

**1 SERVING:** Calories 165 (Calories from Fat 100); Fat 11g (Saturated 2g); Cholesterol 0mg; Sodium 200mg; Carbohydrate 16g (Dietary Fiber 1g); Protein 1g

## SWEET-SOUR DRESSING

¼ **cup vegetable oil**

2 **tablespoons sugar**

2 **tablespoons white vinegar**

1 **tablespoon chopped fresh parsley**

½ **teaspoon salt**

 **Dash of pepper**

 **Dash of red pepper sauce**

Shake all ingredients in tightly covered container. Refrigerate until serving.

# GORGONZOLA AND TOASTED WALNUT SALAD

**QUICK**  Prep: 20 min  6 servings

**Toasted Walnut Dressing (below)**
1 **head radicchio, torn into bite-size pieces**
1 **head Bibb lettuce, torn into bite-size pieces**
½ **cup crumbled Gorgonzola or Roquefort cheese (2 ounces)**
½ **cup ½-inch pieces fresh chives**
⅓ **cup coarsely chopped walnuts, toasted**

**1.** Prepare Toasted Walnut Dressing.

**2.** Toss dressing and remaining ingredients.

**1 SERVING:** Calories 250 (Calories from Fat 215); Fat 24g (Saturated 4g); Cholesterol 5mg; Sodium 210mg; Carbohydrate 5g (Dietary Fiber 2g); Protein 5g

## TOASTED WALNUT DRESSING

⅓ **cup olive or vegetable oil**
⅓ **cup coarsely chopped walnuts, toasted**
2 **tablespoons lemon juice**
1 **clove garlic**
⅛ **teaspoon salt**
**Dash of pepper**

Place all ingredients in blender or food processor. Cover and blend on high speed about 1 minute or until smooth.

**COOKING TIP**

• One fresh lemon will give you about 2 to 3 tablespoons of juice. To get the most juice out of a lemon or lime, it should be at room temperature. Before you squeeze it, roll the lemon back and forth on the counter several times with firm pressure, which helps release the juice.

**COOKING TIP**

• Pesto comes in lots of flavors and is found in the refrigerated and condiment sections of your supermarket. Experiment to see which one you like best.

# Couscous-Pesto Salad

**QUICK**  Prep: 15 min; Cook: 5 min        6 servings

1½  **cups uncooked couscous**
  1  **tablespoon olive or vegetable oil**
  2  **medium zucchini, halved lengthwise and cut into ¼-inch slices**
  1  **large red bell pepper, cut into ½-inch pieces**
  ½  **medium red onion, peeled and cut into 8 wedges**
  2  **cups water**
  1  **container (7 ounces) refrigerated basil pesto**
  2  **tablespoons balsamic or red wine vinegar**

1. Heat water and ½ teaspoon salt if desired to boiling in saucepan over high heat. Stir in couscous. Cover and remove from heat. Let stand 5 minutes.

2. Meanwhile, heat oil in skillet over medium-high heat 1 to 2 minutes. Cook zucchini, bell pepper and onion in oil about 5 minutes, stirring frequently, until vegetables are crisp-tender.

3. Mix couscous, vegetable mixture, pesto and vinegar in bowl. Serve warm, or cover and refrigerate about 30 minutes until chilled.

**1 SERVING:** Calories 350 (Calories from Fat 180); Fat 20g (Saturated 4g); Cholesterol 5mg; Sodium 270mg; Carbohydrate 41g (Dietary Fiber 5g); Protein 9g

# ROASTED BEET SALAD

Prep: 15 min; Bake: 1 hr; Cool: 1 hr    4 servings

- 4 **medium beets (4 to 6 ounces each)**
- ½ **cup Fresh Herb Vinaigrette (below)**
- ¼ **cup orange juice**
- 4 **cups bite-size pieces mixed salad greens**
- 1 **medium orange, peeled and sliced**
- ½ **cup walnut halves, toasted (see page 99) and coarsely chopped**
- ¼ **cup crumbled chèvre (goat) cheese**

**1.** Heat oven to 400°. Remove greens from beets, leaving about ½ inch of stem. Wash beets well. Place in square pan, 8 × 8 × 2 inches. Add ½ cup water to pan. Cover tightly with aluminum foil. Bake about 1 hour or until tender.

**2.** Cool beets 1 hour. Remove skins from beets under running water. Cut beets into slices. Cut each slice in half.

**3.** Prepare Fresh Herb Vinaigrette. Arrange salad greens on 4 salad plates. Top with beets, orange, walnuts and cheese. Drizzle with vinaigrette. Serve with remaining vinaigrette.

**1 SERVING:** Calories 270 (Calories from Fat 205); Fat 23g (Saturated 4g); Cholesterol 8mg; Sodium 75mg; Carbohydrate 14g (Dietary Fiber 3g); Protein 5g

## FRESH HERB VINAIGRETTE

- ½ **cup olive or vegetable oil**
- ¼ **cup white or cider vinegar**
- ¼ **cup orange juice**
- 1 **tablespoon chopped fresh herb leaves (basil, marjoram, oregano, rosemary, tarragon or thyme)**
- 1 **tablespoon chopped fresh parsley**
- 1 **medium green onion, trimmed and finely chopped**

Shake all ingredients in tightly covered container. Shake before serving.

# Homemade Croutons

If you want to add a little extra flair to salads when you're serving guests, try making your own croutons.

Spread one side of dry (not hard) bread with softened butter or margarine, and cut into ½-inch cubes. Or, cut dry (not hard) bread into ½-inch cubes, and toss with olive oil to lightly coat.

Then sprinkle either type of bread cubes with grated Parmesan cheese and Italian seasoning or your favorite herbs and seasonings. Cook in an ungreased heavy skillet over medium heat 4 to 7 minutes, stirring frequently, until golden brown. ■

• To make ahead, wrap filled potato shells airtight and refrigerate up to 24 hours or freeze up to 2 months. Unwrap potatoes and place on a cookie sheet. Bake in a 400° oven about 30 minutes for refrigerated potatoes or about 40 minutes for frozen potatoes, until hot.

# CHEDDAR TWICE-BAKED POTATOES

Prep: 15 min; Bake: 1 hr 35 min      8 servings

  8 **large baking potatoes (russet or Idaho), 8 to 10 ounces each**
      **About ⅓ cup milk**
  ¼ **cup (½ stick) margarine or butter at room temperature**
  ¼ **teaspoon salt**
      **Dash of pepper**
  1 **cup shredded Cheddar cheese (4 ounces)**
  1 **tablespoon chopped fresh chives**
      **Additional chopped fresh chives for garnish, if desired**

**1.** Heat oven to 375°. Scrub potatoes thoroughly with a vegetable brush, but do not peel. Pierce potatoes on all sides with a fork to allow steam to escape while potatoes bake. Place potatoes directly on oven rack.

**2.** Bake potatoes 1 hour to 1 hour 15 minutes or until potatoes feel tender when squeezed gently. (Be sure to use a pot holder because

potatoes will be very hot to the touch.) When potatoes are cool enough to handle, cut lengthwise in half. Scoop out insides into a medium bowl, leaving about a ¼-inch shell in potato skin.

3. Increase oven temperature to 400°.

4. Mash potatoes with potato masher or electric mixer until no lumps remain. Add milk in small amounts, beating after each addition. The amount of milk needed to make potatoes smooth and fluffy depends on the type of potato used.

5. Add margarine, salt and pepper. Beat vigorously until potatoes are light and fluffy. Stir in cheese and 1 tablespoon chives. Fill potato shells with mashed potato mixture. Place on ungreased cookie sheet. Bake potatoes uncovered about 20 minutes or until hot. Sprinkle with additional chives.

**1 SERVING:** Calories 305 (Calories from Fat 100); Fat 11g (Saturated 4g); Cholesterol 15mg; Sodium 260mg; Carbohydrate 47g (Dietary Fiber 4g); Protein 8g

***Horseradish Twice-Baked Potatoes:*** Omit cheese and chives. Stir ¼ cup sour cream and 2 tablespoons prepared horseradish into mashed potato mixture in step 5. Garnish with fresh dill weed if desired.

**SCOOPING POTATO FROM SHELLS**

Using a soup spoon, carefully scoop out the inside of each potato half, leaving about a ¼-inch shell.

# Marbled Potatoes and Carrots

Prep: 20 min; Cook: 25 min       4 servings

**2 medium potatoes (⅔ pound), peeled and cut into pieces**
**4 medium carrots, sliced**
**2 to 3 tablespoons milk**
**2 teaspoons margarine, butter or spread**
**¼ teaspoon salt**
**2 to 3 tablespoons milk**
**1 teaspoon margarine, butter or spread**
**¼ teaspoon dried dill weed**

1. Heat 1 inch water (salted if desired) to boiling in 1-quart saucepan. Add potatoes. Cover and heat to boiling; reduce heat. Cook 20 to 25 minutes or until tender; drain. Shake pan gently over low heat to dry potatoes.

2. Meanwhile, heat 1 inch water (salted if desired) to boiling in another 1-quart saucepan. Add carrots. Cover and heat to boiling; reduce heat. Cook about 15 minutes or until very tender; drain.

3. Mash potatoes until no lumps remain. Beat in 2 to 3 tablespoons milk in small amounts. Add 2 tablespoons margarine and ¼ teaspoon salt. Beat vigorously until potatoes are light and fluffy. Cover to keep warm.

4. Mash carrots until no lumps remain. Beat in 2 to 3 tablespoons milk in small amounts. Beat in 1 teaspoon margarine and the dill weed.

5. Spoon potato mixture into half of small serving bowl; spoon carrot mixture into other half. Pull a small rubber spatula through mixtures to create a marbled design.

**1 SERVING:** Calories 105 (Calories from Fat 25); Fat 3g (Saturated 1g); Cholesterol 2mg; Sodium 200mg; Carbohydrate 20g (Dietary Fiber 3g); Protein 2g

# READ STUFFING

**QUICK** Prep: 15 min; Cook: 5 min          5 cups

- ¾ **cup butter or stick margarine**
- 2 **large stalks celery (with leaves), chopped**
- 1 **large onion, peeled and chopped**
- 9 **cups soft bread cubes (about 15 slices bread)**
- 1½ **teaspoons chopped fresh or ½ teaspoon dried thyme leaves**
- 1 **teaspoon salt**
- ½ **teaspoon ground sage**
- ¼ **teaspoon pepper**

**1.** Melt butter in 4-quart Dutch oven over medium-high heat. Cook celery and onion in butter, stirring occasionally, until tender; remove from heat.

**2.** Toss celery mixture and remaining ingredients. Use to stuff one 10- to 12-pound turkey.

**1 SERVING (ABOUT ½ CUP):** Calories 215 (Calories from Fat 135); Fat 15g (Saturated 9g); Cholesterol 40mg; Sodium 510mg; Carbohydrate 18g (Dietary Fiber 1g); Protein 3g

***Lighter Bread Stuffing:*** For 6 grams of fat and 135 calories per serving, decrease butter to ¼ cup. Heat butter and ½ cup chicken broth to boiling in Dutch oven over medium-high heat. Cook celery and onion in broth mixture.

# $\mathscr{P}$ECAN SWEET POTATOES

Prep: 10 min; Bake: 1 hr; Cook: 2 min     8 servings

**8**   **medium sweet potatoes or yams (about 3 pounds)**

½   **cup packed brown sugar**

¼   **cup (½ stick) margarine or butter**

¼   **cup water**

¾   **teaspoon salt**

⅓   **cup chopped pecans**

**1.** Heat oven to 350°. Scrub sweet potatoes thoroughly with a vegetable brush, but do not peel. Pierce potatoes on all sides with fork to allow steam to escape while potatoes bake. Place potatoes directly on oven rack.

2. Bake potatoes about 1 hour or until tender. (Be sure to use a pot holder because potatoes will be very hot to the touch.)

3. When potatoes are cool enough to handle, gently peel off skins using a paring knife. Cut potatoes into ½-inch slices.

4. Heat brown sugar, margarine, water and salt in skillet over medium heat about 2 minutes, stirring constantly, until mixture is smooth and bubbly. Add potatoes and pecans. Gently stir until potatoes are coated with sauce.

**1 SERVING:** Calories 255 (Calories from Fat 80); Fat 9g (Saturated 1g); Cholesterol 0mg; Sodium 290mg; Carbohydrate 41g (Dietary Fiber 4g); Protein 2g

***Orange Sweet Potatoes:*** Substitute orange juice for the water. Add 1 tablespoon grated orange peel to brown sugar sauce in step 4. Omit pecans.

## SPECIAL TOUCH

### Pear Glasses

You will need:

**4 large martini or margarita glasses or footed dessert dishes**

**Straw, hay or moss**

**4 fresh pears**

**Short pillar or votive candles and uncooked rice or popcorn, if desired**

1. Line glasses with straw.

2. Place 1 pear in each glass. Arrange glasses along center of table.

3. If desired, fill 2 glasses with uncooked rice. Place candles in glasses. Alternate glasses with pears and candles on table.

# Onion and Mushroom Quinoa

**QUICK**   Prep: 10 min; Cook: 20 min        6 servings

| | |
|---|---|
| 1 | teaspoon vegetable oil |
| 1 | cup uncooked quinoa, rinsed and drained |
| 1 | small onion, peeled, quartered and sliced |
| 1 | medium carrot, shredded |
| 1 | small green bell pepper, chopped |
| 1 | cup sliced mushrooms |
| 1 | teaspoon chopped fresh or ¼ teaspoon dried thyme leaves |
| ¼ | teaspoon salt |
| 1 | can (14½ ounces) fat-free vegetable broth |

**1.** Heat oil in 2-quart saucepan over medium heat. Cook quinoa and onion in oil 4 to 5 minutes, stirring occasionally, until light brown.

**2.** Stir in remaining ingredients. Heat to boiling; reduce heat. Cover and simmer about 15 minutes or until liquid is absorbed. Fluff with fork.

**1 SERVING:** Calories 125 (Calories from Fat 25); Fat 3g (Saturated 0g); Cholesterol 0mg; Sodium 410mg; Carbohydrate 24g (Dietary Fiber 3g); Protein 4g

# Pine Nut and Green Onion Pilaf

Prep: 20 min; Cook: 25 min        6 servings

| | |
|---|---|
| 1 | tablespoon margarine or butter |
| 1 | cup uncooked regular long-grain rice |
| 12 | medium green onions, trimmed and sliced |
| 3 | tablespoons pine nuts |
| 2½ | cups fat-free chicken broth |
| 1 | teaspoon grated lemon peel |
| ¼ | teaspoon salt |

**1.** Melt margarine in 3-quart saucepan over medium-high heat. Cook rice, ½ cup of the onions and the nuts in margarine about 5 minutes, stirring occasionally, until nuts are light brown.

**2.** Stir in broth, lemon peel and salt. Heat to boiling, stirring once or twice; reduce heat. Cover and simmer 15 minutes. (Do not lift cover or stir.) Remove from heat; fluff rice lightly with fork. Sprinkle with remaining onions.

**1 SERVING:** Calories 175 (Calories from Fat 45); Fat 5g (Saturated 1g); Cholesterol 0mg; Sodium 560mg; Carbohydrate 29g (Dietary Fiber 1g); Protein 5g

# Spinach Soufflé

Prep: 25 min; Bake: 35 min        4 servings

1   **package (9 ounces) frozen chopped spinach, thawed**

3   **tablespoons all-purpose flour**

½   **teaspoon dried dill weed**

¼   **teaspoon salt**

¼   **teaspoon pepper**

1   **cup milk**

1   **cup shredded Cheddar cheese (4 ounces)**

5   **large eggs**

**1.** Heat oven to 350°. Grease bottom and side of 2-quart casserole with shortening.

**2.** Squeeze spinach to drain; spread on paper towels and pat dry. Mix flour, dill weed, salt, pepper and milk in 2-quart saucepan. Cook over medium-high heat, stirring constantly, until thickened; remove from heat. Stir in cheese and spinach.

**3.** Separate eggs; set egg whites aside. Beat egg yolks in large bowl with wire whisk. Gradually stir in spinach mixture. Beat egg whites in large bowl with electric mixer on high speed until stiff. Gently fold egg whites into egg yolk mixture.

**4.** Spoon spinach mixture into casserole. Bake uncovered 30 to 35 minutes or until golden brown and puffed.

**1 SERVING:** Calories 270 (Calories from Fat 155); Fat 17g (Saturated 9g); Cholesterol 300mg; Sodium 470mg; Carbohydrate 11g (Dietary Fiber 1g); Protein 19g

***Corn Soufflé:*** Omit dill weed. Substitute 1½ cups frozen whole kernel corn, thawed, for the spinach.

**COOKING TIP**

• Soufflés stay fluffy and are easiest to serve when two forks or a fork and spoon are used to divide the servings.

**COOKING TIP**

• You can substitute 2 packages (10 ounces each) frozen asparagus spears for the fresh asparagus. Cook as directed on package.

# *H*AZELNUT-PARMESAN ASPARAGUS

**QUICK**    Prep: 5 min; Cook: 10 min          4 servings

1  **pound asparagus spears**

1  **cup water**

1  **tablespoon margarine or butter**

4  **ounces sliced mushrooms (about 1½ cups)**

¾  **teaspoon chopped fresh or ¼ teaspoon dried basil leaves**

⅛  **teaspoon salt**

⅛  **teaspoon coarsely ground pepper**

1  **tablespoon shredded Parmesan cheese**

2  **tablespoons chopped hazelnuts (filberts)**

**1.** Break off tough ends of asparagus stalks where they snap easily. Discard ends.

**2.** Heat water in skillet to boiling over high heat. Add asparagus. Cover and heat to boiling again. Once water is boiling, reduce heat just enough so water bubbles gently. Cook covered 4 to 6 minutes or until asparagus is crisp-tender. Remove asparagus from water with tongs, allowing extra water to drip off; set aside.

**3.** Meanwhile, melt margarine in skillet over medium-high heat. Stir in mushrooms. Cook 2 to 3 minutes, stirring frequently, until mushrooms are light brown. Add asparagus, basil, salt and pepper to mushrooms in skillet. Stir until vegetables are coated with seasonings. Sprinkle with cheese and hazelnuts.

**1 SERVING:** Calories 85 (Calories from Fat 55); Fat 6g (Saturated 1g); Cholesterol 2mg; Sodium 160mg; Carbohydrate 5g (Dietary Fiber 1g); Protein 4g

# Versatile White Sauce

Instead of serving plain vegetables with an elegant dinner, try impressing company by topping veggies with a beautiful white sauce. Also called Béchamel sauce, this is perfect paired with all sorts of vegetables, as well as meat and fish. Or, you can use it as a creamy sauce in casseroles. Try the many flavored variations of this sauce as well (see recipe variations below).

Prep: 5 min; Cook: 5 min        About 1 cup

- **2 tablespoons butter or stick margarine**
- **2 tablespoons all-purpose flour**
- **¼ teaspoon salt**
- **⅛ teaspoon pepper**
- **1 cup milk**

Melt butter in 1½-quart saucepan over low heat. Stir in flour, salt and pepper. Cook over medium heat, stirring constantly, until mixture is smooth and bubbly; remove from heat. Gradually stir in milk. Heat to boiling, stirring constantly. Boil and stir 1 minute.

**1 SERVING (1 TABLESPOON):** Calories 25 (Calories from Fat 20); Fat 2g (Saturated 1g); Cholesterol 5mg; Sodium 55mg; Carbohydrate 1g (Dietary Fiber 0g); Protein 1g

**Curry Sauce:** Stir in ½ teaspoon curry powder with the flour. Serve with chicken, lamb or shrimp.

**Dill Sauce:** Stir in 1 teaspoon chopped fresh or ½ teaspoon dried dill weed and dash of ground nutmeg with the flour. Serve with fish.

**Mustard Sauce:** Decrease butter to 1 tablespoon and flour to 1 tablespoon. After boiling and stirring sauce 1 minute, stir in 3 tablespoons prepared yellow mustard and 1 tablespoon prepared horseradish. Serve with beef, veal, ham and vegetables. ■

# $\mathcal{S}$TUFFED ZUCCHINI

Prep: 10 min; Cook: 15 min; Bake: 35 min     8 servings

4 **medium zucchini**

1 **medium onion, peeled and chopped**

¼ **cup (½ stick) margarine or butter**

1 **can (4 ounces) chopped green chilies, drained**

1 **jar (2 ounces) diced pimientos, drained**

1½ **cups herb-seasoned stuffing mix (dry)**

¾ **cup shredded mozzarella or Monterey Jack cheese (3 ounces)**

**1.** Heat 2 inches water (salted if desired) to boiling. Add zucchini. Heat to boiling; reduce heat. Cover and simmer just until tender, 8 to 10 minutes; drain. Cool slightly; cut each zucchini lengthwise in half.

**2.** Spoon out pulp; chop coarsely. Place zucchini, cut sides up, in ungreased rectangular baking dish, 13 × 9 × 2 inches.

**3.** Heat oven to 350°.

**4.** Cook and stir onion in margarine in 10-inch skillet until onion is tender. Stir in chopped pulp, chilies, pimientos and stuffing mix. Divide stuffing mixture among zucchini halves. Sprinkle each with cheese. Bake uncovered until hot, 30 to 35 minutes.

**1 SERVING:** Calories 145 (Calories from Fat 70); Fat 8g (Saturated 2g); Cholesterol 5mg; Sodium 330mg; Carbohydrate 14g (Dietary Fiber 2g); Protein 6g

# $\mathscr{B}$ROCCOLI WITH PINE NUTS

**QUICK**  Prep: 5 min; Cook: 15 min  4 servings

1 **cup water**

1½ **pounds broccoli, cut into spears**

¼ **cup (½ stick) butter or stick margarine**

½ **cup pine nuts, almonds or pecans**

**1.** Heat water to boiling in 2-quart saucepan. Add broccoli. Cook uncovered 5 to 7 minutes or until stems are crisp-tender; drain.

**2.** Melt butter in 8-inch skillet over medium heat. Cook pine nuts in butter about 5 minutes, stirring frequently, until golden brown. Stir pine nuts into broccoli.

**1 SERVING:** Calories 235 (Calories from Fat 200); Fat 22g (Saturated 9g); Cholesterol 30mg; Sodium 110mg; Carbohydrate 9g (Dietary Fiber 5g); Protein 5g

## SPECIAL TOUCH

### Green Onion and Flower Bundle

You will need:

**1 bunch fresh green onions**

**Fresh flowers**

**Clear drinking glass (6 to 8 inches high)**

**Twine**

1. Trim ends of tops of onions. Trim stems of flowers so they are shorter than onions.

2. Tie twine around onions and flowers to form a bundle.

3. Fill glass about ½ full with water. Place bundle in glass.

# DESSERTS

**DIPPING STRAWBERRIES**

For each strawberry, poke a fork into stem end, and dip three-fourths of the way into melted white chips, leaving the top of the strawberry and leaves uncoated.

# White Chocolate–Dipped Strawberries

Prep: 10 min; Cook: 10 min; Chill: 30 min     18 to 24 strawberries

18 to 24  **large strawberries with leaves**
    1  **bag (12 ounces) white baking chips (2 cups)**
    1  **tablespoon shortening**
    ½  **cup semisweet chocolate chips**
    1  **teaspoon shortening**

**1.** Cover cookie sheet with waxed paper.

**2.** Rinse strawberries with cool water and pat dry with paper towels.

**3.** Heat white baking chips and 1 tablespoon shortening in saucepan over low heat, stirring constantly, until chips are melted.

**4.** For each strawberry, poke a fork into stem end, and dip three-fourths of the way into melted white chips, leaving top of strawberry and leaves uncoated. Place dipped strawberries on waxed paper–covered cookie sheet.

**5.** Heat semisweet chocolate chips and 1 teaspoon shortening in another small saucepan over low heat, stirring constantly, until chocolate chips are melted. (Or place chocolate chips and shortening in a small microwavable bowl. Microwave uncovered on medium 1 minute; stir. Microwave 2 to 3 minutes longer, until mixture can be stirred smooth.)

**6.** Drizzle melted chocolate chips over dipped strawberries, using a small spoon. Refrigerate uncovered about 30 minutes or until coating is set.

**1 STRAWBERRY:** Calories 125 (Calories from Fat 65); Fat 8g (Saturated 5g); Cholesterol 5mg; Sodium 15mg; Carbohydrate 15g (Dietary Fiber 1g); Protein 1g

**Double Chocolate–Dipped Strawberries:** Substitute 1 package (12 ounces) semisweet or milk chocolate chips for the white baking chips.

# $\mathcal{B}$ANANA—CHOCOLATE CHIP BISCOTTI

Prep: 30 min; Bake: 47 min; Cool: 15 min          32 cookies

1 **cup sugar**

½ **cup (1 stick) butter or stick margarine, softened (see tip)**

½ **cup mashed very ripe banana (1 medium)**

2 **eggs**

1 **teaspoon vanilla**

3 **cups all-purpose flour (see tip)**

3 **teaspoons baking powder**

¼ **teaspoon salt**

½ **cup miniature semisweet chocolate chips**

1. Heat oven to 350°. Grease large cookie sheet.

2. Beat sugar and butter in large bowl with electric mixer on medium speed, or mix with spoon. Beat in banana, eggs and vanilla until smooth. Stir in flour, baking powder and salt. Stir in chocolate chips.

3. Divide dough in half. Shape each half into 10 × 3-inch rectangle on cookie sheet with greased hands (dough will be sticky).

4. Bake about 25 minutes or until toothpick inserted in center comes out clean. Cool on cookie sheet on wire rack 15 minutes.

5. Cut crosswise into ½-inch slices. Turn slices, cut sides down, on cookie sheet. Bake 10 to 12 minutes or until golden brown and dry on top. Turn cookies. Bake about 10 minutes longer or until golden brown. Remove from cookie sheet to wire rack.

**1 COOKIE:** Calories 110 (Calories from Fat 35); Fat 4g (Saturated 2g); Cholesterol 20mg; Sodium 90mg; Carbohydrate 18g (Dietary Fiber 1g); Protein 2g

# $\mathcal{V}$ELVET CRUMB CAKE

Prep: 10 min; Bake: 35 min; Broil: 3 min        8 servings

1½  **cup Original Bisquick baking mix**

½  **cup sugar**

½  **cup milk or water**

2  **tablespoons shortening**

1  **teaspoon vanilla**

1  **egg**
   **Broiled Topping (below)**

1. Heat oven to 350°. Grease and flour square pan, 8 × 8 × 2 or 9 × 9 × 2 inches, or round pan, 9 × 1½ inches.

2. Beat all ingredients except Broiled Topping in large bowl on low speed 30 seconds, scraping bowl constantly. Beat on medium speed 4 minutes, scraping bowl occasionally. Pour into pan.

3. Bake 9-inch square pan 25 to 30 minutes, 8-inch square or 9-inch round pan 30 to 35 minutes or until toothpick inserted in center comes out clean; cool slightly.

4. Prepare Broiled Topping; spread over cake. Set oven control to broil. Broil cake about 3 inches from heat about 3 minutes or until topping is golden brown.

**1 SERVING:** Calories 310 (Calories from Fat 145); Fat 16g (Saturated 5g); Cholesterol 30mg; Sodium 400mg; Carbohydrate 39g (Dietary Fiber 1g); Protein 3g

## BROILED TOPPING

½  **cup flaked coconut**

⅓  **cup packed brown sugar**

¼  **cup chopped nuts**

3  **tablespoons margarine or butter, softened**

2  **tablespoons milk**

Mix all ingredients.

**REMOVING CAKE FROM PAN**

Place wire rack upside down onto cake. Using pot holders, turn rack and pan over together and remove pan.

# Vanilla-Glazed Sour Cream Coffee Cake

Prep: 20 min; Bake: 1 hr; Cool: 15 min    16 servings

½ cup packed brown sugar

½ cup finely chopped nuts

1½ teaspoons ground cinnamon

1½ cups granulated sugar

¾ cup (1½ sticks) margarine or butter at room temperature

1½ teaspoons vanilla

3 eggs

3 cups all-purpose flour

1½ teaspoons baking powder

1½ teaspoons baking soda

¾ teaspoon salt

1½ cups sour cream

Vanilla Glaze (at right)

1. Heat oven to 350°. Grease bottom and side of Bundt cake pan with shortening.

2. Mix brown sugar, nuts and cinnamon; set aside.

3. Beat granulated sugar, margarine, vanilla and eggs in large bowl with electric mixer on medium speed 2 minutes, scraping bowl occasionally.

4. Mix flour, baking powder, baking soda and salt in medium bowl. Beat about one-third of the flour mixture into sugar mixture on low speed until blended. Beat in about ½ cup of the sour cream until blended. Repeat with remaining flour mixture and sour cream.

5. Spread one-third of the batter (about 2 cups) in greased pan. Sprinkle with half of the brown sugar mixture. Repeat layers once. Spread with remaining batter.

6. Bake about 1 hour or until toothpick inserted near center comes out clean. Meanwhile, prepare Vanilla Glaze.

**7.** Place pan on wire rack and cool 5 minutes. Run a knife around edge of pan to loosen cake. Remove cake from pan. To remove cake from pan, place wire rack upside down onto cake. Using pot holders, turn rack and pan over together, and remove pan. Cool 10 minutes.

**8.** Dip a spoon into glaze. Spread glaze over top of cake, letting glaze drip down sides of cake. Serve cake warm or cool.

**1 SERVING:** Calories 370 (Calories from Fat 145); Fat 16g (Saturated 5g); Cholesterol 55mg; Sodium 410mg; Carbohydrate 57g (Dietary Fiber 1g); Protein 5g

**SPREADING GLAZE OVER CAKE**

Dip a small spoon into glaze. Spread glaze over top of cake letting glaze drip down sides of cake.

## VANILLA GLAZE

½  **cup powdered sugar**

¼  **teaspoon vanilla**

**2 to 3  teaspoons milk**

Mix powdered sugar, vanilla and milk until smooth and spreadable.

## COOKING TIP

• Feel free to use your favorite flavor of ice cream, frozen yogurt, or sherbet to top the cake. Instead of candy decorations, you can use colored sugars, edible flowers, sliced fresh fruit or ice cream topping for a special finish.

# 𝒫ARTY ICE CREAM CAKE

Prep: 15 min; Bake: 33 min; Cool: 1 hr; Freeze: 4 hr        16 servings

> 1   **package (1 pound 2¼ ounces) party rainbow chip cake mix**
> 1¼  **cups water**
> ⅓   **cup vegetable oil**
> 3   **eggs**
> 1   **quart ice cream or frozen yogurt (any flavor), slightly softened**
>     **Candy decorations, if desired**

**1.** Heat oven to 350°. Spray just bottom of rectangular pan, 13 × 9 × 2 inches, with cooking spray.

**2.** Beat cake mix, water, oil and eggs in a large bowl with the electric mixer on low speed 2 minutes. Pour batter into the sprayed pan.

3. Bake 28 to 33 minutes or until toothpick inserted in center comes out clean. Place pan on a wire rack. Cool completely, about 1 hour.

4. Spread ice cream over top of cooled cake. Immediately cover and freeze at least 4 hours or until firm.

5. Just before serving, top cake with candy decorations. Cover and freeze any remaining cake.

**1 SERVING:** Calories 265 (Calories from Fat 90); Fat 10g (Saturated 2g); Cholesterol 0mg; Sodium 300mg; Carbohydrate 40g (Dietary Fiber 0g); Protein 4g

**SERVING TIP**

• So the frozen cake won't be too hard to cut, remove it from the freezer 20 to 30 minutes before serving.

## SPECIAL TOUCH

### Floral Vase

You will need:

**Vase (8 to 10 inches high)**

**20-inch-square piece lightweight fabric (If fabric is very thin, you can use spray starch to stiffen it. Let fabric dry before wrapping.)**

**About 1½ yards 1½-inch-wide ribbon**

**Fresh flowers to coordinate with fabric and ribbon**

1. Place vase on center of fabric. Wrap fabric around vase by pulling up the four corners first and then the sides.

2. Wrap ribbon around neck of vase to secure fabric; tie bow.

3. Fill vase with water. Arrange flowers in vase.

# CHOCOLATE SOUFFLÉ CAKES

Prep: 20 min; Bake: 22 min; Cool: 20 min      8 servings

1    **ounce sweet baking chocolate**

1    **tablespoon margarine or butter**

1    **teaspoon instant espresso coffee (dry)**

2    **egg whites**

2    **eggs, separated**

1    **container (8 ounces) vanilla low-fat yogurt**

½    **cup granulated sugar**

¼    **cup packed brown sugar**

¼    **cup all-purpose flour**

¼    **cup baking cocoa**

¼    **teaspoon ground cinnamon**

     **Mocha Topping (below)**

     **Frozen (thawed) fat-free whipped topping, if desired**

**1.** Heat oven to 375°. Spray bottoms only of 8 jumbo muffin cups, 3¾ × 1⅞ inches, with cooking spray. Heat chocolate, margarine and espresso in 1-quart saucepan over low heat, stirring constantly, until melted and smooth; cool slightly.

**2.** Beat 4 egg whites in medium bowl with electric mixer on high speed until stiff peaks form; set aside. Beat egg yolks and yogurt in another medium bowl on medium speed until blended. Gradually beat in granulated sugar, brown sugar and chocolate mixture. Stir in flour, cocoa and cinnamon just until blended. Fold in egg whites. Spoon into muffin cups.

**3.** Bake 20 to 22 minutes or until firm to the touch. Cool 5 minutes (centers of cakes will sink slightly). Remove from muffin cups to wire rack. Cool 15 minutes.

**4.** Meanwhile, prepare Mocha Topping. Place cakes on individual plates. Drizzle with topping. Serve with whipped topping.

**1 SERVING:** Calories 215 (Calories from Fat 45); Fat 5g (Saturated 2g); Cholesterol 55mg; Sodium 80mg; Carbohydrate 38g (Dietary Fiber 1g); Protein 5g

## MOCHA TOPPING

¼    **cup chocolate-flavored syrup**

4    **teaspoons powdered sugar**

½    **teaspoon instant espresso coffee (dry)**

Heat all ingredients in 1-quart saucepan over low heat, stirring constantly, until smooth.

# *P*UMPKIN CHEESECAKE

Prep: 15 min; Bake: 1 hr 25 min; Cook: 2 min    12 servings

1¼  **cups gingersnap cookie crumbs (about twenty 2-inch cookies)**
¼  **cup margarine or butter, melted**
3  **packages (8 ounces each) cream cheese, softened**
1  **cup sugar**
1  **teaspoon ground cinnamon**
1  **teaspoon ground ginger**
½  **teaspoon ground cloves**
1  **can (16 ounces) pumpkin**
4  **eggs**
2  **tablespoons sugar**
12  **walnut halves**
¾  **cup chilled whipping cream**

**1.** Heat oven to 350°.

**2.** Mix cookie crumbs and margarine. Press evenly on bottom of springform pan, 9 × 3 inches. Bake 10 minutes; cool. Reduce oven temperature to 300°.

**3.** Beat cream cheese, 1 cup sugar, the cinnamon, ginger and cloves in 4-quart bowl on medium speed until smooth and fluffy. Add pumpkin. Beat in eggs, one at a time on low speed. Pour over crumb mixture.

**4.** Bake until center is firm, about 1 hour 15 minutes. Cool to room temperature. Cover and refrigerate at least 3 hours but no longer than 48 hours.

**5.** Cook and stir 2 tablespoons sugar and the walnuts over medium heat until sugar is melted and nuts are coated. Immediately spread on a dinner plate or aluminum foil; cool. Carefully break nuts apart to separate if necessary. Cover tightly and store at room temperature up to 3 days.

**6.** Loosen cheesecake from side of pan; remove side of pan. Beat whipping cream in chilled 1½-quart bowl until stiff. Pipe whipped cream around edge of cheesecake; arrange walnuts on top. Refrigerate any remaining cheesecake immediately.

**1 SERVING:** Calories 450 (Calories from Fat 290); Fat 32g (Saturated 17g); Cholesterol 150mg; Sodium 310mg; Carbohydrate 33g (Dietary Fiber 1g); Protein 8g

# BLACK FOREST CHERRY TORTE

Prep: 20 min; Bake: 35 min; Cool: 10 min; Cook: 5 min        12 servings

**Bonnie Butter Cake (page 103)**
**Cherry Filling (below)**
1½ **cups chilled whipping cream**
¼ **cup powdered sugar**
⅓ **bar (4-ounce size) sweet cooking chocolate, grated**

1. Bake Bonnie Butter Cake in 9-inch layers as directed. Cool 10 minutes; remove from pans. Cool completely. Prepare Cherry Filling; refrigerate until chilled.

2. To assemble cake, place 1 layer, top side down, on serving plate. Beat whipping cream and powdered sugar in chilled bowl until very stiff. Form thin rim of whipped cream around edge of layer with decorators' tube or spoon. Fill center with Cherry Filling. Place other layer, top side up, on filling. Gently spread whipped cream on side and top of cake. Gently press chocolate by teaspoonfuls onto side of cake.

3. Place remaining whipped cream in decorators' tube with star tip. Pipe border of whipped cream around top edge of cake. Beginning from center of cake, outline individual portions in spoke design. Place desired number of reserved dipped cherries in each portion. Store torte in refrigerator.

**1 SERVING:** Calories 510 (Calories from Fat 220); Fat 24g (Saturated 10g); Cholesterol 80mg; Sodium 450mg; Carbohydrate 69g (Dietary Fiber 1g); Protein 6g

## CHERRY FILLING

2 **tablespoons cornstarch**
2 **tablespoons sugar**
1 **can (16 ounces) pitted dark sweet cherries**
1 **tablespoon brandy flavoring**

1. Mix cornstarch and sugar in 1-quart saucepan. Drain cherries, reserving syrup. Add enough water to reserved cherry syrup to measure 1 cup; stir into sugar-cornstarch mixture. Cook, stirring constantly, until mixture thickens and boils. Boil and stir 1 minute. Cool to lukewarm.

2. Stir in brandy flavoring. Dip 36 cherries into thickened syrup; reserve for top of cake. Cut remaining cherries into fourths and stir into thickened syrup.

# $\mathcal{B}$READ PUDDING WITH WHISKEY SAUCE

Prep: 15 min; Cook: 5 min; Bake: 45 min        8 servings

**2  cups milk**

**¼  cup (½ stick) margarine or butter**

**½  cup sugar**

**1  teaspoon ground cinnamon or nutmeg**

**¼  teaspoon salt**

**2  eggs, slightly beaten**

**6  cups dry bread cubes (8 slices bread)**

**½  cup raisins, if desired**

**Whiskey Sauce (below)**

**1.** Heat oven to 350°.

**2.** Heat milk and margarine in 2-quart saucepan over medium heat until margarine is melted and milk is hot.

**3.** Mix sugar, cinnamon, salt and eggs in large bowl with wire whisk until well blended. Stir in bread cubes and raisins. Stir in milk mixture. Pour into ungreased 1½-quart casserole or square baking dish, 8 × 8 × 2 inches. Place casserole in rectangular pan, 13 × 9 × 2 inches; pour boiling water into rectangular pan until 1 inch deep.

**4.** Bake uncovered 40 to 45 minutes or until knife inserted 1 inch from edge of casserole comes out clean.

**5.** Meanwhile, prepare Whiskey Sauce. Serve sauce over warm bread pudding. Refrigerate any remaining dessert.

**1 SERVING:** Calories 665 (Calories from Fat 215); Fat 24g (Saturated 6g); Cholesterol 60mg; Sodium 1020mg; Carbohydrate 101g (Dietary Fiber 3g); Protein 14g

## WHISKEY SAUCE

**1  cup packed brown sugar**

**½  cup (1 stick) stick margarine or butter**

**3 to 4  tablespoons bourbon or 2 teaspoons brandy extract**

Heat all ingredients to boiling in heavy 1-quart saucepan over medium heat, stirring constantly, until sugar is dissolved. Serve warm or cool.

## COOKING TIP

• To serve a crowd of 10, double all ingredients in recipe except French bread. Bake in a greased 13 × 9-inch rectangular pan. There's no need to double the Cran-Raspberry Topping.

# CRAN-RASPBERRY BREAD PUDDING

Prep: 15 min; Bake: 55 min; Cook: 5 min    6 servings

1 loaf (8 ounces) or ½ loaf (1-pound size) French bread
2 tablespoons raisins, if desired
3 eggs
⅓ cup granulated sugar
½ teaspoon ground cinnamon
   Dash of salt
1½ cups milk
2 tablespoons packed brown sugar
   Cran-Raspberry Topping (at right)

1. Heat oven to 325°. Grease bottom and sides of square pan, 9 × 9 × 2 inches, with shortening.

2. Tear bread into 1-inch pieces. You should have about 8 cups of bread pieces. Spread bread pieces evenly in greased pan. Sprinkle with raisins.

**3.** Beat eggs, granulated sugar, cinnamon and salt in medium bowl with fork or wire whisk. Beat in milk. Pour milk mixture over bread in pan. Sprinkle with brown sugar.

**4.** Bake uncovered 50 to 55 minutes or until golden brown. Meanwhile, prepare Cran-Raspberry Topping. Serve bread pudding warm with topping.

**1 SERVING:** Calories 410 (Calories from Fat 45); Fat 5g (Saturated 2g); Cholesterol 110mg; Sodium 280mg; Carbohydrate 86g (Dietary Fiber 4g); Protein 9g

## CRAN-RASPBERRY TOPPING

**1  package (10 ounces) frozen raspberries in syrup, thawed**

**1  cup granulated sugar**

**1  cup cranberries**

Drain raspberries in strainer, reserving ½ cup of syrup. Mix syrup and sugar in saucepan. Cook over medium heat, stirring constantly, until mixture thickens and boils. Continue boiling 1 to 2 minutes, stirring constantly. Stir in raspberries and cranberries. Reduce heat just enough so mixture bubbles gently. Cook about 3 minutes, stirring occasionally, until cranberries are tender but do not burst.

### Sticker Garland

You will need:

**12 to 16 round or same-shape self-adhesive stickers**
**About 1 yard thin ribbon or string**

1. Place 1 sticker on ribbon; back with another sticker.

2. Repeat with remaining stickers, spacing them evenly along length of ribbon.

3. Arrange garland along center of table.

# CHOCOLATE MOUSSE

Prep: 25 min; Chill: 2 hr       8 servings

**4  large egg yolks**

**¼  cup sugar**

**1  cup whipping (heavy) cream**

**1  package (6 ounces) semisweet chocolate chips (1 cup)**

**1½  cups whipping (heavy) cream**

**1.** Beat egg yolks in small bowl with electric mixer on high speed about 3 minutes or until thick and lemon colored. Gradually beat in sugar.

**2.** Heat 1 cup whipping cream in 2-quart saucepan over medium heat just until hot.

**3.** Gradually stir at least half of the hot cream into egg yolk mixture, then stir back into hot cream in saucepan. Cook over low heat about 5 minutes, stirring constantly, until mixture thickens (do not boil).

**4.** Stir in chocolate chips until melted. Cover and refrigerate about 2 hours, stirring occasionally, just until chilled.

**5.** Beat 1½ cups whipping cream in chilled medium bowl on high speed until stiff. Fold chocolate mixture into whipped cream. Pipe or spoon mixture into dessert dishes or stemmed glasses. Refrigerate until serving. Store covered in refrigerator.

**1 SERVING:** Calories 390 (Calories from Fat 290); Fat 32g (Saturated 19g); Cholesterol 190mg; Sodium 30mg; Carbohydrate 22g (Dietary Fiber 1g); Protein 4g

**Lighter Chocolate Mousse:** For 13 grams of fat and 225 calories per serving, substitute 2 eggs for the 4 egg yolks, half-and-half for the 1 cup whipping cream and 3 cups frozen (thawed) reduced-fat whipped topping for the whipped 1½ cups whipping cream.

**White Chocolate Mousse:** Substitute white baking chips for the chocolate chips.

## Chocolate Curls and Shavings

To make chocolate curls for garnishing desserts, pull a swivel-bladed vegetable peeler or thin, sharp knife across a block of milk chocolate, using long, thin strokes. The curls will be easier to make if the chocolate is slightly warm, so you can let it stand in a warm place for about 15 minutes before cutting if you like. Semisweet chocolate will make smaller curls. Use a toothpick to lift the curls from the chocolate and to place them on a frosted cake, pie or dessert. Make chocolate shavings the same way by using shorter strokes. ■

# Tiramisu

Prep: 20 min; Chill: 4 hr     9 servings

1   cup whipping (heavy) cream
1   package (8 ounces) cream cheese at room temperature
½   cup powdered sugar
2   tablespoons light rum or ½ teaspoon rum extract
1   package (3 ounces) ladyfingers (12 ladyfingers)
½   cup cold prepared espresso or strong coffee
2   teaspoons baking cocoa
    Maraschino cherries with stems for garnish, if desired

**1.** Pour whipping cream into medium bowl and place in the refrigerator to chill.

**2.** Beat cream cheese and powdered sugar in another medium bowl with electric mixer on medium speed until smooth. Beat in rum on low speed; set aside.

**3.** Beat whipping cream on high speed until stiff peaks form. Gently spoon whipped cream onto cream cheese mixture. To fold together, use a rubber spatula to cut down vertically through the mixtures, then slide spatula across bottom of bowl and up side, turning mixtures over. Rotate bowl one-fourth turn and repeat this down-across-up motion. Continue mixing in this way just until ingredients are blended.

**4.** Split each ladyfinger horizontally in half. Arrange half of them, cut sides up, over bottom of ungreased square pan, 8 × 8 × 2 inches. Drizzle ¼ cup of the cold espresso over the ladyfingers. Spread half of the cream cheese mixture over ladyfingers.

**5.** Arrange remaining ladyfingers, cut sides up, over cream cheese mixture. Drizzle with remaining ¼ cup cold espresso, and spread with remaining cream cheese mixture.

**6.** Sprinkle cocoa over top of dessert. Cover and refrigerate about 4 hours or until filling is firm. Garnish each serving with a cherry.

**1 SERVING.** Calories 240 (Calories from Fat 160); Fat 18g (Saturated 11g); Cholesterol 60mg; Sodium 115mg; Carbohydrate 17g (Dietary Fiber 0g); Protein 3g

*Lighter Tiramisu:* For 8 grams of fat and 165 calories per serving, use reduced-fat cream cheese (Neufchâtel) instead of regular cream cheese. Use 2 cups frozen (thawed) reduced-fat whipped topping for the whipping cream.

# AKED CUSTARD

Prep: 15 min; Bake: 45 min; Cool: 30 min          6 servings

**3** **large eggs, slightly beaten**
**⅓** **cup sugar**
**1** **teaspoon vanilla**
   **Dash of salt**
**2½** **cups very warm milk**
   **Ground nutmeg**

**1.** Heat oven to 350°.

**2.** Mix eggs, sugar, vanilla and salt in medium bowl with wire whisk or fork. Gradually stir in milk. Pour into six 6-ounce custard cups. Sprinkle with nutmeg.

**3.** Place cups in rectangular pan, 13 × 9 × 2 inches, on oven rack. Pour very hot water into pan to within ½ inch of tops of cups.

**4.** Bake about 45 minutes or until knife inserted halfway between center and edge comes out clean. Remove cups from water. Cool about 30 minutes. Unmold and serve warm, or refrigerate and un-mold before serving. Store covered in refrigerator.

**1 SERVING:** Calories 135 (Calories from Fat 45); Fat 5g (Saturated 2g); Cholesterol 115mg; Sodium 120mg; Carbohydrate 16g (Dietary Fiber 0g); Protein 7g

## COOKING TIPS

• Do not use glass custard cups or glass pie plates; they cannot withstand the heat from broiling and may break.

• If you use ramekins instead of a pie plate, place them on a baking sheet before setting them under the broiler to make removing them easier.

# CRÈME BRÛLÉE

Prep: 15 min; Cook: 15 min; Chill: 4 hr        4 servings

4 **large egg yolks**

3 **tablespoons granulated sugar**

2 **cups whipping (heavy) cream**

1 **teaspoon vanilla**

⅓ **cup packed brown sugar**

1. Beat egg yolks in medium bowl with electric mixer on high speed about 3 minutes or until thick and lemon colored. Gradually beat in granulated sugar.

2. Heat whipping cream in 2-quart saucepan over medium heat just until hot.

3. Gradually stir at least half of the hot cream into egg yolk mixture, then stir back into hot cream in saucepan. Cook over low heat 5 to 8 minutes, stirring constantly, until mixture thickens (do not boil). Stir in vanilla.

4. Pour custard into four 6-ounce ceramic ramekins (see tip) or ungreased ceramic pie plate, 9 × 1¼ inches (see tip). Cover and refrigerate at least 2 hours but no longer than 24 hours. Custard must be completely chilled before broiling with brown sugar on top to keep custard from overheating.

5. Set oven control to broil. Sprinkle brown sugar evenly over custard. Broil with tops about 5 inches from heat about 3 minutes or until sugar is melted and forms a glaze. Serve immediately (mixture will be runny), or refrigerate 1 to 2 hours or until slightly firm. Store covered in refrigerator.

**1 SERVING:** Calories 610 (Calories from Fat 380); Fat 42g (Saturated 24g); Cholesterol 340mg; Sodium 60mg; Carbohydrate 54g (Dietary Fiber 2g); Protein 6g

# MENUS FOR WEEKEND MEALS

## Snacks and Sweets

Cheese Fondue, **page 206**
Marinated Peppers, Olives and Cheese, **page 216**
Assorted crackers
White Chocolate–Dipped Strawberries, **page 286**
Chocolate Soufflé Cakes, **page 295**
Sparkling cider

**SPECIAL TOUCH:** An old mirror cleaned with vinegar makes a beautiful platter for serving snacks.

## Sit-Down Dinner

Toast points with garlic cream cheese
Broiled Salmon with Hazelnut Butter, **page 240**
Marbled Potatoes and Carrots, **page 276**
Broccoli with Pine Nuts, **page 285**
Velvet Crumb Cake, **page 289**
Champagne, coffee and tea

**SPECIAL TOUCH:** Dim the lights and use candles during your meal to create a relaxing atmosphere.

## Buffet-Style Party

Italian Stuffed Mushrooms, **page 215**
Sun-Dried Tomato Biscotti with Basil–Cream Cheese Topping, **page 219**
Cider-Glazed Stuffed Pork Roast, **page 260**
*Hazelnut-Parmesan Asparagus, **page 282**
Banana–Chocolate Chip Biscotti, **page 288**
Prepared fruit salad
Sangria, **page 205**

**SPECIAL TOUCH:** To decorate a buffet table, place rings of tea light candles, small flower blossoms, and sprigs of greenery on a tiered cake stand.

## Small Gathering

Spinach-Filled Fish Rolls, **page 248**
Parmesan Sun-Dried Tomato Bread, **page 224**
Pine Nut and Green Onion Pilaf, **page 280**
Crème Brûlée, **page 306**
Citrus Spritzers, **page 199**

**SPECIAL TOUCH:** Decorate serving plates with frosted fruit. Brush clusters of grapes or cranberries with corn syrup and sprinkle with sugar.

## For a Larger Crowd

Jamaican Shrimp, **page 210**
Asiago Cheese and Artichoke Dip, **page 207**
Crunchy Herb-Baked Chicken, **page 249**
Mixed greens with balsamic vinaigrette
Black Forest Cherry Torte, **page 298**
Neapolitan ice cream
Sparkling Cranberry Punch, **page 200**

**SPECIAL TOUCH:** Place plain or chocolate-dipped pirouette cookies on a serving plate next to the punch bowl.

## Last-Minute Meal

Pear and Blue Cheese Salad, **page 268**
Garlic-Ginger Chicken with Fettuccine, **page 250**
Prepared rice pudding
Iced tea with lemon slices

**SPECIAL TOUCH:** Gift wrap can be a fun tablecloth. First, cover your table with a plain white tablecloth. Then cut gift wrap paper slightly smaller than the plain tablecloth and place on top.

*Double recipes that are marked with an asterisk.

# MAKE-AHEAD OR TAKE-ALONG

Whether you're planning a potluck or just planning ahead, these recipes are just the ticket. Do the prep work now and cook later, or pack 'em up for easy transport to the big get-together. Either way, you'll have more time to join in the fun with family and friends!

◀ Tabbouleh with Garbanzo Beans (page 346)

# BEVERAGES

## STRAWBERRY SMOOTHIES

**QUICK** Prep: 5 min    4 servings

1 **pint (2 cups) strawberries**

1 **cup milk**

2 **containers (6 ounces each) strawberry yogurt**

**1.** Reserve 4 strawberries (with green stems) for garnish. Cut out the hull, or "cap," from remaining strawberries.

**2.** Place remaining strawberries, the milk and yogurt in blender. Cover and blend on high speed about 30 seconds or until smooth.

**3.** Pour mixture into 4 glasses. Make a small cut partway up the bottom of the reserved strawberries. Place one on each glass.

**1 SERVING:** Calories 130 (Calories from Fat 20); Fat 2g (Saturated 1g); Cholesterol 10mg; Sodium 80mg; Carbohydrate 24g (Dietary Fiber 2g); Protein 6g

***Strawberry-Banana Smoothies:*** Substitute 1 medium banana, cut into chunks, for 1 cup of the strawberries.

# RANGE SMOOTHIES

**QUICK**   Prep: 5 min          4 servings

1   **quart (4 cups) vanilla frozen yogurt or ice cream, slightly softened**

½   **cup frozen orange juice concentrate, thawed**

¼   **cup milk**

**Orange slices, if desired**

**1.** Place yogurt, orange juice concentrate and milk in blender. Cover and blend on medium speed about 45 seconds, stopping blender occasionally to scrape sides, until mixture is thick and smooth.

**2.** Pour mixture into glasses. Garnish with orange slices.

**1 SERVING:** Calories 260 (Calories from Fat 20); Fat 2g (Saturated 2g); Cholesterol 10mg; Sodium 120mg; Carbohydrate 51g (Dietary Fiber 0g); Protein 10g

# PICED CRAN-APPLE CIDER

Prep: 5 min; Cook: 4 to 6 hr          24 servings

1   **bottle (48 ounces) apple cider**

1   **bottle (48 ounces) cranberry juice cocktail**

⅓   **cup packed brown sugar**

2   **teaspoons whole allspice**

4   **sticks cinnamon, 3 inches long**

**1.** Mix all ingredients in 3½- to 6-quart slow cooker.

**2.** Cover and cook on low heat setting 4 to 6 hours. Remove allspice and cinnamon before serving.

**1 SERVING:** Calories 80 (Calories from Fat 0); Fat 0g (Saturated 0g); Cholesterol 0mg; Sodium 0mg; Carbohydrate 20g (Dietary Fiber 0g); Protein 0g

## Extra-Special Cider

For serving your hot cider, try one of these handy hints:

**Pull out the slow cooker.** When serving hot cider at a buffet, pour heated cider into a slow cooker set on low and let guests help themselves.

**You can make a glass punch bowl safer** for hot beverages by filling it first with hot water and letting it stand about 30 minutes. Pour out water, and slowly add hot cider. ■

## COOKING TIPS

• Tying the allspice and cinnamon in a cheesecloth bag makes them easy to remove from the hot cider. Or if you don't have cheesecloth, place the spices in a paper coffee filter and tie with a piece of kitchen string.

• Fresh orange slices add a pretty touch of color to this ruby-red hot drink. Add them to the cider in the cooker just before serving.

**COOKING TIP**

• This recipe is easy to cut in half for a treat for the family. Just use 2½ cups dry milk, ½ cup cocoa, ⅓ cup sugar, 5½ cups water and 1 teaspoon vanilla in a 2- to 3½-quart slow cooker. You can decide whether you want to include 2 tablespoons instant coffee and ¼ teaspoon ground cinnamon.

# MOCHA COCOA

Prep: 5 min; Cook: 3 to 4 hr    12 servings

    5  cups nonfat dry milk
    1  cup baking cocoa
    ¾  cup sugar
    ¼  cup instant coffee (dry)
    ½  teaspoon ground cinnamon
   11  cups water
    2  teaspoons vanilla

**1.** Mix all ingredients except water and vanilla in 5- to 6-quart slow cooker. Stir in water and vanilla until smooth.

**2.** Cover and cook on low heat setting 3 to 4 hours.

**1 SERVING:** Calories 170 (Calories from Fat 10); Fat 1g (Saturated 1g); Cholesterol 5mg; Sodium 160mg; Carbohydrate 32g (Dietary Fiber 3g); Protein 11g

***Cocoa for Kids:*** Just leave out the coffee and cinnamon to make this recipe more kid-friendly. Serve with plenty of marshmallows to float on top, or stick a candy cane into each mug.

# WASSAIL

Prep: 5 min; Cook: 4 hr    16 servings

    5  cups apple cider
    3  cups dry red wine
    ¼  cup granulated or packed brown sugar
    ½  teaspoon whole cloves
    ¼  teaspoon whole allspice
    1  stick cinnamon, 3 inches long

**1.** Mix all ingredients in 3½- to 6-quart slow cooker.

**2.** Cover and cook on low heat setting 3 to 4 hours. Remove cloves, allspice and cinnamon before serving.

**1 SERVING:** Calories 80 (Calories from Fat 0); Fat 0g (Saturated 0g); Cholesterol 0mg; Sodium 5mg; Carbohydrate 13g (Dietary Fiber 0g); Protein 0g

# APPETIZERS

## $\mathcal{C}$HEESY BEAN DIP

Prep: 10 min; Cook: 40 min     3½ cups

1 **package (16 ounces) process cheese spread loaf with jalapeño chilies, cut into cubes**

1 **can (15 or 16 ounces) refried beans**

1 **can (4 ounces) chopped green chilies, undrained**

    **Tortilla chips, if desired**

1. Spray inside of 2- to 3½-quart slow cooker with cooking spray.

2. Mix cheese, beans and chilies in cooker. Cover and cook on high heat setting 30 to 40 minutes or until cheese is melted. Stir until cheese is smooth.

3. Scrape down side of cooker with rubber spatula to help prevent edge of dip from scorching. Turn to low heat setting.

4. Serve with tortilla chips. Dip will hold up to 4 hours.

**1 TABLESPOON:** Calories 40 (Calories from Fat 25); Fat 3g (Saturated 2g); Cholesterol 10mg; Sodium 140mg; Carbohydrate 1g (Dietary Fiber 0g); Protein 2g

---

**COOKING TIP**

• Sprinkle the top of the dip with chopped fresh cilantro just before serving. The cool mint flavor of cilantro will complement the chilies.

---

**SERVING TIP**

• For a festive presentation, use a variety of colored tortilla chips, such as white, yellow and blue cornmeal chips. Red and green chips also are available during the holidays.

---

## $\mathcal{P}$IZZA FONDUE

Prep: 10 min; Cook: 60 min     6 cups

1 **package (16 ounces) process cheese spread loaf, cut into cubes**

2 **cups shredded mozzarella cheese (8 ounces)**

1 **jar (28 ounces) spaghetti sauce**

½ **cup dry red wine or beef broth**

1 **loaf Italian bread, cut into 1-inch cubes, if desired**

1. Spray inside of 2- to 3½-quart slow cooker with cooking spray.

2. Mix cheeses, spaghetti sauce and wine in cooker. Cover and cook on high heat setting 45 to 60 minutes or until cheese is melted. Stir until cheese is smooth.

3. Scrape down side of cooker with rubber spatula to help prevent edge of fondue from scorching. Turn to low heat setting.

4. Serve with bread cubes and wooden picks or fondue forks for dipping. Fondue will hold up to 4 hours.

**1 TABLESPOON:** Calories 30 (Calories from Fat 20); Fat 2g (Saturated 1g); Cholesterol 5mg; Sodium 120mg; Carbohydrate 2g (Dietary Fiber 0g); Protein 2g

## COOKING TIPS

• The flesh, ribs and seeds of chilies contain burning irritating, oils. Wear plastic gloves when handling. Wash hands and utensils in soapy water, and be especially careful not to rub your face or eyes until the oils have been washed away.

• If you desire a hotter salsa, leave some of the seeds in the jalapeño chili.

# $\mathcal{F}$RESH TOMATO SALSA

Prep: 10 min; Chill: 1 hr        About 3½ cups

**3 medium tomatoes, halved, seeded and chopped**
**1 small green bell pepper, chopped**
**6 medium green onions, trimmed and sliced**
**3 cloves garlic, peeled and finely chopped**
**1 medium jalapeño chili**
**2 tablespoons chopped fresh cilantro**
**2 tablespoons lime juice**
**½ teaspoon salt**
**Flour tortillas or tortilla chips, if desired**

**1.** Place tomato, green pepper, green onion and garlic in bowl.

**2.** Cut stem off jalapeño chili, cut chili lengthwise in half and scrape out seeds. Cut chili into strips, and then finely chop.

**3.** Add cilantro, lime juice and salt. Mix all ingredients. Cover and refrigerate at least 1 hour to blend flavors but no longer than 7 days.

**4.** Serve salsa with flour tortillas or tortilla chips or as an accompaniment to chicken, fish and other main dishes.

**1 SERVING (1 TABLESPOON):** Calories 5 (Calories from Fat 0); Fat 0g (Saturated 0g); Cholesterol 0mg; Sodium 20mg; Carbohydrate 1g (Dietary Fiber 0g); Protein 0g

# $\mathcal{H}$OT REUBEN SPREAD

Prep: 10 min; Cook: 1 hr 30 min      3¼ cups

- 1 **package (8 ounces) cream cheese, softened**
- 1½ **cups shredded Swiss cheese (6 ounces)**
- ¾ **cup drained sauerkraut**
- 2 **packages (2½ ounces each) thinly sliced corned beef, chopped**
- ½ **cup Thousand Island dressing**
  **Pretzel crackers or cocktail rye bread slices, for serving, if desired**

1. Spray inside of 1- to 2½-quart slow cooker with cooking spray.

2. Mix all ingredients except crackers; spoon into cooker. Cover and cook on low heat setting 1 hour to 1 hour 30 minutes or until cheese is melted. Stir until cheese is smooth.

3. Scrape down side of cooker with rubber spatula to help prevent edge of spread from scorching. Turn to low heat setting.

4. Serve with crackers. Spread will hold up to 4 hours.

**1 SERVING (1 TABLESPOON):** Calories 40 (Calories from Fat 25); Fat 3g (Saturated 2g); Cholesterol 10mg; Sodium 100mg; Carbohydrate 1g (Dietary Fiber 0g); Protein 2g

***Hot Reuben Spread Sandwiches:*** Toast slices of rye or pumpernickel bread. Spread about ½ cup Reuben spread over each slice. Pop the open-face sandwiches under the broiler until the tops are hot and bubbly and begin to brown. Serve with big, crisp dill pickles—just like at your favorite deli restaurant!

## COOKING TIP

- Sauerkraut sometimes can be quite salty. Rinsing it in a strainer under cold water can help remove some of the salty flavor.

# ARTICHOKE-CRAB SPREAD

Prep: 15 min; Cook: Low 1 hr 15 min, or High 45 min    3 cups

1 can (14 ounces) artichoke heart quarters, drained and coarsely chopped

1 package (8 ounces) cream cheese, cubed

4 medium green onions, trimmed and sliced

1 cup shredded imitation crabmeat (4 ounces)

½ cup grated Parmesan cheese (1 ounce)

4 teaspoons lemon juice

French baguette or cocktail rye bread slices, for serving, if desired

**1.** Spray inside of 1- to 2½-quart slow cooker with cooking spray.

**2.** Place all ingredients except bread in cooker. Cover and cook on low heat setting 1 hour to 1 hour 15 minutes or high heat setting 30 to 45 minutes or until cream cheese is melted. Stir until cheese is smooth.

**3.** Scrape down side of cooker with rubber spatula to help prevent edge of spread from scorching. Turn to low heat setting.

**4.** Serve with bread slices. Spread will hold up to 3 hours.

**1 SERVING (1 TABLESPOON):** Calories 25 (Calories from Fat 20); Fat 2g (Saturated 1g); Cholesterol 5mg; Sodium 80mg; Carbohydrate 1g (Dietary Fiber 0g); Protein 1g

# $\mathcal{L}$AYERED MEXICAN SNACK PLATTER

**QUICK**    Prep: 20 min        16 servings

    1  **can (15 ounces) refried beans**
    2  **tablespoons salsa, chili sauce or ketchup**
1½  **cups sour cream**
    1  **cup Guacamole (page 116) or prepared guacamole**
    1  **cup shredded Cheddar cheese (4 ounces)**
    2  **medium green onions, trimmed and chopped**
       **Tortilla chips**

**1.** Mix refried beans and salsa. Spread in thin layer on 12- or 13-inch serving plate or pizza pan.

**2.** Spread sour cream over beans, leaving about 1-inch border of beans around edge. Spread guacamole over sour cream, leaving border of sour cream showing.

**3.** Sprinkle cheese over guacamole. Sprinkle onions over cheese. Serve immediately, or cover with plastic wrap and refrigerate until ready to serve. Serve with tortilla chips.

**1 SERVING:** Calories 75 (Calories from Fat 45); Fat 5g (Saturated 2g); Cholesterol 10mg; Sodium 210mg; Carbohydrate 6g (Dietary Fiber 2g); Protein 4g

## Preparing a Cheese Tray

To create an interesting and balanced cheese tray, choose three to five varieties of cheese with different shapes, textures and flavors.

- Plan on 2 to 3 ounces of cheese per person.

- Separate mild cheeses from the sharp and strong-flavored cheeses.

- Serve most cheeses at room temperature to maximize their flavor and aroma.

- Flag or label cheeses so everyone can identify the types and get what they prefer. ■

# $\mathcal{V}$EGGIE TORTILLA ROLL-UPS

Prep: 10 min; Chill: 3 hr        About 30 roll-ups

½  **small red bell pepper, chopped**

½  **cup sour cream**

½  **cup finely shredded Cheddar cheese (2 ounces)**

2  **tablespoons chopped sliced ripe olives**

1  **package (3 ounces) cream cheese at room temperature**

1  **tablespoon chopped fresh parsley**

3  **flavored or plain flour tortillas (8 to 10 inches in diameter)**

**1.** Mix olives, bell pepper, sour cream, Cheddar cheese, parsley and cream cheese in medium bowl. Spread about ½ cup of the cheese mixture over one side of each tortilla. Roll tortilla up tightly. Repeat with remaining tortillas and cheese mixture.

**2.** Wrap each tortilla roll individually in plastic wrap. Refrigerate at least 3 hours but no longer than 24 hours. To serve, cut each tortilla roll into 1-inch slices.

**1 ROLL-UP:** Calories 45 (Calories from Fat 25); Fat 3g (Saturated 2g); Cholesterol 10mg; Sodium 45mg; Carbohydrate 3g (Dietary Fiber 0g); Protein 1g

## COOKING TIP

• For more flavor and variety, use a combination of flavored tortillas for the roll-ups. Spinach and tomato, for example, are a perfect pair on a holiday appetizer platter.

## SPECIAL TOUCH

### Picture Frame Tray

You will need:

**Multiphoto picture frame**

**Vellum paper, waxed paper or parchment paper**

**Coarse salt, uncooked couscous, lentils, or rice, small seeds or nuts, or whole spices or dried herbs**

1. For foods with drips or crumbs, line frame sections with pieces of vellum paper, waxed paper or parchment paper.

2. For foods with a dry crust, such as tartlets or mini pizzas, fill frame sections with coarse salt or other dry material.

3. Place food in frame sections.

# CRAB TORTILLA ROLL-UPS

**QUICK**    Prep: 15 min; Cook: 5 min        4 roll-ups

**Yogurt Salsa (at right)**

12  **imitation crabmeat sticks (about 1 ounce each), chopped**

 1  **cup finely shredded cabbage**

½  **cup finely shredded red bell pepper**

 2  **medium green onions, trimmed and sliced**

¼  **teaspoon red pepper sauce**

¼  **teaspoon salt**

⅛  **teaspoon pepper**

 4  **flour tortillas (10 inches in diameter)**

**1.** Prepare Yogurt Salsa. Mix remaining ingredients except tortillas in 12-inch nonstick skillet. Cook over medium-high heat 3 to 5 minutes, stirring frequently, until hot.

**2.** Spread 3 to 4 tablespoons Yogurt Salsa on each tortilla; top with about ⅔ cup crabmeat mixture. Roll up each tortilla; cut diagonally into thirds.

**1 ROLL-UP:** Calories 320 (Calories from Fat 55); Fat 6g (Saturated 1g); Cholesterol 25mg; Sodium 1240mg; Carbohydrate 49g (Dietary Fiber 4g); Protein 21g

## YOGURT SALSA

½  **cup fat-free plain yogurt**

1  **tablespoon chopped fresh cilantro**

¼  **teaspoon ground cumin**

1  **small tomato, chopped**

2  **medium green onions, trimmed and chopped**

Mix all ingredients.

## SAVORY PECANS

**QUICK**    Prep: 5 min; Bake: 10 min        2 cups

2  **cups pecan halves, walnut halves or peanuts**

2  **medium green onions, trimmed and chopped**

2  **tablespoons butter or stick margarine, melted (see tip)**

1  **tablespoon soy sauce**

¼  **teaspoon ground red pepper (cayenne)**

**1.** Heat oven to 300°.

**2.** Mix all ingredients. Spread pecans in single layer in ungreased jelly roll pan, 15½ × 10½ × 1 inch.

**3.** Bake uncovered about 10 minutes or until pecans are toasted. Serve warm, or cool completely. Store in airtight container at room temperature up to 3 weeks.

**1 SERVING (¼ CUP):** Calories 210 (Calories from Fat 190); Fat 21g (Saturated 3g); Cholesterol 10mg; Sodium 135mg; Carbohydrate 5g (Dietary Fiber 2g); Protein 2g

---

**COOKING TIP**

• For best results, do not use vegetable oil spreads.

---

# CINNAMON-SUGARED NUTS

Prep: 10 min; Bake: 30 min        2 cups

1 tablespoon slightly beaten large egg white

2 cups pecan halves, unblanched whole almonds or walnut halves

¼ cup sugar

2 teaspoons ground cinnamon

¼ teaspoon ground nutmeg

¼ teaspoon ground cloves

**1.** Heat oven to 300°.

**2.** Mix egg white and pecan halves in medium bowl until pecans are coated and sticky.

**3.** Mix remaining ingredients; sprinkle over pecans. Stir until pecans are completely coated. Spread pecans in single layer in ungreased jelly roll pan, 15½ × 10½ × 1 inch.

**4.** Bake uncovered about 30 minutes or until toasted. Cool completely, or serve slightly warm. Store in airtight container at room temperature up to 3 weeks.

**1 SERVING (¼ CUP):** Calories 210 (Calories from Fat 160); Fat 18g (Saturated 1g); Cholesterol 2mg; Sodium 5mg; Carbohydrate 12g (Dietary Fiber 2g); Protein 2g

# BREADS

## OLD-FASHIONED BLUEBERRY MUFFINS

Prep: 10 min; Bake: 25 min          12 muffins

- 1½ cups fat-free plain yogurt
- 1¼ cups all-purpose flour
- 1 cup old-fashioned or quick-cooking oats
- ⅔ cup packed brown sugar
- ¼ cup (½ stick) margarine or butter, softened
- ¼ cup fat-free cholesterol-free egg product or 1 egg, slightly beaten
- 2 teaspoons baking powder
- 1 teaspoon ground cinnamon
- ½ teaspoon baking soda
- ¼ teaspoon ground nutmeg
- ¼ teaspoon salt
- 1 cup fresh or frozen (thawed and drained) blueberries

1. Heat oven to 400°. Place paper baking cup in each of 12 medium muffin cups, 2½ × 1¼ inches, or grease bottoms only of muffin cups.

2. Mix all ingredients except blueberries in large bowl just until flour is moistened (batter will be lumpy). Fold in blueberries.

3. Divide batter evenly among muffin cups. Bake 20 to 25 minutes or until golden brown. Immediately remove from pan.

**1 MUFFIN:** Calories 170 (Calories from Fat 35); Fat 4g (Saturated 1g); Cholesterol 0mg; Sodium 220mg; Carbohydrate 31g (Dietary Fiber 2g); Protein 5g

**COOKING TIP**

• To make ahead, wrap cooled bread tightly in plastic wrap and store at room temperature up to 4 days or refrigerate up to 10 days.

# BANANA-NUT BREAD

Prep: 10 min; Bake: 1 hr 15 min; Cool: 1 hr        1 loaf (18 slices)

1¼ **cups sugar**

½ **cup (1 stick) margarine or butter, at room temperature**

2 **eggs**

3 **medium very ripe bananas**

½ **cup buttermilk**

1 **teaspoon vanilla**

2½ **cups all-purpose flour**

1 **teaspoon baking soda**

1 **teaspoon salt**

1 **cup chopped nuts**

**1.** Heat oven to 350°. Grease bottom only of loaf pan with shortening.

**2.** Mix sugar and margarine in large bowl. Stir in eggs until well mixed.

**3.** Mash bananas with potato masher or fork in medium bowl. You should have about 1½ cups mashed bananas. Add bananas, buttermilk and vanilla to egg mixture. Stir until smooth. Stir in flour, baking soda and salt all at once just until flour is moistened. Stir in nuts. Pour batter into greased pan.

**4.** Bake about 1 hour 15 minutes or until a toothpick inserted in center comes out clean.

**5.** Place pan on wire rack and cool 5 minutes. Loosen sides of bread from pan, using a knife. Carefully tip pan on its side and tap gently to remove bread from pan. Place bread, top side up, on wire rack. Cool completely, about 1 hour, before slicing.

**1 SLICE:** Calories 245 (Calories from Fat 100); Fat 11g (Saturated 2g); Cholesterol 25mg; Sodium 280mg; Carbohydrate 33g (Dietary Fiber 1g); Protein 4g

**BREAD MACHINE**

# CRANBERRY BLUEBERRY BREAD

Prep: 10 min; Cycle time

### 1½-pound recipe (12 slices)

- 1 cup plus 1 tablespoon water
- 3 tablespoons honey
- 2 tablespoons margarine or butter, softened
- 3 cups bread flour
- 1¼ teaspoons salt
- 2 teaspoons bread machine or quick active dry yeast
- ¼ cup dried cranberries
- ¼ cup dried blueberries

### 2-pound recipe (16 slices)

- 1 cup plus 3 tablespoons water
- ¼ cup honey
- 2 tablespoons margarine or butter, softened
- 4 cups bread flour
- 1½ teaspoons salt
- 2 teaspoons bread machine or quick active dry yeast
- ⅓ cup dried cranberries
- ⅓ cup dried blueberries

**1.** Make 1½-pound recipe with bread machines that use 3 cups flour, or make 2-pound recipe with bread machines that use 4 cups flour.

**2.** Measure carefully, placing all ingredients except cranberries and blueberries in bread machine pan in the order recommended by the manufacturer. Add cranberries and blueberries at Raisin/Nut signal.

**3.** Select Sweet or Basic/White cycle. Use Medium or Light crust color. Do not use Delay cycles. Remove baked bread from pan, and cool on wire rack.

**1 SLICE:** Calories 165 (Calories from Fat 20); Fat 2g (Saturated 0g); Cholesterol 0mg; Sodium 270mg; Carbohydrate 35g (Dietary Fiber 2g); Protein 4g

***Cherry Blueberry Bread:*** Substitute the same amount of dried cherries for the dried cranberries.

---

### COOKING TIPS

• If your bread machine doesn't have a Raisin/Nut signal, add the cranberries and blueberries 5 to 10 minutes before the last kneading cycle ends. Check your bread machine's use-and-care book to find out how long the last cycle runs.

• The same amount of yeast is needed for both the 1½-pound and 2-pound loaves.

## COOKING TIPS

• If your bread machine has a 2-pound vertical pan, the loaf will be short but still will have good texture and flavor. If your bread machine has a 2-pound horizontal pan, however, there isn't enough dough to make a good loaf of baked bread.

• If your bread machine doesn't have a Raisin/Nut signal, add the almonds 5 to 10 minutes before the last kneading cycle ends. Check your bread machine's use-and-care book to find out how long the last cycle runs.

• Toast the almonds to give this chocolate bread even more almond boost. Sprinkle the almonds in a heavy skillet. Cook over medium-low heat, stirring them frequently, until they are golden brown and you can smell the toasty almond aroma. Pour them out of the skillet so they don't continue to brown, and let them cool before using.

**BREAD MACHINE**

# ALMOND CHOCOLATE CHIP BREAD

Prep: 10 min; Cycle time

| 1-pound recipe (8 slices) | 1½-pound recipe (12 slices) |
|---|---|
| ¾ cup plus 1 tablespoon water | 1 cup plus 2 tablespoons water |
| 1 tablespoon margarine or butter, softened | 2 tablespoons margarine or butter, softened |
| ¼ teaspoon vanilla | ½ teaspoon vanilla |
| 2 cups bread flour | 3 cups flour |
| ½ cup semisweet chocolate chips | ¾ cup semisweet chocolate chips |
| 2 tablespoons sugar | 3 tablespoons sugar |
| 2 teaspoons dry milk | 1 tablespoon dry milk |
| ½ teaspoon salt | ¾ teaspoon salt |
| 1 teaspoon bread machine or quick active dry yeast | 1½ teaspoons bread machine or quick active dry yeast |
| ¼ cup sliced almonds | ⅓ cup sliced almonds |

1. Make 1-pound recipe with bread machines that use 2 cups flour, or make 1½-pound recipe with bread machines that use 3 cups flour.

2. Measure carefully, placing all ingredients except almonds in bread machine pan in the order recommended by the manufacturer. Add almonds at the Raisin/Nut signal.

3. Select Sweet or Basic/White cycle. Use Medium or Light crust color. Remove baked bread from pan, and cool on wire rack.

**1 SLICE:** Calories 225 (Calories from Fat 65); Fat 7g (Saturated 2g); Cholesterol 0mg; Sodium 320mg; Carbohydrate 37g (Dietary Fiber 2g); Protein 5g

# CHOCOLATE COFFEE BREAD

Prep: 20 min; Cycle time; Rest: 10 min; Rise: 50 min; Bake: 20 min
1 loaf, 16 slices

1 cup water
2 tablespoons margarine or butter, softened
3 cups bread flour
⅓ cup packed brown sugar
1 tablespoon instant coffee granules
1 teaspoon salt
2¼ teaspoons bread machine or quick active dry yeast
½ cup semisweet chocolate chips
1 egg, beaten
1 teaspoon instant coffee granules
1 tablespoon granulated sugar

1. Measure carefully, placing all ingredients except chocolate chips, egg, 1 teaspoon instant coffee granules and the granulated sugar in bread machine pan in the order recommended by the manufacturer. Add chocolate chips at the Raisin/Nut signal.

2. Select Dough/Manual cycle. Do not use Delay cycles.

3. Remove dough from pan, using lightly floured hands. Cover and let rest 10 minutes on lightly floured surface.

4. Grease large cookie sheet. Shape dough into 10 × 3-inch rectangle on cookie sheet. Cover and let rise in warm place 40 to 50 minutes or until double. (Dough is ready if indentation remains when touched.)

5. Heat oven to 400°. Make 5 diagonal slashes, ¼ inch deep, across top of loaf, using sharp knife. Make 5 additional slashes in opposite direction to make X-shaped cuts. Brush egg over top of loaf. Mix 1 teaspoon coffee granules and the granulated sugar; sprinkle over loaf. Bake 18 to 20 minutes or until loaf is golden brown and sounds hollow when tapped. Remove from cookie sheet to wire rack; cool.

**1 SLICE:** Calories 140 (Calories from Fat 30); Fat 3g (Saturated 1g); Cholesterol 0mg; Sodium 170mg; Carbohydrate 26g (Dietary Fiber 1g); Protein 3g

## COOKING TIPS

• To make ahead, cover shaped dough on cookie sheet with plastic wrap. Refrigerate from 4 hours up to 24 hours. Before baking, remove plastic wrap, cover with kitchen towel and let rise in a warm place about 2 hours or until double. Then top and bake.

• If your bread machine doesn't have a Raisin/Nut signal, add chocolate chips 5 to 10 minutes before last kneading cycle ends. Check your bread machine's use-and-care book for how long the last cycle runs.

# Honey Mustard Bread

Prep: 10 min; Cycle time

### 1½-pound recipe (12 slices)

- ¾ cup plus 1 tablespoon water
- 2 tablespoons honey
- 2 tablespoons mustard
- 2 tablespoons margarine or butter, softened
- 3 cups bread flour
- ½ teaspoon salt
- ½ teaspoon paprika
- 1½ teaspoons bread machine or quick active dry yeast

### 2-pound recipe (16 slices)

- 1 cup water
- 3 tablespoons honey
- 3 tablespoons mustard
- 3 tablespoons margarine or butter, softened
- 4 cups bread flour
- ¾ teaspoon salt
- 1 teaspoon paprika
- 1¾ teaspoons bread machine or quick active dry yeast

**1.** Make 1½-pound recipe with bread machines that use 3 cups flour, or make 2-pound recipe with bread machines that use 4 cups flour.

**2.** Measure carefully, placing all ingredients in bread machine pan in the order recommended by the manufacturer.

**3.** Select Basic/White cycle. Use Medium or Light crust color. Do not use Delay cycles. Remove baked bread from pan, and cool on wire rack.

**1 SLICE:** Calories 145 (Calories from Fat 20); Fat 2g (Saturated 1g); Cholesterol 0mg; Sodium 150mg; Carbohydrate 29g (Dietary Fiber 1g); Protein 4g

## Refrigerating Dough

One of the joys of the bread machine is you can easily make a dough and keep it in the refrigerator until you want to bake it. Doughs without egg will keep up to 48 hours in the refrigerator and doughs with egg should be stored no more than 24 hours.

Remove the dough from the bread machine pan, and shape it into a ball. Place it in a bowl greased with shortening or nonstick cooking spray. Grease or spray the top of the dough, and cover with plastic wrap and then with a damp cloth. Place the bowl in the refrigerator. When you are ready to bake the dough, shape it and let it rise, covered, in a warm place about 1½ to 2 hours or until double. Bake the dough as the recipe instructs.

As to freezing dough, follow "bake first, then freeze" for better-quality baked goods. Doughs can lose some of their rising power after freezing. ■

# OATMEAL SUNFLOWER BREAD

Prep: 10 min; Cycle time

| 1½-pound recipe (12 slices) | 2-pound recipe (16 slices) |
|---|---|
| **1 cup water** | **1¼ cups water** |
| **¼ cup honey** | **¼ cup honey** |
| **2 tablespoons margarine or butter, softened** | **2 tablespoons margarine or butter, softened** |
| **3 cups bread flour** | **4 cups bread flour** |
| **½ cup old-fashioned or quick-cooking oats** | **⅔ cup old-fashioned or quick-cooking oats** |
| **2 tablespoons dry milk** | **2 tablespoons dry milk** |
| **1¼ teaspoons salt** | **1¼ teaspoons salt** |
| **2¼ teaspoons bread machine or quick active dry yeast** | **2½ teaspoons bread machine or quick active dry yeast** |
| **½ cup sunflower nuts** | **⅔ cup sunflower nuts** |

**1.** Make 1½-pound recipe with bread machines that use 3 cups flour, or make 2-pound recipe with bread machines that use 4 cups flour.

**2.** Measure carefully, placing all ingredients except nuts in bread machine pan in the order recommended by the manufacturer. Add nuts at the Raisin/Nut signal.

**3.** Select Basic/White cycle. Use Medium or Light crust color. Do not use Delay cycles. Remove baked bread from pan, and cool on wire rack.

**1 SLICE:** Calories 205 (Calories from Fat 45); Fat 5g (Saturated 1g); Cholesterol 0mg; Sodium 280mg; Carbohydrate 36g (Dietary Fiber 2g); Protein 6

## COOKING TIPS

• If your bread machine doesn't have a Raisin/Nut signal, add the nuts 5 to 10 minutes before the last kneading cycle ends. Check your bread machine's use-and-care book to find out how long the last cycle runs.

• This nutty oatmeal bread makes a fabulous Santa Fe Meatloaf Sandwich. Spread tomato jam or your favorite salsa on two slices of bread. Layer slices of cold meatloaf, Monterey Jack cheese, canned chopped green chilies, avocado slices and shredded lettuce on one slice of bread. Top with remaining slice of bread. It has a wonderfully rich, zippy flavor.

# CARAWAY RYE BREAD

Prep: 10 min; Cycle time

---

## COOKING TIPS

• If your bread machine has a 2-pound vertical pan, the loaf will be short but still will have good texture and flavor. If your bread machine has a 2-pound horizontal pan, however, there isn't enough dough to make a good loaf of baked bread.

• To make this bread picture perfect, try this delicious tangy cheese spread. Mix a 3-ounce package of softened cream cheese with 2 tablespoons milk until smooth and creamy. Stir in ½ cup finely shredded aged Swiss cheese and 1 tablespoon of chopped fresh chives or green onion. This makes about ⅔ cup Swiss Cheese and Chives spread, so cover and refrigerate leftovers—if there are any!

---

### 1-pound recipe (8 slices)

- ¾ cup water
- 2 teaspoons margarine or butter, softened
- 1½ cups bread flour
- ½ cup rye flour
- 1 tablespoon dry milk
- 1 tablespoon sugar
- 1 teaspoon salt
- ⅛ teaspoon caraway seed
- 1¼ teaspoons bread machine or quick active dry yeast

### 1½-pound recipe (12 slices)

- 1 cup plus 3 tablespoons water
- 1 tablespoon margarine or butter, softened
- 2 ,½ cups bread flour
- ¾ cup rye flour
- 2 tablespoons dry milk
- 2 tablespoons sugar
- 1½ teaspoons salt
- ¾ teaspoon caraway seed
- 2¼ teaspoons bread machine or quick active dry yeast

**1.** Make 1-pound recipe with bread machines that use 2 cups flour, or make 1½-pound recipe with bread machines that use 3 cups flour.

**2.** Measure carefully, placing all ingredients in bread machine pan in the order recommended by the manufacturer.

**3.** Select Basic/White cycle. Use Medium or Light crust color. Remove baked bread from pan, and cool on wire rack.

**1 SLICE:** Calories 125 (Calories from Fat 10); Fat 1g (Saturated 0g); Cholesterol 0mg; Sodium 310mg; Carbohydrate 27g (Dietary Fiber 2g); Protein 4g

# SANDWICHES

## CHICKEN SALAD SANDWICHES

**QUICK** Prep: 15 min    4 sandwiches

1½  **cups chopped cooked chicken or turkey**
½   **cup mayonnaise or salad dressing**
¼   **teaspoon salt**
¼   **teaspoon pepper**
1   **medium stalk celery, chopped**
1   **small onion, peeled and chopped**
8   **slices bread**

**1.** Mix all ingredients except bread.

**2.** Spread chicken mixture on each of 4 slices bread. Top with remaining bread.

**1 SANDWICH:** Calories 450 (Calories from Fat 280); Fat 31g (Saturated 6g); Cholesterol 60mg; Sodium 630mg; Carbohydrate 27g (Dietary Fiber 2g); Protein 18g

***Lighter Chicken Salad Sandwiches:*** For 9 grams of fat and 270 calories per serving, use fat-free mayonnaise.

## GARDEN VEGETABLE WRAPS

**QUICK** Prep: 15 min    4 wraps

½   **cup cream cheese (4 ounces)**
4   **flour tortillas (8 or 10 inches in diameter)**
1   **cup lightly packed spinach leaves**
1   **large tomato, thinly sliced**
¾   **cup shredded carrot**
8   **slices (1 ounce each) Muenster or Monterey Jack cheese**
1   **small yellow bell pepper, chopped**

**1.** Spread 2 tablespoons of the cream cheese over each tortilla. Top with spinach and tomato to within 1 inch of edge. Sprinkle with carrot. Top with cheese slices. Sprinkle with bell pepper.

**2.** Roll up tortillas tightly. Serve immediately, or wrap securely with plastic wrap and refrigerate no longer than 24 hours.

**1 WRAP:** Calories 460 (Calories from Fat 270); Fat 30g (Saturated 18g); Cholesterol 35mg; Sodium 660mg; Carbohydrate 31g (Dietary Fiber 3g); Protein 20g

**COOKING TIP**

• These fun, portable sandwiches have endless possibilities. Try different flavors of cream cheese, chopped fresh broccoli, sliced green onions or shredded zucchini. Or add your favorite cheeses and deli meats.

**COOKING TIP**

• If you have leftover rice from another dinner, stir $\frac{1}{2}$ cup of it into the filling for these wraps.

# SOUTH-OF-THE-BORDER WRAPS

**QUICK**   Prep: 15 min; Cook: 3 min      4 wraps

1   **can (8 ounces) kidney beans, rinsed and drained**
1   **can (8 ounces) whole kernel corn, drained**
$\frac{1}{2}$   **small bell pepper, chopped**
$\frac{1}{2}$   **cup chunky-style salsa**
1   **tablespoon chopped fresh cilantro or parsley**
4   **flour tortillas (8 or 10 inches in diameter)**
$\frac{1}{2}$   **cup shredded Cheddar cheese (2 ounces)**

**1.** Mix beans, corn, pepper, salsa and cilantro in bowl.

**2.** Place tortillas on clean counter or on waxed paper. Spread about $\frac{1}{2}$ cup of bean mixture over each tortilla to within 1 inch of edge. Sprinkle 2 tablespoons cheese over each tortilla.

**3.** Fold opposite sides of each tortilla up toward center about 1 inch over filling (the sides will not meet in the center). Roll up tortilla, beginning at one of the open ends. Place wraps, seam sides down, in microwavable dish.

**4.** Microwave uncovered on high 1 minute. Rotate dish $\frac{1}{4}$ turn. Microwave 1 minute to 1 minute 30 seconds longer.

**1 WRAP:** Calories 335 (Calories from Fat 90); Fat 10g (Saturated 4g); Cholesterol 15mg; Sodium 800mg; Carbohydrate 53g (Dietary Fiber 6g); Protein 14g

# ITA SANDWICHES

**QUICK**  Prep: 10 min; Chill: 20 min          8 sandwiches

- **8  pita breads (6 inches in diameter)**
- **½  pound cooked sliced turkey**
- **½  pound cooked sliced roast beef**
- **8  tomato slices**
- **½  cup alfalfa sprouts**
- **Peppery Mustard Sauce (below)**
- **Horseradish Sauce (below)**

**1.** Make Peppery Mustard Sauce and Horseradish Sauce.

**2.** Split each pita bread halfway around edge with knife; separate to form pocket. Place 2 slices turkey or roast beef in each pocket; top with tomato slice and sprouts. Serve sandwiches with Peppery Mustard Sauce and Horseradish Sauce.

**1 SANDWICH:** Calories 470 (Calories from Fat 235); Fat 26g (Saturated 5g); Cholesterol 55mg; Sodium 420mg; Carbohydrate 37g (Dietary Fiber 2g); Protein 24g

## PEPPERY MUSTARD SAUCE

- **¾  cup olive oil**
- **3  tablespoons lemon juice**
- **2  tablespoons grainy mustard**
- **1  teaspoon cracked black pepper**

Combine all ingredients in blender or food processor; cover and blend or process until smooth. Store tightly covered in refrigerator.

## HORSERADISH SAUCE

- **½  cup sour cream**
- **2  tablespoons horseradish**
- **2  tablespoons apple cider**

Mix all ingredients in small bowl. Cover and refrigerate until chilled, about 20 minutes.

# $\mathcal{S}$UBMARINE SANDWICH

**QUICK**   Prep: 15 min        6 servings

- 1 loaf (1 pound) French bread
- ¼ cup (½ stick) butter or stick margarine, softened
- 4 ounces Swiss cheese, sliced
- ½ pound salami, sliced
- 2 cups shredded lettuce
- 2 medium tomatoes, thinly sliced
- 1 medium onion, peeled and thinly sliced
- ½ pound fully cooked ham, thinly sliced
- 1 medium green bell pepper, thinly sliced
- ¼ cup Italian dressing
- 6 long wooden picks or small skewers

**1.** Cut bread horizontally in half. Spread butter over bottom half.

**2.** Layer cheese, salami, lettuce, tomatoes, onion, ham and pepper on bread.

**3.** Drizzle with dressing. Top with remaining bread half. Secure loaf with picks. Cut into 6 serving pieces.

**1 SERVING:** Calories 605 (Calories from Fat 315); Fat 35g (Saturated 15g); Cholesterol 90mg; Sodium 1780mg; Carbohydrate 46g (Dietary Fiber 3g); Protein 30g

# MAIN DISHES

## Multi-bean Soup

Prep: 10 min; Cook: 10 hr; Finishing Cook: 15 min          12 servings

- 1 package (20 ounces) 15- or 16-dried bean soup mix, sorted and rinsed
- ½ pound smoked beef sausage ring, cut into ¼-inch slices
- 1 large onion, peeled and chopped
- 10 cups water
- 1½ teaspoons dried thyme leaves
- 1 teaspoon salt
- ½ teaspoon pepper
- 2 medium carrots, shredded
- 1 can (14½ ounces) diced tomatoes, undrained

**1.** Mix all ingredients except carrots and tomatoes in 5- to 6-quart slow cooker. Cover and cook on high heat setting 8 to 10 hours or until beans are tender.

**2.** Stir in carrots and tomatoes. Cover and cook on high heat setting about 15 minutes or until hot.

**1 SERVING:** Calories 210 (Calories from Fat 55); Fat 6g (Saturated 3g); Cholesterol 10mg; Sodium 660mg; Carbohydrate 35g (Dietary Fiber 6g); Protein 10g

### COOKING TIPS

• The shredded carrots are added at the end so they don't overcook and disappear into the soup. Also, the tomatoes are added after the beans are tender because the acid in the tomatoes can prevent the beans from becoming tender during the long, slow cooking.

• If you have small amounts of various leftover dried beans in your cupboard, mix them together to make 2¼ cups of beans, and use them instead of purchasing a package of bean soup mix. Or use a 16-ounce package of dried beans for the bean soup mix, but use only 8 cups of water and ¾ teaspoon salt.

• Add a secret ingredient to this soup for additional flavor and color—stir in 1 cup canned pumpkin when you add the carrots and tomatoes.

## COOKING TIPS

- Cutting the fish into 1-inch pieces will be a snap if you use fish steaks that are 1 inch thick or use thicker cuts of fish fillets. Any firm-fleshed fish, such as halibut, haddock, swordfish, pollack, tuna or red snapper, works well in this soup. If fish is frozen, thaw it in the refrigerator or under cold running water before cutting it into pieces and adding it to the soup.

- The red cayenne pepper in this chowder packs a little punch, but if you prefer a chowder that's a little more tame, use black pepper instead. If you like really fiery chowder, pass a bottle of red pepper sauce at the table.

# PEPPERY FISH CHOWDER WITH RICE

Prep: 15 min; Cook: Low 9 hr, or High 4 hr;
Finishing Cook: 45 min        10 servings

2  medium stalks celery, chopped
1  medium bell pepper, chopped
1  medium onion, peeled and chopped
2  cloves garlic, peeled and finely chopped
2  cans (14½ ounces each) diced tomatoes, undrained
½  cup uncooked instant rice
2  cups eight-vegetable juice
1  cup dry white wine or vegetable broth
1  tablespoon Worcestershire sauce
1  teaspoon salt
¼  teaspoon ground red pepper (cayenne)
1  pound firm-fleshed fish steak, cut into 1-inch pieces
3  tablespoons chopped fresh parsley

**1.** Mix all ingredients except fish and parsley in 3½- to 6-quart slow cooker. Cover and cook on low heat setting 7 to 9 hours or high heat setting 3 to 4 hours or until rice is tender.

**2.** Stir in fish and parsley. Cover and cook on high heat setting 30 to 45 minutes or until fish flakes easily with fork.

**1 SERVING:** Calories 90 (Calories from Fat 10); Fat 1g (Saturated 0g); Cholesterol 20mg; Sodium 540mg; Carbohydrate 13g (Dietary Fiber 2g); Protein 9g

# $\mathcal{S}$ummertime Chicken Gazpacho

Prep: 25 min; Chill: 1 hr    8 servings

3 slices white bread, crusts removed

3 cloves garlic, peeled

2 tablespoons lemon juice

10 medium unpeeled tomatoes, diced

6 medium green onions, trimmed and finely chopped

2 medium cucumbers, peeled and diced

2 medium red bell peppers, diced

1 can (46 ounces) spicy eight-vegetable juice

2 tablespoons balsamic vinegar

½ teaspoon salt

1 cup cubed cooked chicken

Croutons, if desired

**1.** Place bread, garlic and lemon juice in food processor or blender. Cover and process until bread forms fine crumbs.

**2.** Place bread crumb mixture in large bowl. Stir in remaining ingredients except chicken and croutons. Place half of the bread crumbs and vegetable mixture (about 7 cups) in food processor or blender. Cover and process until smooth. Repeat in small batches if necessary.

**3.** Stir smooth vegetable mixture into vegetable mixture remaining in bowl. Stir in chicken. Cover and refrigerate at least 1 hour until chilled. Serve with croutons.

**1 SERVING:** Calories 125 (Calories from Fat 20); Fat 2g (Saturated 0g); Cholesterol 15mg; Sodium 680mg; Carbohydrate 23g (Dietary Fiber 5g); Protein 9g

# Savory Cabbage and Pork Soup

Prep: 20 min; Cook: Low 9 hr, or High 5 hr      8 servings

1   pound boneless country-style pork ribs, cut into 1-inch pieces
4   medium carrots, cut into ¼-inch slices
2   medium stalks celery, chopped
1   medium potato, peeled and cut into ½ × ¼-inch pieces
1   medium onion, peeled and chopped
4   cups chopped cabbage (about 1 medium head)
¼   cup packed brown sugar
4   cups water
1   teaspoon crushed red pepper
½   teaspoon salt
½   teaspoon pepper
4   chicken bouillon cubes
1   can (28 ounces) crushed tomatoes, undrained

Mix all ingredients in 3½- to 6-quart slow cooker. Cover and cook on low heat setting 8 to 9 hours or high heat setting 4 to 5 hours or until pork and vegetables are tender.

**1 SERVING:** Calories 215 (Calories from Fat 65); Fat 7g (Saturated 2g); Cholesterol 35mg; Sodium 920mg; Carbohydrate 21g (Dietary Fiber 4g); Protein 14g

# ORIENTAL PORK SOUP

Prep: 15 min; Cook: Low 9 hr, or High 4 hr; Finishing Cook: Low 1 hr
6 servings

- 1 **pound chow mein meat (see tip)**
- 2 **medium carrots, cut into julienne strips**
- 4 **medium green onions, trimmed and cut into 1-inch pieces**
- 1 **clove garlic, peeled and finely chopped**
- ¼ **cup soy sauce**
- ½ **teaspoon finely chopped gingerroot**
- ⅛ **teaspoon pepper**
- 1 **can (49½ ounces) ready-to-serve chicken broth**
- 1 **cup sliced mushrooms**
- 1 **cup bean sprouts**

**1.** Cook chow mein meat in 10-inch skillet over medium heat 8 to 10 minutes, stirring occasionally, until brown; drain.

**2.** Mix meat and remaining ingredients except mushrooms and bean sprouts in 3½- to 6-quart slow cooker. Cover and cook on low heat setting 7 to 9 hours or high heat setting 3 to 4 hours.

**3.** Stir in mushrooms and bean sprouts. Cover and cook on low heat setting about 1 hour or until mushrooms are tender.

**1 SERVING:** Calories 220 (Calories from Fat 115); Fat 13g (Saturated 4g); Cholesterol 50mg; Sodium 1720mg; Carbohydrate 6g (Dietary Fiber 1g); Protein 21g

## COOKING TIPS

• Coarsely ground fresh pork is sometimes labeled "chow mein meat." If it isn't available at your store, use regular ground pork, chicken or turkey. Drained canned sliced mushrooms and bean sprouts come in handy when you don't have the fresh on hand.

• Spoon a mound of hot cooked rice into each bowl of soup before serving, and sprinkle with some sliced green onion tops.

# VEGETABLE-BEEF SOUP

Prep: 20 min; Cook: 30 min        7 servings

3 cups cut-up cooked beef

4 cups canned beef broth

1 cup frozen corn kernels

2 medium potatoes, cubed

2 medium tomatoes, chopped

1 medium carrot, thinly sliced

1 medium stalk celery, sliced

1 cup frozen cut green beans

1 cup frozen green peas

¼ teaspoon pepper

Place beef and broth in 4-quart Dutch oven. Stir in remaining ingredients. Heat to boiling; reduce heat to low. Cover and simmer about 30 minutes or until vegetables are tender.

**1 SERVING:** Calories 235 (Calories from Fat 80); Fat 9g (Saturated 4g); Cholesterol 50mg; Sodium 440mg; Carbohydrate 19g (Dietary Fiber 3g); Protein 22g

## SPECIAL TOUCH

### Cabinet Door Tray

You will need:

**12 x 15-inch cabinet door**

**Decorative drawer pulls or handles**

**1 sheet (8½ x 11 inches) decorative paper, if desired**

**Four 4- or 6-inch fence post end caps, if desired**

1. Drill holes (if needed) on short sides of door.

2. Attach drawer pulls.

3. Line tray with decorative paper, if desired.

To add height and dimension to your buffet table, place the tray on fence post end caps.

*Note:* Cabinet door and fence post end caps are available at hardware stores.

# ℬEEF STEW WITH SUN-DRIED TOMATOES

Prep: 20 min; Cook: Low 9 hr, or High 5 hr; Finishing Cook: 15 min
6 servings

| | |
|---|---|
| 1 | **cup sun-dried tomatoes (not oil-packed)** |
| 1½ | **pounds beef stew meat** |
| 12 | **medium new potatoes, cut in half** |
| 1 | **medium onion, peeled and cut into 8 wedges** |
| 1 | **bag (8 ounces) baby-cut carrots** |
| 2 | **cups water** |
| 1½ | **teaspoons seasoned salt** |
| 1 | **bay leaf** |
| ¼ | **cup cold water** |
| 2 | **tablespoons all-purpose flour** |

**1.** Soak tomatoes in water as directed on package; drain and coarsely chop.

**2.** Mix tomatoes and remaining ingredients except ¼ cup water and the flour in 3½- to 6-quart slow cooker. Cover and cook on low heat setting 8 to 9 hours or high heat setting 3 to 5 hours or until beef and vegetables are tender.

**3.** Mix ¼ cup water and flour; gradually stir into beef mixture. Cover and cook on high heat setting 10 to 15 minutes or until slightly thickened. Remove bay leaf.

**1 SERVING:** Calories 310 (Calories from Fat 100); Fat 11g (Saturated 4g); Cholesterol 60mg; Sodium 600mg; Carbohydrate 34g (Dietary Fiber 5g); Protein 24g

### COOKING TIPS

• You can also try chuck, tip or top or bottom round steak in this recipe. Get a 1-inch-thick piece of boneless steak, trim the extra fat and cut the steak into 1-inch pieces.

• When fresh tomatoes are plentiful, you can add 2 cups chopped fresh tomatoes with the flour mixture instead of using the sun-dried tomatoes.

• If you're serving a smaller crowd, you can cut the ingredient amounts in half and cook the chili in a 3-quart saucepan. Decrease the cooking time by about 10 minutes.

• For a cool zing, mix a tablespoon or 2 of fresh lime juice into 1 cup of sour cream to spoon on top of the chili. Sprinkle with chopped fresh cilantro or sliced green onions.

# CHILI FOR A CROWD

Prep: 10 min; Cook: 1 hr 45 min       12 servings

| | |
|---|---|
| 4 | medium onions, peeled and chopped |
| 2 | pounds ground beef |
| 2 | cans (28 ounces each) diced tomatoes, undrained |
| 1 | can (8 ounces) tomato sauce |
| 1½ | tablespoons chili powder |
| 1 | tablespoon sugar |
| 2 | teaspoons salt |
| 2 | cans (15 to 16 ounces each) kidney beans, undrained |

**1.** Cook onions and beef in 4-quart Dutch oven over medium heat about 15 minutes, stirring occasionally, until beef is brown. Place large strainer over medium bowl, or place colander in large bowl. Spoon beef mixture into strainer to drain fat. Discard fat.

2. Return beef mixture to Dutch oven. Stir in tomatoes with their liquid, tomato sauce, chili powder, sugar and salt. Heat to boiling over high heat. Reduce heat just enough so mixture bubbles gently. Cook uncovered 1 hour 15 minutes.

3. Stir beans with their liquid into chili. Heat to boiling over high heat. Reduce heat just enough so chili bubbles gently. Cook uncovered about 15 minutes longer, stirring occasionally, until chili is thickened.

**1 SERVING:** Calories 280 (Calories from fat 110); Fat 12g (Saturated 4g); Cholesterol 45mg; Sodium 960mg; Carbohydrate 28g (Dietary Fiber 7g); Protein 22g

### SERVING TIPS

• Gather the gang and serve a "make it your way" chili bar. Provide toppings of sour cream, salsa, shredded cheeses, chopped red onion, chopped ripe olives and chopped avocado. Have baskets filled with croutons, tortilla chips, crackers, corn muffins and breadsticks for chili dipping.

• For an extra treat, offer purchased bread bowls or tortilla bowls (available at your supermarket) to serve the chili in.

## SPECIAL TOUCH

### Tortilla Holders

You will need:

**Aluminum foil**

**Empty soup or vegetable cans (2 or 3 inches in diameter)**

**6 flour tortillas (12 inches in diameter)**

**⅓ cup olive or vegetable oil**

**3 tablespoons chili powder, ground cinnamon or ground nutmeg**

1. Heat oven to 325°. Wrap aluminum foil around outside of cans. Spray foil with cooking spray.

2. Cut each tortilla in half. Mix oil and chili powder. Brush about 1½ teaspoons oil mixture over 1 side of each tortilla half. Roll uncoated side of tortilla around foil-wrapped can.

3. Place tortilla, rolled edge down, in baking pan. Bake 5 minutes. While still warm, unwrap tortilla slightly to remove from can. Repeat with remaining tortillas. Cool. Use to hold breadsticks, pretzel rods or carrot and celery sticks.

# Tabbouleh
## WITH GARBANZO BEANS

Prep: 15 min; Stand: 1 hr      4 servings

1½  **cups boiling water**

¾  **cup uncooked bulgur**

**Lemon-Garlic Dressing (at right)**

3  **medium tomatoes, chopped**

8  **medium green onions, trimmed and chopped**

1  **medium green bell pepper, chopped**

1  **cup chopped cucumber**

¾  **cup chopped fresh parsley**

3  **tablespoons chopped fresh or 1 tablespoon dried mint leaves, crumbled**

1  **can (15 to 16 ounces) garbanzo beans, drained**

**1.** Pour boiling water over bulgur in medium bowl. Let stand 1 hour.

**2.** Prepare Lemon-Garlic Dressing. Drain any remaining water from bulgur. Stir remaining ingredients into bulgur. Toss with dressing.

**1 SERVING:** Calories 305 (Calories from Fat 65); Fat 7g (Saturated 1g); Cholesterol 0mg; Sodium 1350mg; Carbohydrate 60g (Dietary Fiber 15g); Protein 15g

### LEMON-GARLIC DRESSING

- ¼ cup lemon juice
- 1 tablespoon olive or vegetable oil
- ¾ teaspoon salt
- ¼ teaspoon pepper
- 3 cloves garlic, peeled and finely chopped

Shake all ingredients in tightly covered container.

# ANICOTTI

Prep: 15 min; Bake: 1 hr 30 min      7 servings

- 1 jar (32 ounces) chunky-style spaghetti sauce
- 2 packages (10 ounces each) frozen chopped spinach, thawed and well drained
- 1 container (12 ounces) small curd creamed cottage cheese
- 1 cup grated Parmesan cheese (4 ounces)
- 1 tablespoon snipped fresh or 1 teaspoon dried oregano leaves
- ¼ teaspoon pepper
- 14 uncooked manicotti shells
- 2 cups shredded mozzarella cheese (8 ounces)

**1.** Heat oven to 350°.

**2.** Spread ⅓ of the spaghetti sauce in ungreased rectangular baking dish, 13 × 9 × 2 inches. Mix spinach, cottage cheese, Parmesan cheese, oregano and pepper. Fill uncooked manicotti shells with spinach mixture; arrange on spaghetti sauce in dish.

**3.** Pour remaining spaghetti sauce evenly over shells, covering completely; sprinkle with mozzarella cheese. Cover and bake until shells are tender, about 1 hour 30 minutes.

**1 SERVING:** Calories 450 (Calories from Fat 145); Fat 16g (Saturated 8g); Cholesterol 35mg; Sodium 1270mg; Carbohydrate 55g (Dietary Fiber 5g); Protein 27g

**COOKING TIP**

• For variety, mix up your cheeses! Try Vermont white Cheddar, or even a mixture of half sharp Cheddar and half Monterey Jack cheese with jalapeño peppers, in this great-tasting comfort food.

# Macaroni and Cheese

Prep: 25 min; Cook: 5 min; Bake: 25 min        4 servings

- **2  cups uncooked elbow macaroni**
- **¼  cup (½ stick) butter or stick margarine**
- **¼  cup all-purpose flour**
- **½  teaspoon salt**
- **¼  teaspoon pepper**
- **¼  teaspoon ground mustard**
- **¼  teaspoon Worcestershire sauce**
- **2  cups milk**
- **2  cups shredded sharp Cheddar cheese (8 ounces)**

**1.** Heat oven to 350°.

**2.** Cook and drain macaroni as directed on package.

**3.** Meanwhile, melt butter in 3-quart saucepan over low heat. Stir in flour, salt, pepper, mustard and Worcestershire sauce. Cook over low heat, stirring constantly, until mixture is smooth and bubbly; remove from heat. Stir in milk. Heat to boiling, stirring constantly. Boil and stir 1 minute; remove from heat. Stir in cheese until melted.

**4.** Gently stir drained macaroni into cheese sauce. Pour into ungreased 2-quart casserole. Bake uncovered 20 to 25 minutes or until bubbly.

**1 SERVING:** Calories 605 (Calories from Fat 305); Fat 34g (Saturated 21g); Cholesterol 100mg; Sodium 790mg; Carbohydrate 51g (Dietary Fiber 2g); Protein 26g

*Lighter Macaroni and Cheese:* For 10 grams of fat and 375 calories per serving, decrease butter to 2 tablespoons. Use fat-free (skim) milk and substitute 1½ cups reduced-fat Cheddar cheese (6 ounces) for the 2 cups regular sharp Cheddar cheese.

# Vegetarian Cannellini Bean Lasagna

Prep: 40 min; Bake: 1 hr; Stand: 10 min    12 servings

- 9 uncooked lasagna noodles (9 ounces)
- 1 medium onion, peeled and chopped
- ½ green bell pepper, chopped
- 2 cloves garlic, peeled and finely chopped
- 2 cans (15 ounces each) chunky Italian-style tomato sauce
- 1 can (19 ounces) cannellini beans, rinsed and drained
- ¾ teaspoon fennel seeds
- ½ teaspoon sugar
- 1 container (15 ounces) fat-free ricotta cheese
- ¼ cup shredded Parmesan cheese (1 ounce)
- 3 cups frozen cut leaf spinach, thawed and squeezed to drain
- 1½ cups finely shredded mozzarella cheese (6 ounces)

**1.** Heat oven to 350°. Spray rectangular baking dish, 13 × 9 × 2 inches, with cooking spray. Cook and drain lasagna noodles as directed on package.

**2.** Spray 12-inch nonstick skillet with cooking spray; heat over medium-high heat. Cook onion, bell pepper and garlic in skillet about 3 minutes, stirring occasionally, until vegetables are crisp-tender. Stir in tomato sauce, beans, fennel seeds and sugar; reduce heat to medium. Cook 5 to 10 minutes, stirring occasionally, until sauce is slightly thickened.

**3.** Mix ricotta cheese, 2 tablespoons of the Parmesan cheese and the spinach. Spread about 1 cup tomato sauce mixture in baking dish. Top with 3 noodles. Spread with half of ricotta mixture. Top with about 1½ cups tomato sauce mixture, ½ cup of the mozzarella cheese, 3 noodles, remaining ricotta mixture, remaining tomato sauce mixture and remaining 3 noodles. Sprinkle with remaining 1 cup mozzarella cheese and remaining 2 tablespoons Parmesan cheese.

**4.** Cover and bake 45 minutes. Uncover and bake 10 to 15 minutes more or until top is light golden brown and mixture is bubbly. Let stand 5 to 10 minutes before serving.

**1 SERVING:** Calories 260 (Calories from Fat 55); Fat 6g (Saturated 2g); Cholesterol 10mg; Sodium 610mg; Carbohydrate 40g (Dietary Fiber 6g); Protein 17g

## COOKING TIP

• If you're making a casserole and don't want the hassle of scrubbing any baked-on bits from the pan afterward, line the casserole dish with heavy-duty aluminum foil and grease or spray with cooking spray before filling and baking.

# $\mathcal{V}$EGETABLE LASAGNA

Prep: 20 min; Bake: 55 min; Stand: 10 min      6 servings

 1  **medium zucchini, shredded**

 2  **cups spaghetti sauce**

 1  **package (10 ounces) frozen chopped spinach, thawed**

1½  **cups reduced-fat cottage cheese or ricotta cheese (12 ounces)**

⅓  **cup grated Parmesan cheese (1½ ounces)**

 2  **tablespoons chopped fresh or 1½ teaspoons dried oregano leaves**

 1  **can (4 ounces) mushroom stems and pieces**

 8  **purchased precooked or oven-ready lasagna noodles (each about 7 × 3 inches)**

 2  **cups shredded mozzarella cheese (8 ounces)**

**1.** Mix zucchini and spaghetti sauce in medium bowl.

**2.** Drain thawed spinach in strainer, then squeeze out excess moisture from spinach, using paper towels or a clean kitchen towel, until spinach is dry.

**3.** Mix spinach, cottage cheese, Parmesan cheese and oregano in medium bowl. Drain mushrooms in strainer. Spread ½ cup of the sauce mixture in ungreased square pan.

**4.** Top sauce mixture in pan with 2 noodles, placing them so they do not overlap or touch the sides of the pan because they will expand as they bake. Spread one fourth of the remaining sauce mixture (about ½ cup) over noodles.

**5.** Drop one quarter of the spinach mixture by small spoonfuls over the sauce mixture; spread carefully, pulling with the tines of a fork if necessary. Sprinkle with one quarter of the mushrooms and ½ cup of the mozzarella cheese.

**6.** Repeat layering three more times, beginning with 2 more noodles and following directions in steps 4 and 5. Bake immediately or cover with plastic wrap and then with aluminum foil and refrigerate up to 24 hours, if desired. (The plastic wrap keeps the lasagna from touching the aluminum foil while being refrigerated.)

**7.** Heat oven to 400°. Remove plastic wrap from lasagna, then cover lasagna again with aluminum foil. Bake 45 minutes. Carefully remove foil and continue baking about 10 minutes longer or until lasagna is bubbly around edges. Remove from oven and let stand 10 minutes before serving.

**1 SERVING:** Calories 425 (Calories from Fat 115); Fat 13g (Saturated 6g); Cholesterol 30mg; Sodium 1030mg; Carbohydrate 53g (Dietary Fiber 4g); Protein 28g

# $\mathcal{C}$OLD POACHED SALMON WITH HERB MAYONNAISE

Prep: 25 min; Cook: 19 min; Chill: 2 hr     6 servings

- 2 **cups water**
- 1 **cup dry white wine, nonalcoholic white wine or apple juice**
- 1 **teaspoon salt**
- ¼ **teaspoon dried thyme leaves**
- ¼ **teaspoon dried oregano leaves**
- ⅛ **teaspoon ground red pepper (cayenne)**
- 1 **small onion, peeled and sliced**
- 4 **black peppercorns**
- 4 **sprigs cilantro**
- 2 **pounds salmon or other medium-firm fish fillets**
  **Herb Mayonnaise (below)**
  **Lemon wedges, if desired**

**1.** Heat all ingredients except fish, Herb Mayonnaise and lemon wedges to boiling in 12-inch skillet; reduce heat to low. Cover and simmer 5 minutes.

**2.** Cut fish into 6 serving pieces. Place fish in skillet; add water to cover if necessary. Heat to boiling; reduce heat to low. Simmer uncovered about 14 minutes or until fish flakes easily with fork.

**3.** Carefully remove fish with slotted spatula; drain on wire rack. Cover and refrigerate about 2 hours or until chilled.

**4.** Prepare Herb Mayonnaise. Serve fish with Herb Mayonnaise and lemon wedges.

**1 SERVING:** Calories 375 (Calories from Fat 260); Fat 29g (Saturated 5g); Cholesterol 100mg; Sodium 350mg; Carbohydrate 1g (Dietary Fiber 0g); Protein 28g

## HERB MAYONNAISE

- ¾ **cup mayonnaise or salad dressing**
- 1½ **tablespoons chopped fresh or 1½ teaspoons dried dill weed or tarragon leaves**
- 1 **tablespoon chopped fresh chives**
- 1 **tablespoon chopped fresh parsley**
- 1 **tablespoon lemon juice**
- 1½ **teaspoons Dijon mustard**
  **Dash of ground red pepper (cayenne)**

Mix all ingredients. Cover and refrigerate until serving.

# $\mathcal{C}$HICKEN MANICOTTI

Prep: 15 min; Bake: 1 hr 30 min        7 servings

| 1 | jar (26 to 30 ounces) tomato pasta sauce |
| 1 | teaspoon garlic salt |
| 1½ | pounds chicken breast tenders |
| 14 | uncooked manicotti shells (8 ounces) |
| 2 | cups shredded mozzarella cheese (8 ounces) |
| | Chopped fresh basil leaves, if desired |

**1.** Heat oven to 350°. Spread about 1 cup of the pasta sauce in an ungreased rectangular pan, 13 × 9 × 2 inches.

**2.** Sprinkle garlic salt over chicken. Fill uncooked manicotti shells with chicken, stuffing chicken from each end of shell. Place filled shells on pasta sauce in pan.

**3.** Pour remaining pasta sauce evenly over shells, covering shells completely with sauce. Sprinkle with cheese.

**4.** Cover pan with aluminum foil and bake about 1 hour 30 minutes or until shells are tender. Sprinkle with basil.

**1 SERVING:** Calories 435 (Calories from Fat 115); Fat 13g (Saturated 5g); Cholesterol 75mg; Sodium 880mg; Carbohydrate 46g (Dietary Fiber 3g); Protein 36g

## COOKING TIP

• To make ahead, tightly wrap pan of unbaked manicotti (before adding cheese) with plastic wrap, and then with aluminum foil, and freeze up to 1 month. Thaw, wrapped, in refrigerator 12 hours or until completely thawed. Sprinkle with cheese, remove plastic wrap, then cover again with foil and bake as directed.

## SPECIAL TOUCH

### Fall Harvest Bowl

You will need:

**Clean peat pot liner (10 to 12 inches in diameter)**

**Natural excelsior (wood shavings), straw or hay**

**Variety of fresh fall fruits and vegetables (apples, baby artichokes, beets, bell peppers, garlic, mushrooms, pears, mini pumpkins, squash, turnips)**

**About 1 yard 2-inch-wide ribbon**

1. Line peat pot with excelsior

2. Arrange fruits and vegetables in pot.

3. Tie ribbon around pot into bow.

*Note:* Peat pot liners are used in hanging flower pots and are available at your local nursery. You'll find them in many sizes.

# CHICKEN TETRAZZINI

Prep: 20 min; Bake: 30 min          6 servings

1 package (7 ounces) spaghetti, broken into thirds

¼ cup (½ stick) butter or stick margarine

¼ cup all-purpose flour

½ teaspoon salt

¼ teaspoon pepper

1 cup chicken broth

1 cup whipping (heavy) cream

2 tablespoons dry sherry or water

2 cups cubed cooked chicken or turkey

1 can (4 ounces) sliced mushrooms, drained

½ cup grated Parmesan cheese (2 ounces)

**1.** Heat oven to 350°.

**2.** Cook and drain spaghetti as directed on package.

**3.** Meanwhile, melt butter in 2-quart saucepan over low heat. Stir in flour, salt and pepper. Cook, stirring constantly, until mixture is smooth and bubbly; remove from heat. Stir in broth and whipping cream. Heat to boiling, stirring constantly. Boil and stir 1 minute.

**4.** Stir spaghetti, sherry, chicken and mushrooms into sauce. Pour spaghetti mixture into ungreased 2-quart casserole. Sprinkle with cheese. Bake uncovered about 30 minutes or until bubbly in center.

**1 SERVING:** Calories 480 (Calories from Fat 260); Fat 29g (Saturated 15g); Cholesterol 110mg; Sodium 680mg; Carbohydrate 34g (Dietary Fiber 2g); Protein 22g

***Lighter Chicken Tetrazzini:*** For 12 grams of fat and 320 calories per serving, decrease butter to 2 tablespoons and Parmesan cheese to ¼ cup, and substitute fat-free (skim) milk for the whipping cream.

# TUFFED PEPPERS

Prep: 15 min; Cook: 15 min; Bake: 1 hr        6 servings

- **6 large bell peppers (any color)**
- **1 pound lean ground beef**
- **2 tablespoons chopped onion**
- **1 cup cooked rice**
- **1 teaspoon salt**
- **1 clove garlic, peeled and finely chopped**
- **1 can (15 ounces) tomato sauce**
- **¾ cup shredded mozzarella cheese (3 ounces)**

**1.** Cut thin slice from stem end of each bell pepper to remove top of pepper. Remove seeds and membranes. Cook peppers in enough boiling water to cover in 4-quart Dutch oven about 5 minutes; drain.

**2.** Cook beef and onion in 10-inch skillet over medium heat 8 to 10 minutes, stirring occasionally, until beef is brown; drain. Stir in rice, salt, garlic and 1 cup of the tomato sauce; cook until hot.

**3.** Heat oven to 350°.

**4.** Stuff peppers with beef mixture. Stand peppers upright in ungreased square baking dish, 8 × 8 × 2 inches. Pour remaining tomato sauce over peppers.

**5.** Cover and bake 45 minutes. Uncover and bake about 15 minutes longer or until peppers are tender. Sprinkle with cheese.

**1 SERVING:** Calories 290 (Calories from Fat 125); Fat 14g (Saturated 6g); Cholesterol 50mg; Sodium 930mg; Carbohydrate 24g (Dietary Fiber 4g); Protein 21g

***Lighter Stuffed Peppers:*** For 3 grams of fat and 190 calories per serving, substitute ground turkey breast for the ground beef and use reduced-fat cheese.

# CABBAGE ROLLS

Prep: 20 min; Bake: 45 min     4 servings

12  cabbage leaves
1  pound lean ground beef
½  cup uncooked instant rice
1  can (15 ounces) tomato sauce
½  teaspoon salt
⅛  teaspoon pepper
1  medium onion, peeled and chopped
1  clove garlic, peeled and finely chopped
1  can (4 ounces) mushroom pieces and stems, undrained
1  teaspoon sugar
½  teaspoon lemon juice
1  tablespoon cornstarch
1  tablespoon water

**1.** Cover cabbage leaves with boiling water. Cover and let stand about 10 minutes or until leaves are limp. Remove leaves; drain.

**2.** Heat oven to 350°.

**3.** Mix beef, rice, ½ cup of the tomato sauce, the salt, pepper, onion, garlic and mushrooms. Place about ⅓ cup beef mixture at stem end of each leaf. Roll leaf around beef mixture, tucking in sides. Place cabbage rolls, seam sides down, in ungreased square baking dish, 8 × 8 × 2 inches.

**4.** Mix remaining tomato sauce, the sugar and lemon juice; pour over cabbage rolls.

**5.** Cover and bake about 45 minutes or until beef mixture is no longer pink in center.

**6.** Remove cabbage rolls to platter. Pour liquid in baking dish into 1-quart saucepan. Mix cornstarch and water; stir into liquid. Heat to boiling, stirring constantly. Boil and stir 1 minute. Pour sauce over cabbage rolls.

**1 SERVING:** Calories 355 (Calories from Fat 155); Fat 17g (Saturated 6g); Cholesterol 65mg; Sodium 1120mg; Carbohydrate 30g (Dietary Fiber 4g); Protein 25g

**Lighter Cabbage Rolls:** For 2 grams of fat and 245 calories per serving, substitute ground turkey breast for the ground beef.

**Corned Beef Cabbage Rolls:** Substitute 1 pound chopped cooked corned beef for the ground beef.

# OVERNIGHT LASAGNA

Prep: 15 min; Cook: 30 min; Bake: 1 hr 10 min; Stand: 15 min
6 servings

- 1 pound ground beef
- 1 medium onion, peeled and chopped
- 1 clove garlic, peeled and crushed
- ⅓ cup chopped fresh or 2 tablespoons dried parsley leaves
- 1 tablespoon sugar
- 2 tablespoons chopped fresh or 1½ teaspoons dried basil leaves
- 1 teaspoon seasoned salt
- 1 can (16 ounces) whole tomatoes, undrained
- 1 can (10¾ ounces) condensed tomato soup
- 1 can (6 ounces) tomato paste
- 2½ cups water
- 12 uncooked lasagna noodles (about 12 ounces)
- 1 container (12 ounces) creamed cottage cheese
- 2 cups shredded mozzarella cheese (8 ounces)
- ¼ cup grated Parmesan cheese (1 ounce)

**1.** Cook, stirring, ground beef, onion and garlic in 4-quart Dutch oven until beef is brown; drain. Stir in parsley, sugar, basil, seasoned salt, tomatoes, tomato soup, tomato paste and water; break up tomatoes.

**2.** Heat to boiling, stirring occasionally; reduce heat. Simmer uncovered 20 minutes.

**3.** Spread 2 cups of the sauce mixture in ungreased rectangular baking dish, 13 × 9 × 2 inches. Top with 4 noodles. Spread half of the cottage cheese over noodles; spread with 2 cups of the sauce mixture. Sprinkle with 1 cup of the mozzarella cheese. Repeat with 4 noodles, remaining cottage cheese, 2 cups of the sauce mixture and remaining mozzarella cheese. Top with remaining noodles and sauce mixture; sprinkle with Parmesan cheese. Cover with plastic wrap and then with aluminum foil and refrigerate up to 12 hours.

**4.** Heat oven to 350°. Remove plastic wrap, then cover again with aluminum foil. Bake covered 30 minutes. Uncover and bake until hot and bubbly, 30 to 40 minutes longer. Let stand 15 minutes before cutting.

**1 SERVING:** Calories 425 (Calories from Fat 155); Fat 17g (Saturated 8g); Cholesterol 55mg; Sodium 1160mg; Carbohydrate 41g (Dietary Fiber 3g); Protein 30g

## COOKING TIP

• To make ahead, cover unbaked lasagna with plastic wrap, and then with aluminum foil and refrigerate up to 24 hours or freeze up to 2 months. Remove plastic wrap, then cover again with aluminum foil. Bake 45 minutes. Uncover and bake refrigerated lasagna 15 to 20 minutes longer or frozen lasagna 35 to 45 minutes longer until hot and bubbly.

# *I*TALIAN SAUSAGE LASAGNA

Prep: 15 min; Cook: 55 min; Bake: 45 min; Stand: 15 min          8 servings

- 1 **pound bulk Italian sausage or ground beef**
- 1 **medium onion, peeled and chopped**
- 1 **clove garlic, peeled and chopped**
- 3 **tablespoons chopped fresh parsley**
- 1 **tablespoon chopped fresh or 1 teaspoon dried basil leaves**
- 1 **teaspoon sugar**
- 1 **can (15 ounces) tomato sauce**
- 1 **can (14½ ounces) whole tomatoes, undrained**
- 8 **uncooked lasagna noodles (from 16-ounce package)**
- 1 **container (15 ounces) ricotta cheese or small curd creamed cottage cheese (2 cups)**
- ½ **cup grated Parmesan cheese (2 ounces)**
- 1 **tablespoon chopped fresh or 1½ teaspoons dried oregano leaves**
- 2 **cups shredded mozzarella cheese (8 ounces)**

1. Cook sausage, onion and garlic in skillet over medium heat about 5 minutes, stirring occasionally, until sausage is no longer pink. Place strainer over medium bowl, or place colander in large bowl. Spoon sausage mixture into strainer to drain fat; discard fat.

2. Return sausage mixture to skillet. Stir in 2 tablespoons of the parsley, the basil, sugar, tomato sauce and tomatoes with their liquid. Break up tomatoes with a spoon or fork.

3. Heat mixture to boiling over medium-high heat, stirring occasionally. Reduce heat just enough so mixture bubbles gently. Cook uncovered about 45 minutes, stirring occasionally, until sauce is slightly thickened.

4. After sauce has been cooking about 25 minutes, cook and drain noodles as directed on package.

5. While noodles are cooking, mix ricotta cheese, ¼ cup of the Parmesan cheese, the oregano and remaining 1 tablespoon parsley.

6. Heat oven to 350°. Spread half of the sauce (about 2 cups) in ungreased rectangular pan. Top with 4 noodles. Spread half of the ricotta cheese mixture (about 1 cup) over noodles. Sprinkle with 1 cup of the mozzarella cheese.

7. Repeat layers by adding remaining sauce, noodles, ricotta cheese mixture and mozzarella cheese. Sprinkle with remaining ¼ cup Parmesan cheese.

**8.** Cover with aluminum foil and bake 30 minutes. Carefully remove foil, and continue baking about 15 minutes longer or until lasagna is bubbly around edges and looks very hot. Remove from oven and let stand 15 minutes before serving.

**1 SERVING:** Calories 415 (Calories from Fat 200); Fat 22g (Saturated 10g); Cholesterol 65mg; Sodium 1090mg; Carbohydrate 28g (Dietary Fiber 2g); Protein 28g

## Iced Wine Bottle

You will need:

**Empty green or clear wine bottle**

**Uncooked rice**

**1 bunch (about 12 inches long) flexible branches (willow or grapevine)**

**1 bunch (18 to 20 inches long) flexible branches (willow or grapefine)**

**Twine**

**Empty half-gallon milk carton**

1. Clean and completely dry inside of bottle. Fill bottle with rice to prevent cracking. Cork or cover top with plastic wrap. Wrap and tie each branch bunch in middle and at both ends, using twine. Wrap 12-inch bunch around middle of bottle, and tie with twine to secure. Secure ends of longer bunch to opposite sides of the bunch on the bottle to make a handle, using twine.

2. Cut milk carton to a height of 7 inches. Place bottle inside carton. Fill carton with water; freeze overnight or until solid.

3. To remove frozen bottle from carton, place carton briefly in warm water. Pour rice out of bottle. Fill bottle with chilled wine or water. Place on liner or plate to catch the water as the ice melts.

# $\int$TUFFED PASTA SHELLS

Prep: 20 min; Cook: 12 min; Bake: 30 min          6 servings

|     |     |
| --- | --- |
| 12 | uncooked jumbo pasta shells |
| 1 | pound lean ground beef |
| 1 | medium onion, peeled and chopped |
| 1½ | teaspoons chili powder |
| 1 | package (3 ounces) cream cheese at room temperature |
| ¼ | cup taco sauce |
| ½ | cup taco sauce |
| 1 | cup shredded Colby-Monterey Jack cheese (4 ounces) |
| ½ | cup crushed corn chips |
| ½ | cup sour cream |
| 4 | medium green onions with tops, trimmed and sliced |

**1.** Cook and drain pasta shells as directed on package.

**2.** Cook ground beef and onion in skillet over medium-high heat 5 to 6 minutes, stirring occasionally, until beef is brown; drain.

**3.** Stir chili powder, cream cheese and ¼ cup taco sauce into beef in skillet. Heat over medium-low heat 2 to 3 minutes, stirring occasionally, until cheese is melted. Remove skillet from heat.

**4.** Heat oven to 350°. Spray square pan with cooking spray.

**5.** Drain pasta shells in a strainer or colander. Fill shells with beef mixture, using about 2 tablespoons for each shell. Place filled shells in sprayed pan. Pour ½ cup taco sauce over shells.

**6.** Cover with aluminum foil and bake 20 minutes. Remove pan from oven. Sprinkle Colby-Monterey Jack cheese and corn chips over shells. Bake uncovered about 10 minutes longer or until cheese is melted. Garnish pasta shells with sour cream and green onions.

**1 SERVING:** Calories 585 (Calories from Fat 270); Fat 30g (Saturated 14g); Cholesterol 90mg; Sodium 340mg; Carbohydrate 53g (Dietary Fiber 3g); Protein 29g

***Lighter Stuffed Pasta Shells:*** For 24 grams of fat and 540 calories per serving, use 1 pound lean ground turkey instead of the ground beef and use reduced-fat cream cheese (Neufchâtel), available in 8-ounce packages.

## COOKING TIP

• To make ahead, cover and refrigerate pan of unbaked stuffed pasta shells up to 24 hours. Increase first bake time to 25 minutes.

# FAVORITE MEAT LOAF

Prep: 10 min; Bake: 1 hr 30 min; Stand: 5 min        6 servings

- 1 **pound ground beef**
- ½ **pound ground pork**
- 1 **cup milk**
- 1 **tablespoon Worcestershire sauce**
- ¼ **teaspoon pepper**
- ¼ **teaspoon celery salt**
- ¼ **teaspoon garlic salt**
- ¼ **teaspoon ground mustard**
- ¼ **teaspoon ground sage**
- 1 **egg, beaten**
- 3 **slices white bread, torn into pieces**
- 1 **small onion, peeled and chopped**

**1.** Heat oven to 350°.

**2.** Mix all ingredients. Spread in ungreased loaf pan, 9 × 5 × 3 inches.

**3.** Bake 1 hour 30 minutes or until beef mixture is no longer pink in center and juice is clear. Let stand 5 minutes; remove from pan.

**1 SERVING:** Calories 340 (Calories from Fat 170); Fat 19g (Saturated 7g); Cholesterol 105mg; Sodium 370mg; Carbohydrate 17g (Dietary Fiber 1g); Protein 26g

## COOKING TIP

• For added flavor, spread the top of the meat loaf with ketchup, barbecue sauce or salsa before baking.

# $\mathcal{H}$AM AND SCALLOPED POTATOES

Prep: 20 min; Cook: 5 min; Bake: 1 hr 40 min; Stand: 10 min          6 servings

- **6** medium boiling or baking potatoes, peeled
- **3** tablespoons margarine or butter
- **1** small onion, peeled and finely chopped
- **3** tablespoons all-purpose flour
- **1** teaspoon salt
- **¼** teaspoon pepper
- **2½** cups milk
- **1½** cups diced fully cooked ham
- **1** tablespoon margarine or butter

**1.** Heat oven to 350°. Grease 2-quart casserole.

**2.** Cut potatoes into enough thin slices to measure about 4 cups.

**3.** Melt 3 tablespoons margarine in 2-quart saucepan over medium heat. Cook onion in margarine about 2 minutes, stirring occasionally, until tender. Stir in flour, salt and pepper. Cook, stirring constantly, until smooth and bubbly; remove from heat.

**4.** Stir milk into sauce. Heat to boiling, stirring constantly. Boil and stir 1 minute. Stir in ham.

**5.** Spread potatoes in casserole. Pour sauce over potatoes. Dot with 1 tablespoon margarine.

**6.** Cover and bake 30 minutes. Uncover and bake 1 hour to 1 hour 10 minutes longer or until potatoes are tender. Let stand 5 to 10 minutes before serving.

**1 SERVING:** Calories 295 (Calories from Fat 115); Fat 13g (Saturated 4g); Cholesterol 25mg; Sodium 1040mg; Carbohydrate 33g (Dietary Fiber 2g); Protein 13g

# SALADS AND SIDES

## 24-HOUR FRUIT SALAD

Prep: 30 min; Cook: 5 min; Chill: 12 hr        8 servings

**Whipped Cream Dressing (below)**

2 **cans (20 ounces each) pineapple chunks in juice, drained and 2 tablespoons juice reserved for dressing**

1 **can (16½ ounces) pitted light or dark sweet cherries, drained**

3 **oranges, cut into small chunks**

1 **cup miniature marshmallows**

**1.** Prepare Whipped Cream Dressing.

**2.** Gently toss dressing and remaining ingredients in large glass or plastic bowl. Cover and refrigerate at least 12 hours to blend flavors but no longer than 24 hours. Store remaining salad covered in refrigerator.

**1 SERVING:** Calories 255 (Calories from Fat 90); Fat 10g (Saturated 6g); Cholesterol 80mg; Sodium 35mg; Carbohydrate 40g (Dietary Fiber 3g); Protein 4g

## WHIPPED CREAM DRESSING

2 **large eggs, beaten**

2 **tablespoons sugar**

2 **tablespoons white vinegar or lemon juice**

2 **tablespoons reserved pineapple juice**

1 **tablespoon butter or stick margarine**

**Dash of salt**

¾ **cup whipping (heavy) cream**

**1.** Heat all ingredients except whipping cream just to boiling in 1-quart saucepan over medium heat, stirring constantly; cool.

**2.** Beat whipping cream in chilled medium bowl with electric mixer on high speed until stiff. Fold in egg mixture.

*Lighter 24-Hour Salad:* For 3 grams of fat and 180 calories per serving, omit Whipped Cream Dressing. For dressing, reserve ¼ cup pineapple juice; fold juice into 2 cups frozen (thawed) reduced-fat whipped topping.

### COOKING TIP

• You can substitute 2 cans (11 ounces each) mandarin orange segments, drained, for the cut-up oranges.

# $\mathcal{S}$EVEN-LAYER SALAD

Prep: 15 min; Cook: 10 min; Chill: 2 hr          6 servings

12  slices bacon

 6  cups ready-to-eat mixed salad greens (from 10-ounce bag)

 8  medium radishes, thinly sliced

 5  medium green onions, trimmed and thinly sliced

 2  medium stalks celery, thinly sliced

 1  package (10 ounces) frozen green peas, thawed

1½  cups mayonnaise or salad dressing

 ½  cup shredded Cheddar cheese or grated Parmesan cheese (2 ounces)

**1.** Cook bacon in skillet over low heat 8 to 10 minutes, turning occasionally, until bacon is evenly browned and crisp. Drain bacon on paper towels. When bacon is cool enough to handle, crumble into small pieces.

**2.** Place salad greens in bowl. Layer radishes, onions, celery, bacon and peas on salad greens. Spread mayonnaise over peas, covering top completely and sealing to edge of bowl. Sprinkle with cheese.

**3.** Cover and refrigerate at least 2 hours to blend flavors but no longer than 12 hours. Just before serving, toss if desired. Store any remaining salad covered in refrigerator.

**1 SERVING:** Calories 535 (Calories from Fat 470); Fat 52g (Saturated 10g); Cholesterol 48mg; Sodium 700mg; Carbohydrate 11g (Dietary Fiber 4g); Protein 10g

# ℘ESTO MACARONI SALAD

Prep: 10 min; Cook: 10 min; Chill: 2 hr      6 servings

- 3 **cups uncooked medium shell macaroni**
- 1 **tablespoon olive or vegetable oil**
- 1 **container (8 ounces) pesto**
- 4 **Italian plum tomatoes, each cut into 4 wedges**
- ½ **cup small pitted ripe olives**
- ¼ **cup white wine vinegar**
- 4 **cups coarsely shredded spinach**
   **Grated Parmesan cheese**

1. Cook macaroni as directed on package; drain. Rinse in cold water; drain and toss with oil.

2. Mix pesto, tomatoes, olives and vinegar in large bowl. Arrange 2 cups of the macaroni and 2 cups of the spinach on pesto mixture; repeat with remaining macaroni and spinach.

3. Cover and refrigerate at least 2 hours but no longer than 24 hours. Toss; sprinkle with cheese.

**1 SERVING:** Calories 470 (Calories from Fat 215); Fat 24g (Saturated 15g); Cholesterol 150mg; Sodium 220mg; Carbohydrate 56g (Dietary Fiber 5g); Protein 13g

**COOKING TIP**

• Oil and vinegar is used in place of mayonnaise in this recipe, making it perfect to pack for picnic lunches.

# Gazpacho Pasta Salad with Tomato-Lime Dressing

**QUICK** Prep: 15 min; Cook 15 min          4 servings

**Tomato-Lime Dressing (below)**

1 package (8 ounces) farfalle (bow-tie) pasta

1 large tomato, seeded and coarsely chopped

1 small cucumber, coarsely chopped

1 small bell pepper, coarsely chopped

4 medium green onions, trimmed and sliced

½ green Anaheim chili, seeded and chopped

1 can (2¼ ounces) sliced ripe olives, drained

¼ cup chopped fresh cilantro

**1.** Prepare Tomato-Lime Dressing. Cook and drain pasta as directed on package.

**2.** Mix pasta and remaining ingredients in large bowl. Pour dressing over mixture; toss. Serve immediately, or cover and refrigerate until serving.

**1 SERVING:** Calories 320 (Calories from Fat 90); Fat 10g (Saturated 2g); Cholesterol 0mg; Sodium 350mg; Carbohydrate 62g (Dietary Fiber 4g); Protein 5g

## TOMATO-LIME DRESSING

¼ cup tomato juice

2 tablespoons olive or vegetable oil

2 tablespoons lime juice

¼ teaspoon salt

⅛ teaspoon pepper

1 clove garlic, peeled and finely chopped

Shake all ingredients in tightly covered container.

# ARTICHOKE-PEPPER PASTA SALAD

<u>**QUICK**</u>    Prep: 10 min; Cook: 15 min        6 servings

2⅔ cups uncooked fusilli (corkscrew) pasta (8 ounces)

1 jar (7 ounces) roasted red bell peppers

1 jar (2 ounces) sliced mushrooms

1 jar (6 to 7 ounces) marinated artichoke hearts, undrained

2 tablespoons shredded Parmesan cheese

½ teaspoon pepper

2 tablespoons pine nuts

3 tablespoons chopped fresh basil leaves, if desired

1. Cook and drain pasta as directed on package. Rinse thoroughly with cold water.

2. Meanwhile, drain bell peppers in strainer, then cut into small pieces. Place peppers in large bowl. Drain mushrooms in strainer and add to peppers.

3. Add artichoke hearts with their liquid, cheese and pepper to vegetables in bowl. Mix all ingredients thoroughly.

4. Add pasta to vegetable mixture and toss. Sprinkle with nuts and basil.

**1 SERVING:** Calories 195 (Calories from Fat 35); Fat 4g (Saturated 1g); Cholesterol 0mg; Sodium 180mg; Carbohydrate 36g (Dietary Fiber 4g); Protein 8g

***Main-Dish Artichoke-Pepper Pasta Salad:*** For 4 main-dish servings, add 1 cup chopped cooked chicken or turkey.

## SPECIAL TOUCH

### Lined Salad Plates

You will need:

**Clear glass plates: one dinnersize (about 10 inches) and one salad plate (about 8 inches) per place setting**

**Cards, photographs, torn art paper, flowers, leaves or other flat objects**

1. Place cards or other flat objects on the larger plates.

2. Set smaller plates on top.

# CURRIED TURKEY SALAD

Prep: 5 min; Cook: 10 min; Chill: 4 hr     6 servings

1½ **cups uncooked elbow macaroni**
1 **package (10 ounces) frozen green peas, thawed**
¾ **cup mayonnaise or salad dressing**
2 **teaspoons curry powder**
2 **cups cut-up cooked turkey breast**
½ **cup shredded Cheddar cheese (2 ounces)**
4 **medium green onions, trimmed and sliced**
1 **medium stalk celery, sliced**
   **Lettuce leaves, if desired**

1. Cook and drain macaroni as directed on package. Rinse with cold water; drain. Rinse frozen peas with cold water to separate; drain.

2. Mix mayonnaise and curry powder in large bowl. Stir in macaroni, peas and remaining ingredients except lettuce. Cover and refrigerate 2 to 4 hours to blend flavors. Serve on lettuce.

**1 SERVING:** Calories 465 (Calories from Fat 250); Fat 28g (Saturated 6g); Cholesterol 60mg; Sodium 290mg; Carbohydrate 34g (Dietary Fiber 4g); Protein 23g

# SWEET-SOUR COLESLAW

**QUICK** Prep: 5 min; Cook: 10 min        6 servings

1 **egg**

¼ **cup sugar**

¼ **cup vinegar**

2 **tablespoons water**

2 **tablespoons margarine or butter**

1 **teaspoon salt**

½ **teaspoon dry mustard**

1 **pound green cabbage, finely shredded or chopped**

1 **small bell pepper, chopped**

**1.** Beat egg until thick and lemon-colored.

**2.** Heat sugar, vinegar, water, margarine, salt and mustard to boiling, stirring constantly. Gradually stir at least half of the hot mixture into egg; then stir into hot mixture in saucepan.

**3.** Cook over low heat, stirring constantly, until thickened, about 5 minutes. Pour over cabbage and bell pepper; toss.

**1 SERVING:** Calories 80 (Calories from Fat 35); Fat 4g (Saturated 1g); Cholesterol 2mg; Sodium 350mg; Carbohydrate 10g (Dietary Fiber 1g); Protein 2g

**COOKING TIP**

• For the best flavor, cover and refrigerate this coleslaw for 2 to 4 hours before serving.

# COLD CUCUMBER SALAD

**QUICK**   Prep: 5 min; Cook: 5 min        12 servings

½ **cup sugar**

⅓ **cup water**

1 **teaspoon white pepper**

½ **teaspoon salt**

1½ **cups cider vinegar**

4 **large cucumbers, peeled and thinly sliced**

¼ **cup chopped fresh parsley**

**1.** Mix sugar, water, white pepper and salt in medium saucepan. Heat mixture over medium-high heat to boiling and boil until sugar is dissolved; remove from heat and cool. Stir in vinegar.

**2.** Pour mixture over cucumber slices; sprinkle with parsley. Cover and refrigerate until ready to serve.

**1 SERVING:** Calories 50 (Calories from Fat 0); Fat 0g (Saturated 0g); Cholesterol 0mg; Sodium 100mg; Carbohydrate 13g (Dietary Fiber 1g); Protein 1g

# THREE-BEAN SALAD

Prep: 20 min; Chill: 3 hr        6 servings

1 **can (15 to 16 ounces) cut green beans, drained**

1 **can (15 to 16 ounces) wax beans, drained**

1 **can (15 to 16 ounces) kidney, black or garbanzo beans, rinsed and drained**

4 **medium green onions, trimmed and chopped**

¼ **cup chopped fresh parsley**

1 **cup Italian dressing**

1 **tablespoon sugar**

2 **cloves garlic, peeled and finely chopped**

**1.** Mix beans, onions and parsley in medium glass or plastic bowl.

**2.** Mix dressing, sugar and garlic. Pour over salad; toss. Cover and refrigerate at least 3 hours to blend flavors, stirring occasionally.

**3.** Just before serving, spoon bean mixture into bowl with slotted spoon.

**1 SERVING:** Calories 200 (Calories from Fat 90); Fat 10g (Saturated 2g); Cholesterol 0mg; Sodium 640mg; Carbohydrate 27g (Dietary Fiber 7g); Protein 8g

# $\mathcal{C}$OUNTRY POTATO SALAD

Prep: 15 min; Cook: 40 min; Chill: 4 hr          10 servings

- 6 **medium potatoes**
- ¼ **cup Italian dressing**
  **Cooked Salad Dressing (below) or 1 cup mayonnaise**
- 2 **medium stalks celery, sliced**
- 1 **medium cucumber, chopped**
- 1 **large onion, peeled and chopped**
- 6 **radishes, thinly sliced**
- 4 **hard-cooked eggs, chopped**

**1.** Heat 1 inch water (salted if desired) to boiling. Add potatoes. Cover and heat to boiling; reduce heat. Cook until tender, 30 to 35 minutes. Drain and cool slightly.

**2.** Peel potatoes; cut into cubes (about 6 cups). Toss warm potatoes with Italian dressing in 4-quart glass or plastic bowl. Cover and refrigerate at least 4 hours. Prepare Cooked Salad Dressing.

**3.** Add celery, cucumber, onion, radishes and eggs to potatoes. Pour Cooked Salad Dressing over top; toss. Refrigerate until chilled. Immediately refrigerate any remaining salad.

**1 SERVING:** Calories 290 (Calories from Fat 200); Fat 22g (Saturated 4g); Cholesterol 100mg; Sodium 210mg; Carbohydrate 20g (Dietary Fiber 2g); Protein 5g

## COOKED SALAD DRESSING

- 2 **tablespoons all-purpose flour**
- 1 **tablespoon sugar**
- 1 **teaspoon dry mustard**
- ¾ **teaspoon salt**
- ¼ **teaspoon pepper**
- 1 **egg yolk, slightly beaten**
- ¾ **cup milk**
- 2 **tablespoons vinegar**
- 1 **tablespoon margarine or butter**

**1.** Mix flour, sugar, mustard, salt and pepper in 1-quart saucepan. Mix egg yolk and milk; slowly stir into flour mixture. Cook over medium heat, stirring constantly, until mixture thickens and boils. Boil and stir 1 minute; remove from heat.

**2.** Stir in vinegar and margarine. Place plastic wrap directly on surface; refrigerate until cool, at least 1 hour.

# $\mathcal{D}$UCHESS POTATOES

Prep: 20 min; Cook: 35 min; Bake: 15 min        12 servings

**12**  **medium potatoes, peeled**

**⅔ to 1**  **cup milk**

**½**  **cup margarine, butter or spread, softened**

**½**  **teaspoon salt**

**Dash of pepper**

**4**  **eggs, beaten**

**Margarine, butter or spread, melted**

**1.** Cut potatoes into large pieces if desired. Heat 1 inch water (salted if desired) to boiling in Dutch oven. Add potatoes. Cover and heat to boiling; reduce heat. Cook whole potatoes 30 to 35 minutes, pieces 20 to 25 minutes, or until tender; drain. Shake pan gently over low heat to dry potatoes.

**2.** Heat oven to 425°. Grease cookie sheet.

**3.** Mash potatoes until no lumps remain. Beat in milk in small amounts (amount of milk needed to make potatoes smooth and fluffy depends on kind of potatoes). Add ½ cup margarine, the salt and pepper. Beat vigorously until potatoes are light and fluffy. Add eggs; beat until blended.

**4.** Drop potato mixture by 12 spoonfuls into mounds onto cookie sheet. Or place in decorating bag with star tip and form rosettes or pipe a border around meat or fish. Brush with melted margarine. Bake about 15 minutes or until light brown.

**1 SERVING:** Calories 240 (Calories from Fat 115); Fat 13g (Saturated 3g); Cholesterol 70mg; Sodium 260mg; Carbohydrate 28g (Dietary Fiber 2g); Protein 5g

# SCALLOPED POTATOES

Prep: 20 min; Cook: 12 hr          8 servings

- **6  medium potatoes, cut into ⅛-inch slices**
- **1  can (10¾ ounces) condensed cream of onion soup**
- **1  can (5 ounces) evaporated milk (⅔ cup)**
- **1  jar (2 ounces) diced pimientos, undrained**
- **½  teaspoon salt**
- **¼  teaspoon pepper**

**1.** Spray inside of 3½- to 6-quart slow cooker with cooking spray.

**2.** Mix all ingredients; pour into cooker. Cover and cook on low heat setting 10 to 12 hours or until potatoes are tender.

**1 SERVING:** Calories 155 (Calories from Fat 25); Fat 3g (Saturated 1g); Cholesterol 10mg; Sodium 460mg; Carbohydrate 30g (Dietary Fiber 2g); Protein 4g

## COOKING TIPS

• Vary the taste by using whatever cream soup you have on hand, such as cream of mushroom, chicken or broccoli. You may want to add a thinly sliced small onion or ¼ teaspoon onion powder if you decide not to use the onion soup.

• For the cheese lovers in your family, sprinkle about ½ cup of their favorite shredded cheese over the top of the potatoes. Cover and let stand a few minutes so the cheese becomes warm and melty.

# $\mathcal{D}$O-AHEAD MASHED POTATOES

Prep: 15 min; Cook: 30 min; Chill: up to 24 hr; Bake: 45 min      8 servings

- **9** **medium potatoes, peeled and cut into large pieces**
- ¾ **cup milk**
- ½ **cup whipping (heavy) cream**
- ½ **cup (1 stick) margarine or butter**
- **1** **teaspoon salt**
  **Dash of pepper**

**1.** Add 1 inch of water and ¼ teaspoon salt, if desired, to large saucepan. Cover and heat to boiling over high heat. Add potato pieces. Cover and heat to boiling again. Reduce heat just enough so water bubbles gently.

2. Cook covered 20 to 25 minutes or until potatoes are tender. The cooking time will vary, depending on the size of the potato pieces and the type of potato used. Drain potatoes in strainer.

3. Return drained potatoes to saucepan, and cook over low heat about 1 minute to dry them. While cooking, shake pan often to keep potatoes from sticking and burning.

4. Place potatoes in medium bowl and mash with a potato masher or electric mixer until no lumps remain.

5. Heat milk, whipping cream, margarine, salt and pepper in small saucepan over medium-low heat, stirring occasionally, until margarine is melted. Measure out ¼ cup of the milk mixture; cover and refrigerate.

6. Add remaining milk mixture in small amounts as needed to potatoes, mashing after each addition. You may not need all the milk because the amount needed to make potatoes smooth and fluffy depends on the type of potato used. Beat vigorously until potatoes are light and fluffy.

7. Spray casserole with cooking spray. Spoon potatoes into sprayed casserole. Bake immediately, or cover and refrigerate up to 24 hours.

8. Heat oven to 350°. Pour reserved milk mixture over potatoes. Bake uncovered 40 to 45 minutes or until potatoes are hot. Just before serving, stir potatoes.

**1 SERVING:** Calories 280 (Calories from Fat 155); Fat 17g (Saturated 5g); Cholesterol 20mg; Sodium 470mg; Carbohydrate 29g (Dietary Fiber 2g); Protein 4g

***Do-Ahead Garlic Mashed Potatoes:*** Peel and finely chop 1 or 2 cloves garlic. Add to potatoes before mashing in step 4.

**SERVING TIP**
• For extra flavor, sprinkle 1 cup crushed herb-seasoned croutons or shredded Parmesan cheese over mashed potatoes. Or place purchased basil pesto in a resealable plastic bag, snip off a tiny corner and drizzle pesto over potatoes.

## COOKING TIPS

• Make soft bread crumbs by tearing the bread into small pieces. It's best to use a firm bread that is a couple of days old. Fresh, soft bread will give you a stuffing that is too moist and soggy.

• To add a little sweetness to this stuffing, add 1½ cups chopped apples and ½ cup raisins with the pecans.

# Pecan Bread Stuffing

Prep: 20 min; Cook: 5 hr      8 servings

4   cups soft bread crumbs (about 6 slices bread)
1   cup crushed saltine crackers (about eighteen 2-inch squares)
1   cup chopped pecans
1   large onion, peeled and chopped
2   medium stalks celery, chopped
⅔   cup vegetable or chicken broth
½   cup fat-free cholesterol-free egg product
¼   cup margarine or butter, melted
½   teaspoon pepper
½   teaspoon rubbed sage
    Chopped fresh parsley, if desired

**1.** Spray inside of 2- to 3½-quart slow cooker with cooking spray.

**2.** Mix bread crumbs, cracker crumbs, pecans, onion and celery in cooker.

**3.** Mix remaining ingredients except parsley; pour into cooker. Toss to coat ingredients. Cover and cook on low heat setting 4 to 5 hours or until stuffing is slightly puffed and brown around the edges. Sprinkle with parsley.

**1 SERVING:** Calories 405 (Calories from Fat 180); Fat 20g (Saturated 3g); Cholesterol 0mg; Sodium 720mg; Carbohydrate 49g (Dietary Fiber 3g); Protein 10g

# CREAMY WILD RICE

Prep: 15 min; Cook: 9 hr          10 servings

1½  **cups uncooked wild rice**

2¼  **cups water**

½  **teaspoon rubbed (crumbled) sage**

½  **teaspoon salt**

¼  **teaspoon pepper**

1  **medium onion, peeled and chopped**

1  **can (10¾ ounces) condensed cream of celery soup**

1  **can (10¾ ounces) condensed cream of mushroom soup**

¼  **cup chopped fresh parsley**

**1.** Mix all ingredients except parsley in 5- to 6-quart slow cooker.

**2.** Cover and cook on low heat setting 8 to 9 hours or until wild rice is tender. Stir in parsley.

**1 SERVING:** Calories 405 (Calories from Fat 115); Fat 13g (Saturated 2g); Cholesterol 0mg; Sodium 1360mg; Carbohydrate 69g (Dietary Fiber 11g); Protein 14g

## COOKING TIPS

• Wash wild rice in water before cooking it. Place the rice in a bowl of cold water and swirl it around with your hand a bit. When the water becomes cloudy, drain the rice. Repeat the process until the water remains clear.

• Toast some chopped nuts, such as walnuts or pecans, to add crunch and flavor to this creamy dish. Half a cup of nuts, either stirred in or sprinkled on top, should do the trick.

**COOKING TIP**

• If you are a little short on time, a tablespoon of dried parsley flakes can be used instead of the fresh parsley, and ¼ teaspoon of garlic powder can be used for the garlic cloves.

# FRENCH VEGETABLE RATATOUILLE

Prep: 20 min; Cook: 8 hr     8 servings

- **1** small eggplant (1 pound), peeled and cut into ½-inch cubes (about 5 cups)
- **4** medium tomatoes, quartered
- **1** medium zucchini, sliced
- **1** medium green bell pepper, cut into strips
- **1** medium onion, peeled and sliced
- **2** cloves garlic, peeled and finely chopped
- **¼** cup chopped fresh parsley
- **2** tablespoons olive or vegetable oil
- **1** teaspoon salt
- **1** teaspoon dried basil leaves
- **¼** teaspoon pepper

Mix all ingredients in 3½- to 6-quart slow cooker. Cover and cook on low heat setting 6 to 8 hours or until vegetables are tender.

**1 SERVING:** Calories 70 (Calories from Fat 35); Fat 4g (Saturated 1g); Cholesterol 0mg; Sodium 300mg; Carbohydrate 10g (Dietary Fiber 3g); Protein 2g

# SPICY BLACK-EYED PEAS

Prep: 5 min; Cook: 4 hr; Finishing Cook: 10 min        8 servings

1 **pound dried black-eyed peas (2 cups), sorted and rinsed**
1 **medium onion, peeled and chopped**
6 **cups water**
1 **teaspoon salt**
½ **teaspoon pepper**
¾ **cup medium or hot salsa**

**1.** Mix all ingredients except salsa in 3½- to 6-quart slow cooker. Cover and cook on high heat setting 3 to 4 hours or until peas are tender.

**2.** Stir in salsa. Cover and cook on high heat setting about 10 minutes or until hot.

**1 SERVING:** Calories 145 (Calories from Fat 10); Fat 1g (Saturated 0g); Cholesterol 0mg; Sodium 360mg; Carbohydrate 35g (Dietary Fiber 11g); Protein 13g

## COOKING TIPS

• Cooked greens, such as spinach, mustard or collards, are the perfect mate for black-eyed peas. Serve the greens with red wine vinegar to splash on top. Warm cornbread with molasses completes the meal.

• For an extra-special touch, top each serving with sour cream and a big spoonful of salsa.

# EASY BAKED BEANS

Prep: 10 min; Cook: Low 5 hr, or High 2 hr 30 min        10 servings

2 **cans (28 ounces each) vegetarian baked beans, drained**
1 **medium onion, peeled and chopped**
⅔ **cup barbecue sauce**
½ **cup packed brown sugar**
2 **tablespoons ground mustard (dry)**

Mix all ingredients in 3½- to 6-quart slow cooker. Cover and cook on low heat setting 4 to 5 hours (or high heat setting 2 hours to 2 hours 30 minutes) or until desired consistency.

**1 SERVING:** Calories 190 (Calories from Fat 10); Fat 1g (Saturated 0g); Cholesterol 0mg; Sodium 940mg; Carbohydrate 43g (Dietary Fiber 8g); Protein 10g

## COOKING TIP

• To halve the recipe, cut the ingredients in half, and cook in a 2- to 3½-quart slow cooker. Spoon the beans over squares of hot corn bread or split corn bread muffins. Sprinkle with shredded Cheddar cheese and sliced green onion.

**SERVING TIP**

• Spark up the taste of a plain hot dog or hamburger by spooning on this colorful relish. Or stir a few tablespoons into fat-free mayonnaise, and use it to dress up a crisp tossed salad.

# CARROT AND CELERY RELISH

Prep: 20 min; Cook: High 2 hr 45 min; Finishing Cook: 15 min; Cool: 2 hr
2½ cups

| | |
|---|---|
| 4 to 5 | medium carrots, coarsely shredded |
| 4 | medium stalks celery, sliced |
| 1 | small green bell pepper, chopped |
| ⅔ | cup sugar |
| ½ | cup white vinegar |
| 2 | teaspoons salt |
| 1 | teaspoon celery seed |
| 2 | teaspoons cornstarch |
| 2 | teaspoons cold water |

1. Mix all ingredients except cornstarch and water in 2- to 3½-quart slow cooker. Cover and cook on high heat setting 2 hours to 2 hours 30 minutes or until vegetables are tender.

2. Mix cornstarch and water; stir into vegetable mixture. Cover and cook on high heat setting about 15 minutes or until thickened. Cool about 2 hours.

3. Spoon relish into container. Cover and store in refrigerator up to 3 weeks.

**1 SERVING (1 TABLESPOON):** Calories 20 (Calories from Fat 0); Fat 0g (Saturated 0g); Cholesterol 0mg; Sodium 125mg; Carbohydrate 5g (Dietary Fiber 0g); Protein 0g

# CHUNKY CINNAMON APPLESAUCE

Prep: 20 min; Cook: 2 hr        8 servings

- 8    medium Granny Smith apples or other tart cooking apples, peeled and quartered
- ⅔    cup sugar
- ¾    cup apple juice
- 2    tablespoons margarine or butter, melted
- 1    teaspoon ground cinnamon

**1.** Mix all ingredients in 3½- to 6-quart slow cooker. Cover and cook on high heat setting 1 hour 30 minutes to 2 hours or until apples begin to break up. Stir well to break up larger pieces of apples.

**2.** Serve warm or chilled. To chill, cool about 2 hours, then spoon sauce into container; cover and refrigerate until chilled.

**1 SERVING:** Calories 170 (Calories from Fat 25); Fat 3g (Saturated 1g); Cholesterol 0mg; Sodium 40mg; Carbohydrate 39g (Dietary Fiber 3g); Protein 0g

## COOKING TIPS

• We liked the chunkiness of this applesauce, but if you and your family like a smoother sauce, use a potato masher to break up the apple pieces.

• For a pretty, delicate red applesauce that is packed with cinnamon flavor, stir ⅓ cup red cinnamon candies into the applesauce during the last 30 minutes of cooking.

## SERVING TIP

• Applesauce is good served with your favorite pork recipe or as a topping for pancakes or waffles. Or, serve topped with a splash of heavy whipping cream to make a memorable homemade dessert.

# DESSERTS

## OUTRAGEOUS DOUBLE CHOCOLATE— WHITE CHOCOLATE CHUNK COOKIES

Prep: 15 min; Bake: 14 min per sheet; Cool: 2 min     About 2 dozen

- 1 bag (24 ounces) semisweet chocolate chips (4 cups)
- 1 cup (2 sticks) butter or stick margarine, softened (see tip)
- 1 cup packed brown sugar
- 1 teaspoon vanilla
- 2 large eggs
- 2½ cups all-purpose flour (see tip)
- 1½ teaspoons baking soda
- ½ teaspoon salt
- 1 package (6 ounces) white baking bars, cut into ¼- to ½-inch chunks
- 1 cup pecan or walnut halves

**1.** Heat oven to 350°. Heat 1½ cups of the chocolate chips in 1-quart saucepan over low heat, stirring constantly, until melted. Cool to room temperature, but do not allow chocolate to become firm.

**2.** Beat butter, brown sugar and vanilla in large bowl with electric mixer on medium speed until light and fluffy. Beat in eggs and melted chocolate until light and fluffy. Stir in flour, baking soda and salt. Stir in remaining 2½ cups chocolate chips, the white baking bar chunks and pecan halves.

**3.** Drop dough by level ¼ cupfuls or #16 cookie/ice cream scoop about 2 inches apart onto ungreased cookie sheet.

**4.** Bake 12 to 14 minutes or until set (centers will appear soft and moist). Cool 1 to 2 minutes; remove from cookie sheet to wire rack.

**1 COOKIE:** Calories 375 (Calories from Fat 200); Fat 22g (Saturated 12g); Cholesterol 40mg; Sodium 200mg; Carbohydrate 42g (Dietary Fiber 2g); Protein 4g

# WHITE CHOCOLATE CHUNK—MACADAMIA COOKIES

Prep: 10 min; Bake: 12 min per sheet; Cool: 2 min
About 2½ dozen

**COOKING TIPS**

• Do not use a vegetable oil spread.

• Do not use self-rising flour.

- 1 cup packed brown sugar
- ½ cup granulated sugar
- ½ cup (1 stick) butter or stick margarine, softened (see tip)
- ½ cup shortening
- 1 teaspoon vanilla
- 1 large egg
- 2¼ cups all-purpose flour (see tip)
- 1 teaspoon baking soda
- ¼ teaspoon salt
- 1 package (6 ounces) white baking bars, cut into ¼- to ½-inch chunks
- 1 jar (3½ ounces) macadamia nuts, coarsely chopped

**1.** Heat oven to 350°.

**2.** Beat sugars, butter, shortening, vanilla and egg in large bowl with electric mixer on medium speed until light and fluffy, or mix with spoon. Stir in flour, baking soda and salt (dough will be stiff). Stir in white baking bar chunks and nuts.

**3.** Drop dough by rounded tablespoonfuls about 2 inches apart onto ungreased cookie sheet.

**4.** Bake 10 to 12 minutes or until light brown. Cool 1 to 2 minutes; remove from cookie sheet to wire rack.

**1 COOKIE:** Calories 185 (Calories from Fat 100); Fat 11g (Saturated 3g); Cholesterol 8mg; Sodium 110mg; Carbohydrate 21g (Dietary Fiber 1g); Protein 2g

# COCONUT CREAM MACAROONS

Prep: 15 min; Bake: 14 min per sheet; Cool: 30 min; Stand: 30 min
About 3½ dozen

- **3  packages (7 ounces each) flaked coconut (7⅔ cups)**
- **1  cup all-purpose flour (see tip)**
- **½  teaspoon salt**
- **1  can (14 ounces) sweetened condensed milk**
- **⅔  cup canned cream of coconut (not coconut milk)**
- **1  tablespoon vanilla**
- **¼  teaspoon almond extract**
- **1  large egg**
- **1  bag (6 ounces) semisweet chocolate chips (1 cup), if desired**
- **1  tablespoon vegetable oil, if desired**

**1.** Heat oven to 350°. Line cookie sheet with aluminum foil or cooking parchment paper.

**2.** Sprinkle 1 cup of the coconut over aluminum foil. Bake 5 to 7 minutes, stirring occasionally, until golden brown; cool. Reserve aluminum foil for baking cookies.

3. Mix toasted coconut, remaining coconut, the flour and salt in large bowl. Beat milk, cream of coconut, vanilla, almond extract and egg in medium bowl until well mixed. Pour milk mixture over coconut mixture; stir until well mixed.

4. Drop mixture by heaping tablespoonfuls about 2 inches apart onto foil on cookie sheet.

5. Bake 12 to 14 minutes or until golden brown (cookies will be soft in center and set at edges). Immediately slide aluminum foil with cookies from cookie sheet to wire rack. Cool completely, about 30 minutes.

6. Heat chocolate chips and oil in 1-quart saucepan over low heat, stirring constantly, until chips are melted. Drizzle over cookies. Let stand about 30 minutes or until chocolate is set.

**1 COOKIE:** Calories 140 (Calories from Fat 70); Fat 8g (Saturated 6g); Cholesterol 10mg; Sodium 85mg; Carbohydrate 16g (Dietary Fiber 1g); Protein 2g

# CHOCOLATY MERINGUE STARS

Prep: 15 min; Bake: 30 min per sheet; Cool: 5 min        About 4 dozen

   3 **large egg whites**
 ½ **teaspoon cream of tartar**
 ⅔ **cup sugar**
   2 **tablespoons plus 1 teaspoon baking cocoa**
     **About ⅓ cup ground walnuts**

1. Heat oven to 275°. Line cookie sheet with aluminum foil or cooking parchment paper.

2. Beat egg whites and cream of tartar in medium bowl with electric mixer on medium speed until foamy. Beat in sugar, 1 tablespoon at a time; continue beating until stiff and glossy. Do not underbeat. Fold in cocoa. (Batter will not be mixed completely; there will be some streaks of cocoa.)

3. Place meringue in decorating bag fitted with large star tip (#4). Pipe 1¼-inch stars onto cookie sheet. Sprinkle lightly with walnuts; brush excess nuts from cookie sheet.

4. Bake 25 to 30 minutes or until outside is crisp and dry (meringues will be soft inside). Cool 5 minutes; remove from cookie sheet to wire rack. Store in airtight container.

**1 COOKIE:** Calories 10 (Calories from Fat 0); Fat 0g (Saturated 0g); Cholesterol 0mg; Sodium 5mg; Carbohydrate 3g (Dietary Fiber 0g); Protein 0g

**COOKING TIP**

• Anyone with allergies to wheat will be grateful to have this recipe. Not only are they yummy little cookies, they are wonderfully wheat-free (and low-calorie, too).

**COOKING TIP**

• If the dough is sticky when pressing the crust into the pan, try dipping your fingers in a little flour.

# *L*USCIOUS LEMON BARS

Prep: 10 min; Bake: 50 min; Cool: 1 hr    16 bars

- 1 **cup all-purpose flour**
- ½ **cup (1 stick) margarine or butter at room temperature**
- ¼ **cup powdered sugar**
- 1 **cup granulated sugar**
- 2 **teaspoons grated lemon peel, if desired**
- 2 **tablespoons lemon juice**
- ½ **teaspoon baking powder**
- ¼ **teaspoon salt**
- 2 **eggs**

**1.** Heat oven to 350°.

**2.** Mix flour, margarine and powdered sugar. Press into bottom and ½ inch up sides of ungreased square pan, 8 × 8 × 2 inches.

**3.** Bake crust 20 minutes.

**4.** Meanwhile, beat granulated sugar, lemon peel, lemon juice, baking powder, salt and eggs in medium bowl with electric mixer on high speed about 3 minutes or until light and fluffy.

**5.** Carefully pour lemon filling over hot crust.

**6.** Bake 25 to 30 minutes or until no indentation remains when touched lightly in center. Place pan on wire rack. Cool completely, about 1 hour. For bars, cut into 4 rows by 4 rows.

**1 BAR:** Calories 160 (Calories from Fat 55); Fat 6g (Saturated 1g); Cholesterol 26mg; Sodium 80mg; Carbohydrate 21g (Dietary Fiber 0g); Protein 2g

---

**SERVING TIP**

• To dress up these lemony bars, sprinkle them with a delicate dusting of powdered sugar. Just place a small amount of powdered sugar in a small strainer, and shake it over the pan of cooled lemon bars.

---

## SPECIAL TOUCH

### Screen and Lemon Bowl

You will need:

**1 square (14 to 15 inches) fine metal mesh window screening (Window screening is sold in rolls at hardware stores. Cut screening to desired size with scissors or wire cutters.)**

**1 square (10 to 11 inches) fine metal mesh window screening**

**1 large white plate (10 or 11 inches in diameter)**

**1 large white shallow bowl (9 or 10 inches in diameter)**

**7 or 8 fresh whole lemons**

**Whole cloves and star anise, if desired**

1. Fold over 1 inch on edges of squares of screening so edges are smooth.

2. Set plate on center of table. Place large screen on plate; set bowl on top of screen.

3. Place 4 or 5 lemons in bowl. Place small screen over lemons; top with remaining lemons.

If desired you can stud the lemons with whole cloves and place star anise on screens.

*Note:* Use any size plate and bowl, and cut the screen into squares slightly larger than your plate and bowl.

# $\mathcal{G}$OOEY CARAMEL BROWNIES

Prep: 10 min; Cook: 10 min; Bake: 30 min; Cool: 1 hr     48 brownies

  **2**   packages (4 ounces each) sweet baking chocolate
  **½**   cup (1 stick) margarine or butter
  **1½** cups all-purpose flour
  **1**   cup sugar
  **½**   teaspoon baking powder
  **½**   teaspoon vanilla
  **¼**   teaspoon salt
  **2**   eggs
  **1**   package (14 ounces) vanilla caramels
  **¼**   cup milk
  **1**   package (6 ounces) semisweet chocolate chips (1 cup)
  **1**   cup coarsely chopped nuts, if desired

**1.** Heat oven to 350°. Grease bottom and sides of rectangular pan, 13 × 9 × 2 inches, with shortening.

**2.** Heat sweet baking chocolate and margarine in large saucepan over low heat, stirring frequently, until chocolate is melted. Remove saucepan from heat.

**3.** Stir flour, sugar, baking powder, vanilla, salt and eggs into chocolate mixture until well mixed. Spread batter in greased pan. Bake 15 minutes.

**4.** Meanwhile, heat caramels and milk in small saucepan over low heat, stirring frequently, until melted and smooth.

**5.** Remove brownies from oven. Spread caramel mixture over warm brownies. Sprinkle with chocolate chips and nuts.

**6.** Bake 10 to 15 minutes or just until brownies begin to pull away from sides of pan. Place pan on a wire rack. Cool completely, about 1 hour. For brownies, cut into 8 rows by 6 rows.

**1 BROWNIE:** Calories 130 (Calories from Fat 55); Fat 6g (Saturated 3g); Cholesterol 15mg; Sodium 55mg; Carbohydrate 19g (Dietary Fiber 1g); Protein 1g

# CREAM CHEESE BROWNIES

Prep: 25 min; Bake: 50 min          48 brownies

1 cup (2 sticks) butter or stick margarine (see tip)
4 ounces unsweetened baking chocolate
  Cream Cheese Filling (below)
2 cups sugar
2 teaspoons vanilla
4 large eggs
1½ cups all-purpose flour (see tip)
½ teaspoon salt
1 cup coarsely chopped nuts

**1.** Heat oven to 350°. Grease bottom and sides of rectangular pan, 13 × 9 × 2 inches, with shortening.

**2.** Melt butter and chocolate in 1-quart saucepan over low heat, stirring frequently. Remove from heat; cool 5 minutes.

**3.** Prepare Cream Cheese Filling; set aside.

**4.** Beat chocolate mixture, sugar, vanilla and eggs in large bowl with electric mixer on medium speed 1 minute, scraping bowl occasionally. Beat in flour and salt on low speed 30 seconds, scraping bowl occasionally. Beat on medium speed 1 minute. Stir in nuts. Spread 1¾ cups of the batter in pan. Spread filling over batter. Drop remaining batter in mounds randomly over filling. Carefully spread to cover cream cheese layer.

**5.** Bake 45 to 50 minutes or until toothpick inserted in center comes out clean. Cool in pan on wire rack. For brownies, cut into 8 rows by 6 rows. Store covered in refrigerator.

**1 BROWNIE:** Calories 165 (Calories from Fat 100); Fat 11g (Saturated 4g); Cholesterol 30mg; Sodium 110mg; Carbohydrate 15g (Dietary Fiber 1g); Protein 2g

## CREAM CHEESE FILLING

2 packages (8 ounces each) cream cheese, softened
½ cup sugar
2 teaspoons vanilla
1 large egg

Beat all ingredients until smooth.

***Lighter Cream Cheese Brownies:*** For 6 grams of fat and 120 calories per serving, substitute ½ cup unsweetened applesauce for ½ cup of the butter and 2 eggs plus 4 egg whites for the 4 eggs. Decrease nuts to ½ cup. Use reduced-fat cream cheese (Neufchâtel), softened, in Cream Cheese Filling.

**COOKING TIPS**

• Margarine spreads with at least 65% vegetable oil can be used.

• If using self-rising flour, omit salt.

# TOFFEE BARS

Prep: 20 min; Bake: 30 min; Cool: 30 min      32 bars

1  **cup (2 sticks) butter or stick margarine, softened (see tip)**
1  **cup packed brown sugar**
1  **teaspoon vanilla**
1  **large egg yolk**
2  **cups all-purpose flour (see tip)**
¼  **teaspoon salt**
⅔  **cup milk chocolate chips or 3 bars (1.55 ounces each) milk chocolate, broken into small pieces**
½  **cup chopped nuts**

**1.** Heat oven to 350°.

**2.** Mix butter, brown sugar, vanilla and egg yolk in large bowl. Stir in flour and salt. Press dough in ungreased rectangular pan, 13 × 9 × 2 inches.

**3.** Bake 25 to 30 minutes or until very light brown (crust will be soft). Immediately sprinkle chocolate chips on hot crust. Let stand about 5 minutes or until soft; spread evenly. Sprinkle with nuts. Cool 30 minutes in pan on wire rack. For bars, cut into 8 rows by 4 rows while warm for easiest cutting.

**1 BAR:** Calories 135 (Calories from Fat 70); Fat 8g (Saturated 2g); Cholesterol 5mg; Sodium 100mg; Carbohydrate 15g (Dietary Fiber 0g); Protein 1g

# ℬLUEBERRY-LEMON TART

Prep: 15 min; Bake: 10 min; Chill: 2 hr    12 servings

- 35 reduced-fat vanilla wafer cookies, crushed (1½ cups)
- 1 egg white, beaten
- 1 tablespoon margarine or butter, melted
- 1¼ cups fat-free (skim) milk
- 1 package (4-serving size) lemon instant pudding and pie filling mix
- 1½ teaspoons grated lemon peel
- 1 cup frozen fat-free whipped topping, thawed
- Blueberry Topping (below)

**1.** Heat oven to 400°. Lightly spray tart pan with removable bottom, 9 × 1 inch, with cooking spray. Mix crushed cookies, egg white and margarine until crumbly. Press in bottom and up side of pan. Bake 8 to 10 minutes or until light golden brown; cool.

**2.** Beat milk, pudding mix and lemon peel in medium bowl with electric mixer on low speed about 2 minutes or until smooth. Chill 5 minutes.

**3.** Fold in whipped topping. Spread over crust. Cover and refrigerate at least 2 hours until chilled. Serve with Blueberry Topping. Store covered in refrigerator.

**1 SERVING:** Calories 120 (Calories from Fat 20); Fat 2g (Saturated 1g); Cholesterol 0mg; Sodium 200mg; Carbohydrate 25g (Dietary Fiber 1g); Protein 2g

## BLUEBERRY TOPPING

- 3 tablespoons water
- 2 tablespoons sugar
- 1 teaspoon cornstarch
- 1½ cups fresh or frozen blueberries
- 1 tablespoon lemon juice

Mix water, sugar and cornstarch in 1-quart saucepan. Stir in ½ cup of the blueberries. Heat to boiling; reduce heat to medium-low. Cook about 5 minutes or until slightly thickened. Stir in lemon juice; remove from heat. Cool 10 minutes. Stir in remaining 1 cup blueberries. Cover and refrigerate at least 1 hour until chilled.

# CHERRY-BERRIES ON A CLOUD

Prep: 15 min; Bake: 15 min; Chill: 8 hr    10 to 12 servings

**Pastry Crust (below)**
1 **package (8 ounces) cream cheese, softened**
¾ **cup sugar**
1 **teaspoon vanilla**
2 **cups whipping (heavy) cream**
2½ **cups miniature marshmallows**
1 **can (21 ounces) cherry pie filling**
1 **teaspoon lemon juice**
2 **cups sliced strawberries (1 pint) or 1 package (16 ounces) frozen strawberries, thawed**
1 **cup fresh or frozen (thawed) sliced peaches**

**1.** Prepare and bake Pastry Crust.

**2.** Beat cream cheese, sugar and vanilla in large bowl with electric mixer on medium speed until smooth. Beat whipping cream in chilled medium bowl with electric mixer on high speed until stiff. Fold whipped cream and marshmallows into cream cheese mixture; spread over crust. Cover and refrigerate at least 8 hours but no longer than 48 hours.

**3.** Mix pie filling, lemon juice, strawberries and peaches. Cut dessert into serving pieces; serve with fruit mixture. Cover and refrigerate any remaining dessert.

**1 SERVING:** Calories 650 (Calories from Fat 370); Fat 41g (Saturated 19g); Cholesterol 80mg; Sodium 310mg; Carbohydrate 67g (Dietary Fiber 2g); Protein 5g

## PASTRY CRUST

1½ **cups all-purpose flour**
1 **cup margarine or butter, softened**
½ **cup powdered sugar**

**1.** Heat oven to 400°.

**2.** Beat all ingredients with electric mixer on low speed 1 minute, scraping bowl constantly. Beat on medium speed about 2 minutes or until creamy.

**3.** Spread in ungreased rectangular pan, 13 × 9 × 2 inches. Bake 12 to 15 minutes or until edges are golden brown. Cool completely. (For quick cooling, place in freezer 10 to 15 minutes.)

**COOKING TIP**

• If using self-rising flour, omit baking powder and salt.

# JELLY ROLL

Prep: 20 min; Bake: 15 min; Cool: 30 min        10 servings

3 **large eggs**

1 **cup granulated sugar**

⅓ **cup water**

1 **teaspoon vanilla**

¾ **cup all-purpose (see tip) or 1 cup cake flour**

1 **teaspoon baking powder**

¼ **teaspoon salt**

**Powdered sugar**

**About ⅔ cup jelly or jam**

1. Heat oven to 375°. Line jelly roll pan, 15½ × 10½ × 1 inch, with waxed paper, aluminum foil or cooking parchment paper; generously grease waxed paper or foil with shortening.

2. Beat eggs in small bowl with electric mixer on high speed about 5 minutes or until very thick and lemon colored. Pour eggs into medium bowl. Gradually beat in granulated sugar. Beat in water and vanilla on low speed. Gradually add flour, baking powder and salt, beating just until batter is smooth. Pour into pan, spreading to corners.

3. Bake 12 to 15 minutes or until toothpick inserted in center comes out clean. Immediately loosen cake from edges of pan and turn upside down onto towel generously sprinkled with powdered sugar. Carefully remove paper. Trim off stiff edges of cake if necessary. While cake is hot, carefully roll cake and towel from narrow end. Cool on wire rack at least 30 minutes.

4. Unroll cake and remove towel. Beat jelly slightly with fork to soften; spread over cake. Roll up cake. Sprinkle with powdered sugar.

**1 SERVING:** Calories 240 (Calories from Fat 20); Fat 2g (Saturated 1g); Cholesterol 65mg; Sodium 135mg; Carbohydrate 43g (Dietary Fiber 0g); Protein 3g

# ℒEMON CHIFFON CAKE

Prep: 20 min; Bake: 1 hr 15 min; Cool: 2 hr          12 servings

- **2  cups all-purpose (see tip) or 2¼ cups cake flour**
- **1½  cups sugar**
- **3  teaspoons baking powder**
- **1  teaspoon salt**
- **¾  cup cold water**
- **½  cup vegetable oil**
- **2  teaspoons vanilla**
- **1  tablespoon grated lemon peel**
- **7  large egg yolks (with all-purpose flour) or 5 large egg yolks (with cake flour)**
- **1  cup large egg whites (about 8)**
- **½  teaspoon cream of tartar**

**1.** Move oven rack to lowest position. Heat oven to 325°.

**2.** Mix flour, sugar, baking powder and salt in large bowl. Beat in water, oil, vanilla, lemon peel and egg yolks with electric mixer on low speed until smooth.

**3.** With clean beaters, beat egg whites and cream of tartar in large bowl with electric mixer on high speed until stiff peaks form. Gradually pour egg yolk mixture over beaten egg whites, folding in with rubber spatula just until blended. Pour into ungreased angel food cake pan (tube pan), 10 × 4 inches.

**4.** Bake about 1 hour 15 minutes or until top springs back when touched lightly. Immediately turn pan upside down onto heatproof funnel or bottle. Let hang about 2 hours or until cake is completely cool. Loosen side of cake with knife or long metal spatula; remove from pan.

**1 SERVING:** Calories 295 (Calories from Fat 108); Fat 12g (Saturated 2g); Cholesterol 125mg; Sodium 360mg; Carbohydrate 42g (Dietary Fiber 1g); Protein 6g

## COOKING TIPS

- If using self-rising flour, omit baking powder and salt.

- Top this cake with yummy Lemon Glaze. Melt ⅓ cup butter or stick margarine (not vegetable oil spread) in 1½-quart saucepan over low heat; remove from heat. Stir in ½ teaspoon grated lemon peel. Stir in 2 cups powdered sugar and 1½ teaspoons lemon juice. Stir in 2 to 4 tablespoons additional lemon juice, 1 tablespoon at a time, until smooth and consistency of thick syrup.

# Vanilla Cheesecake with Cherry-Berry Topping

Prep: 15 min; Bake: 40 min; Cool: 30 min; Chill: 3 hr      8 servings

**Graham Cracker Crust (below)**
2 **packages (8 ounces each) cream cheese at room temperature**
½ **cup sugar**
½ **teaspoon vanilla**
2 **eggs**
**Cherry-Berry Topping (at right)**

1. Heat oven to 325°. Prepare Graham Cracker Crust. While crust is chilling, continue with the recipe.

2. Beat cream cheese in large bowl with electric mixer on medium speed until smooth. Gradually beat in sugar and vanilla until smooth. Beat in eggs, one at a time.

3. Pour cheesecake mixture into crust and spread evenly. Bake about 40 minutes or until filling is set. Place pan on a wire rack. Cool 30 minutes.

4. Cover cheesecake and refrigerate at least 3 hours but no longer than 48 hours. While cheesecake is chilling, prepare Cherry-Berry Topping.

5. Serve cheesecake with topping. Store covered in refrigerator.

**1 SERVING:** Calories 450 (Calories from Fat 295); Fat 31g (Saturated 18g); Cholesterol 135mg; Sodium 360mg; Carbohydrate 52g (Dietary Fiber 2g); Protein 8g

## GRAHAM CRACKER CRUST

1½ **cups graham cracker crumbs (20 squares)**
¼ **cup sugar**
⅓ **cup margarine or butter, melted**

Mix the cracker crumbs, sugar and margarine. Press firmly and evenly against bottom and side of ungreased pie pan, 9 × 1¼ inches. Cover and refrigerate about 30 minutes or until firm.

## CHERRY-BERRY TOPPING

- **1  pint (2 cups) strawberries**
- **1  can (21 ounces) cherry pie filling**
- **1  teaspoon lemon juice**

Rinse the strawberries with cool water, and pat dry with paper towels. Cut out the hull with the point of a paring knife. Cut the strawberries lengthwise into slices. Mix the strawberries, pie filling and lemon juice in a medium bowl. Cover and refrigerate topping until you are ready to serve the cheesecake.

# TURTLE CHEESECAKE

Prep: 30 min; Bake: 50 min; Cool: 1 hr; Chill: 2 hr        12 servings

- **1½  cups finely crushed vanilla wafer cookies (about 40 cookies)**
- **¼  cup (½ stick) butter or stick margarine, melted (see tip)**
- **2  packages (8 ounces each) cream cheese, softened**
- **½  cup sugar**
- **2  teaspoons vanilla**
- **2  eggs**
- **¼  cup hot fudge topping**
- **1  cup caramel topping**
- **½  cup coarsely chopped pecans**

**1.** Heat oven to 350°. Mix cookie crumbs and butter in medium bowl. Press firmly against bottom and side of pie plate, 9 × 1¼ inches.

**2.** Beat cream cheese, sugar, vanilla and eggs in large bowl with electric mixer on low speed until smooth. Pour half of the mixture into pie plate.

**3.** Add hot fudge topping to remaining cream cheese mixture in bowl; beat on low speed until smooth. Spoon over vanilla mixture in pie plate. Swirl mixtures slightly with tip of knife.

**4.** Bake 40 to 50 minutes or until center is set. (Do not insert knife into cheesecake because the hole may cause cheesecake to crack as it cools.) Cool at room temperature 1 hour. Refrigerate at least 2 hours until chilled. Serve with caramel topping and pecans. Store covered in refrigerator.

**1 SERVING:** Calories 440 (Calories from Fat 235); Fat 26g (Saturated 13g); Cholesterol 90mg; Sodium 340mg; Carbohydrate 46g (Dietary Fiber 1g); Protein 6g

---

### COOKING TIP

• Margarine spreads with at least 65% vegetable oil can be used.

# ALMOND CHEESECAKE
## WITH RASPBERRY SAUCE

Prep: 20 min; Bake: 1 hr; Cool: 45 min; Chill: 3 hr          16 servings

- ½  **cup crushed reduced-fat graham crackers (6 squares)**
- 2  **packages (8 ounces each) reduced-fat cream cheese (Neufchâtel), softened**
- ⅔  **cup sugar**
- ½  **cup fat-free cholesterol-free egg product or 2 eggs**
- ½  **teaspoon almond extract**
- 2  **cups vanilla low-fat yogurt**
- 2  **tablespoons all-purpose flour**
   **Raspberry Sauce (below)**
- 1  **tablespoon sliced almonds, if desired**
   **Fresh raspberries, if desired**

**1.** Heat oven to 300°. Spray springform pan, 9 × 3 inches, with cooking spray. Sprinkle crushed crackers over bottom of pan.

**2.** Beat cream cheese in medium bowl with electric mixer on medium speed until smooth. Add sugar, egg product and almond extract. Beat on medium speed about 2 minutes or until smooth. Add yogurt and flour. Beat on low speed until smooth. Carefully spread batter over crackers in pan.

**3.** Bake 1 hour. Turn off oven; cool in oven 30 minutes with door closed. Remove from oven; cool on wire rack 15 minutes. Carefully remove side of pan. Cover and refrigerate at least 3 hours.

**4.** Meanwhile, prepare Raspberry Sauce. Garnish cheesecake with sauce, almonds and fresh raspberries. Store covered in refrigerator.

**1 SERVING:** Calories 170 (Calories from Fat 65); Fat 7g (Saturated 4g); Cholesterol 20mg; Sodium 160mg; Carbohydrate 24g (Dietary Fiber 2g); Protein 5g

## RASPBERRY SAUCE

- 2  **cups fresh or frozen (thawed and drained) raspberries**
- 2  **tablespoons water**
- 3  **tablespoons sugar**
- ¼  **teaspoon almond extract**

Place all ingredients in food processor. Cover and process until smooth. Press through sieve to remove seeds.

# $\mathcal{R}$ICH CHOCOLATE FUDGE CAKE

Prep: 15 min; Cook: 10 min; Bake: 35 min; Cool: 1 hr 15 min        12 servings

- 1 **cup semisweet chocolate chips**
- ½ **cup (1 stick) margarine or butter**
- ½ **cup all-purpose flour**
- 4 **eggs, separated into yolks and whites**
- ½ **cup sugar**
- ½ **cup semisweet chocolate chips**
- 2 **tablespoons margarine or butter**
- 2 **tablespoons corn syrup**

**1.** Heat oven to 325°. Grease bottom and side of round pan, 9 × 1¼ inches, with shortening.

**2.** Heat 1 cup chocolate chips and ½ cup margarine in saucepan over low heat, stirring constantly, until chocolate is melted. Cool 5 minutes.

**3.** Stir flour into melted chocolate mixture until smooth. Stir in egg yolks until well blended.

**4.** Beat egg whites in large bowl with electric mixer on high speed until foamy. Beat in sugar, 1 tablespoon at a time, until soft peaks form.

**5.** Gently stir chocolate mixture into egg whites. Spread in greased pan. Bake 30 to 35 minutes or until a thin crust forms and toothpick inserted in center comes out clean.

**6.** Place pan on wire rack and cool 10 minutes. Run a knife around edge of pan to loosen cake. Remove cake from pan. To remove cake from pan, place wire cooling rack upside down onto cake. Using pot holders, turn rack and pan over, and remove pan. Place another rack upside down on bottom of cake, and turn racks and cake over so cake is right side up. Trim top edges of cake where crust overhangs side. Cool cake completely, about 1 hour.

**7.** Place cooled cake on serving plate, using a second plate and method in step 6.

**8.** Heat ½ cup chocolate chips, 2 tablespoons margarine and the corn syrup in saucepan over low heat, stirring constantly, until chocolate is melted and mixture is smooth.

**9.** Spread melted chocolate mixture over top of cake, allowing some to drizzle down side of cake.

**1 SERVING:** Calories 360 (Calories from Fat 205); Fat 23g (Saturated 9g); Cholesterol 75mg; Sodium 150mg; Carbohydrate 36g (Dietary Fiber 2g); Protein 4g

---

**COOKING TIPS**

• Margarine spreads with at least 65 percent vegetable oil can be used.

• For easier cleanup, heat the margarine in a microwavable mixing bowl on high for 30 to 45 seconds until melted, then add remaining ingredients for the cake.

---

# $\mathcal{F}$UDGY BROWNIE CAKE WITH RASPBERRY SAUCE

Prep: 15 min; Bake: 45 min; Cool: 20 min          8 servings

1½  **cups sugar**

¾  **cup all-purpose flour**

¾  **cup (1½ sticks) margarine or butter, melted (see tip)**

½  **cup baking cocoa**

1½  **teaspoons vanilla**

¼  **teaspoon salt**

3  **eggs**

**Raspberry Sauce (below)**

**Fresh raspberries for garnish, if desired**

1. Heat oven to 350°. Grease bottom and side of pan with shortening. Sprinkle a small amount of flour over greased surface, shake pan to distribute flour evenly, then turn pan upside down and tap bottom to remove excess flour.

2. Mix sugar, flour, margarine, cocoa, vanilla, salt and eggs in medium bowl. Pour into greased and floured pan.

3. Bake 40 to 45 minutes or until top appears dry. Meanwhile, prepare Raspberry Sauce.

4. Cool cake 10 minutes, then remove from pan and place on wire rack. Cool cake, and serve with sauce. If desired, garnish with fresh raspberries.

**1 SERVING.** Calories 420 (Calories from Fat 180); Fat 20g (Saturated 5g); Cholesterol 80mg; Sodium 300mg; Carbohydrate 59g (Dietary Fiber 4g); Protein 5g

## RASPBERRY SAUCE

3  **tablespoons sugar**

2  **teaspoons cornstarch**

⅓  **cup water**

1  **package (10 ounces) frozen raspberries in syrup, thawed and undrained**

Mix sugar and cornstarch in saucepan. Stir in water and raspberries. Cook over medium heat, stirring constantly, until mixture thickens and boils. Continue boiling 1 minute, stirring constantly. Remove saucepan from heat. Strain sauce through a strainer to remove seeds if desired. Serve sauce slightly warm or cool.

**COOKING TIPS**

• Save some time by preparing this stunning, rich torte a day ahead; it keeps well covered in the refrigerator.

• Try grinding the nuts ¼ cup at a time—it will keep them from getting too oily.

# CHOCOLATE HAZELNUT TORTE

Prep: 10 min; Cook: 5 min; Bake: 45 min        10 servings

| | |
|---|---|
| **6** | **ounces sweet cooking chocolate** |
| **¾** | **cup margarine or butter** |
| **4** | **eggs, separated** |
| **⅛** | **teaspoon salt** |
| **¾** | **cup sugar** |
| **¾** | **cup ground hazelnuts (filberts)** |
| **2** | **tablespoons hazelnut liqueur or coffee** |
| | **Whole hazelnuts** |

**1.** Heat oven to 375°. Grease and flour springform pan, 8 × 2½ inches.

**2.** Heat chocolate and margarine in medium saucepan over low heat until melted; cool 5 minutes.

**3.** Beat egg whites and salt in medium bowl on high speed until stiff.

**4.** Beat egg yolks and sugar on medium speed until lemon colored; stir into chocolate mixture. Stir in ground hazelnuts and liqueur. Gently fold chocolate mixture into egg whites; pour into pan.

**5.** Bake 40 to 45 minutes until top is dry and knife inserted in center comes out slightly wet. Cool completely; remove from pan. Garnish with whole hazelnuts.

**1 SERVING:** Calories 330 (Calories from Fat 210); Fat 24g (Saturated 6g); Cholesterol 85mg; Sodium 220mg; Carbohydrate 28g (Dietary Fiber 1g); Protein 5g

MAKE-AHEAD OR TAKE-ALONG   **405**

# MAKE-AHEAD OR TAKE-ALONG MENUS

## Snacks and Sweets

Cinnamon-Sugared Nuts, *page 322*

Veggie Tortilla Roll-Ups, *page 319*

Rich Chocolate Fudge Cake, *page 401*

Outrageous Double Chocolate–White Chocolate Chunk Cookies, *page 384*

Mocha Cocoa, *page 312*

**SPECIAL TOUCH:** For an informal party, try a dessert potluck—invite your friends to prepare and share their favorite treat.

## Sit-Down Dinner

Ham and Scalloped Potatoes, *page 362*

French Vegetable Ratatouille, *page 380*

Honey Mustard Bread, *page 330*

Chocolate Hazelnut Torte, *page 404*

Wine, coffee and tea

**SPECIAL TOUCH:** Line 4 dessert dishes with straw, place a whole fresh pear in each, and arrange along the center of your table.

## Buffet-Style Party

Layered Mexican Snack Platter, *page 317*

Savory Pecans, *page 321*

Italian Sausage Lasagna, *page 358*

Garlic bread

Mixed greens with sliced red bell pepper and Italian dressing

Almond Cheesecake with Raspberry Sauce, *page 400*

Toffee Bars, *page 392*

Wassail, *page 312*

**SPECIAL TOUCH:** Attach a gift tag to a party favor like cookies wrapped in tissue paper, write names on the tags, and place in a bowl on the buffet table.

## Small Gathering

Cheesy Bean Dip, *page 313*

Garden Vegetable Wraps, *page 333*

Gazpacho Pasta Salad with Tomato-Lime Dressing, *page 366*

Vanilla Cheesecake with Cherry-Berry Topping, *page 398*

Fruit juice spritzers

**SPECIAL TOUCH:** Use festive serving trays for salads, available at party stores and supermarkets.

## For a Larger Crowd

Pizza Fondue, *page 313*

Chili for a Crowd, *page 344*

Crusty bread

White Chocolate Chunk–Macadamia Cookies, *page 385*

Assorted ice creams with toppings

Spiced Cran-Apple Cider, *page 311*

**SPECIAL TOUCH:** In the fall months, a hollowed pumpkin works well as a punch bowl or soup tureen.

## Last-Minute Meal

Chicken Salad Sandwiches, *page 333*

Pretzels or potato chips

Cold Cucumber Salad, *page 372*

Chocolate cupcakes

Strawberry Smoothies, *page 310*

**SPECIAL TOUCH:** For an easy table topper, float flowers in a clear glass or small bowl and set on center of the table.

# Good Times—Guaranteed!

Wouldn't it be great to call up your friends on the spur of the moment and invite them over for dinner? Or, wouldn't you love to welcome the whole family to your house around the holidays? Inviting guests over for a meal can be fun and enjoyable. If you're cooking for company or just looking for some fresh and simple new ideas, read on to learn Betty Crocker's secrets to success—every time!

## GOOD COMPANY

Whether you're cooking for your family or you've decided to have some friends over, the people around your table are the first part of Betty's Success Formula:

Good Company
+ **Good Food**
+ **Good Setting**
+ **Good Planning**
*Great Time!*

If cooking for company is new territory to you, don't begin by throwing a huge bash. It's all right to start small. A great get-together can be as simple as inviting a friend or two over for a glass of wine. As your comfort level increases, so will the number of guests you will feel comfortable inviting. Here are some helpful questions to ask yourself as you begin planning.

### What's the Occasion?

The occasion itself will set the tone for your get-together. Is it a casual gathering of friends and family or a special celebration that you'll remember for years to come? Is it tied to a theme such as the Super Bowl or the Oscars? Are you planning a wine tasting,

pre-concert drinks or a holiday cookie exchange? Will it be casual or fancy?

### Who's Coming?

Narrowing down who is coming will help you to decide the kind of gathering to have, such as a cocktail party, sit-down dinner or a backyard barbecue. Does your guest list include your three best friends from college, six of your in-laws or a dozen of your neighbors? Next, think about your guests. Are they food adventurers or more conservative? Are they health conscious or does counting fat grams make them cringe? Do you have a mix of ages from your 6-year-old niece to your 80-year-old grandparents? Are there vegetarians in the bunch or anyone with food allergies? You'll be prepared if you know ahead of time.

### Do Guests Have Special Needs?

If guests tell you that they're on a special diet, perhaps low-cholesterol, diabetic, salt-restricted or vegetarian, do your very best to accommodate them. For example, if you have your heart set on serving turkey for Thanksgiving, but one guest is vegetarian, go ahead and roast a turkey. Just make sure there are other meatless dishes your guest can enjoy. For other diets, here are a few suggestions.

**Use low-fat or nonfat ingredients** in some of the dishes. (This works really well for dips and toppings.)

**Go light on the salt** when making the meal, and let guests sprinkle it on at the table.

**Serve sauces on the side** and let everyone add salad dressing and butter to taste.

**Make plenty of the food that fits** the special diet, such as rice, pasta, potatoes and vegetables.

**Have a back-up bowl of cut-up fresh fruit** or berries as a "light" alternative if you're planning on serving a rich dessert.

## Where and When Will It Be?

Next, figure out where your gathering will be, such as at your house or apartment, a party room, your backyard or at a park. The location will help you decide who and how many people to invite. If you live in an apartment, you may want to keep your guest list small. If the get-together will be at the park, invite the whole crowd. Think about the time of day and time of year, too. Will your guests arrive for a spring brunch, a tailgate party before a football game or dessert after the theater on a frosty winter night?

## What's the Budget?

Is your budget more in line with a potluck supper or a multicourse menu with matching wine choices? The amount of money that you plan to spend will help you decide how many people to invite and what to serve. For instance, having friends over for brunch, for coffee and dessert or for snacks and drinks may fit your budget better than a five-course sit-down dinner.

# GOOD FOOD

Serving tasty food turns a good time into a great time! This second element of Betty Crocker's Success Formula can be the most challenging but also the most fun part of your get-together.

## What Should I Serve?

All of those "Good Company" questions that you answered earlier should make planning your menu a little easier. Here are some pointers to help you dream up the perfect menu. (Also, check out pages 107, 195, 307 and 405 for menu ideas.)

**Plan the main course first.** It could be meat-based, such as Beef Kabobs with Chilied Plum Sauce (page 158); a blend of meat, vegetables and starch such as Pasta with Beef, Broccoli and Toma-toes (page 64); or meatless, such as Creamy Corn and Garlic Risotto (page 50). Then plan side dishes, appetizers and desserts to complement your main course.

**Consider where you'll serve the food.** How you plan to serve the food will help you decide what type of food to have. Your guests can "lap it" with sandwiches, but if steak and potatoes are on the menu, a sit-down meal would be a better bet.

**Make sure flavors go together.** A strongly flavored main dish needs a milder-flavored side dish for balance; a subtle main dish works well with a boldly flavored side dish. If the meal has been on the heavier side, choose a light dessert; if the meal was a bit lighter, why not finish with something indulgent and rich?

**Involve your senses—sight, taste, smell and touch.** Keep flavors, colors, shapes, textures and temperatures in mind. For example, serve spicy with mild; white or brown with red, yellow or green; tiny pieces with big chunks; creamy with crispy; and hot dishes with cold.

**Mix up the temperatures.** Planning a combination of temperatures will not only free up space in your oven and on your stove top, it will also add variety to your menu. Choose some foods than can be served cold (such as salad or a chilled soup), some that should be served piping hot (for example roast chicken or hot apple crisp) and some that are best at room temperature (think cake or cookies).

**Check oven temperatures.** If four of your recipes call for four different oven settings and you want to serve them all at the same time, you may want to reconsider your selections or check to see if some of them can be made ahead.

**Think about the time of day and time of year.** Timing is important when planning a menu. People usually expect a lighter meal at lunch and more hearty dinners. But, if you're planning a late-night dinner, you may want to consider smaller portions than you would serve at 5:00 or 6:00 P.M. The season and the weather also make a difference. You wouldn't want to serve chili on a sweltering evening in July or a frozen ice-cream pie when it's cold and snowing in January. And don't forget to take advantage of seasonal, fresh produce.

**Serve what you love to cook and eat.** If you serve good food that you like to make, your friends and family are sure to enjoy it, too.

## How Much Food Do I Need?

Nothing is worse than realizing that the main dish is almost gone and the platter hasn't made it all the way around the table. But having mountains of leftovers isn't much better. How do you strike that happy balance between enough but not too much?

It's better to err on the side of having too much. But know your guests, too. Are they hearty eaters or do they have smaller appetites? Taking your guests'

---

## Impromptu Eats in a Flash

For last-minute gatherings, here are some quick-to-fix ideas that you can pull together with foods from your pantry, refrigerator or freezer.

**Snacks and munchies,** such as potato and tortilla chips, salsa, bean dip, honey-roasted nuts, crackers, cheese, olives and packaged gourmet cookies all can be last-minute lifesavers. Just arrange them in attractive serving dishes or baskets.

**Pasta,** olive oil, a little fresh garlic and some Parmesan cheese can be tossed together for a simple but delicious main dish in minutes.

**Flour tortillas** can wrap up a variety of fix-it-fast fillings, such as canned black beans, cut-up cooked chicken or sliced deli meats, for a meal in minutes. Salsa, sour cream and shredded cheese all make great toppers.

**Eggs** can be scrambled, fried or filled and folded into an omelet to make a quick any-time-of-day meal.

**Ice cream** can be topped with a splash of liqueur or maple syrup and sprinkled with fresh berries or coconut for a spur-of-the-moment dessert.

**Pick up the phone.** Full-meal help is only a phone call away to your favorite restaurant, deli or pizzeria. ■

preferences into consideration, use these guidelines for how much to serve grown-ups. (For kids, serve about two-thirds of these amounts.)

## How Much Food Should I Make?

| | Per person: |
|---|---|
| **Appetizers** | 4 to 5 per hour |
| **Fruits/Vegetables** | ½ to ⅔ cup |
| **Meat/Poultry/Fish** | |
| Boneless | 4 to 6 ounces, uncooked |
| Bone-in | 6 to 8 ounces, uncooked |
| **Pasta/Rice/Grains** | |
| Main dish | 1 cup |
| Side dish | ½ cup |
| **Salad** | |
| Tossed | 1 to 1½ cups |
| Vegetable/fruit | ½ cup |
| **Sauces/Dips/Dressings** | 2 to 3 tablespoons |
| **Soups** | ¾ cup to 1 cup |

**Check the number of servings.** The recipes that you choose will help by telling how many servings (and sometimes what size) they make, for example, 6 servings, 40 bars, 3 cups or 8 slices. Keep in mind that serving sizes are just guidelines. For instance, a

4-serving main-course recipe might feed only two hearty eaters if it's served alone, but if you add an appetizer and several sides it may serve six.

**Plan for the unexpected guest.** Just to be on the safe side, make or buy enough food for at least two "invisible" guests. This way, you're covered if your guests are extra hungry or if someone shows up unexpectedly.

**Let friends bring something.** If friends or family offer to bring something, don't hesitate to say yes—but make sure to specify what you want or need. If a salad, an appetizer or a dessert would help you out, let them know the other types of food you are serving so that they can bring a complementary dish. If your friend offers to bring something that just doesn't fit your menu, you can always suggest a bottle of wine or a loaf of bread from the bakery instead.

## How Should I Serve the Food?

The way food looks can affect how it tastes. With just a smidgen of effort, your food will make a fabulous first impression. Remember, the garnish is the finishing touch, so add it just before serving. Here are a few ideas to get you started.

## Quick Fixes for Unexpected Guests

What happens if a friend brings an unexpected guest to your house? First, smile nicely, welcome the guest, then work a little magic. Here's how.

**Stretch a meal** by making extra pasta, couscous, rice or potatoes.

**Slice some extras** by cutting the meat or chicken a little thinner or cutting a casserole into smaller squares.

**Make up the plates** in the kitchen instead of passing the food. People tend to eat more when they help themselves.

**Slip in an extra course** by setting out munchies before dinner; or serve an extra plate of store-bought cookies with dessert or coffee.

**Take a smaller portion** for yourself.

**Remember to cook extra next time** for that "invisible" guest! ▪

**Drop** sprigs of mint in a pitcher of fruit punch.

**Float** slices of lemons, limes, oranges or maraschino cherries in glasses of lemonade or iced tea.

**Arrange** sprigs of fresh herbs on serving platters or trays.

**Decorate** a serving plate with frosted fruit. Brush clusters of grapes or cranberries with a little corn syrup, and sprinkle with sugar.

**Drizzle** melted white baking chips in a simple pattern over a frosted chocolate cake.

## What Beverages Should I Serve?

Beverage choices are nearly endless—punch, tea, coffee, lemonade, soft drinks, sparkling cider, water, juice, alcoholic beverages and more. But don't feel as though you have to offer huge selection of choices. A small sampling will do just fine. Consider a good mix of beverages, though, such as

### How Many Drinks Do I Serve?

How much you serve depends on the following:

**The occasion:** Sunday brunch or Saturday evening cocktails?

**Your guests:** Do they sip drinks or drink a little more?

**The length of the get-together:** A before-concert buffet versus a game-day picnic.

**Your budget:** Guests may offer to bring a bottle of wine.

| | Purchase this amount . . . | For this many servings . . . |
|---|---|---|
| **Wine** | 1 bottle (750 milliliters) | four 6-ounce servings |
| **Liquor** | 1 bottle (750 milliliters) | sixteen 1½-ounce shots |
| **Punch** | 1 gallon | 24 servings |

a few hot and a few cold choices, some caffeinated and some caffeine-free and some heavy-tasting such as cola and others light such as 7-Up. Also, don't feel pressure to have a full bar, or any hard liquor for that matter. If you do choose to serve alcoholic beverages, wine and beer will be perfectly acceptable for most of your gatherings. If you want to serve hard liquor but also want to keep it simple, stick to one or two mixed drinks that tie in with the theme of your gathering, such as rum-spiked eggnog at Christmas or margaritas for a south-of-the-border dinner. Here's a clever solution that accommodates drinkers and nondrinkers: Serve a simple fruit punch with a pitcher of rum or whiskey on the side, and let guests spike their own drinks if they wish. This works great with holiday eggnog and hot cider, too.

### Great Food and Wine Pairs

Here are some pairing pointers when choosing a wine to go with your meal.

**Hearty** foods such as beef and chili need a heavier, more tannic wine that is bold enough to stand up to the food, such as Cabernet Sauvignon or Shiraz.

**Lighter** foods such as grilled fish and chicken, which would be overwhelmed by a heavier wine, marry well with a light wine with some acidity, such as Sauvignon Blanc or some Chardonnays.

**Sweet** foods and dishes with some degree of sweetness (think teriyaki or fruit-based sauces) are best paired with a wine that also has a touch of sweetness, such as Riesling. If the food is sweeter than the wine, it can make the wine taste dry and "puckery."

**Sour** foods such as sauces made with lemons, limes and vinegar cut the tartness of a wine and make a full-bodied wine taste sweet and thin. Instead, choose a wine that also has some acidity, such as Sauvignon Blanc.

**Spicy, smoked and heavily seasoned** foods are best when served with light, fruity wines that tend to cool the heat, such as Pinot Noir and Sauvignon Blanc.

Although there may be a lot of good matches in the food and wine world, it's important to remember that there is no single perfect wine for any one food. If you like a wine, drink it with food you like also, and you're sure to have a super match.

## Food and Wine Pairings

| Food | Wine | Food | Wine |
|---|---|---|---|
| **Beef** | | **Fish and Shellfish** | |
| Burgers | Cabernet, Zinfandel | Crab, Lobster, Shrimp | Chardonnay, Sauvignon Blanc |
| Roast | Cabernet, Shiraz/Syrah | Fish, mild-flavored | Sauvignon Blanc |
| Stew | Cabernet, Merlot | (halibut, sole) | |
| **Cheese** | | Fish, strong-flavored | Chardonnay |
| Blue | Port | (tuna, swordfish) | |
| Brie | Chardonnay, Champagne | Salmon | Chardonnay, Pinot Noir |
| Cheddar | Cabernet, Zinfandel | **Lamb** | Cabernet |
| Feta or goat cheese | Sauvignon Blanc | **Pasta** | |
| **Chicken** | | Alfredo | Chardonnay |
| Barbecued | Shiraz/Syrah, Cabernet, Zinfandel | Lasagna | Merlot, Zinfandel |
| | | Pesto | Sauvignon Blanc |
| Grilled/Roasted | Chardonnay | Tomato and meat sauce | Chianti, Zinfandel |
| **Chili** | Cabernet | **Pizza** | Merlot, Zinfandel |
| **Chocolate** | Cabernet, Port | **Pork** | |
| **Desserts** | Champagne, Riesling | Chops | Merlot, Shiraz/Syrah |
| **Ethnic Dishes** | | Ribs, barbecued | Zinfandel |
| Chinese | Riesling, Gewürztraminer, Sauvignon Blanc | Ham | Shiraz/Syrah, Riesling |
| | | Sausage | Cabernet, Zinfandel |
| Indian | Gewürztraminer, Sauvignon Blanc | **Salads** | Riesling, Sauvignon Blanc |
| Mexican | Zinfandel | **Turkey** | Gewürztraminer, Pinot Noir |
| Thai | Sauvignon Blanc | | |

# GOOD SETTING

You don't have to own a 12-place-setting service of bone china with matching crystal goblets to set a beautiful table. What you have on hand will work just fine. Even if all you own are bits and pieces, you can make it work. The good news is, mix-and-match is in! So get out your dishes, flatware and glasses and have fun.

Although glass and china are always elegant, there's also a time and place for paper and plastic, such as a picnic or pool party. We'll show you how to set any table with extra-special touches to make it all look terrific.

Here are some dishes, flatware and glasses that are nice to have. Of course, you don't have to have all of these items, but you may want to begin adding some of these pieces to your collection.

## Plates and Dishes

Salad/dessert plate

Dinner plate

Soup/fruit bowl

Bread and butter plate, optional (not pictured)

Charger plate

Cup and saucer

## Flatware

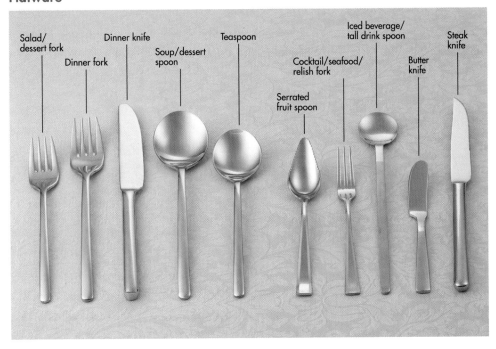

Salad/dessert fork

Dinner fork

Dinner knife

Soup/dessert spoon

Teaspoon

Serrated fruit spoon

Cocktail/seafood/relish fork

Iced beverage/tall drink spoon

Butter knife

Steak knife

## Glasses and Specialty Glasses for Cocktails and Mixed Drinks

Flute (champagne) · Wine (red) · Brandy · Cordial · Juice · Beer mug · Margarita · Pilsner

Goblet (water) · Wine (white) · Sherry · Highball/cooler/iced beverage · Double old-fashioned · Martini

## Deciding on a Serving Style

The type of food you're serving, your guests and the type of gathering you're having will help you decide how to serve the meal. Basically, there are two main serving styles: sit-down and buffet.

### Choosing a Sit-Down

Just like the name says, with this serving style your guests sit down at a table. If you're serving a meal that requires a sturdy plate and utensils to eat, such as spaghetti, a sit-down meal will be more comfortable for your guests than "lapping it." At a sit-down meal, you have a few serving options.

**You can pass the food** around the table, family style. This makes for a more casual, comfortable meal.

**You can dish up the plates** in the kitchen and serve them. This can feel more elegant and is especially nice for garnishing or arranging the food in a special way.

**You can do a combination of the two,** serve the salad, but pass the rest of the dishes.

Here are some things to keep in mind while planning a sit-down meal.

**If you are serving drinks and appetizers** before the meal, don't wait too long before serving dinner or your guests may be too full for the meal.

**Pay attention to the pacing of the meal.** At a long meal, allow for a comfortable amount of time between courses so guests don't feel rushed but not so much that they start to get restless.

**When guests are finished** or have almost finished eating, that's your cue to get ready for the next course, but don't clear the table until everyone is done eating.

**Set a beautiful table** for your sit-down meal. Here's a quick refresher course.

- **Plates** should be placed about 1 inch from the edge of the table with the forks on the left and the knife (blade toward the plate) and spoon to the right.

- **Bread-and-butter plates,** if used, should be placed above the forks. If bread or rolls are not being served, you can replace the bread-and-butter plate with the salad plate.

Place setting for a casual meal

Place setting for a formal meal

- **Salad plates** are placed to the left of the forks if salad is served with the main course. The salad fork can be placed on either side of the dinner fork if salad is served with the main course.

- **Flatware pieces** used first are placed farthest from the plate. For example, if salad is served first, the salad fork goes to the left of the dinner fork. As you use your utensils for each course, work your way in toward the plate.

- **Dessert flatware** is usually brought to the table with dessert. If you want to leave it on the table throughout the meal, place it above the top of the dinner plate.

- **Glassware** is arranged above the knife. The water glass is usually at the tip of the knife, with beverage and/or wine glasses to the right of the water glass.

- Cups and saucers for coffee and tea, if serving with the main meal, are placed slightly above and to the right of the spoon. Or they can be brought out later when dessert is served.

- Napkins can be placed either on the center of the dinner plate, to the left of the forks, or tucked inside the water glass. (Check out page 418 for some great napkin-folding suggestions.)

## Choosing a Buffet

Buffet-style dining can be very casual (think picnics) or elegant (think dessert parties) and adapts to just about any menu. With a buffet, all the food is set out in a central place and guests take a plate and help themselves. A buffet also can be combined with sit-down dining. Guests serve themselves from a buffet set up on a side table or counter, then sit at the main table.

Here are some things to keep in mind when you're planning a buffet-style meal.

**Consider your menu.** Not all foods are well suited to a buffet. Your guests will be juggling a plate, glass and flatware, so the food should be easy to eat and require little or no cutting. For example, lasagna is a good buffet food, but spaghetti may be too messy if your guests have to balance a plate on their laps.

**If you're inviting a large group,** plan to have two platters for each food. When one platter is almost empty, you can fix up the next one and make a quick switch. If the food you are serving is cold or room temperature, you can even prepare the second platter ahead of time.

**Have enough seating.** Buffets are great if you don't have one table that's big enough to seat all of your guests. But you still need enough spots for people to sit down, unless you're planning a cocktail party and serving just appetizers and finger foods.

**Plan your buffet table.** It's easy to set up a lovely buffet by using these simple tips.

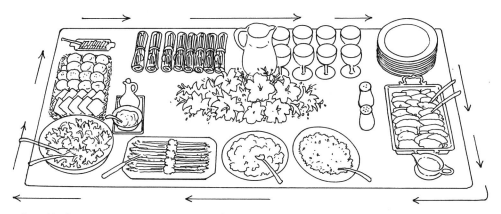

Full-meal buffet

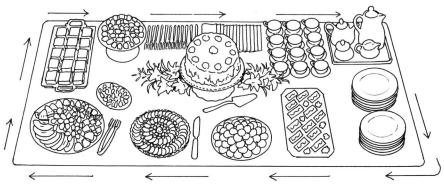

Dessert buffet

- **Set up the buffet** where it's most convenient—on the dining room table, a picnic table, two card tables placed together, a kitchen counter or desk. Or set up "stations" at smaller tables. Guests could get the main course at one table and dessert and coffee at another.

- **If your buffet table is small,** you can use a separate table or counter to lay out the glasses, flatware and napkins.

- **Table placement** is the secret to a guest-friendly buffet. Put the buffet in the center of the room, so guests can help themselves from all sides of the table. For a large group, set up identical lines on each side of the table. Or push the table against the wall to save space, leaving three sides open for serving.

- **Avoid a traffic jam** by setting up a separate area for beverages where guests can serve themselves.

- **For a multilevel buffet table,** use upside-down boxes or turned-over pans or bowls (make sure they're sturdy). Cover them with large pieces of fabric or napkins, and place serving platters, plates or bowls securely on top.

- **Place the centerpiece** where it can be admired but where it won't get in the way as guests help themselves to the food.

- **Arrange the food** so that items that go together (such as chips and dip or mashed potatoes and gravy) are near each other. This way, guests can help themselves without backtracking.

- **Set out name cards** by unusual foods or ones that contain nuts, for those guests who may be allergic.

- **Pretend that you're a guest** and walk through your set-up buffet table. You'll quickly find out what adjustments you need to make.

# Mixing and Matching

Don't worry if you're short of dishes, silverware or glassware. It's great to mix old and new, such as casual pottery plates for the main course and your grandmother's special dessert service to show off your cake. You can add to your collection by:

**Shopping.** Check out garage and estate sales or consignment shops where you can find full or partial sets at terrific bargains. You can also pick up inexpensive plates, bowls and glassware at restaurant supply, discount and outlet stores or by shopping post-holiday sales.

**Choosing white for your basic plates.** They can be mixed-and-matched more easily with your other dishes and dressed up or down.

**Borrowing.** That's what parents and friends are for! Let's say that you have four yellow plates, and your neighbor across the street has four white ones. Perfect—service for eight! Or if you're short a place setting, give the guest of honor the "special" mismatched one.

**Renting.** For larger gatherings, you can supplement the dishes you have with rentals. Your local party rental center should offer a selection of dishes, flatware and serving pieces from which to choose.

# Dressing Up the Table

If you have a linen closet filled with lovely matching tablecloths, special runners for the holidays, decorative place mats and fancy napkins, great, by all means use them! But, if your linen closet is lacking, here are some ideas for setting a festive table.

## Tablecloths and Table Runners

Use a tablecloth for casual or more formal occasions, but especially if your table isn't in good condition. A tablecloth should be big enough so that it hangs 18 to 20 inches over the edge on all sides.

**Check out your tablecloth ahead** so you have time to iron out any creases.

**Improvise with lengths** of inexpensive colorful fabric or even with a clean, pretty sheet. (Try layering them, too.)

**Wrapping paper** or white butcher paper are great for birthday parties or picnics—don't forget the crayons!

**Table runners** are another way to dress up your table. Use a runner on its own or layered with a coordinating tablecloth.

## Place Mats

Place mats tend to be more casual than a tablecloth, but they can be used along with a tablecloth or table runner to add pizzazz. They're also a great way to show off a beautiful wood table instead of hiding it under a tablecloth. Here are some ideas if your place mats don't all match or if you're short a place mat or two.

**Put "odd" place mats** at each end of the table or set the "odd" place mat in front of the guest of honor.

**Check out the selection** of fabulous paper place mats available at paper goods and party supply stores.

**Use squares of fabric, mirrored glass squares or decorative art papers** that coordinate with your theme or color scheme.

**Layer place mats** of different sizes, textures and colors for a casual look.

**For the holidays,** use large gold or silver doilies. Place doilies underneath the dinner plates on the tablecloth or on each place mat. Sprinkle the table with gold and silver confetti.

### Napkins

Dress your table to impress your guests with these three easy ways to fold napkins. These napkin folds work best if you use large, square fabric or heavier paper napkins. You don't have to iron napkins before folding them, but they turn out a little nicer and hold their shape better if you do.

In addition to these creative napkin folds, here are a few other ways to add color and flair to your table with napkins.

**Use decorative kitchen towels** (colorful stripes or checks look fun) or bandanas in place of formal napkins for a picnic or casual meal.

**Accessorize your napkins** with some pretty napkin rings, strings of beads, ribbon or raffia. You can tuck in a fresh herb sprig like rosemary for an extra-special touch.

**Good quality paper napkins** in plenty of attractive colors and patterns are available at party supply stores. These are great for casual occasions and cocktail parties.

**All your napkins don't need to match.** It can be even more fun to use a couple of coordinating colors or decorative prints and patterns and alternate them on the table.

**Napkins have plenty of other uses** as well: line a bread basket filled with warm dinner rolls; drape on a tray where you will stack coffee and tea cups; or fold a thick napkin into quarters and use as a trivet for a serving platter or bowl.

## Flatware Holder

**1.** Fold the napkin into quarters. Position napkin so the four points are at the top; roll down top layer about half way.

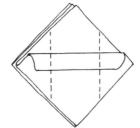

**2.** Fold the opposite corners under.

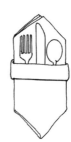

**3.** Tuck flatware into the napkin's "pocket."

## The Fan

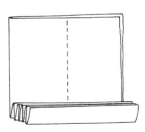 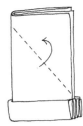 

**1.** Open the napkin to full size. Fold in half, bringing the left edge to the right edge. Starting at the bottom, make accordion pleats two-thirds of the way up.

**2.** Fold in half with the accordion pleating on the outside. Fold on the dotted line, laying the right side along the accordion pleat.

**3.** Fold the overlap on the left toward the front.

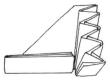 

**4.** Rest the overlap on the table or plate, and let the fan open so it's facing toward you.

## Goblet Twist

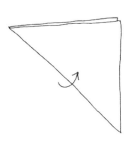 

**1.** Fold napkin in half diagonally into a triangle.

**2.** Roll up tightly from the diagonal fold. Fold in half and place in goblet.

# Serving with Style

If you like having guests over, or even just jazzing up your weeknight table, here are some items you may like to add to your serving collection.

### BASKETS

For serving bread, rolls and muffins. Napkins or pretty dish towels make nice basket liners.

### CHEESE BOARD AND CHEESE PLANE

An attractive way to present cheese and accompaniments including crackers, bread and fruit.

### CAKE STAND

An elegant way to serve cakes as well as pies, tarts, cookies, appetizers, cheese and fruit. (You can also create a beautiful buffet centerpiece by stacking two or three stands on top of one another.) Some cake stands have a domed cover, which helps protect the food and keep it fresh.

### CRUET WITH STOPPER

An elegant way to serve salad dressings, vinegars and oils. Bring it to the table, and let guests dress their salad to their taste.

### DESSERT DISHES, FOOTED

A fun and pretty way to serve ice cream, custard, fruit, nuts and candy or to use for small table centerpieces (see page 279).

### CHAFING DISH

A covered dish that has a small warming unit, such as a candle or canned cooking fuel, for keeping foods hot.

### FONDUE POT AND SKEWERS

Can be used for cheese or dessert fondue, and for keeping dips, sauces and gravies hot.

### ICE BUCKET WITH TONGS

An attractive way to serve ice with cold beverages.

### STRAINER, SMALL

For garnishing desserts with a sprinkling of powdered sugar, baking cocoa or ground cinnamon.

### PUNCH BOWL, 1½-GALLON SIZE

An easy way to serve large quantities of punch.

### VASES

In several shapes and sizes.

### SALAD BOWL WITH SERVERS

A nice way to serve salad on a buffet or for passing it at the table.

### WARMING TRAY

A plug-in electric tray that keeps food warm at the table or on a buffet.

### SQUEEZE BOTTLES

Fill with sauces and toppings. Use to make fancy drizzles and designs over desserts and soups or on individual plates and serving platters.

### WINE COOLER

Keeps wine chilled without ice.

## Centerpieces

We've created lots of easy-to-make table decorations to give you fresh ideas. Look for them throughout the book with the recipes. Centerpieces don't need to be expensive or time-consuming to make. Most can be assembled with things that you already have around the house or can pick up at the supermarket.

**Fill a wooden bowl** with natural items such as dried berries, fruit, flowers or leaves, pinecones and whole nuts. This is especially pretty for a Thanksgiving feast or a fall harvest supper. (1)

**Place whole lemons and limes** and lemon leaves in a clear tall container, vase or wide bowl. (2)

**Fill a wire basket** with an assortment of shiny, metallic ornaments.

**Drape strands of twinkling white lights** (battery operated) down the center of your table.

## Flowers

Instead of a centerpiece, you could also try a bunch of flowers or a few simple stems to add instant color to your table. Have all your vases somehow vanished? Look around your house for creative containers. Drinking glasses, jelly jars, mixing bowls, and olive oil and perfume bottles make instant flower holders. Just make sure your guests can see easily around and over the arrangement.

**Arrange colorful flowers** in a tea kettle or small watering can. (3)

**Wrap a vase** with fabric or decorative art paper, and tie with a ribbon to match your bouquet. (4)

**Cut sweetheart roses** down to size and tuck into short glasses or teacups.

**Float a flower** in a dish at each person's place.

**Tuck fresh herbs and flowers** into small bottles or juice glasses filled with water.

### Candles

Candles are one of the simplest ways to set the stage for a memorable evening. From short and stubby votives to tall and skinny tapers, the shape, size and color possibilities are endless. One tip: Be sure to use unscented candles at the dinner or buffet table so a fragrance doesn't overpower the taste and smell of the food.

Just about any container that you have in your kitchen cupboard can double as a candleholder—coffee cup saucers, martini or wine glasses, empty salt and pepper shakers with the tops removed, small baking tins or decorative molds.

**Fill a large cast-iron skillet** with candles and whole spices or nuts. (5)

**Place rings of tea light candles,** small flower blossoms and sprigs of greenery on a tiered cake stand. (6)

**Cluster candles** of different sizes and shapes in the center of the table on a square of mirrored glass.

**Float candles and flowers** in a shallow bowl.

# GOOD PLANNING

Now that you've decided what your gathering is all about and thought of what you'd like to serve, it's time to move on to the final part of the Success Formula—Good Planning. So what is good planning? It's plotting out a time schedule, shopping and, for larger gatherings, making lists. In short, planning is the key to success.

## Food Preparation

A lot of your planning will center around food. Here are some meal-related planning tips.

**Gather your recipes.** Pull together all of the recipes you'll be using before you start. If you have recipes from several cookbooks or magazines, put sticky notes on the pages so that you can find them quickly.

**Read your recipes.** This will help you avoid choosing foods that all need last-minute preparation or two dishes that need to go into the oven at the same time but at different temperatures. Reading your recipes also will help you plan your timetable, "to do" list and shopping list.

**Make a preparation timetable.** Recipes will tell you what foods can be made ahead of time and what you need to do just before serving. For instance, if your dessert has to chill for 12 hours, plan on making it the day before. Other recipes might require you to beat the whipping cream or scoop the ice cream minutes before serving. Tack your timetable in a place you'll be likely to see it—like on the fridge!

**Work with your space.** Don't overestimate the amount of cooking space you have. Are you planning on cooking the turkey and the potatoes in the same oven at the same time? Before the big day, you'll want to put the roasting pan for the turkey and the casserole for the potatoes in the oven to make sure they will fit side by side. How about your stove top? Will all the saucepans you need fit on the burners? Do you have enough refrigerator space, or should you stash a cooler packed with ice on the back porch for items such as beverages?

## Lists Can Be Lifesavers

One of the best ways to organize your get-together is to make good lists. If you write everything down, you won't forget anything. Plus, you'll get a better sense of the big picture of your gathering and how to fit everything into your schedule. Here are some lists that you may want to make.

### Guest List

Even with terrific food and a fabulous table setting, it's the people that really make the party. There's no right or wrong answer when it comes to choosing how many guests to invite, but there are some general guidelines. First, consider what kind of get-together you are having and how much space you have. Think about your comfort and energy levels, too. A few friends over for drinks will be much less draining than a house full of people.

Once you have an approximate head count, you'll know the quantity of food, beverages and other supplies to buy. (To determine the amounts of food you'll need, see "How Much Food Should I Make?" on page 410.) You'll also have an idea of how many places to set at the table or how many chairs to have on hand if you're serving buffet style.

### Before the Party "To Do" List

These are the things that you can get done ahead of time, from 2 weeks to 1 day before your party. This list may include shopping, preparing recipes ahead of time, cleaning the house, buying flowers, setting the table, decorating and so on. Jot down key dates on your calendar, such as when to order the cake from the bakery and flowers from the florist. Check items off your list as you get them done. (Doesn't that feel good?)

### Day of the Party "To Do" List

Although much of your party preparation can be done prior to the actual day, there are some things that can't be done in advance. Some of the tasks that should definitely be on the "day of the party" list include making a shopping run for last-minute items, defrosting food, chopping vegetables, decorating the cake and lighting the candles. Don't forget to schedule some time for yourself! Be sure to leave enough time to relax and get ready so you aren't just hopping out of the shower when the first guests arrive.

### Shopping List

Once you've thought of all the tasks you need to do, it's time to pull together your actual shopping list. Here's a foolproof way to draw one up.

**Jot down your complete menu.** Be sure to include beverages and other fixings you might need, such as mustard for the burgers or ice for the lemonade.

**Read through the recipes** and write down the ingredients and the amounts you'll need for each one. Then look for repeated ingredients and add them up. For example, 2 cups sour cream for the dip, about 1 cup for topping the baked potatoes and ½ cup for the cake you're baking makes a grand total of 3½ cups.

(Round that up to 4 cups. It's best to have a little extra just to be on the safe side.)

**Double-check your pantry** to find out what staples (such as flour, sugar, canned tomatoes, chicken broth and paper towels) you have on hand and what you'll need to stock up on.

**Attach any coupons** right to your list.

**Write down any prepared foods that you plan to pick up,** such as fresh bread, salads from the deli or a sheet cake from the bakery. You'll probably have to pick these up at the last minute, so make sure they're also on your "day of the party" list.

**Write down all the extras you'll need:** wine and beer, cocktail napkins, toothpicks with frilly ends, paper birthday decorations, flowers, candles. Next to each item or group of items, write down where you need to go to get them: the liquor store, paper goods warehouse, florist.

**Group your list by the places you'll need to go to pick up your items.** If you're shopping all at once, use your list to plan your route. Buy nonrefrigerated items first, and save the ice for last. If it's a hot day, you may want to bring along a cooler, especially if you're making more than one food stop.

# HELPFUL NUTRITION AND COOKING INFORMATION

## NUTRITION GUIDELINES

We provide nutrition information for each recipe that includes calories, calories from fat, fat, saturated fat, cholesterol, sodium, carbohydrate, fiber and protein. Individual food choices can be based on this information.

**Following is the recommended intake for a daily diet of 2,000 calories as set by the Food and Drug Administration:**

| Total Fat | Less than 65g |
|---|---|
| Saturated Fat | Less than 20g |
| Cholesterol | Less than 300mg |
| Sodium | Less than 2400mg |
| Total Carbohydrate | 300g |
| Dietary Fiber | 25g |

### Criteria Used for Calculating Nutrition Information

- The first ingredient was used wherever a choice is given (such as ⅓ cup sour cream or plain yogurt).

- The first ingredient amount was used wherever a range is given (such as 3- to 3½-pound cut-up broiler-fryer chicken).

- "If desired" ingredients and recipe variations were not included (such as "sprinkle with brown sugar, if desired").

- Only the amount of a marinade or frying oil that is estimated to be absorbed by the food during preparation or cooking was calculated.

### Ingredients Used in Recipe Testing and Nutrition Calculations

- Ingredients used for testing represent those that the majority of consumers use in their homes: large eggs, 2% milk, 80%-lean ground beef, canned ready-to-use chicken broth and vegetable oil spread containing not less than 65 percent fat.

- Fat-free, low-fat or low-sodium products were not used, unless otherwise indicated.

- Solid vegetable shortening (not butter, margarine, nonstick cooking sprays or vegetable oil spread as they can cause sticking problems) was used to grease pans, unless otherwise indicated.

### Equipment Used in Recipe Testing

We use equipment for testing that the majority of consumers use in their homes. If a specific piece of equipment (such as a wire whisk) is necessary for recipe success, it is listed in the recipe.

- Cookware and bakeware without nonstick coatings were used, unless otherwise indicated.

- No dark-colored, black or insulated bakeware was used.

- When a pan is specified in a recipe, a metal pan was used; a baking dish or pie plate means oven-proof glass was used.

- An electric hand mixer was used for mixing only when mixer speeds are specified in the recipe directions. When a mixer speed is not given, a spoon or fork was used.

# COOKING TERMS GLOSSARY

We often use these common cooking terms in the recipes in this book.

**Beat:** Mix ingredients vigorously with spoon, fork, wire whisk, hand beater or electric mixer until smooth and uniform.

**Boil:** Heat liquid until bubbles rise continuously and break on the surface and steam is given off. For rolling boil, the bubbles form rapidly.

**Chop:** Cut into coarse or fine irregular pieces with a knife, food chopper, blender or food processor.

**Cube:** Cut into squares ½ inch or larger.

**Dice:** Cut into squares smaller than ½ inch.

**Grate:** Cut into tiny particles using small, rough holes of grater (often used for citrus peel or chocolate).

**Grease:** Rub the inside surface of a pan with shortening, using pastry brush, piece of waxed paper or paper towel, to prevent food from sticking during baking (as for some casseroles).

**Julienne:** Cut into thin, matchlike strips, using knife or food processor (used for vegetables, fruits, meats).

**Mix:** Combine ingredients in any way that distributes them evenly.

**Sauté:** Cook foods in hot oil or margarine over medium-high heat with frequent tossing and turning motion.

**Shred:** Cut into long thin pieces by rubbing food across the holes of a shredder, as for cheese, or by using a knife to slice very thinly, as for cabbage.

**Simmer:** Cook in liquid just below the boiling point on top of the stove; usually after reducing heat from a boil. Bubbles will rise slowly and break just below the surface.

**Stir:** Mix ingredients until uniform consistency. Stir once in a while for "stirring occasionally," often for "stirring frequently" and continuously for "stirring constantly."

**Toss:** Tumble ingredients (such as green salad) lightly with a lifting motion, usually to coat evenly or mix with another food.

# METRIC CONVERSION CHART

## Volume

| U.S. Units | Canadian Metric | Australian Metric |
|---|---|---|
| ¼ teaspoon | 1 mL | 1 ml |
| ½ teaspoon | 2 mL | 2 ml |
| 1 teaspoon | 5 mL | 5 ml |
| 1 tablespoon | 15 mL | 20 ml |
| ¼ cup | 50 mL | 60 ml |
| ⅓ cup | 75 mL | 80 ml |
| ½ cup | 125 mL | 125 ml |
| ⅔ cup | 150 mL | 170 ml |
| ¾ cup | 175 mL | 190 ml |
| 1 cup | 250 mL | 250 ml |
| 1 quart | 1 liter | 1 liter |
| 1½ quarts | 1.5 liters | 1.5 liters |
| 2 quarts | 2 liters | 2 liters |
| 2½ quarts | 2.5 liters | 2.5 liters |
| 3 quarts | 3 liters | 3 liters |
| 4 quarts | 4 liters | 4 liters |

## Weight

| U.S. Units | Canadian Metric | Australian Metric |
|---|---|---|
| 1 ounce | 30 grams | 30 grams |
| 2 ounces | 55 grams | 60 grams |
| 3 ounces | 85 grams | 90 grams |
| 4 ounces (¼ pound) | 115 grams | 125 grams |
| 8 ounces (½ pound) | 225 grams | 225 grams |
| 16 ounces (1 pound) | 455 grams | 500 grams |
| 1 pound | 455 grams | ½ kilogram |

## Measurements

| Inches | Centimeters |
|---|---|
| 1 | 2.5 |
| 2 | 5.0 |
| 3 | 7.5 |
| 4 | 10.0 |
| 5 | 12.5 |
| 6 | 15.0 |
| 7 | 17.5 |
| 8 | 20.5 |
| 9 | 23.0 |
| 10 | 25.5 |
| 11 | 28.0 |
| 12 | 30.5 |
| 13 | 33.0 |

## Temperatures

| Fahrenheit | Celsius |
|---|---|
| 32° | 0° |
| 212° | 100° |
| 250° | 120° |
| 275° | 140° |
| 300° | 150° |
| 325° | 160° |
| 350° | 180° |
| 375° | 190° |
| 400° | 200° |
| 425° | 220° |
| 450° | 230° |
| 475° | 240° |
| 500° | 260° |

**Note:** The recipes in this cookbook have not been developed or tested using metric measures. When converting recipes to metric, some variations in quality may be noted.

# INDEX